Later Life

Later Life

The Social Psychology of Aging

Edited by

Victor W. Marshall

SAGE PUBLICATIONS
The Publishers of Professional Social Science
Beverly Hills   London   New Delhi

For information address:

SAGE Publications, Inc.
275 South Beverly Drive
Beverly Hills, California 90212

SAGE Publications India Pvt. Ltd.
M-32 Market
Greater Kailash I
New Delhi 110 048 India

SAGE Publications Ltd
28 Banner Street
London EC1Y 8QE
England

Printed in the United States of America

Library of Congress Cataloging-in-Publication Data

Main entry under title:

Later life.
  Bibliography: p.
  Contents: Dominant and emerging paradigms in the social psychology of aging / Victor W. Marshall—The subjective construction of self and society / Carol D. Ryff—Socialization in old age—a Meadian perspective / Neena Chappell and Harold L. Orbach—[etc.]
  1. Gerontology. 2. Old age—Social aspects. 3. Aged—Psychology. I. Marshall, Victor W.
HQ1061.L357 1985   305.2′6   85-19581
ISBN 0-8039-2547-6
ISBN 0-8039-2548-4 (pbk.)

FIRST PRINTING

Contents

Acknowledgments

Through no fault of the publisher, this book has been long in gestation. I therefore wish to give special thanks to the contributors for their patience and understanding. The original idea for the book came from Tony Harris, social psychologist and good friend for almost two decades. The commitment to the topic emerged at an informal caucus over coffee at a meeting of the Gerontological Society, in Portland, Oregon, a decade ago. Don Spence and Jim Dowd, contributors here, were present along with a few other good colleagues, and we deplored the dismal state of theory in the sociology of aging. To these colleagues, who know who they are, I am grateful. I am also particularly grateful to Vern Bengtson for moral support in this project and for the years of theoretical adventure we have shared. My work on this project and, more generally, in the sociology of aging, has been generously supported by the National Health Research Development Program of Health and Welfare Canada, through its award of a National Health Scientist grant to me, and by the Laidlaw Foundation, who honored me with the Laidlaw Award in support of my research in aging and long-term care. Indirectly, but tangibly, this project has been assisted by the Program in Gerontology, University of Toronto, and by the nourishing atmosphere of my own Department of Behavioural Science. I am grateful also to Joanne Daciuk for her work in compiling the name index for this volume, and to Terry Hendrix and Judy Selhorst of Sage Publications for their help in seeing the book through to completion. I am thankful for all this support. Most of all, I want to thank Joanne Gard Marshall for her encouragement and for just continuing to be Joanne.

1

Dominant and Emerging Paradigms in the Social Psychology of Aging

VICTOR W. MARSHALL

First chapters are usually written last, and this chapter is no exception. In these "last words" I attempt to place the chapters that follow in contexts, to describe and justify the purpose of the collection. I have the advantage over my collaborators in this volume because their chapters are in my hands as I write. I shall attempt to impose a "logic" on the contents and organization of the book that may well have been opaque to the authors, some of whom may be quite surprised at the contextualization of their chapters. From the beginning, my goal was to represent theoretical developments in the social psychology of aging, but the book came to be progressively more focused as the various authors agreed to participate in it. The book's "reconstituted logic" will be of greater interest to the reader than its evolving logic. To an extent I have perhaps drawn some of the authors into being co-conspirators in the service of my own theoretical project. They may not fully agree with that project or with my critiques of much of the theory in the social psychology of aging, which I characterize as the antithesis of what is found in these pages. Nonetheless, assured of their good will if not their complete agreement, I will describe what I take to be the unifying foci of this book.

Authors were selected on the basis of a very personal judgment (though one informed by the reception of their work by the scientific community) that their work showed, or showed the promise of, innovative theory development in the social psychology or micro-sociology of aging. They were asked to develop chapters representing their most recent theoretical work, with an explicit request that they be bold, innovative, and free in theorizing. The overall goal is to stimulate the development of theoretical ideas in a field where these are scarce. Many of the authors see the greatest promise for theoretical development in reintroducing some important strands of theory from the past, or in showing how some "classical" theory has contemporary relevance for the social psychology of aging.

In a recent review, Maddox and Campbell (1985, p. 4) argue that "the social scientific study of aging needs, but currently lacks, widely shared paradigms that would provide common conceptualization of issues, standard measurements, and clearly defined research agendas for the systematic testing of hypotheses derived from theory." Rosow (1985, p. 62) has expressed agreement with an earlier view expressed by Clausen (1972) that there is no basis for a general theory of the life course and that we should attempt to develop theory at the middle range. John (1984, p. 92) goes further and argues, "To the extent that one can characterize theoretical developments in social gerontology, the trend has been away from a search for a special as well as an universal theory of aging. It is wise to abandon these endeavors since any effort along these lines will remain fruitless as long as material and ideal conditions vary from country to country and over time."

The social psychology of aging has been long on data and short on ideas. In less than a half century of intense activity, it has made remarkable progress in measurement but less progress at the level of meaning. Much time and energy has been thrown away on trifling issues and it is still not clear that our understanding of aging and later life has reached a level of sophistication over that which has been with us through the ages, well prior to any disciplined attempt by social scientists to develop systematic, theoretical knowledge. The field has from its origins had a "social problems" focus to the detriment of systematic theorizing. Theory is not doing well in the social psychology or sociology of aging.

Nonetheless, this is a book of and about theory in social gerontology, particularly in the social psychology of aging. The authors represented here are not in agreement as to fine points of theory and no doubt would disagree vigorously on theory-building strategies. However, they do share a commitment to theory as well as a sense of uneasiness about the current state of theory. In addition to their belief in the value of theory, it may safely be said that they agree with the following goals of this book:

(1) The theoretical contributions represented in the book recognize that aging individuals are embedded in social structural contexts that have their own historical and social imperatives and dynamics.

(2) The book constitutes, implicitly and explicitly, a critique of prevailing atheoretical and/or structural-functionalist approaches that now predominate in social gerontology.

(3) The book will introduce, or reintroduce, the basic elements of an "interpretive" perspective, based in Weberian sociology, symbolic interactionist sociology, and phenomenological psychology and social psychology.

In the remainder of this chapter, I will address these three goals and briefly suggest the ways in which the various chapters contribute to them.

AGING AND LATER LIFE IN CONTEXT

Attempting to understand the relationship between the individual and society has been one of the major themes in the sociological enterprise, yet perhaps no sociologist has stated this goal better than C. Wright Mills. In his classic, *The Sociological Imagination*, Mills (1959, p. 3) wrote as follows:

> The facts of contemporary history are also facts about the success and the failure of individual men and women. When a society is industrialized, a peasant becomes a worker; a feudal lord is liquidated or becomes a businessman. When classes rise or fall, a man is employed or unemployed; when the rate of investment goes up or down, a man takes new heart or goes broke. When wars happen, an insurance salesman becomes a rocket launcher; a store clerk, a radar man; a wife lives alone; a child grows up without a father. Neither the life of an individual nor the history of a society can be understood without understanding both.

Mills (1959, p. 4) notes that, in their everyday-life worlds, people rarely connect their individual lives with the societal context, their "personal troubles" with "public issues." This is because they lack "the quality of mind essential to grasp the interplay of man and society, of biography and history, of self and world." This quality of mind, Mills asserts, is precisely the key element in the sociological imagination.

Any review of the sociology of aging must, by these criteria, find it sorely lacking in such imagination. There has been little focus on the societal contexts of aging due to a strong social psychological cast to the field. Simultaneously, the emphasis on the individual has ignored context in several ways. The older individual has all too often been seen in isolation. So, when a recent textbook defines the sociology of aging as "the scientific study of the interaction of older people in society" (Harris & Cole, 1980, p. 12), the definition may be viewed as too narrowly social psychological and too focused on later life.

The strong emphasis in the sociology of aging on the adjustment of the individual to the society has served to decontextualize the aging experience by taking societal arrangements as comparatively non-problematic. In an early and influential development, Ernest W. Burgess submitted a memo to the Committee on Social Adjustment of the Social Sciences Research Council, calling attention to the absence of information about the behavior and adjustment of the aged. Burgess also acknowledged that society could be characterized as maladjusted to the individual or to its older population, rather than the reverse (Calhoun, 1978, p. 105). However, the bulk of his own work and that of such colleagues as Cavan (1949) at Chicago stressed the adaptation or adjustment of the individual to the society. Whether measured by degree of social integration or more psychological variables such as morale or life satisfaction, the adjustment of the aging individual became the dependent variable of choice for hundreds of investigations over the ensuing decades. No equivalent measure or conceptualization of the "adjustment" of the society to the individual ever gained prominence in the research armamentarium of gerontology. Even disengagement theory, which did attempt to provide a theory linking the individual and societal levels of analysis, in practice stimulated research focused on individual aging people and their adjustment to the society. Social change or the social dynamics surrounding disengagement rarely have been addressed in this theoretical tradition.

The emphasis on individual adjustment pervaded the field of social gerontology until the early 1980s and is still a major theme in the social psychology of aging (for a review and critique, see Marshall, 1981; Marshall & Tindale, 1978-1979).

Context has also been ignored because of the predominance of the social survey and of multivariate analysis in the sociology of aging (and in sociology in general). Sociological descriptions focused on variables and the relationships between variables, rather than on whole people in real-life situations. People were, in a sense, first decomposed into variables and then lost, as the relationships between variables were explored instead of the relationships between people. Field studies employing participant observation or other approaches to describe people in situations have been rare in the sociology of aging.

The failure to place aging and the aged in context adequately has also suffered from the ahistorical cast of theory. The largest theoretical debate in the social psychology of aging, that between activity theory and disengagement theory (see, for example, Cumming & Henry, 1961;

Maddox, 1965, 1966; Palmore, 1968; and the review of this debate in Orbach, 1974), totally ignores the historical context in which either disengagement or continuing high levels of activity in later life might be maintained. There has been a remarkable lack of vision in the goal of explanation. Thus, in seeking for the correlates of morale or life satisfaction, investigators have measured such factors as health status, economic status, and social participation. These three sets of variables explain the greatest variance in life satisfaction. However, only rarely have these variables been taken as dependent. Each could be considered as implicated in long causal chains, and when efforts would be made to explain them, the explanation would most likely lead the investigator to a consideration of social structure and broader aspects of social context. More relevant to this volume, it is the linkage between the proximate causal variables such as those found to be highly predictive of life satisfaction and structural variables that has been neglected.

Even at the microsociological level of an analysis, there has been little interest in viewing the social situation of the aging individual in structural terms. A basic distinction can be made between the acting individual and the social structuring of his or her social world. The central thrust of most of the chapters in this volume emphasizes a view of the individual as "acting," which is to say, participating actively in fashioning a life course. The image of human nature put forth here is of a creature capable of exercising choice. However, choice can be exercised only if alternatives are available, and this immediately raises questions about social struture.

THE LIMITATIONS OF
STRUCTURAL FUNCTIONALISM

The second major goal of this book is to posit a critique of prevailing atheoretical and/or structural-functionalist approaches that now predominate in social gerontology. The two most influential North American theoretical approaches in social gerontology are both structural-functionalist in their theoretical grounding. These are "age stratification theory," propounded by Matilda White Riley and associates (Foner, 1972, 1974, 1984; Foner & Kertzer, 1978; Riley, 1971, 1976, 1978, 1985; Riley, Johnson, & Foner, 1972), and the modernization thesis, which has been articulated principally by Donald Cowgill (1974; Cowgill & Holmes, 1972) and by Erdman Palmore and associates (Palmore & Manton, 1974; Palmore & Whittington, 1971) but which was anticipated by Burgess (1960) and even by Durkheim in *The Division of Labor* (1964/1893). A third major theoretical approach, prominent in the work of Burgess but also expressed in the work of Irving Rosow on social integration and social roles of the aged (Rosow, 1974, 1976, 1985), is equally influenced by structural-functionalism. This may be called the "role theory" perspective on aging, but it has many variants (e.g., Blau, 1981; Neugarten, Moore, & Lowe, 1965).

Structural-functionalism (hereafter referred to simply as "functionalism") is something of a dirty word in some contemporary social psychology circles, and this is unfortunate in that the term refers to a major theoretical perspective, itself internally differentiated, that has contributed greatly to social science knowledge.

As Merton (1957) has pointed out, "function" is a term with many meanings both in popular and scientific discourse. Functionalist analysis has been criticized as being teleological, in attempting to explain a phenomenon in relation to the ends to which it is directed. As a simple example, the social institution of retirement might be explained by its function of removing older people from the labor force so as to reduce the possibility of conflict between young and old age groups (as in Cowgill, 1974). However, functional analysis is not in principle teleological and, shorn of teleology and carefully applied, becomes one form of causal analysis (Davis, 1959; Levy, 1967).

In this stripped-down version, functional analysis is completely formal or abstract, being simply a way of mapping causal relationships (as, for example, in stating the equation describing a regression line). However, to be theoretically interesting at all, we must reserve the term "functionalism" to refer to a set of theoretical approaches that look upon society as a system with certain needs whose fulfillment is required if the system is to be maintained or is to survive.

As philosopher Carl Hempel (1965, pp. 304-305) explains:

> The kind of phenomenon that a functional analysis is invoked to explain is typically some recurrent activity or some behavior pattern in an individual or a group, such as a physiological mechanism, a neurotic trait, a culture pattern or a social institution. And the principal objective of the analysis is to exhibit the contribution which the behavior pattern makes to the preservation or the development of the individual or the group in which it occurs. Thus, functional analysis seeks to understand a behavior pattern or a sociocultural institution by determining the role it plays in keeping the given system in proper working order or maintaining it as a going concern.

However, maintenance of a system is extended by some, through analogies to biological organisms, to assume that systems naturally tend toward equilibrium. No support is found for that position in these pages, even though it is found in such a major theoretical perspective in the sociology of aging as the "age stratification" perspective. Similarly, the assumption that society has certain basic needs or requisites, important in the sociological functionalism of Parsons (1951, chap. 2) and Levy (1952, chap. 4) and in the anthropological functionalism of Malinowski (1939), has influenced the disengagement theory of aging and the modernization theory, in both of which the social institution of retirement would be seen as meeting a social system need to process role incumbents out of status positions in order to make room for new entrants. Such a functional requisite assumption can be accepted only with considerable qualification. Societal survival, the criterion against which requisite functional need is defined, is itself difficult to define (Aberle et al., 1950; Levy, 1952, p. 137).

The functionalist emphasis on the contribution that any societal element makes to the functioning of the whole society, coupled with a Durkheimian priority being given to the whole over the parts, informs much of the social psychology of aging that deals with age-related loss of social integration. Rosow and Burgess both appear to judge the integration of the individual into the society primarily in terms of activities relevant to societal survival. Hence, loss of economic function and important familial (parenting and conjugal) roles are the critical aspects of age-related status loss leading to what Burgess (1960) describes as the "role-less role" of the aged, and what Rosow characterizes as tenuous, informal, or "non-role" role types (Rosow, 1985).

From a nonfunctionalist perspective, however, exclusion of the aged from functions deemed by some to be critical for the survival of the society is not taken as ruling out other means of social integration. The issue might seem trivial except that social integration has been such a dominant concern in the sociology and social psychology of aging. Social relationships are based on more than societal survival functions. Unruh (1983) has recently explored alternative bases for social integration through participation in "social worlds." Many old and young people find meaningful social integration in a life with others in society through participating in social worlds such as "stamp collecting" or "ballroom dancing." From a societal survival perspective, participation in such social worlds appears trivial, yet just such participation often forms genuine and meaningful bases of meaning and social identity across the life course.

A central problem with functionalist analysis is the tendency to see any social unit or behavior pattern solely in terms of its functions for the survival of the larger whole (be this a society or a group or collectivity at a more bounded level of analysis). Much of individual or social life, it may be argued, is afunctional. It does not contribute to the maintenance of any social system, nor does it particularly threaten that existence (that is, it is not dysfunctional either). If we focus on functional aspects of behavior or of social structure, we may miss a great deal of social life.

In summary, by encouraging the investigator to think systematically about the relationships of social units and behavioral patterns to each other and to larger systems of social interaction, functionalism has been a valuable theoretical perspective. On the negative side, structural-functionalism is limited by difficulties in defining what shall be taken to be a social system and by what criteria the "needs" of this system are to be met if the system is to survive. The implicit and often explicit assumption that social mechanisms act in some "natural" way to foster survival (or, in weaker versions of functionalism, to preserve or restore equilibrium) cannot be justified a priori and is an unfortunate holdover from the organic analogy so important in the formulation of this perspective (Radcliffe-Brown, 1935). Some social systems do have built-in mechanisms to restore equilibrium or to foster system survival. However, these do not act by some systems logic of their own and their existence and functioning must be treated as matters requiring investigation.

Perhaps more trenchant than these criticisms, though certainly flowing from them, is the critique of functionalism as overly deterministic. Paradoxically, this critique is most centrally launched against Parsons's version of structural-functionalism, which, in turn, incorporates his "voluntaristic theory of action" (Parsons, 1937/1949). Parsons attempted to build a theory of the social system on functionalist premises that incorporated a notion of an "acting," choosing person. However, to provide the stability of the social system that his functionalism implied, he gave great priority to socialization and the internalization of values, which constrained choice greatly. Social system requirements were served by social institutions composed of role behavior. The motivations for correct role behavior were incorporated into individuals as "need-dispositions." As Giddens (1976, p. 16) puts it:

In his earlier writings at least, Parsons specifically sought to incorporate a "voluntaristic" frame within his approach. But Parsons . . . went on to identify voluntarism with the "internalization of values" in personality and hence with psychological motivation ("need-disposition"). *There is no action in Parsons'"action frame of reference"*, only behaviour which is propelled by need-dispositions or role-expectations.

It may be noted that this version of functionalism, with its emphasis on the priority of socialization and the importance of role-behavior in relation to social institutions and, ultimately, social system maintenance, underlies the majority of theoretically informed research in social gerontology, as expressed in conventional role theory approaches (Blau, Neugarten et al., Riley, Rosow, as mentioned above) and in the age stratification perspective. There is a determinism here (even implied in Rosow, who deplores the inadequacy of socialization mechanisms in later life; see Rosow, 1974) that derives from the organic metaphor of the varieties of functionalism but that stands in contrast to the relative indeterminism and voluntarism underlying the chapters in this volume.

AN INTERPRETIVE
SOCIAL PSYCHOLOGY OF AGING

Turning now to the third unifying goal of this volume, we find a commitment to what might be called the "interpretive" perspective. This is not to say that all the authors so label themselves, but in the imposed logic allowed in introductory chapters I would characterize their work in this way. The interpretive perspective contrasts with the determinism, with the emphasis on system, and with assumptions as to equilibrium and systems-maintenance processes found in structural-functionalism.

The contrast between what is here called the "interpretive" perspective and other perspectives has been drawn in a number of ways. It is not a goal of the present chapter or volume to advocate any rigid dichotomization of theoretical perspectives. I will later suggest that reconciliation would be a more laudable goal. However, some gains in understanding can be made by looking at a few of the contrasts, considered as establishing polar types of theorizing.

Wilson (1970) contrasts the "normative" and "interpretive" paradigms within sociology. He sees the former as consisting of two major ideas: that interaction is essentially rule governed and that sociological explanation is properly deductive in its form, following the model of the natural sciences (Wilson, 1970, pp. 59-66). Wilson finds the interpretive paradigm rooted in symbolic interactionism and ethnomethodology. Individuals are here seen not as acting out roles but as "role-taking." That is, people impute motives and sentiments to others and perceive their behavior as meaningful and, on the basis of these imputations, devise a course of action for themselves. Social life is thus improvisational, based on an "interpretive process in which meanings evolve and change over the course of the interaction" (Wilson, 1970, p. 67). The characteristics of any description of the emergence and continual change of social interaction, seen in these terms, make attempts at deductive explanation in principle inadequate. From a methodological point of view, accounts of interaction rely on the development of a shared understanding between the sociologist and those whose interaction is being studied, on the one hand, and on shared understanding among colleagues, on the other.

Dawe (1970) draws a contrast between the "first" and "second" sociologies, or sociologies of "order" and of "control." The first, which is exemplified by structural-functionalism, gives priority to the social system over the individual and sees socialization processes acting with such efficiency as to render social norms not just regulative but *constitutive* of the self (Dawe, 1970, p. 209). In contrast, in the second sociology, society is seen as "the creation of its members; the product of their construction of meaning, and of the action and relationships through which they attempt to impose that meaning on their historical situations" (Dawe, 1970, p. 216).

Geertz (1983, p. 19) also contrasts structural-functionalism and the interpretive paradigm:

> Many social scientists have turned away from a laws and instances ideal of explanation toward a cases and interpretations one, looking less for the sort of thing that connects planets and pendulums and more for the sort that connects chrysanthemums and swords.... analogies drawn from the humanities are coming to play the kind of role in sociological understanding that analogies drawn from the crafts and technology have long played in physical understanding.

Whereas structural-functionalists have seen social life as analogous to mechanistic or, more often, organic systems (the machine or the body), social scientists in the interpretive paradigm draw on the humanities for their analogies and view life as analogous to a game, to the theater, to the text, or to other aspects of everyday life (Geertz, 1983).

Problems of definitional ambiguity are as evident in respect to the interpretive paradigm as anywhere else in the theoretical domains discussed above. However, in searching for a common theoretical tie for the present chapters, we can turn to Max Weber as an exemplary figure. According to Weber (1978, p. 4), sociology is "a science concerning itself with the interpretive understanding of social action and thereby with a causal explanation of its course and consequences. We shall speak of 'action' insofar as its subjective meaning takes account of the behavior of others and is thereby oriented in its course."

Weber emphasizes that sociology studies meaningful social behavior. As a sociologist such as Schutz (who drew heavily on Weber) or a philosopher such as G. H. Mead emphasized, human beings attempt to form an understanding of their own behavior through the perspective of the others with whom they interact. They try to see themselves and their experience "through the eyes of the other" by "taking the role of the other." Some interpretive sociologists, especially those who draw on the symbolic interactionist perspective, emphasize that people develop a concept of self that can be thought of as a kind of model or cognitive map of the individual in relationships with other people. This model, the self-concept, is both influenced by the feedback received from other people and influencer of the behavior of the individual. For example, if many important or "significant" others routinely act toward older people as if those people were incapable of maintaining independence, those older people are highly likely to develop a view of themselves as dependent and, on the basis of this self-attribution, to act in a dependent manner, thereby reinforcing the views of the significant others.

Also within this general rubric of the interpretive perspective, phenomenological sociologists such as Schutz and Berger emphasize that reality itself is socially constructed through the collaborative definitional and meaning-sharing activities of people. Our social world is therefore, in many respects, a world of meaning. However, it is not entirely fragile, as meanings become reified: They often take on a reality independent of their authors, and this reality sets constraints on individual behavior. For example, the greater the proportion of societal members who believe that an elderly widow should not remarry, the more difficult it will be for the individual to violate that shared consensus.

However, interpretive sociologists tend to emphasize the looseness of societal consensus and the extent to which many alternative and frequently conflicting sets of societal expectations can be brought to bear in any given situation. They therefore argue that expectations of "norms" are frequently *invoked* as legitimations or justifications for behavior *after the fact,* or when someone questions the behavior, but that norms rarely determine behavior or cause patterning of behavior.

This places interpretive approaches at odds with normative and structural-functionalist approaches, which are based on a conceptualization of the social system in terms of status positions to which expectations for behavior (norms or bundles of norms called "roles") are attached and that lead to systematic patterning of behavior.

Interpretive sociologists stress people's attempts to make sense of their experience in the world, and to obtain their objectives by trying to influence the definitions and meanings of other participants or by controlling information through deception, the "stage management" of personal and social appearances, and negotiating or bargaining. Social life, in this view, is constantly in flux. There is a constant tension between the stability that follows from social structural constraint and from a certain degree of consensus and the instability that follows from the fact of human willfulness or, as interpretive sociologists would say, the intentionality of humans.

This assumption that humans are willful creatures who interact strategically in self-interest is a key perspectival link to macrosociologies within the conflict tradition. Collins (1981, p. 990) argues that "the dynamics as well as the the inertia in any causal explanation of social structure must be micro-situational; all macroconditions have their effects by impinging upon actors' situational motivations." Denzin (1983, p. 136) argues that "experience and interaction filter structure, giving every moment of a reified structure unique meaning and interpretation. In this sense, all structures, if they are to affect the fate and development of individuals, even in unintended, or unanticipated, ways, must be realized interactionally and phenomenologically." Without an image of individuals in microsituations characterized by conflict or its containment, it would be impossible to address macrosocial or structural issues through a conflict perspective.

The interpretive approach does not lack for a conceptualization of structure. In fact, it suffers from too many alternative ways of dealing with social structure.

Collins, much influenced by ethnomethodology, argues that in principle all social structures are reducible or subject to "micro-translation" into chains of "interaction rituals" (he exempts only three "pure" macro variables: dispersion of individuals in geographical space, duration of social process, and number of individuals involved in the interaction) and that "the sum of all sequences of individual experience in the world would constitute all the possible sociological data" (Collins, 1981, p. 987). Denzin takes a contrasting stance, arguing that while social structure is realized through interaction, reification often occurs, and social structure has not only an interactional and phenomenological character but a historical one as well (Denzin, 1983, p. 136). Treating social structure as at least in some respects irreducible and resistant to human willfulness is consonant with Weber's own macrosociological analyses and with Schutz's emphasis on the historical legacy of relevance structures that form the context of social interaction.

The charge that the interpretive approach has neglected social structure, although not in principle sustainable, has some validity as laid against the practice of some interpretive sociologists. Symbolic interactionism has often been judged the astructural version of role theory, in contrast to structural-functional versions such as were discussed earlier in this chapter. Recently, however, the two approaches have been seen as complementary and mutually enriching in linking micro and macro levels of analysis (Heiss, 1981; Stryker, 1981). A concern with conceiving social structure in interpretive terms pervades this book and represents this move toward reconciliation.

ORGANIZATION OF THE BOOK

Each chapter in this volume stands on its own, and readers may wish to sample them selectively or proceed on the basis of their own interests. However, a reading of the chapters in the published sequence does provide one organization of the work that is perhaps more useful to those not highly familiar with the interpretive perspective.

Although the objectives of the second and third chapters are both very ambitious, they have been placed early in the book for the principal reason that, more explicitly and densely than the other chapters, they convey the fundamental assumptions about human nature that underlie the interpretive perspective. Ryff draws heavily on insights from phenomenological psychology; Chappell and Orbach restrict their attention to social behaviorist George Herbert Mead, whose work stands as a major foundation of symbolic interactionism. Both chapters present an image of the human being as acting, rather than simply reacting. Perception itself is seen as an active process such that the social and physical world, as context for the individual, is itself mediated by intentionality, just as is the nature of the response to external and internal stimuli.

In Chapter 2, psychologist Carol Ryff provides an entrée to the perspective that is appropriate in many respects. She attempts "to generate new and renewed theoretical interest in phenomenological and interpretive approaches to the study of aging." She lists several points of agreement and disagreement among scholars who can be grouped within the perspective. Her approach is not simply multidisciplinary but interdisciplinary, seeking to integrate insights from psychology and sociology. The breadth of her scope is also evident in her attempt to show the analytical payoff of this theoretical approach in terms of its ability to organize data—a goal pursued quite consistently in subsequent chapters as well. Ryff is also aware of the conceptual difficulties of linking the individual to social context and her suggested partial solution is through the concept of "life events." Her analysis of developmental change *as perceived by persons* aging over their life course, in relation to developmental theory *as articulated by theorists* exemplifies one of the major tasks of the interpretive social psychologist: to bring together descriptions of individual and social life that are simultaneously meaningful to actors and observers.

In this chapter and elsewhere in this volume, the sociological perspective of symbolic interactionism is included as a major contribution to the interpretive perspective. The term "symbolic interaction" itself refers to a diversity of approaches that nonetheless acknowledge an intellectual indebtedness to George Herbert Mead. In Chapter 3, Neena Chappell and Harold Orbach describe Mead's perspective and its implications for aging, but they are at pains to separate their interpretation of Mead from the symbolic interactionist perspective. This perspective, or rather set of perspectives, was given shape by many of Mead's students, notably Herbert Blumer, who took over Mead's course at Chicago following his death (Turner, 1982, p. 322). The chapter by Chappell and Orbach deals primarily with Mead the behaviorist, whereas other chapters treat the somewhat distinct symbolic interactionist tradition heavily influenced by Mead.

The principal contributions that Mead's thought promises for the social psychology of aging lie, in the view of Chappell and Orbach, in three areas: Mead's view of temporality, his concept of the "problematic situation," and his views on the uniqueness of the individual. We live in the present but our present influences both our construction of the past and our anticipation of the future. Mead's perspective emphasizes constant change, novelty, and emergence, with the self changing in response to problematic situations. The self is not a thing or object, but a process. The self-as-object (the "me") exists only as a moment in the process of the self. This view is not universally accepted and represents a major point of difference between Meadian and alternative perspectives on the self. Similarly, Chappell and Orbach emphasize that Mead's conception of the development of the self is at odds with that of many other sociologists, including Brim, Riley, and Rosow, whose work is influential in the study of aging.

An additional point made in Chapter 3 should be stressed. This is that many contemporary sociologists do not employ the concept of role in the same way as did Mead. Mead used the term to describe assumption of the attitude of the other, or role-taking. He did not use the word "role" to refer to a set of expectations attached to a status position. Mead's usage is reflected in the work of many but not all contemporary symbolic interactionists, whose social psychology contrasts with the use of the role construct in normative and structural-functionalist sociology.

Whereas Chappell and Orbach deal exclusively with the fruitfulness of Mead's insights for the social psychology of aging, Donald Spence, in Chapter 4, examines one aspect of the Meadian legacy as realized in the theoretical insights of Anselm Strauss. Here there is no hesitation in invoking the symbolic interactionist tradition, including contemporary symbolic interactionists.

In Spence's chapter we find a discussion of some of the issues raised by Chappell and Orbach, but phrased in terms of other contributors to this perspective. Thus, his review of Dewey's description of habitual and nonhabitual conduct relates directly to Chappell and Orbach's discussion of the problematic situation in Mead.

The most important processes discussed in this chapter are those dealing with transformations in identity in relation to age and aging; the key concept is that of "career," which embodies assumptions about limits to determinism and the emergence of new social realities over time. Based on the notion of career, as articulated by Strauss and others (see also Chapter 5 in this volume), Spence describes four elements of a theoretical model. These are the concept of emergence, the dimension of time, bargaining, and "statuses and functions." The first two of these relate quite directly to the Meadian notions described in Chapter 3. Statuses and functions in this view are given life in contrast to their static conceptualization in structural-functionalism by being conceptualized as "career set." The concept of bargaining is a major vehicle for grasping the active, emergent nature of career-set behavior. As Strauss emphasizes, change rather than stability ought to be taken for granted in our theorizing. Norms are not then the major basis for societal stability that the structural-functionalists would have us believe. Consensus on norms is not necessarily high, normative behavior has its own emergent properties, and norms are invoked to account for behavior more than they are followed as constraints on behavior.

While the first four chapters lay a general theoretical foundation for an interpretive social psychology of aging, illustrated with research questions, data, and anecdotal accounts, the four chapters that follow deal with specific topics in the social psychology of aging. In Chapter 5, I have outlined a theoretical framework for understanding some of the implications of the fact that people die for individuals and for the life in a society. The relevance of this topic for age-related concerns has been established only recently as the social location of death has come to be concentrated in the later years of the life course. My perspective draws heavily on symbolic interactionist notions of career or status passage and even more on the phenomenological sociologies of Schutz, Berger, and Luckmann. I have attempted to preserve some of the insights of structural-functionalism as a means of dealing, at a macro level, with the problematics of death and dying and of societal response to it; yet I have attempted to avoid the reification, determinism, and strain toward equilibrium found in most functionalist accounts. In the contemporary era, in societies such as our own, individuals are seen as actively seeking, in collaboration with others, to construct the final chapters of their aging and dying careers. The metaphor in this instance is, like the types of metaphors noted earlier in this chapter through the work of Geertz, drawn from the humanities rather than the sciences.

James Dowd's chapter, "The Old Person as Stranger," like my own, seeks to link micro and macro issues and to focus on the social and historical context of the aging individual. Dowd's chapter is predicated on his view that old people in contemporary America (at least) are culturally estranged. He attempts to describe the nature of inter-generational estrangement in relation to age and class stratification. To do so, he posits the outlines of a social psychology of age relations that avoids the limitations of positivistic analysis and sees people as simultaneously producers and products of their worlds.

Older people are strangers, Dowd argues, because of economic and social remoteness. This is due, however, to neither structural nor psychological factors alone. Concretely, Dowd sees a generational watershed based on pre- and post-1920s generations and based on ideological differences and generational *Weltanschauung*. The complexity of his argument cannot concern us here, but the bases of the differences themselves touch closely on the human nature assumptions that differentiate the interpretive perspective from normative and functionalist approaches.

Although differences in worldviews and ideologies inevitably follow from the flow of successive generations through society, the particular nature of such change is also affected by such factors as economic structure and demographic composition. Analyzing these factors, Dowd displays the complementarity between an interpretive psychology and sociology: The perspective is useful to relate broadly based, often conflictual aspects of social structural change to the lives of individuals. But these are issues rarely raised by scholars within the perspective. Dowd's chapter, therefore, perhaps pushes the perspective toward its limits.

The social relationships that older people have to others has been the most enduring topic for social psychological analysis in the field of aging. The quantity and, in lesser degree, the quality of such ties has been described to test activity, disengagement, and role theories of aging; to measure degree of social integration; and, in more recent years, to assess degree of social support.

Only in recent years has network theory been taken from the conceptual warehouse of sociology and systematically applied to these issues. In Chapter 7, Barry Wellman and Alan Hall do precisely this. There are many varieties of network theory (and some view it not as theory but as methodology), but the approach Wellman and Hall take is consistent with the overall theme of this volume. They focus on social support systems in relation to health care of the aged, treating these as an example of social networks. However, in their chapter the basic aspects of network theory are more broadly defined and reviewed.

Recent network analysis, as reviewed by Wellman and Hall, is explicitly structural: It focuses on "the characteristics of the pattern of ties between actors in a social system rather than on the characteristics of the individual actors themselves." As such, it provides an important set of conceptual tools to describe both the immediate and distal social contexts of individuals. Personal or ego-centered social networks can be described for individuals using interview data or other social survey data, that have considerable utility for addressing many issues in the social psychology of aging.

While Wellman and Hall emphasize that social network analysis provides a structuralist alternative to "normative" theorizing, the approach is not antithetical to the voluntarism or intentionality assumed in interpretive sociology. Rather, social network analysis can be used to describe the "opportunity structure" that constrains choice. People can make voluntaristic choices only if the choices are available in the first place. Social network theory can usefully describe many of the limits to voluntarism posed by what Wellman and Hall call "the social distribution of possibilities."

Moreover, as Wellman and Hall also emphasize, social networks cannot be treated merely as "observers' constructs." The empirical study of community ties that they report illustrates this approach. Significant social network ties do not automatically imply social support; support and other networks cross community boundaries; social networks are highly differentiated in meaning and function.

Sarah Matthews, in Chapter 8, analyzes a specific type of social relationship: friendship. Her analysis harks back to Ryff's discussion of the phenomenology of the life course and also to Wellman and Hall's discussion of social networks. Many an interview schedule or questionnaire in research on the social psychology of aging has asked people how many friends they have. Friends have been considered of major importance in the lives of older people and loss of friends is one of the important negative features of aging. Although the spousal relationship is considered more important, friendship is thought to increase in salience with aging, friendship relationships compensating to some degree for kin relationships lost through death.

The researcher can far more easily count friendships if he or she is willing to ask few questions about their meaning. Matthews, drawing on "topical oral biographies," aims specifically at a description of the meaning of "friendship." She sees actors as formulating and resourcing typologies of friendship and the observer-sociologist as faced with the problem of inducing a set of constructs from the actors' constructs. While in normative sociology it may be problematic that there is no widely shared definition of friendship, from the interpretive perspective "this lack of a universal definition poses few problems for social actors who are content to rely on context to supply meaning and rarely question whether or not their meanings in fact are shared."

Matthews identifies three aspects of friendship that are unique to old age. One is that friendship is increasingly precarious with aging. Friends are lost through death and friendships are harder to maintain due to physical fragility and health problems. A second feature is that old people, having longer biographies than the young, tend to have accumulated more friendships over their lifetimes and to have friendships of longer duration than the young. Third, friendships are affected by the position of the aged in the demographic structure of the society. Young people are likely to have more relationships (not necessarily friendships) with people older than themselves, whereas the opposite is true for the old. Matthews relates these features of later-life friendship to "friendship styles," "the expectations about friendships, built up through the life course, that are brought to old age."

The interpretive context that must be investigated if later-life friendship is to be studied therefore encompasses the concrete relationships of a whole life course or set of life courses. The two concluding chapters of the volume seek to place the individual in even wider sociohistorical contexts.

In chapter 9, Martin Kohli takes the life course not as given but as socially constructed. In a sense his chapter approaches issues similar to those of Ryff, in Chapter 2, but from a more macrosociological perspective. The temporal context of his analysis is of long duration, extending well beyond the life course of any individual. Over time, Kohli argues, the social structures of the life course have increased in salience, have become more closely tied to chronological age, and have become more closely tied to the division of labor. Large-scale social changes such as the growth of salaried labor and the administrative apparatus contribute to the increased structuring of the life course.

Kohli's description of the structural problems for which the institutionalization of the life course might be a solution reflects a functionalist argument but goes well beyond functionalism by incorporating conflict and emphasizing the dynamic aspects of the social construction of reality over historical time. Searching for a "nonnormative action theory," he turns to Mead and Schutz.

Moreover, the institutionalization of the life course is seen as a dynamic process of the social construction of reality. Kohli's chapter represents an attempt to draw an interpretive and structural perspective together into one analysis. While this analysis is set in terms of a broad sweep of sociohistorical change, the issues dealt with are germane to several current theoretical questions in the social psychology of aging, including age stratification theory (just how concrete are age strata?), normative role theories of later life (does the institutionalization of the life course have an impact in terms of normative constraint?), and the debate as to whether or not we are moving to an age-irrelevant society (is the short-term indication of decreased chronologization of the life course an indication of long-term erosion of age stratification?).

The book concludes with a contribution from Vern Bengtson that is at once a plea for explicit theorizing and for comparative analysis in the social psychology of aging. In terms of this book, Bengtson's concern to relate the individual to various interpretive contexts at the levels of social and family network, community, society, and historical time emphasizes the interrelatedness of many of the preceding chapters. His chapter also emphasizes the perspective of the interpreter, and the problematics of his or her life-world.

To ground his argument, Bengtson draws on his own research studies, "because I know their flaws, as well as their virtues, only too well." These are a major cross-cultural study of retirement; a cross-cultural study of modernization and its impact on the individual; a study of attitudes toward death in relation to age, gender, ethnic, and other contextual variables; and a study of intergenerational relationships in relation to value orientations.

Bengtson emphasizes the value of theory and argues that it is best derived and employed through explicitly comparative research. The logic of explicit comparisons is equally applicable to the social psychologist and the macro-sociologist (and, indeed, that distinction is a false one much of the time).

When universal theories of aging are tested, any apparent universality disappears, at least in the studies reported by Bengtson. A major reason for this lies in cross-cultural variability in the meanings of theoretical constructs and resultant problems in their measurement. For Bengtson this is largely a methodological problem to be solved by careful pretesting of data-gathering instruments, back-translation, and use of key informants. The issues may be more fundamental than this, and other authors in this book might see these difficulties as in principle irresolvable. Yet, Bengtson strikes a sympathetic chord when he says that "the search for 'universals' is virtually irresistible in science, as is the tendency toward reduction." Explicit theorizing, even the formulation of lawlike propositions, and explicitly comparative testing of such theory is "particularly useful in avoiding unwarranted claims to universality." The testing of deterministic models can increase recognition of the indeterminism that, the interpretive sociologists would assert, in fact characterizes life in society.

There is quite obviously a tension within the covers of this volume, despite the central thrust toward the interpretive social psychology of aging that I have described. These authors, however, thrive on tension. It is only consonant with the assumptions about human nature and the social world made in interpretive sociology that there should be continuing, ever-emergent problems to be addressed. If the chapters that follow foster such emergence, taken either singly or collectively, then the book will have served a useful purpose.

REFERENCES

Aberle, D. F., Cohen, A. K., Davis, A. K., Levy, M. J., Jr., & Sutton, F. X. (1950). The functional prerequisites of society. *Ethics, 60*, 100-111.
Blau, Z. S. (1981). *Aging in a changing society* (2nd ed.). New York: Franklin Watts.

Burgess, E. W. (1960). Aging in Western culture. In E. W. Burgess (Ed.), *Aging in Western societies* (pp. 3-28). Chicago: University of Chicago Press.

Calhoun, R. B. (1978). *In search of the new old: Redefining old age in America, 1945-1970.* New York: Elsevier.

Cavan, R. S., Burgess, E. W., Havighurst, R. J., & Goldhamer, H. (1949). *Personal adjustment in old age.* Chicago: Science Research Associates.

Clausen, J. (1972). The life course of individuals. In M. W. Riley, M. Johnson, & A. Foner (Eds.), *Aging and society: Vol. 3. A sociology of age stratification* (pp. 457-514). New York: Russell Sage Foundation.

Collins, R. (1981). On the microfoundations of macro-sociology. *American Journal of Sociology, 86,* 984-1014.

Collins, R. (1985). *Three sociological traditions.* New York: Oxford University Press.

Cowgill, D. (1974). Aging and modernization: A revision of the theory. In J. F. Gubrium (Ed.), *Late life: Communities and environmental policy* (pp. 123-145). Springfield, IL: Charles C Thomas.

Cowgill, D., & Holmes, L. (1972). *Aging and modernization.* New York: Appleton-Century-Crofts.

Cumming, E., & Henry, W. (1961). *Growing old: The process of disengagement.* New York: Basic Books.

Davis, K. (1959, December). The myth of functional analysis as a special method of sociology and anthropology. *American Sociological Review, 10.*

Dawe, A. (1970). The two sociologies. *British Journal of Sociology, 21,* 207-218.

Denzin, K. (1983). Interpretive interactionism. In G. Morgan (Ed.), *Beyond method: Strategies for social research* (pp. 129-146). Beverly Hills, CA: Sage.

Durkheim, E. (1964). *The division of labor in society.* New York: Free Press. (Original work published 1893)

Foner, A. (1972). The polity. In M. W. Riley, M. Johnson, & A. Foner (Eds.), *Aging and society: Vol. 3. A sociology of age stratification* (pp. 115-159). New York: Russell Sage.

Foner, A. (1974). Age stratification and age conflict in political life. *American Sociological Review, 39,* 187-196.

Foner, A. (1984). The issues of age conflict in political life. In V. Garms-Homolová, E. M. Hoerning, & D. Schaeffer (Eds.), *Intergenerational relationships* (pp. 170-175). Lewiston and Toronto: C. J. Hogrefe.

Foner, A., & Kertzer, D. (1978). Transitions over the life course: Lessons from age-set societies. *American Journal of Sociology, 83,* 1081-1104.

Geertz, C. (1983). *Local knowledge: Further essays in interpretive anthropology.* New York: Basic Books.

Giddens, A. (1976). *New rules of sociological method: A positive critique of interpretative sociologies.* New York: Basic Books.

Harris, D. K., & Cole, W. E. (1980). *Sociology of aging.* Boston: Houghton Mifflin.

Heiss, J. (1981). Social roles. In M. Rosenberg & R. H. Turner (Eds.), *Social psychology: Sociological perspectives* (pp. 94-129). New York: Basic Books.

Hempel, C. G. (1965). The logic of functional analysis. In C. G. Hempel (Ed.), *Aspects of scientific explanation* (pp. 297-330). New York: Free Press.

John, R. (1984). Prerequisites of an adequate theory of aging: A critique and a reconceptualization. *Mid-American Review of Sociology, 9*(2), 79-108.

Levy, M. J., Jr. (1952). *The structure of society.* Princeton, NJ: Princeton University Press.

Levy, M. J., Jr. (1967). Structural-functional analysis. In D. L. Sills (Ed.), *International encyclopedia of the social sciences* (Vol. 6, pp. 21-29). New York: Free Press.

Maddox, G. L. (1965). Fact and artifact: Evidence bearing on disengagement theory. *Human Development, 8,* 117-130.

Maddox, G. L. (1966). Persistence of life style among the elderly. *Proceedings of the 7th International Congress of Gerontology* (pp. 309-311).

Maddox, G. L., & Campbell, R. I. (1985). Scope, concepts, and methods in the study of aging. In R. H. Binstock & E. Shanas (Eds.), *Handbook of aging and the social sciences* (2nd ed., pp. 3-31). New York: Van Nostrand Reinhold.

Malinowski, B. (1939). The group and the individual in functional analysis. *American Journal of Sociology, 44,* 938-964.

Marshall, V. W. (1981). State of the art lecture: The sociology of aging. In J. Crawford (Ed.), *Collection III* (pp. 76-144). Winnipeg: Canadian Association on Gerontology.

Marshall, V. W., & Tindale, J. A. (1978-1979). Notes for a radical gerontology. *International Journal of Aging and Human Development, 9*(2), 163-175.

Merton, R. K. (1957). Manifest and latent functions. In R. K. Merton (Ed.), *Social theory and social structure* (rev. ed., pp. 19-84). New York: Free Press.

Mills, C. W. (1959). *The sociological imagination.* New York: Oxford University Press.

Neugarten, B. L., Moore, J. W., & Lowe, J. C. (1965). Age norms, age constraints, and adult socialization. *American Journal of Sociology, 70,* 710-717.

Orbach, H. L. (1970). *The disengagement theory of aging, 1960-1970: A case study of scientific controversy.* Doctoral dissertation, University of Michigan.

Palmore, E. (1968). The effects of aging on activities and attitudes. *Gerontologist, 8,* 259-263.

Palmore, E., & Manton, K. (1974). Modernization and the status of the aged: International correlations. *Journal of Gerontology, 29*(2), 205-210.

Palmore, E., & Whittington, F. (1971). Trends in the relative status of the aged. *Social Forces, 50,* 84-91.

Parsons, T. (1949). *The structure of social action.* New York: Free Press. (Original work published 1937)

Parsons, T. (1951). *The social system.* New York: Free Press.

Radcliffe-Brown, A. R. (1935). On the concept of function in social science. *American Anthropologist, N. S., 37,* 394-402.

Riley, M. W. (1971). Social gerontology and the age stratification of society. *Gerontologist, 11,* 79-87.

Riley, M. W. (1976). Age strata in social systems. In R. Binstock & E. Shanas (Eds.), *Handbook of aging and the social sciences* (pp. 189-217). New York: Van Nostrand Reinhold.

Riley, M. W. (1978). Aging, social change, and the power of ideas. *Daedalus, 107*(4), 39-52.

Riley, M. W. (1985). Age strata in social systems. In R. Binstock & E. Shanas (Eds.), *Handbook of aging and the social sciences* (2nd ed., pp. 369-411). New York: Van Nostrand Reinhold.

Riley, M. W., Johnson, M., & Foner, A. (Eds.). (1972). *Aging and society: Vol. 3. A sociology of age stratification.* New York: Russell Sage.

Rosow, I. (1974). *Socialization to old age.* Berkeley: University of California Press.

Rosow, I. (1976). Status and role change through the life span. In R. H. Binstock & E. Shanas (Eds.), *Handbook of aging and the social sciences* (pp. 457-482). New York: Van Nostrand Reinhold.

Rosow, I. (1985). Status and role change through the life cycle. In R. H. Binstock & E. Shanas (Eds.), *Handbook of aging and the social sciences* (2nd ed., pp. 62-93). New York: Van Nostrand Reinhold.

Stryker, S. (1981). Symbolic interactionism: Themes and variations. In M. Rosenberg & R. H. Turner (Eds.), *Social psychology: Sociological perspectives* (pp. 3-29). New York: Basic Books.

Turner, J. H. (1982). *The structure of sociological theory.* Homewood, IL: Dorsey.

Unruh, D. R. (1983). *Invisible lives: Social worlds of the aged.* Beverly Hills, CA: Sage.

Weber, M. (1978). *Economy and society: An outline of interpretive sociology* (2 vols., G. Roth & C. Wittich, Eds.). Berkeley: University of California Press.

Wilson, T. P. (1970). Normative and interpretive paradigms in sociology. In J. D. Douglas (Ed.), *Understanding everyday life* (pp. 57-79). Chicago: Aldine.

2

The Subjective Construction of Self and Society: An Agenda for Life-Span Research

CAROL D. RYFF

Some of us long for enlivened theoretical discussion as we go about our business of doing aging research. My longings are ministered to in this chapter as I attempt to generate new and renewed theoretical interest in phenomenological and interpretive approaches to the study of aging. As a first step in this endeavor, I review key proponents and propositions of these perspectives. An interdisciplinary sketch is provided drawing on the influence of phenomenology in psychology and the interpretive perspective in sociology. My intent is to crystallize fundamental assumptions and objectives of these approaches so that they might be better understood. Compared to mainstream theories in the social sciences, phenomenological and interpretive perspectives have had minor impact. Part of the difficulty may stem from the struggle required to discern what these approaches actually mean.

Still, the well-nourished, well-balanced scholar cannot live by theory alone. Many have perhaps discounted the writings of phenomenologists because they failed to get beyond overly abstract, concept-laden discussions into more concrete directives for generating knowledge or conducting research. As such a directive, a second section of the chapter reviews the phenomenologists' program of research on the subjective experience of personal change in adulthood and aging. This section illustrates how phenomenological and interpretive objectives can be translated to empirical questions. Our studies capture certain of the objectives detailed in the opening section but fail to address others. I therefore discuss how the program of research is being expanded to respond to other guiding themes of phenomenology and interpretive sociology.

A final section moves from our specific program of research into territory that is at once more grandiose and more precarious. Though the concern for inner, subjective meaning is a central strength of phenomenological and interpretive perspectives, it is also a central limitation. One immersed in these approaches can easily produce models that are overly personological and oblivious to the strictures and opportunities of the surrounding social order. Thus reappears the age-old question of how to connect the inner experience of the individual with the surrounding external world. Drawing on empirical examples, I propose that the study of adult life events could provide a useful nexus for joining these realms. The proposal addresses theoretical issues as well, such as the argument that psychology and sociology are inextricably linked as they try to explain change within their own systems. The chapter closes with proposals aimed at provoking new empirical directions regarding undying theoretical issues.

SUBJECTIVE EXPERIENCE AND INNER MEANINGS

The significance of phenomenological and interpretive approaches for the social sciences varies as a function of the sources examined. Different proponents have emphasized various themes and these have been differentially translated in psychology and sociology. Rather than attempt a uniform summary, I have selected for discussion representative works that capture prominent guiding assumptions. The discussion is organized according to the phenomenological tradition within psychology and the interpretive tradition in sociology. An enormous literature underlies any such review, and the reader is encouraged to consult original sources for a thorough introduction to these approaches. My aim here is to sketch key assumptions and concerns deriving from representative works so as to examine their relevance for the study of adulthood and aging.

The Phenomenological Tradition
Within Psychology

I have been trained as a psychologist. As such, my initial exposure to phenomenology came within the psychological realm. Historical accounts within this literature traced the origins of phenomenology to the philosophical writings of Edmund Husserl (1859-1938). Working in an era in which positivism was at the helm, Husserl argued that objectivism, causal determinism, and mind/body dualism distorted the phenomena being studied. Cartesian dualism assumed that human life "can be neatly divided in what is physical—and therefore observable like any non-human physical process—and what is mental, or supposedly private, subjective, and inaccessible to observation" (Bernstein, 1978, p. 138). Believing that the psychology of his era was essentially bound to the physical, Husserl advocated examining direct experience in the context of the everyday world, the "Lebenswelt." His aim was to discover the "essence of things" and the method he conceived was a laborious process wherein objects are brought to "self-givenness in intuition" (Lauer, 1965, p. 62). This meant getting away from mathematical formulas or psychological constructs that were being substituted for human experience and going back to the experiences themselves.

Specific to psychology, Husserl argued that too much emphasis had been placed on interpreting or classifying human experience rather than finding out what human experience actually is. In this sense, he advocated a kind of pure description without interpretation or explanation. To understand reality as immediately given, one must free oneself of judgments or preconceptions, that is, "bracket" one's presuppositions so as to understand reality as immediately given without bias or assumption. Other themes associated with Husserl's work are intentionality (he was much influenced by the work of Brentano); the transcendental epoché, which referred to the act of pure philosophical reflection (the methods for which were never entirely clear); essential intuition (the perception of a perception; for instance, a recollection of a judgment); and the life-world (Lebenswelt), which referred to the world of commonsense language and everyday experience. Husserl is associated with the general aim of understanding human subjectivity. "For true nature in its proper scientific sense is a product of the spirit that investigates nature, and thus, the science of nature presupposes the science of the spirit" (Husserl, in Lauer, 1965, p. 189).

Phenomenology within experimental psychology. Because of the obscurity of his writings and method, Husserl's work did not yield a unified conception of phenomenology. It did, however, influence an array of philosophical elaborations and psychological applications (see Spiegelberg, 1972). Within experimental psychology, phenomenology has been more generally contrasted with behaviorism (Wann, 1964), which encompassed many of the same emphases (e.g., objectivism, positivism, determinism) against which Husserl was reacting in his day. MacLeod (1964) attempted to add further clarity to the distinction between the phenomenologist and the experimentalist by noting that the former would accept as subject matter all the data of experience (i.e., subjective as well as objective experiences), and that the former would begin observation of phenomena by suspending biases or putting implicit assumptions into brackets (i.e., concepts such as reinforcement or stimulus generalization would not be postulated). With regard to bias, MacLeod recognized the impossibility of suspending all bias or preconception, but stressed the need for identifying one's bias and shifting systematically from one bias to the next. MacLeod also provided a much-needed clarification of the difference between the phenomenological approach and the introspectionism of Titchener. For Titchener, introspection meant analyzing the data of experience into their irreducible elements (e.g., sensations and images) through disciplined observation. The introspectionist begins with the initial assumption that experience can be reducible to a finite number of conscious elements and attributes, a kind of bias the phenomenologist would attempt to bracket. More important, the phenomenologist would give much greater emphasis to meaning: the meaning of experience for the experiencing subject, a meaning that was something separate from the reduction of experience to basic sensations and images. MacLeod (1964, p. 68) states that there is no experience devoid of meaning: "Even a pinpoint of light in a dark room has meaning in that it is white and not red, small and not large, out there in space and not in here in me."

Phenomenological psychologists have conducted research in the traditional experimental areas of perception, learning, and memory. The Duquesne Studies in Phenomenological Psychology (Giorgi, Fischer, & Von Eckartsberg, 1971; Giorgi, Fischer, & Murray, 1975; Giorgi, Knowles, & Smith, 1979) have provided a forum for many such endeavors. Colaizzi (1971), for example, analyzed the learner's perception of learning material at various phases in a learning experiment with nonsense syllables. Subjects were interrupted to provide descriptions of their experience. They spoke about the apparatus, instructions, experimenter, interruption, and unfamiliar letters, which clarified that the *meaning* of the learning situation included all of these, not just the nonsense syllables. The facts, contexts, and meanings were much broader than typically would have been reported. Similarly, in a phenomenological approach to memory, Sardello (1978) critiqued the unmeaningful study of memory (as with nonsense syllables) and the traditional focus on storage, acquisition, and retrieval. He argued that memory should be studied in the life-world rather than the laboratory and that memory must be treated as an experience rather than an impersonal, abstract fact. Overall, these works emphasized the total range of experiences a person has in psychological experiments and the meaning the experiment has for the individual. Further clarification of phenomenology's influence on traditional experimental topics is provided by Valle and King (1978).

Phenomenology within the personality and clinical realm. Within the personality realm, phenomenology has been closely related to humanistic and existential psychologies (Gatchel & Mears, 1982; Hall & Lindzey, 1978; Massey, 1981; Mischel, 1981; Pervin, 1980). The concern is with assessing the individual's subjective impressions or experiences and examining how these relate to external behavior and social circumstances.

> Modern phenomenology does not deny that there is a material or objective reality, but it focuses on consciousness and the individual's unique perception of a material or objective reality. It claims that reality is a private affair and that the appearance of things in the mind is more important than whatever actuality exists apart from human awareness. This view point is therefore concerned with the study of subjective personal experiences of reality. Descriptions and analyses of reality are made according to the individual's unique frame of reference. (Gatchel & Mears, 1982, p. 417)

Thus, phenomenology reflects an approach to the study of personality rather than a specific theory with formal postulates aimed at explaining disorders or adaptive functioning.

Phenomenology has been articulated extensively within the clinical realm, the therapeutic context where it is important to understand the subjective experiences of the individual. Carl Rogers (1961), for example, stresses understanding people in terms of how they view themselves and the world around them. He has developed a theory of psychotherapy concerned with subjective personal experiences of reality.

> As he [the client] finds someone else listening acceptantly to his feelings, he little by little becomes able to listen to himself. He begins to receive the communications from within himself—to realize that he is angry, to recognize when he is frightened, even to realize when he is feeling courageous. As he becomes more open to what is going on within him he becomes able to listen to feelings which he has always denied and repressed. He can listen to feelings which have seemed to him so terrible or disorganizing, or so abnormal, or so shameful, that he has never been able to recognize their existence in himself. (Rogers, 1961, p. 63)

The descriptions and analyses of reality are made according to the individual's unique frame of reference and the supportive context provided by the therapist enables the client to explore personal feelings and become more accepting of them. George Kelly's (1955) psychology of personal constructs represents another phenomenological perspective in personality. Kelly's model focuses on how behavior and thought are determined by the individual's interpretation and construction of reality. It is a cognitive model that assumes behavior and personality are a function of belief systems and thinking processes within the individual. The emphasis on styles of thinking and perceiving contrasts with psychodynamic theories that focus on concepts such as motivation, needs, and drives. For Kelly, people operate much like scientists in generating constructs and hypotheses about their lives and what happens to them. The process of psychotherapy aims to elaborate, test, or modify these constructs. Both Rogers and Kelly stress understanding reality as the person sees or experiences it and build their program of therapy on altering the individual's view of self and the world around him or her.

Within existential psychology, phenomenology has been seen as a method for studying the inner world of experience. It describes experience using the language of experience—a vocabulary of commonplace, everyday words as opposed to technical, scientific terms. Boss (1963) and Binswanger (1963) have stressed understanding human functioning rather than explaining it, thereby rejecting a concern for causality. They have also been suspicious of theory, mind-body dualism, and experimentation. The principles of existential counseling following from these views have been summarized by Anderson (1978). These include noninstrumentality (seeing the relationship in nontechnical, nondirective terms), self-centeredness (viewing the client's self as the primary focus of counseling), encounter (the counselor's willingness to confront the patient directly when appropriate), and incurable crisis (the aim is not to cure human crises because they are viewed as an inevitable part of the human condition). Phenomenology's role is to provide the means or methods for understanding the person's subjective experience of distress.

Throughout the perspectives discussed above, one can discern a continuum along which the works were integrated with the methods of science. Rogers and Kelly, for example, both attempted to study the individual's subjective experiences with objective measures (structured interviews, content analyses, Q-sort methods, and objective tests). At the other extreme one might consider Binswanger's case of Ellen West (1958), which reveals a style of writing that is evocative, poetic, and oriented toward imagery rather than technical terminology. In this work, the ties are stronger with literature than with scientific methodology. Thus, while phenomenology has led personality researchers to be concerned with how individuals experience themselves and their worlds, there has been considerable disparity regarding whether or not such aims can be pursued within the usual framework of the scientific method.

The Interpretive Tradition Within Sociology

Phenomenology did not evolve as a unified conception of principles in psychology. So, too, in sociology the interpretive or hermeneutic approach has multiple meanings depending on the sources examined. In general, however, the interpretive perspective provided an alternative to the oversocialized conception of the individual provided by mainstream sociological theory (see Marshall, 1978-1979; Wrong, 1961). As in the emergence of phenomenology in psychology, the reaction was against positivism and strongly deterministic views of the individual. The new alternatives emphasized the individual's ability to gain control or mastery over the surrounding life situations. In addition, emphasis was given to the meanings held by the individual, to issues of identity, and to negotiating one's social relationships. In this view, "norms are not something 'out there' to be learned, and internalized, and which thence determine behavior; rather, norms are viewed as claims involved in, and outcomes of, continuous negotiations processes" (Marshall, 1978-1979, p. 348). To add substance to these differing perspectives, brief summaries will be provided of the work of Schutz (1967) and Berger and Luckmann (1966).

Meaningful action and the interpretive function. Alfred Schutz (1967) saw the goal of interpretive sociology as the study of social behavior "by interpreting its subjective meaning as found in the intentions of individuals. The aim, then, is to interpret the actions of individuals in the social world and the ways in which individuals give meaning to social phenomena" (p. 6). Schutz was concerned with the interpretation of one's own experiences and those of others, with the establishment of meaning, and with the nature of ideal types. In his view, objectivity was made possible through the use of theoretical constructs known as "ideal types." Thus he was influenced by the work of Max Weber as well as by the theory of meaning of Edmund Husserl.

Schutz was also interested in Weber's concept of meaningful action. From Weber's perspective, all social relationships and structures could be reduced to the most elementary forms of individual behavior. Though complex phenomena in the social world had meaning, it was meaning held at the level of individual action.

> The action of the individual and its intended meaning alone are subject to interpretive understanding. Further, it is only by such understanding of individual action that social science can gain access to the meaning of each social relationship and structure, constituted as these are, in the last analysis, by the action of the individual in the social world. (Schutz, 1967, p. 6)

Thus for Schutz the meaning of actions must first be understood at the individual level, with the meaning of social relationships and social structures following from these.

Elaborating his interest in the concept of meaning, Schutz examined the distinction between actions that are meaningful and those without meaning. He also studied the distinction between subjective and objective meaning, between directly experienced social reality and indirectly experienced social reality, and between observational and motivational understanding. He provided a foundation for the theory of intersubjective understanding and discussed the differences in meaning between self-explication and interpretation of another person's experience. Again he argued that understanding of another must begin with explication of one's own experience.

> First we must study the genuine understanding of actions which are performed without any communicative intent. The action of the wood-cutter would be a good example. Second we would examine cases where such communicative intent was present. The latter type of action involves a whole new dimension, the using and interpreting of signs. (Schutz, 1967, p. 113)

He therefore moved from the study of meaningful actions to consideration of the symbolic system by which meaning is communicated.

With regard to the structure of the social world, Schutz examined concepts such as social action, social relationship, and ideal types. "When sociology undertakes to interpret a concrete action, it has the act already given to it as a datum. From the act it tries to draw inferences about the motives that would be typical of a person acting in this way.

In the process, recourse is had to a personal ideal type" (Schutz, 1967, p. 229). The understanding of social actions and social relationships was based on the conception of the ideal type and the motivations associated with such an ideal figure. Finally, Schutz outlined what he saw as the problems of interpretive sociology, including the formulation of causal adequacy in the social sciences, meaning adequacy, and the problem of relevance. Throughout these discussions, he agreed with Weber that the social sciences should be value free.

The Social Construction of Knowledge

Berger and Luckmann (1966) proposed a treatise in the sociology of knowledge. In it, they argued that reality is socially constructed. Thus knowledge or what is real depends on the social context.

> What is "real" to a Tibetan monk may not be "real" to an American businessman. The "knowledge" of the criminal differs from the "knowledge" of the criminologist. It follows that specific agglomerations of "reality and knowledge" pertain to specific contexts, and that these relationships will have to be included in an adequate sociological analysis of these contexts. (Berger & Luckmann, 1966, p. 3)

Numerous philosophers influenced Berger and Luckmann's perspective. The term "sociology of knowledge" came from the German philosopher Max Scheler. The root proposition that consciousness is determined by social being was derived from Marx. In Nietzsche Berger and Luckmann examined the social significance of deception, self-deception, and the role of illusion as a necessary condition of life. And from Dilthey they drew emphasis on the inevitable historicity of human thought and hence the relativity of all perspectives on human events.

Like many researchers in this tradition, they were concerned with the relationship between subjective meanings and objective realities. They examined reality as it is available to the common sense of the ordinary members of society. Like Schutz (1967, p. 34), they believed that objectivation occurs through language and social interaction: "Human expressivity is capable of objectivation, that is, it manifests itself in products of human activity that are available both to their producers and to other men as elements of a common world."

Berger and Luckmann begin with an emphasis on subjective constructions and then move to the analysis of socialization into roles. Society has objective reality by the processes of institutionalization and legitimation and has subjective reality by the processes of internalization and socialization. While the individual internalizes what is objectivated as reality in his or her society, not all elements of subjective awareness originate in socialization (e.g., awareness of one's own body).

> Subjective biography is not fully social. The individual apprehends himself as being both inside and outside society. This implies that the symmetry between objective and subjective reality is never a static, once-for-all state of affairs. (Berger & Luckmann, 1966, pp. 133-134)

Individual decisions and actions are not given prominent emphasis in their model, though they do discuss these topics. Individualism for them is linked to unsuccessful socialization. That is, when the socialization process has failed the individual must choose between discrepant realities and identities and face the question "Who am I?"

> This opens a Pandora's box of "individualistic" choices, which eventually become generalized regardless of whether one's biographical course was determined by the "right" or the "wrong" choices. The "individualist" emerges as a specific social type who has at least the potential to migrate between a number of available worlds and who has deliberately and awarely constructed a self out of the "material" provided by a number of available identities. (p. 171)

In this regard, autonomy, self-direction, and capacity for individual choice constitute a "specific social type" for Berger and Luckmann. Though reality is socially constructed in their view, individuals are basically guided by the social order except in the anomalous case in which socialization has failed.

Still, Berger and Luckmann's model is not entirely deterministic, as they discuss the dialectics between identity and social structure. The formation and maintenance of identity are determined by the social structure, but, conversely, these identities "react upon the given social structure, maintaining it, modifying it, or even reshaping it. Societies have histories in the course of which specific identities emerge; these histories are, however, made by men with specific identities" (p. 173). Historical change for them occurs then in the interplay between individual consciousness and social structure. Radical changes in the social structure (as during periods of revolution) produce changes in the psychological reality, which in turn may further influence the social structure.

Berger and Luckmann argue that sociologists must guard against reifying social phenomena with a purely structural analysis. Social phenomena are not laws of the universe but are continually evolving in history. Sociology must be conducted in continuous conversation with history and philosophy. For Berger and Luckmann (1966, p. 189) the proper object of sociology "is society as part of the human world, made by men, inhabited by men, and in turn, making men, in an ongoing historical process."

Links to ethnomethodology and symbolic interactionism. Other empirical and theoretical works in sociology have ties to the interpretive or phenomenological orientation. For example, Garfinkel's (1967) studies in ethnomethodology examine practical activities in practical circumstances with practical reasoning. Similar to Husserl's emphasis on the life-world, the concern is with commonplace activities in daily life and how individuals produce and manage their everyday affairs. Garfinkel (1967, p. 37) spoke of the need to make commonplace scenes visible: "The seen but unnoticed backgrounds of everyday activities are made visible and are described from a perspective in which persons live out the lives they do, have the children they do, feel the feelings, think the thoughts, enter the relationships they do, all in order to permit the sociologist to solve his theoretical problems." Such a perspective has been used to examine decision making in such settings as suicide prevention centers, coroner's offices, jury situations, and outpatient psychiatric clinics.

The human construction of social reality, a recurrent theme within the interpretive approach, is also emphasized in the literature of symbolic interactionism. Marshall (1978-1979, p. 349), in contrasting normative sociology's emphasis on the individual's incorporation and internalization of external reality, describes the imagery of the symbolic interactionist: "The actor portrays an individual who searches for meaning, who constructs his identity, and who seeks to direct his interactions with others in ways compatible with his sense of identity." Philosopher George Herbert Mead (1934) was concerned with inner experience and saw the need to go beyond the behaviorism of Watson prominent in his era, which focused solely on the external. However, he contended that one got to the inside realm by way of the outside realities:

> Social psychology is behavioristic in the sense of starting off with an observable activity—the dynamic, on-going social process, and the social acts which are its component elements—to be studied and analyzed scientifically. But it is not behavioristic in the sense of ignoring the inner

experience of the individual—the inner phase of the process or activity. On the contrary, it is particularly concerned with the rise of such experience within the process as a whole. It simply works from the outside to the inside instead of from the inside to the outside, so to speak, in its endeavor to determine how such experience does arise in the process. (pp. 7-8)

Following from the above position, Mead proposed that human beings attempt to form understanding of their own behavior through the perspective of the other. People try to see themselves and their experiences by taking the role of the other, seeing through the eyes of the other. Thus the feedback received from significant others plays an important part in identity development from this perspective. These selective aspects of symbolic interactionism, particularly the concern with inner experience and the construction of one's identity, parallel general concerns within the interpretive approach.

PHENOMENOLOGICAL AND INTERPRETIVE THEMES

As can be seen from the preceding review, a wide array of researchers have contributed to or been guided by phenomenological and interpretive writings. In psychology, interested scholars have applied their concern for subjective experience and the construction of meaning to traditional experimental and clinical domains. These applications have resulted in the implementation of different types of experiments and the practice of new forms of therapy. In sociology, the emphasis has been on expanding the theoretical framework guiding the subjective construction of self and society. The interest has been more conceptual than empirical. Running through these endeavors, one can discern various themes. Though not all the theorists addressed the same issues, certain recurrent assumptions or goals are stated. I will discuss these themes in detail in the following section, with the intent of identifying the essential meanings in these diverse approaches. Once key objectives are in hand, their import for the study of adulthood and aging can be assessed more easily.

(1) Phenomenological and interpretive approaches emphasize a person that is active and intentional. People construct their own meanings and identities; they exercise control over their lives and are guided by internal convictions and goals. Within psychology, this view of the person was a reaction to reigning behavioral orientations that saw the individual as shaped, controlled, and determined by forces in the

surrounding environment. In sociology, the position was a reaction against oversocialized views of the individual that saw the person as merely internalizing values and norms of society and following stable, socially prescribed roles. Historically, it is perhaps worth recalling the social contexts that fostered the more controlled, deterministic views of the person. Dawe (1970, p. 207), for example, cites the Enlightenment, the French Revolution, and the Industrial Revolution as leading to a sociology that gave focus to concepts such as "authority, the group, the sacred and, above all, the organic community." Presumably the need was to construe a social world that was orderly and predictable and individuals who were controlled and responsive to authority. However, social contexts change and with them the basic nature of the individual may be reworked. The phenomenological and interpretive writings stress an individual who has the capacity for and the need to be self-directing, intentional, and guiding his or her own destiny. These writings are not new, nor is the call for a more active conception of the person. During the heyday of positivism, there were prominent advocates of intentional, goal-oriented models of the person (such as Brentano and Dilthey). The newness, however, stems from the growing interest in translating these models into research strategies that can *evidence* intentionality, its sources, and its impact. Thus the active person theme has a long-standing tradition in the theoretical or philosophical realm. Its appearance in the empirical realm has yet to receive significant notice or recognition.

(2) Phenomenologists and interpretive sociologists speak of a person concerned with meaning that pertains to the surrounding world and to oneself. Phenomenological researchers in psychology ask participants in experimental studies about the meaning of the experiment for them—what they thought about or noticed during laboratory studies of learning, perception, or memory. Phenomenological or existential therapists emphasize how individuals construe themselves and experience their personal feelings. Interpretive sociologists in turn focus on how individuals make meaning of their actions. Schutz, for example, gave considerable attention to the question of what distinguishes meaningful actions from those without meaning. The emphasis then is not just on behavior but the meaning of behavior, or action, as constructed by the person. Again, while prevailing paradigms have focused on what people *do* in terms of their external behavior or social roles, these alternative models give as much attention to the *meaning* of people's actions for themselves and for their surrounding worlds. A critical concern with this theme, as with the one discussed above, is how

to address the question of meaning and meaningful action on the empirical level.

(3) A third theme emerging from these perspectives is that human conduct must be understood from the point of view of the person. In contrast to the views that saw the subjective realm as unobservable and inaccessible, these alternative approaches saw the subjective realm as the starting point for understanding objective reality. Husserl, for example, advocated a kind of pure description without interpretation or explanation in order to understand reality as immediately given; Rogers based his theory of psychotherapy on subjective personal experiences of reality; Schutz argued that even complex social phenomena must first be understood on the level of the individual; and Berger and Luckmann began their treatise with an emphasis on subjective constructions. Many of these theorists, acknowledging the importance of the subjective realm, were also interested in the relationship between the subjective and the objective. Schutz studied the distinction between subjective and objective meaning, Berger and Luckmann believed that objectivation occurs through language and social interaction, and Mead addressed the question of how the "outside" influences the "inside." In combination, these views elevated the inner experiences of the individual to a new level of importance in the social sciences.

(4) A corollary to the emphasis on subjective or personal experiences of reality is the concern for studying the Lebenswelt, the life-world. Husserl first advocated investigation of the life-world. Later, Berger and Luckmann addressed how reality is structured in the commonsense world of everyday life. More recently, ethnomethodologists have examined practical situations in the real world and practical decision making within them. The aim in these endeavors, as Husserl might have put it, is to get away from empty word abstractions and into the world as it is actually experienced. Thus, in contrast to the tendency of current research to generate jargon and concepts, the concern for the life-world calls for understanding the world as we actually live in it, attending to the everyday issues that matter to us, and exploring them with the language we use to communicate. Such appeals have an enticing ring for many, but again the challenge is to translate the life-world imperative into research strategies and actions.

(5) The contextual and historical relativity of what we know is emphasized in various phenomenological and interpretive works. Berger and Luckmann cautioned researchers against reifying their constructs to make them universal. Instead, they reminded us that our knowledge about human experience and social structure is time and

culture bound. The Tibetan monk's reality differs from that of the American businessman. Taken to heart, this relativity changes considerably the scope of the usual scientific objectives. Rather than search for sweeping generalizations about human experience or social structure, we must content ourselves with the unending task of monitoring changing human experiences in changing social worlds.

I have taken some liberties in formulating the above parallels. The guiding themes were given greater emphasis in some works and less in others. Lest my drawing of convergence seem overdone, I have also tried to identify points on which the phenomenological and interpretive writers are are not in agreement. These are detailed below.

(1) The question of whether the social sciences should be value free or value directed is discussed by many of the perspectives mentioned above. Among the sociological writers, Weber, Schutz, Berger, and Luckmann stress the importance of conducting social science from the standpoint of neutrality. On the other hand, one can find in the discipline alternative views. Dawe (1970, p. 215), for example, has argued that values shape sociology from beginning to end:

> In other words, the problems of order and control are problems of value and, to the extent that they penetrate sociology in the logical progression suggested here, it follows that values shape the discipline from beginning to end. This is not to say that ethical arguments about those values can be settled within sociology itself; this would be circular. But it is to say that values play a much more pervasive role in sociology than is allowed by the conventional wisdom of value-neutrality.

From a psychological perspective, Giorgi (1970) has made a similar argument, stating that it is impossible to be free of values or bias totally. Rather than pretend to achieve a kind of impartiality, he advocates that scientists make clear their biases and preferences at the outset. His view is that of a science that admits to its guiding biases, but makes every effort to make them explicitly known. This issue of whether the researcher can or should be value free is ever present in the selection of a topic of study, the choice of guiding theory, operationalization of the question, and the application of findings. One could argue that the question itself evokes a certain value perspective. In any case, it is a significant point of disagreement among phenomenological and interpretive approaches and, as such, produces considerable divergence regarding the activities of the scientist.

(2) Many of the writings covered address identity or the emergence and formation of the self. Sociological perspectives tend to emphasize the inherently social nature of identity. For example, Mead argues that we come to know ourselves through taking the perspective of the other, seeing ourselves through their eyes. He speaks of moving from the outside to the inside, that is, following how social structure and social roles give definition to the person. Similarly, Berger and Luckmann focus on processes of institutionalization, internalization, and socialization in understanding human conduct. For them, individualism is a failure of socialization when one must choose between discrepant realities and identities in answering the question "Who am I?" In contrast, psychological perspectives tend to be more personological in formulating the emergence and development of identity. Rogers stresses that the person must listen, with the assistance of a supportive therapist, to his or her own feelings in achieving self-development. Moreover, as development progresses, identity becomes less and less social.

> Less and less does he look to others for approval or disapproval; for standards to live by; for decisions and choices. He recognizes that it rests within himself to choose; that the only question that matters is, "Am I living in a way which is deeply satisfying to me, and which truly expresses me?" This I think is perhaps the most important question for the creative individual. (Rogers, 1961, p. 119)

Other clinical perspectives in psychology have shared this view. Jung (1954, p. 175) speaks of "deliverance from convention" as being critical to self-development. In becoming more individuated, one casts aside cultural standards acquired in early life. Similarly, Maslow (1955) describes self-actualization as leading to greater autonomy, self-direction, detachment, and self-sufficiency. Thus these perspectives see the individual as functioning at a higher level, becoming more differentiated and developed when he or she steps out of the strictures of societal norms and standards. These "growth theories" have been criticized as leading to narcissism, egocentrism, and alienation (see Ryff, 1985, for a review of these issues). This issue aside, the point for the present perspective is that the conceptions of self-development have varied considerably, depending on whether the guiding lens is interpretive and sociological or phenomenological and psychological. Though antipositivistic consensus is strong among these perspectives, the fundamental discrepancy between viewing the person versus the social group as central to identity and self-development persisted.

(3) The methodological implications following from phenomeno-logical and interpretive approaches reveal anything but consensus. Husserl's methods, to begin with, were notoriously unclear. Thus later researchers carried them in widely differing directions. Some advocated a general antiscience position in which phenomenology became the rationale for discounting the scientific method. Existential therapists, for example, referred to phenomenology as their method and from this position wrote about their patients in a way that was more literary and evocative than scientific and precise (e.g., Binswanger, 1958). This tradition can be traced in part to the works of Dilthey (see Giorgi, 1970), a nineteenth-century philosopher who drew inspiration from aesthetics, literature, and historical studies rather than mathematics and the natural sciences. Dilthey argued that the subjective matter of the human sciences could not be observed directly nor could theories be formulated that could be tested by experiments. Theory must rather be approached indirectly with awareness of the complexities of life. This tradition, though less prominent in the history of psychology, was concerned with description, meaning, intentional relations, and understanding behavior and consciousness in context. It contrasted with the more known and accepted tradition that began with Wundt and evolved through James and Titchener. The emphasis here was on controlled observation, experimentation, measurement, and explanation. Some phenomenol-ogists attempted to work within these guidelines (see the Duquesne Studies noted earlier) though they tried to expand them to include more subjective data sources. Also focused on the individual's subjective experience, Rogers and Kelly worked with objective measures (struc-tured tests, content analyses, Q-sorts). In sum, the question of whether phenomenology and interpretive sociology prescribe quantitative versus qualitative, structured versus unstructured, open-ended versus closed procedures is far from resolved.

I have argued elsewhere (Ryff, 1984) that the concern for human experience, its meaning for the individual, its connections to the world in which the person lives, does not dictate any particular methodology. Certainly phenomenology has revitalized interests in spontaneous reports, personal narrative, and protocol analysis (Colaizzi, 1978). Such methods enable persons to describe in their own words experiences they are having. But these paths to understanding human experience are not problem free. The condensing and interpretation of the protocol is open to the bias of the researcher. Such procedures are also unfair to the inarticulate and less verbal. Observational methods (Filstead, 1970) entail a further mix of advantages and disadvantages. Thus the aims of phenomenological and interpretive approaches are best served by employing a wide range of methodological procedures. Such a position is not hedging; rather, it is an acknowledgment that the strengths and weaknesses of more qualitative methods complement those of the more quantitative variety.

In sum, I have identified a number of recurrent themes in phenomenological and interpretive writings as well as pointed to significant differences. The aim has been to synthesize key assumptions and objectives of these approaches. What then are their implications for how we conduct research? In general, these perspectives have not been translated extensively to the empirical level. The difficulty may stem from the fact that many of the guiding theorists were philosophers rather than empirical scientists. Still, if their impact is to be felt, the guiding abstractions must enter the realm of knowledge generation through empirical activity. The following section moves the discussion in this direction.

THE EMPIRICAL TRANSLATION

Without translation to research strategies, the preceding perspectives are little more than rhetoric about what is wrong with our conception of the person and what is lacking in the questions we ask. Thus in making the case for the phenomenological and interpretive perspectives it is critical to demonstrate how one can not only endorse the underlying metatheoretical positions, but carry them through to the design and implementation of research. Such research will then influence the kind of knowledge we accumulate about human experience and its social context. By way of illustration, the following section will summarize a series of studies conducted by me and my colleagues dealing with the subjective experience of personal change. Clearly, our research does not embody the full range of objectives of a phenomenological orientation. Rather, it reflects beginning steps to translate the guiding principles into research action.

Illustrative Case:
The Subjective Organization of Personality
in Adulthood and Aging

The general content of this research addresses people's personal experiences of change as they age. It relates to the extensive literature, theoretical and empirical, on adult personality development (Costa &

McCrae, 1980; Neugarten, 1977; Ryff, 1984). Among the prominent questions guiding this research is whether personality processes in the second half of life are characterized by change or stability. That is, do the general traits and personal characteristics of the individual change with aging? Do individuals who are aggressive and achievement oriented in early life remain so in later adulthood, or do they become passive and accommodating? A variety of theoretical frameworks have postulated that there are systematic, age-related changes that occur with regard to personality functioning in adulthood and aging. Jung (1933), for example, discusses the increasing introversion or interiority that comes with age, and the sex-role reversals that occur between men and women—that is, men begin expressing their more nurturant, feminine qualities and women begin discovering their more masculine, assertive natures. Numerous longitudinal and cross-sectional studies have been conducted to establish evidence for change or stability in personality in aging. Our research question in the midst of this controversy has been whether adults *see themselves changing as they age.* That is, do they have an awareness that certain personal characteristics have increased in prominence with age while others have subsided? Or do they see their personal qualities as basically stable so that they have the same characteristics as when they were younger? In short, how do they subjectively construct their own personal characteristics over the course of adulthood? The research is phenomenological in its concern with adults' subjective experience of themselves. How the studies relate to the larger phenomenological agenda detailed earlier will be examined following a review of specific findings.

Before presenting specific studies, I will summarize the general model guiding the program of research. Theoretical guidance has been drawn from Erikson's (1950, 1959) formulation of the stages of generativity versus stagnation and integrity versus despair; Buhler's (1935; Buhler & Massarik, 1968) writings on basic life tendencies, especially the tendencies of creative expansion and upholding internal order; the Jungian (1933) process of self-illumination in old age; and Neugarten's descriptions (1968, 1973, 1977) of the executive processes of middle age and the process of interiority in old age. Again, the question has been whether individuals see themselves changing in ways suggested by these theories. (For a discussion of the extent to which theory should guide phenomenological research, see Ryff, 1984.)

With regard to assessment procedures, structured self-report inventories have been employed. That is, the richness and subjective purity of spontaneous reports have been traded for data that cannot be manipulated by our own interpretive biases. The procedures also eliminate problems associated with different levels of articulateness among participants, and they improve the potential for subsequent refutation or replication of the findings. We might add that our long-term goals are to combine these more quantitative, structured procedures with more open-ended, unstructured approaches. As stated earlier, our view is that phenomenology does not prescribe particular methods and that the topics of interest are best examined from multiple perspectives.

The question of subjectively perceived change has been investigated by use of instructional variation. That is, participants have completed the personality inventories according to varying instructions aimed at assessing how they would rate themselves in the present (concurrent instruction), what they recall being like in the past (retrospective instruction), and what they anticipate they will be like in the future (prospective instruction). Comparisons among these outcomes are then used to provide a measure of subjective change. Finally, most of the studies have included men and women and various combinations of three age groups (young adults and middle- and old-aged adults). As the studies have been published elsewhere, the discussion here will focus only on key questions and findings.

Self-perceived change in values. A first study (Ryff & Baltes, 1976) examined self-perceived change in the domain of values. The question was whether adults perceived that their values had, or possibly would, change as they aged. The Rokeach model of values (1973), which differentiates instrumental from terminal values, was the assessment procedure. "Instrumental" values refer to desirable modes of conduct such as being ambitious, capable, or courageous. "Terminal" values are desirable end-states of existence, such as having a sense of accomplishment, freedom, or happiness. When we considered the context of developmental theories—particularly the description of the executive processes of middle age (Neugarten, 1968), which stressed such qualities as being active, controlling, and achievement-oriented, and the old-aged process of turning inward, becoming more reflective and contemplative (Buhler, 1935; Jung, 1933; Neugarten, 1973)—we hypothesized that instrumental values would have greater salience in middle age, and that terminal values would be more prominent in old age. The subjective change hypothesis was that individuals would be aware of their changing value preferences over time. Two groups of women, one middle aged (n = 57; average age = 43.1) and one old aged (n = 62; average age = 70.4), rated their values under various concurrent, retrospective, and prospective instructional conditions. The findings showed that middle-aged women had comparatively higher preference for instrumental values, and they anticipated that this preference would decline in old age. That is, they expected themselves to become less instrumentally oriented in old age. The older women, on the other hand, showed less of a preference for instrumental values in the present but recalled that such values were more important to them when they were middle aged. As the values instrument is ipsative in nature (i.e., the score on instrumental values determines the score on terminal values), the reverse change patterns were obtained for the terminal value preferences. Thus the findings from this first study supported the view that there were age differences in value preferences and, moreover, that women saw themselves changing in accord with these differences. Following from these outcomes, the next study attempted to broaden the subjective inquiry to the personality realm.

Subjective change in personality. To identify what aspects of personality might be likely to show perceived change in the middle- to old-age transition, relevant developmental theories were again reviewed. The literature (Buhler, 1935; Erikson, 1959; Jung, 1933; Neugarten, 1968, 1973, 1977) presented an image of middle age that stressed traits such as being independent, bold, active, achievement oriented, energetic, controlled, and powerful. The vision of old age, however, revealed an emphasis on characteristics such as being reflective, philosophical, contemplative, accepting, accommodating, hedonistic, and non-work oriented. Following from these descriptions, I looked for personality inventories that could operationalize the characteristics. The scales of achievement, dominance, social recognition, and play were selected from the Personality Research Form (Jackson, 1967). The first three were predicted to be most salient in middle age, while the last was predicted to be more salient in old age. Because these scales were predicted to show perceived changes, they were jointly referred to as "developmental" scales. To differentiate aspects of personality showing subjective change from those showing perceived stability, four control scales also were administered. These included measures of abasement, defendence, impulsivity, and order, characteristics that had not been included in the previous theoretical descriptions. Finally, the Rokeach values measure was again utilized, with the hope of replicating the previous finding and examining its relevance for men. The study was conducted with 160 individuals divided equally by age and gender (see Ryff, 1982a).

The first outcome replicated the previous study (Ryff & Baltes, 1976), showing that women gave greater priority to instrumental values during middle age than old age, and they perceived themselves changing subjectively in the same fashion. The replication was particularly interesting given the sampling differences between the two studies, with the former including highly educated groups and the latter having more representative educational levels among the two age groups (specific sampling details are provided in the published studies). A similar pattern was not obtained for men, whose overall preferences were for terminal values during both age periods. It is possible that men do not experience change in values orientations, or that a shift from instrumental to terminal values occurs at an earlier period in the life span for men.

The predicted outcomes for the developmental scales were obtained, but only for middle-aged men. Their scores on achievement, dominance, and social recognition were higher than the ratings of old-aged men, and they anticipated that such qualities would become less salient to them in old age. The play scale, also as predicted, showed the reverse pattern, with scores being lower in middle age than in old age. Old-aged men, on the other hand, rated themselves lower on the developmental scales and did not see themselves changing over time. The outcomes for women were in the predicted direction, but the differences were not significant. Finally, the control scale of abasement, defendence, impulsivity, and order showed no age differences and no subjective change processes. As predicted, people did not see themselves changing on these dimensions of personality as they aged.

Following a similar research design, Ryff and Migdal (1984) investigated self-perceived personality change in the transition from young adulthood to middle age. Theoretical guidance was provided by Erikson's description of intimacy as the psychosocial task of young adulthood and generativity as the psychosocial task of middle age. According to Erikson, "intimacy" refers to interpersonal relationships where close friendships, affiliations, sexual unions, and self-disclosure with significant others are salient. Generativity in Erikson's model denotes a transition to a broader social orientation, an interest in teaching and guiding younger generations, and a concern with improving the nature of society. As in the previous study, an attempt was made to operationalize these constructs with structured personality inventories, including the Personality Research Form (Jackson, 1967) and the Jackson Personality Inventory (Jackson, 1976). Intimacy was measured by scales of affiliation, interpersonal affect, and succorance;

generativity by scales of breadth of interest, dominance, and innovation. Four control scales (abasement, anxiety, organization, and risk taking) were also used, with the aim of showing perceived stability. The usual concurrent, retrospective, and prospective instructions were employed, and the sample consisted of 100 women divided equally among young adulthood (18-30) and middle age (40-55).

As predicted, women of both age groups saw intimacy as more salient in their self-assessments during young adulthood than during middle age. In terms of self-perceived change, young adult women saw intimacy as more prominent in their present self-perceptions than they anticipated it would be when they reached middle age, while middle-aged women recalled that intimacy was more salient in their self-images during young adulthood. For the generativity scales, middle-aged women rated themselves higher in the present than they recalled being in young adulthood, thereby supporting the predictions. The young adult women showed the reverse pattern, in which their concurrent ratings were higher than their prospective ratings. Thus the prediction of perceived change on generativity measures was only partially supported. Finally, the control scales supported the predictions showing no systematic variation from the period of young adulthood to middle age.

As a whole, the studies described above provided mixed evidence for the subjective experience of personality change in adulthood and aging. Supportive findings were obtained on some measures for some age groups and occasionally for only one sex. The less than uniform outcomes may have been due to individual differences in the subjective experience of personality change. In other words, while adults may see personal change in themselves over time, their perceptions may not be organized systematically by age or by personality dimension. It may, in fact, be more of an idiographic process. Another possible interpretation is that the developmental theories guiding the investigations may not have identified the key dimensions of change being experienced. Perhaps the participants must become the "theorists" through more open-ended, exploratory procedures in order to tap the personality qualities on which people show pervasive subjective change. A third alternative explication for the mixed findings was that the above studies did not utilize assessment procedures sufficiently connected to the underlying theories. The problem may have been one of operationalization. The scales employed had been developed for other purposes and populations and were, at best, approximations of the developmental process of interest. This third possibility served as a basis for the next study.

Toward developmental dimensions of personality. Four dimensions of personality were selected from previous theoretical formulations as targets for scale construction. Two, generativity and integrity, came from Erikson's (1950) psychosocial stage theory of development. As noted before, the former dimension referred to having a concern for guiding the next generation and a sense of responsibility to those younger in age. Integrity was defined as adapting to the triumphs and disappointments of being and to viewing one's past life as inevitable, appropriate, and meaningful. The third dimension of complexity was derived from Neugarten's (1968) discussion of the "executive processes" of personality in adulthood. It referred to being actively engaged in a complex environment and to manipulating and controlling activities selectively in multiple spheres. Interiority, the final dimension, described the "turning inward" that had been addressed by several theorists (Buhler, 1935; Jung, 1933; Neugarten, 1973). It referred to one who was freely relinquishing signs of external status and becoming more reflective, contemplative, and individuated. The scale construction and refinement procedures are detailed in Ryff and Heincke (1983).

With regard to predictions, generativity and complexity were viewed as key personality issues of middle age, while integrity and interiority were seen as prominent in old age. This meant that individuals would perceive the two former qualities as salient in their self-perceptions during middle age, while the two latter qualities would be of increasing significance in old age. The sample consisted of 270 individuals divided by gender and age group (young adulthood, middle age, old age). The first age group was included for comparative purposes. The measures were completed according to the usual concurrent, retrospective, and prospective instructions.

The prediction of perceived change was supported for the scale of generativity, the dimension drawn from Erikson (1950). Self-perceptions of generativity were higher for the middle-aged ratings than for any other period. Such a finding included several patterns of perceived change, including the anticipated change of young adults, the recalled change of old-aged persons, and both the anticipated and recalled change of middle-aged persons. Regardless of actual age, all participants saw themselves as being the most generativity oriented in middle age. Integrity, also proposed by Erikson (1950), revealed the predicted high scores for self-perceptions focused on old age. Thus old persons rated themselves higher on this dimension than they recalled being in the past, and young adults and middle-aged individuals anticipated scoring higher on integrity in old age than they saw themselves in the present.

The findings for the interiority scale were complicated, showing a variety of age and gender differences. There seemed to be little consensus regarding the inevitability or desirability of becoming more inward in the later years. For the complexity scale, measuring a sense of being in command and in control of a diverse environment, the outcomes supported the predicted age differences but not the patterns of self-perceived change. While the middle-aged group rated themselves higher on this dimension than the other two age groups, none of the participants indicated recalled or anticipated change on this dimension over time. This finding is perhaps related to the cohort issue (Baltes, Cornelius, & Nesselroade, 1978; Elder, 1981a). Perhaps the juggling of multiple demands and responsibilities growing out of changing sex-role norms has left current middle-aged individuals, those caught between old and new role expectations, with a strong sense of complexity in themselves that appears to be stable over time.

The control scales that had been used in previous work (Ryff, 1982a) were again employed in this study. Three of the scales (abasement, impulsivity, order) replicated the previous finding of no perceived change across these age periods. The defendence scale showed subjective change in the direction of all age groups seeing themselves as becoming less defensive in old age. This was also the only scale on which clear gender differences were obtained, with men scoring higher than women. The lack of gender differences for the majority of scales across all three age groups was an unexpected outcome given that previous research on self-perceived personality change had shown gender differences and that recent theoretical perspectives (Gilligan, 1979, 1982; Rossi, 1980) had questioned the utility of existing life-span theories for women.

Ties to the Phenomenological Agenda

The studies described above were conducted to investigate whether people experience change in themselves as they age. The issue was how individuals subjectively construct their personal qualities over the course of adulthood. Theories of adult personality development were consulted to identify what personal qualities might be likely to change. These qualities were then operationalized with a variety of personality instruments, which were then administered under different instructional conditions. Overall the findings suggested that adults do have a subjective sense of change and stability in themselves as they age. Two samples of women showed that they saw their values changing from an instrumental orientation in middle age to a terminal orientation in old age. Self-perceived personality change was shown on a variety of measures, but the clearest patterns were obtained for the dimensions of generativity and integrity drawn from Erikson's theory. Finally, the control scales repeatedly demonstrated self-perceived stability.

Clearly the above studies need to be conducted with additional samples to strengthen the consistency and generalizability of the findings. Even at this early stage in the program of research, it is useful to evaluate the studies in light of the guiding assumptions of the phenomenological and interpretive approaches. The empirical discussion focused on the specifics of research design, measurement instruments, sample size, and patterns of outcomes. This information, though necessary for a meaningful research presentation, loses the thread of the larger phenomenological objectives formulated earlier. How does our empirical research respond to those guiding themes? How might we implement them more effectively? What can be done to strengthen the empirical translation of these alternative approaches? These are the questions that will be examined in the remainder of this section.

A first theme emphasized seeing people as active, intentional, and exercising control over their own lives. The study of self-perceived personality change would not appear to be a strong testimony to this theme. One's personal sense of change in aging would seem to be a far cry from taking charge of one's destiny. I would argue, however, that people's subjective experiences of change are, in fact, compatible with an active, self-directed conception of the person. For example, when we ask people to tell us what they will be like in the future, the question presupposes that their personal expectations will play some role in what actually occurs. Whether the participants draw on ideal types, aging stereotypes, or personal observations, their projection into the future may indicate a preparation or readiness for change, and may thereby be a partial determinant of what they become. Thus asking about future expectations illuminates how people subjectively construct themselves forward in time, reveals the implicit theories or end-states that guide their personal visions, and may foretell certain contours of their future realities. The retrospective components of the research also reflect an active, intentional view of the person. As Cohler (1982) has argued, people continually reconstruct their past lives. He believes they do this to see consistency and stability in themselves. Though we have argued that people need to see change in themselves, the point is that retrospective accounts are constructions under the control of the individual. Our memories of the past are continually revised as a function of new experiences in the present. It is perhaps important to distinguish between adaptive and maladaptive reconstructions—from those that influence present feelings, motivations, and cognitions in ways that are beneficial to those that have detrimental effects. In this regard, Gergen and Gergen (1983) have discussed stable, progressive, and regressive self-narratives corresponding to one's improving or diminishing self-assessments over time. Such narratives are viewed as essential to giving one's life a sense of meaning and direction. Thus looking ahead to one's future as well as looking back over one's life are potential mechanisms by which the person can be active and intentional. Our past memories, constructed by us, say much about who we were and currently are, while our future dreams or fears tell much of what we might become.

A second phenomenological and interpretive theme emphasized a person concerned with meaning in his or her own life and in the surrounding world. For the present research, we might ask what meaning self-perceived changes have for the person: What is the significance of seeing oneself as more generative in middle age while more oriented toward integrity in old age? Does one feel positive, negative, or indifferent about such changes? Gergen and Gergen (1983) have identified important queries that may contribute to the building of meaning in one's narrative, including such questions as the following: Am I improving? Is my life happier now? Are my abilities declining? Am I maintaining the high standards to which I once committed myself? Am I growing as a person? To answer these questions, the person must think not only about the directionality of his or her personal change (whether certain qualities have become more pronounced, others less so), but what these changes mean in terms of his or her overall life pattern. Are they good and desired changes, or dreaded and feared turns that signal a worsening of the individual's personal condition? Does the person see the changes as under his or her own control, or as the result of outside, unexpected forces? Such questions, though important for the individual at all ages, would seem particularly salient in old age. They are the kinds of self-explorations that prompt the life review (Butler, 1963), with its heightened call to find the meaning in one's life. Such meaning-seeking activities have not yet been included in our empirical program of research. Our future imperative therefore is to address not only how adults see themselves change as they age, but what meaning their personal changes have for them.

Phenomenological and interpretive perspectives argue that human conduct must be understood from the point of view of the person. Our research may seem to violate this objective, as the work has been strongly theory-guided. That is, we have relied on developmental theories to formulate our questions and to select our measures. Such procedures may be at odds with those we study, so that the existing theories of adult personality development may impose a kind of preformed meaning system that has little to do with the concerns and experiences of individuals in our research. Would we not be better off simply asking directly whether our participants see themselves change, and, if so, in what ways? We would argue that though more open-ended exploratory procedures would be a useful addition to our empirical endeavors, the decision to work within a theory-guided framework need not be viewed as contrary to phenomenological objectives. Theories are, after all, human constructions. They are created by individuals and represent particular experiences of reality. The beginnings of theory construction are, in fact, in the best phenomenological tradition, given the emphasis on detailed accounting of experience and careful formulation of meaning. The question then becomes whether the theorist's construction fits the experiences of others. Has Erikson (1950), for example, identified psychological changes that people can relate to and can see happening in themselves? Such a question is ultimately empirical. To answer a priori that every individual has a unique frame of reference is to ignore the possibility for similarities in people's experiences of themselves, their relationships with others, and their surrounding social worlds. The consistency of our data on certain issues, particularly the heightened sense of generativity in middle age and integrity in old age, suggests that Erikson has captured the experiences of others. The interiority dimension, in contrast, showed a wide range of individual differences, thereby indicating that the underlying theories had not tapped such a nomothetic process. Thus, though we concur that more open-ended procedures will strengthen our research program and bring us close to the viewpoints of those we study, our theory-guided orientation has also contributed new knowledge regarding subjective experiences of personal change.

The study of the Lebenswelt, the life-world, is a prominent theme in phenomenological and interpretive writings. Defined as the world of everyday activities and concerns, the life-world concept encourages researchers to make their work more naturalistic, more tied to the spheres in which people actually conduct their lives. Though the research presented thus far has not addressed this issue, our recent studies have tried to contextualize self-perceived changes by linking them to the actual life experiences adults are having. For example, we have examined subjective change as a result of widowhood (Dunn & Ryff, 1982) and fatherhood (Zeren & Ryff, 1984). Widows reported declines in life satisfaction following the loss of spouse, while fathers saw themselves as becoming more nurturant, less impulsive, more generative, and having greater purpose in life following fatherhood. Another study (Ryff & Dunn, 1985) has looked at a composite of stressful life experiences and related them to personality development with the finding that men's personal growth ratings seem better accounted for by their life experiences than women's. In combination, these studies have tried to link the personal experience of change and concomitant personality development with the actual experiences people are having. Life events thus become a means of translating the life-world into the empirical realm. Other ways of attending to the life-world might focus on adults' interpersonal relationships, their social organizations, or their surrounding physical worlds. These topics are not new to the social scientist. What is new is the aim of investigating these realms more as people actually experience them than as they are construed by the scientist.

The contextual and historical relativity of what we know is the final theme extracted from the phenomenological and interpretive perspectives. Applied to the study of self-perceived changes, we must ask how these patterns of change might vary by historical period or by cultural context. There is some evidence that American society as a whole has become more introspective and inward looking in recent years (Veroff, Douvan, & Kulka, 1981). If we are becoming more inner oriented, what are we thinking about? Similarly, does the content of one's introspection vary according to one's cultural setting? Are our inner thoughts more tied to achievements and life stresses than to political or religious concerns as may be true in other settings? Though we have yet to include such historical and cultural comparisons in our empirical research, they have been considered on a theoretical level (see Ryff, 1982b, 1985), and we are careful not to overgeneralize our current findings beyond their respective samplings and settings.

In summary, I have provided a detailed evaluation of the phenomenological and interpretive themes in our research. These studies do not exemplify all of the objectives detailed earlier, but the omissions are instructive. They point to new research directions (e.g., the need to ask people about the meaning of their personal changes) and sharpen previous questions (e.g., how do people's expectations about future change in themselves influence what actually occurs?). Thus, the linking of theoretical or metatheoretical goals with specific research studies strengthens connections in both directions. Phenomenology generates an expanded range of research questions, while the empirical findings substantiate and fine tune the guiding questions.

FUTURE DIRECTIONS:
JOINING THE INNER AND OUTER REALMS

The phenomenological and interpretive agenda as formulated thus far emphasizes an active, intentional person concerned with the meaning of human experience. Were one to endorse this position and draw on it to formulate research, one would risk the creation of a personological model that neglects the surrounding sociocultural world. Thus the strengths of these approaches in calling for a person who is self-directing and able to confer meaning are simultaneously their essential weaknesses. In their zeal to correct the overdrawn determinism of the positivistic conceptions, these theorists generated a new set of problems that exaggerate the choices of the individual and ignore the constraints of the surrounding social order. Such difficulties are more apparent in the psychological realm, where they are fueled by the traditional disciplinary focus on the person. The key challenge then becomes that of finding the balance, of putting together the inner experiences and intentional activities of the individual with the options and limits of the surrounding world. It is a task of joining the inside realm with the outside realm.

A good deal of research on adult development and aging has missed this connection. The focus has been primarily on the inner, personological realm or the outer, sociostructural realm. I will note a number of these works and contrast them with perspectives that have aimed for more of a synthesis. Finally, the study of life events will be proposed as a potentially meaningful nexus between the two realms. I will argue, in fact, that in the move from descriptive to explanatory research, personologists must look outward to the social order and social structuralists must look inward to the person to understand fully processes of change.

Research in Adult Development and Aging

A variety of psychological studies have examined the changing personal characteristics, beliefs, and concerns of adults as they age. These works deal with the inner realm in their focus on intrapsychic changes. Vaillant (1977), for example, conducted a longitudinal study of adult men that explored their adaptive ego mechanisms and basic styles of adaptation. In terms of developmental changes, the study supported Erikson's stages, though it included a new stage labeled "career consolidation." Gould (1978) also proposed a model of growth and change in adult life (based on studies of men and women) that involved a series of stages of adult consciousness in which the individual was striving to get beyond the constraints and ties of childhood consciousness. Each stage was characterized by major false assumptions that must be confronted and corrected so that a fuller, more independent adult consciousness could be achieved. Emphasizing the adult development of women, Gilligan (1979, 1982) has argued for the importance of attachments, intimacy, and relationships across the life cycle. The emotional, intimate aspects of caring for others are, in her view, central aspects of the adult woman's growth and change. Less theoretically driven, though focused on issues of personal continuity or discontinuity over time, are the Berkeley studies of adult life (Eichorn et al., 1981). The question here has been whether personality profiles in adolescence predict an individual's personality characteristics in adulthood. Viewed in combination, these perspectives illustrate a kind of personological approach to adult development and aging. The emphasis is on the individual and his or her changing personal characteristics. Though certain of the studies examine work or family life, the focus is on intrapsychic processes, personality characteristics, and personal concerns as they evolve across adult life.

The study of social roles, rewards, and obligations provides an alternative approach to adult development and aging. In contrast to the intrapsychic phenomena emphasized above, these perspectives emphasize how individuals internalize social roles, which then provide expectations for their behavior. Developmentally, the concern is with the ways in which people are channeled into positions and roles based on age criteria. Riley's age stratification model (Riley, 1976; Riley, Johnson, & Foner, 1972), for example, emphasizes the differences between age strata and the flow of successive cohorts through time. Each cohort has different experiences, income, education, attitudes, and so on. Within this model, age is the criterion for the allocation of roles, rewards, and obligations. Similarly, Neugarten (Neugarten & Hagestad, 1976; Neugarten, Moore, & Lowe, 1965) has emphasized the impact of age norms and age constraints on adult development. Individuals experience age-related transitions across the life course as a function of the cultural age system. Based on socially shared expectations and definitions, the life course is structured by age into differing positions, privileges, and obligations. Rosow (1974) has also focused on adult socialization and the processes by which people learn new values and behaviors appropriate to their changing roles in adulthood and aging. His emphasis has been on the problematic socialization to old age in which the norms and expectations are unclear, the teachers are few, and the position itself is devalued. Despite these differing emphases, such models approach the study of adulthood and aging from the societal vantage point. The concern is with the age-related allocation of rewards and resources, the internalization of social roles, and the learning of new values and behaviors appropriate for different aging positions. Society, through cultural norms and sanctions, defines the age experience and its changing contours over time.

The above works provide sharp contrasts between individual versus societal perspectives on adult development and aging. The differences between personological and social structural approaches permeate every level of the research endeavor, from the choice of guiding questions to selection of measures, samples, and procedures of analysis. Certain scholars have realized the need to put the person and the society together and have attempted to do so in their own works. Levinson (1978, 1981), for example, conducted an extensive study of psychosocial development in which the "life structure" was formulated as the boundary between personality structure and the social structure. He postulated various structure-building and structure-changing phases across the life course as the men he studied dealt with internal change in themselves and external changes in their environments (primarily in their occupational and family contexts). Another integrative approach is represented by Riegel's (1975) dialectical interpretation of adult development. He focused on crises as constructive confrontations in life course development and argued that the sequences of crises in adult development are codetermined by inner-biological, individual-psychological, cultural-sociological, and outer-physical progressions. Through the careers of well-known scientists, Riegel demonstrated these multiple dimensions and showed how the individual both changes and is changed by society. Finally, Elder (1981b) has put the individual and the societal realm together through his joint interests in history, institutional changes, and personality. In specifying the linkages between social structural and psychological variables, he has emphasized the social psychological aspects of settings (perceived options, constraints, pressures) and the interpersonal aspects of personality (self-other concepts). In his work on the Great Depression, Elder illustrates how economic deprivations influenced the lives of differing generations of children. In so doing, he demonstrates the interaction between historical conditions and human biography.

Though laudable in their aims, these attempts at synthesis betray disciplinary allegiance. Levinson emphasizes the social structure and operationalizes it in the family and occupational realm, though he is generally blind to the larger forces of society that may influence the development of adult men. His strength is in formulating the process of change from the person's point of view. Riegel's perspective in turn is generally without empirical translation or testing, and his illustrations are also more individualistic and psychological. In contrast, Elder's analysis is more informative with regard to how the social structure influences personality (e.g., how social status or group membership creates identity) than with regard to the ways personality influences the social structure. As a sociologist, he is naturally more adept at formulating society's influence on the individual. Given these kinds of trained biases, it is useful to ask whether we might ever get beyond our own disciplinary imprinting. Can we realistically expect psychologists to work with social structural variables, and at the same time ask sociologists to investigate the subtleties of personality development? In my view, synthesis is not likely to come from one scholar trying to wear two hats, a choice that can well lead to an unkempt appearance, but rather from rethinking how better to unite our respective hats. As the western movie meaningfully joins the headgear of cowboys and Indians, we need a theme or motif that might integrate the study of the inner and outer realms in adulthood and aging. I would like to propose the study of life events as a possible theme for synthesizing personological and sociostructural approaches to adult development.

Life Events as Nexus

The study of life events has received considerable attention in recent years, largely because of the burgeoning interest in the topic of stress. Recently, life-span developmentalists (Brim & Ryff, 1980; Danish, Smyer, & Nowak, 1980; Hultsch & Plemons, 1979) have reexamined life events with a greater emphasis on their developmental features such as timing, anticipatory socialization, and so on. In pursuing these interests, translating them to researchable topics, and reviewing related works, I began to see possible connections between the personologist and the sociostructuralist. To illustrate my glimmers of hope, I will draw on our research as well as the work of Dennis Hogan, a sociologist focused on the constraints and options of adult behavior posed by the social structure. While we have looked more at person variables and the inner experiences of the developing person than has Hogan, our research programs connect through the study of similar life events.

Hogan (1980, 1981) has studied the timing and sequencing of various adult life events. In particular, he has examined the completion of formal schooling, the beginning of one's first job, and marriage. Drawing on demographic data, he has shown how the timing of these events has been constrained during certain historical periods, as in postwar years, during which the ages for these events become more concentrated. These fluctuations are discussed in terms of changing age norms, sanctions, and social timetables. He addresses the application of norms to the sequencing of life events as well, and shows how sequencing varies by cohort. He then examines the effects of sequencing on later occupational and earnings attainments. Beginning with the hypothesized normative pattern of going from school to work to marriage, he investigates the impact of deviating from this norm for occupational and earnings attainments. Thus Hogan's variables are the externals—social norms, occupational status, and economic earnings. His life events represent visible, demographic status transitions, and his methods involve large, carefully selected samples and complex statistical analyses. Working within this general model, he shows when men of certain cohorts experienced certain life events and demonstrates the impact on their later social advancements. This brief summary does not do justice to his specific findings, but it illustrates the more socio-structural approach to the study of adult life events. It is this orientation that I wish to contrast and coordinate with the orientation of my associates and me.

Given my interests in inner, subjective experience, it is not surprising that we have studied adult life events from the inside, looking at their psychological meaning and impact for the person. A first study (Fallo-Mitchell & Ryff, 1982) examined women's views regarding the ideal time to experience certain adult life events, such as marriage, first job, and first child. Thus we were interested in the subjective side of the life experience—the person's sense as to when certain life events should be experienced. The study was conducted with three age groups of women (20 to 30, 40 to 50, 60 to 70) and showed that younger women preferred later ages for family events and earlier ages for educational and occupational events than older women. Though based on a cross-sectional design, the findings were interpreted from a cohort perspective. Apart from specific outcomes, the study illustrates the internal, personal side of the life events equation. It also shows how complex social phenomena such as timing norms have their origins in individual belief systems.

Other related studies have examined subjective psychological changes resulting from particular life events. Again, in contrast to Hogan's research, in which the impact of life events is gauged in terms of occupational and earnings attainments, we have focused on the impact of life events on people's internal, subjective changes. Thus self-perceived changes have been monitored in the experiences of widowhood (Dunn & Ryff, 1983), fatherhood (Zeren & Ryff, 1984), and pregnancy (Dietrich & Ryff, 1984). Variables have included measures of life satisfaction, locus of control, and a wide range of personality variables (e.g., nurturance, affiliation, impulsivity). Another study (Ryff & Dunn, 1985) has examined the impact of cumulative life stresses on personality development. Various life event ratings were used to predict scores on measures of personality development such as generativity and integrity. Overall, then, these studies begin with the life event and examine its meaning for the person (views about when it should occur) and its impact (views as to how one changed in the experience).

The above summaries provide a surface view of life events research as conducted according to two widely differing orientations. The concern for social structure in the one and intrapsychic processes in the other would appear to be separate agendas. And yet when one reflects on any particular life event, such as marriage or divorce, it seems obvious that the information derived from both lines of inquiry is essential to a thorough understanding of the experience for the person and for society. Our research must illuminate how large social forces influence human destinies as well as tell us what the experiences mean on the individual level. The joint focus on similar life events would seem to be an avenue for merging these differing endeavors. Moreover, advantages work in both directions when such perspectives are put together. On the one hand, those interested in the external, visible aspects of life events are sensitized to transitions that may be overrated or overlooked. The former instance may refer to life events that are so well anticipated and rehearsed, for which the social norms are so clear, that their impact on the person is relatively small. Menopause, empty nest, or certain career promotions may be such events—there are noticeable external changes, but their internal impact for the individual may be of minimal significance. Researchers are also sensitized to the emergence of new events that would otherwise be overlooked because they are not yet a part of the normative social structure. Midlife crisis might be such an example, though it has become less a "hidden event" due to its popular coverage in recent years. In contrast, those interested in the internal, psychological aspects of life events learn more about the precise magnitude of certain adult experiences. Though younger women may espouse later ages for marriage, one must consult the demographer or sociologist to learn of the actual incidence of later marriages. Similarly, the intrapsychic researcher is sensitized to the sociocultural impact of converging individual choices. The choice to limit family size, for example, begins at the individual level, but has broad implications for many levels of society when jointly endorsed by millions of individuals. In sum, a life events linking of sociostructural and personological research does provide a more complete picture of individual development and social change. The inner meanings and goals of the person are interwoven with the constraints and opportunities of the external environment. We achieve a more balanced view of the intentions of individuals played out against the forces of society.

From Description to Explanation

Beyond the advantages gained from a sociostructural and personological focus on life events, there is another level at which interdisciplinary exchange seems inevitable and unavoidable. The move from descriptive research—in which the content and directionality of change are charted—to explanatory research in which the antecedents or causes of change are identified—signals the exchange. Featherman (1984) has recently provided half of this argument. According to his analysis, causal understanding of individual developmental changes must be based on a population level of analysis. He sees life-span theories as largely personological in their formulation of individual development. Such models cannot account for their empirical observations. In order to explain psychological development, one must look to the societal and biogenetic processes that create the conditions for individual variability and malleability. Thus, from Featherman's perspective, individual development is the outcome of societal and communal adaptations to changing environmental conditions, and such adaptations must be examined on a population level of analysis.

In the context of the present discussion, Featherman is asserting that the personological/psychological approaches to individual development must look to the demographic/sociological perspectives on social change to explain the individual patterns of change. It is a provocative argument, and one that is persuasively presented. His model does not, however, examine what accounts for change and variability in the societal or biogenetic realm. Where does he turn to explain change in population variables? To address those questions would seem to require, at some point, return to the personological level, where individual actions become the catalyst for larger collective change, which then redefines the conditions for what is developmentally possible, and so on. That is, population variables may well set the stage or account for profiles of human development, but to understand change in the population processes requires an eventual return to the individual level. In short, the social sciences are inextricably bound when it comes to explanatory research.

It is useful to draw on our personological program of research to elaborate this point. We are interested in charting subjective personality processes. In recent studies, we have looked at life events (e.g., fatherhood, widowhood) as possible antecedents to change in personal development. This beginning level of explanatory analysis remains quite personological. However, to understand or predict change in our antecedent variables (i.e., the experience of particular life events), we must look to the larger sociocultural conditions that prevent or facilitate the occurrence of certain life events at certain times. We must, as Featherman argues, consult the demographer or sociologist to learn of the larger societal trends that are affecting our individual progressions. Conversely, to understand—or, more important, to predict—change in population processes, demographers must consult the personological realm, where individual beliefs and actions are the seeds of large-scale social change. Thus, as social scientists, we are plagued or blessed, depending on one's point of view, with having to look outside our own disciplines to understand change and transformation in our own variables. Our knowledge of the inner and outer realms advances through acknowledgment of this interdependence.

SUMMARY

William James completed his Gifford Lectures, delivered at Edinburgh from 1901 to 1902, with a discussion of the objective and the subjective in the world of our experience. In his usual inimitable style, he spoke of the subjective realm as follows:

> That unsharable feeling which each one of us has of the pinch of his individual destiny as he privately feels it rolling out on fortune's wheel may be disparaged for its egotism, may be sneered at as unscientific, but it

is the one thing that fills up the measure of our concrete actuality, and any would-be existant that should lack such a feeling, or its analogue, would be a piece of reality only half made up. (James, 1958, p. 376)

In this chapter I have drawn on phenomenological and interpretive perspectives to stimulate renewed interest in topics related to James's concerns such as subjective experience, intentionality, the construction of meaning, and the life-world. Theoretical works tied to these concerns were reviewed briefly, and their implications for empirical endeavors were illustrated with our ongoing program of research.

It is my hope that new research directions for adulthood and aging will come from such discussion. The expanded agenda, for example, might address the purposes, goals, and intentions of aging adults. It might also examine the ways in which they see themselves as self-determining. Where do they not have this sense? How do they construct the meaning in their lives? What assists or deflects in this process? Have we, as researchers, attended sufficiently to their point of view? Are we aware of the everyday world as they actually live in it? Have we connected their inner experience with the external social conditions? How might we? Such are the many questions following from phenomenological and interpretive works that may spur a broadened research agenda in aging.

Finally, a comment about reinventing the wheel. When one writes about grand topics—free will and determinism, subjectivity and objectivity, the individual and society—there is the haunting concern of redundancy, of saying what has been said before. In response to these worries, a slight twist in the metaphor may be useful. Rather than reinventing the wheel, one can think of contributing to its forward momentum.

REFERENCES

Anderson, T. G. (1978). Existential counseling. In R. S. Valle & M. King (Eds.), *Existential-phenomenological alternatives for psychology.* New York: Oxford University Press.

Baltes, P. B., Cornelius, S. W., & Nesselroade, J. R. (1978). Cohort effects in behavioral development: Theoretical and methodological perspectives. In W. A. Collins (Ed.), *Minnesota Symposium on Child Psychology* (Vol. 11). Hillsdale, NJ: Erlbaum.

Berger, P. L., & Luckmann, T. (1966). *The social construction of reality.* Garden City, NY: Doubleday.

Bernstein, R. J. (1976). *The restructuring of social and political theory.* Philadelphia: University of Pennsylvania Press.

Binswanger, L. (1958). The case of Ellen West. In R. May, E. Angel, & H. F. Ellenberger (Eds.), *Existence*. New York: Basic Books.

Binswanger, L. (1963). *Being-in-the-world: Selected papers of Ludwig Binswanger*. New York: Basic Books.

Boss, M. (1963). *Psychoanalysis and Daseinsanalysis*. New York: Basic Books.

Brim, O. G., Jr., & Ryff, C. D. (1980). On the properties of life events. In P. B. Baltes & O. G. Brim, Jr. (Eds.), *Life-span development and behavior* (Vol. 3). New York: Academic Press.

Buhler, C. (1935). The curve of life as studied in biographies. *Journal of Applied Psychology, 19,* 405-409.

Buhler, C., & Massarik, F. (Eds.). (1968). *The course of human life*. New York: Springer.

Butler, R. N. (1963). The life review: An interpretation of reminiscence in the aged. *Psychiatry, 26,* 65-76.

Cohler, B. J. (1982). Personal narrative and life course. In P. B. Baltes & O. G. Brim, Jr. (Eds.), *Life-span development and behavior* (Vol. 4). New York: Academic Press.

Colaizzi, P. F. (1971). Analysis of the learner's perception of learning material at various phases of a learning process. In A. Giorgi, W. F. Fischer, & R. Von Eckartsberg (Eds.), *Duquesne studies in phenomenological psychology* (Vol. 1). Pittsburgh: Duquesne University Press.

Colaizzi, P. F. (1978). Psychological research as the phenomenologist views it. In R. S. Valle & M. King (Eds.), *Existential-phenomenological alternatives for psychology*. New York: Oxford University Press.

Costa, P. T., Jr., & McCrae, R. P. (1980). Still stable after all these years: Personality as a key to some issues in aging. In P. B. Baltes & O. G. Brim, Jr. (Eds.), *Life-span development and behavior* (Vol. 3). New York: Academic Press.

Danish, S. J., Smyer, M. A., & Nowak, C. A. (1980). Developmental intervention: Enhancing life-event processes. In P. B. Baltes & O. G. Brim, Jr. (Eds), *Life-span development and behavior* (Vol. 3). New York: Academic Press.

Dawe, A. (1970). The two sociologies. *British Journal of Sociology, 21,* 207-218.

Dietrich, J. C., & Ryff, C. D. (1984). *Normative psychological development during pregnancy*. Unpublished manuscript, Fordham University, Bronx, NY.

Dunn, D. D., & Ryff, C. D. (1982). *Self-perceived adjustment in widowhood: Age differences, sex differences, and the role of mediating variables*. Paper presented at the meetings of the Gerontological Society, Boston.

Eichorn, D. H., Clausen, J. A., Haan, N., Honzik, M. P., & Mussen, P. H. (Eds.). (1981). *Present and past in middle life*. New York: Academic Press.

Elder, G. H., Jr. (1981a). Social history and life experience. In D. H. Eichorn, J. A. Clausen, N. Haan, M. P. Honzik, & P. H. Mussen (Eds.), *Present and past in middle life*. New York: Academic Press.

Elder, G. H., Jr. (1981b). History and the life course. In D. Bertaux (Ed.), *Biography and society*. Beverly Hills, CA: Sage.

Erikson, E. (1950). *Childhood and society*. New York: W. W. Norton.

Erikson, E. (1959). Identity and the life cycle. *Psychological Issues, 1,* 18-164.

Fallo-Mitchell, L., & Ryff, C. D. (1982). Preferred timing of female life events: Cohort differences. *Research on Aging, 4,* 249-267.

Featherman, D. L. (1984). Individual development and aging as a population process. In J. Nesselroade & A. V. Eye (Eds.), *Individual development and social change: Explanatory analysis*. New York: Academic Press.

Filstead, W. J. (Ed.). (1970). *Qualitative methodology*. Chicago: Markham.

Garfinkel, H. (1967). *Studies in ethnomethodology.* Englewood Cliffs, NJ: Prentice-Hall.

Gatchel, R. J., & Mears, F. G. (1982). *Personality: Theory, assessment, and research.* New York: St. Martin's.

Gergen, K. J., & Gergen, M. M. (1983). Narratives of the self. In T. Sarbin & K. Scheibe (Eds.), *Studies in social identity.* New York: Praeger.

Gilligan, C. (1979). Woman's place in man's life cycle. *Harvard Educational Review, 49,* 431-446.

Gilligan, C. (1982). Adult development and women's development: Arrangements for a marriage. In J. Z. Giele (Ed.), *Women in the middle years.* New York: John Wiley.

Giorgi, A. (1970). *Psychology as a human science: A phenomenologically based approach.* New York: Harper & Row.

Giorgi, A., Fischer, W. F., & Von Eckartsberg, R. (Eds.). (1971). *Duquesne studies in phenomenological psychology* (Vol. 1). Pittsburgh: Duquesne University Press.

Giorgi, A., Fischer, W. F., & Murray, E. L. (Eds.). (1975). *Duquesne studies in phenomenological psychology* (Vol. 2). Pittsburgh: Duquesne University Press.

Giorgi, A., Knowles, R., & Smith, D. L. (Eds.). (1979). *Duquesne studies in phenomenological psychology* (Vol. 3). Pittsburgh: Duquesne University Press.

Gould, R. (1978). *Transformations.* New York: Simon & Schuster.

Hall, C. S., & Lindzey, G. (1978). *Theories of personality* (3rd ed.). New York: John Wiley.

Hogan, D. P. (1980). The transition to adulthood as a career contingency. *American Sociological Review, 45,* 261-276.

Hogan, D. P. (1981). *Transitions and social change: The early lives of American men.* New York: Academic Press.

Hultsch, D. R., & Plemons, J. K. (1979). Life events and life-span development. In P. B. Baltes & O. G. Brim, Jr. (Eds.), *Life-span development and behavior* (Vol. 2). New York: Academic Press.

Jackson, D. N. (1967). *Personality research form manual.* Goshen, NY: Research Psychologists Press.

Jackson, D. N. (1976). *Jackson Personality Inventory manual.* Goshen, NY: Research Psychologists Press.

James, W. (1958). *The varieties of religious experience.* New York: Mentor.

Jung, C. G. (1933). *Modern man in search of a soul.* New York: Harcourt Brace Jovanovich.

Jung, C. G. (1954). *The development of personality.* Princeton, NJ: Princeton University Press.

Kelly, G. A. (1955). *The psychology of personal constructs.* New York: W. W. Norton.

Lauer, Q. (1965). *Phenomenology and the crisis of philosophy.* New York: Harper Torchbooks.

Levinson, D. J. (1978). *The seasons of a man's life.* New York: Alfred A. Knopf.

Levinson, D. J. (1981). Exploration in biography: Evolution of the individual life structure in adulthood. In A. I. Rabin, J. Aronoff, A. M. Barclay, & R. A. Zucker (Eds.), *Further explorations in personality.* New York: John Wiley.

MacLeod, R. B. (1964). Phenomenology: A challenge to experimental psychology. In T. W. Wann (Ed.), *Behaviorism and phenomenology: Contrasting bases for modern psychology.* Chicago: University of Chicago Press.

Marshall, V. W. (1978-1979). No exit: A symbolic interactionist perspective on aging. *International Journal of Aging and Human Development, 9,* 345-358.

Maslow, A. (1955). Deficiency motivation and growth motivation. In M. R. Jones (Ed.), *Nebraska Symposium on Motivation, 1955*. Lincoln: University of Nebraska Press.

Massey, R. F. (1981). *Personality theories: Comparisons and syntheses*. New York: D. Van Nostrand.

Mead, G. H. (1934). *Mind, self, and society*. Chicago: University of Chicago Press.

Mischel, W. (1981). *Introduction to personality* (3rd ed.). New York: Holt, Rinehart & Winston.

Neugarten, B. L. (1968). The awareness of middle age. In B. L. Neugarten (Ed.), *Middle age and aging*. Chicago: University of Chicago Press.

Neugarten, B. L. (1973). Personality change in late life: A developmental perspective. In C. Eisdorfer & M. P. Lawton (Eds.), *The psychology of adult development and aging*. Washington, DC: American Psychological Association.

Neugarten, B. L. (1977). Personality and aging. In J. E. Birren & K. W. Schaie (Eds.), *Handbook of the psychology of aging*. New York: Van Nostrand Reinhold.

Neugarten, B. L., & Hagestad, G. O. (1976). Age and the life course. In R. Binstock & E. Shanas (Eds.), *Handbook of aging and the social sciences*. New York: Van Nostrand Reinhold.

Neugarten, B. L., Moore, J. W., & Lowe, J. C. (1965). Age norms, age constraints, and adult socialization. *American Journal of Sociology, 70*, 710-717.

Pervin, L. A. (1980). *Personality: Theory, assessment, and research* (3rd ed.). New York: John Wiley.

Riegel, K. F. (1975). Adult life crises: A dialectic interpretation of development. In N. Datan & L. H. Ginsberg (Eds.), *Life-span developmental psychology: Normative life crises*. New York: Academic Press.

Riley, M. W. (1976). Age strata in social systems. In R. Binstock & E. Shanas (Eds.), *Handbook of aging and the social sciences*. New York: Van Nostrand Reinhold.

Riley, M. W., Johnson, M., & Foner, A. (Eds.) (1972). *Aging and society: A sociology of age stratification* (Vol. 3). New York: Russell Sage.

Rogers, C. R. (1961). *On becoming a person*. Boston: Houghton Mifflin.

Rokeach, M. (1973). *The nature of human values*. New York: Free Press.

Rossi, A. S. (1980). Life-span theories and women's lives. *Signs: Journal of Women in Culture and Society, 6* , 4-32.

Ryff, C. D. (1982a). Self-perceived personality change in adulthood and aging. *Journal of Personality and Social Psychology, 42*, 108-115.

Ryff, C. D. (1982b). Successful aging: A developmental approach. *Gerontologist, 22*, 209-214.

Ryff, C. D. (1984). Personality development from the inside: The subjective experience of change in adulthood and aging. In P. B. Baltes & O. G. Brim, Jr. (Eds.), *Life-span development and behavior* (Vol. 6). San Diego, CA: Academic Press.

Ryff, C. D. (1985). Adult personality development and the motivation for personal growth. In D. A. Kleiber & M. L. Maehr (Eds.), *Advances in motivation and achievement: Volume 4. Motivation and adulthood*. Greenwich, CT: JAI.

Ryff, C. D., & Baltes, P. B. (1976). Value transitions and adult development in women: The instrumentality-terminality sequence hypothesis. *Developmental Psychology, 12*, 567-568.

Ryff, C. D., & Dunn, D. D. (1985). A life-span developmental approach to the study of stressful events. *Journal of Applied Developmental Psychology, 6*, 113-127.

Ryff, C. D., & Heincke, S. G. (1983). The subjective organization of personality in adulthood and aging. *Journal of Personality and Social Psychology, 44,* 807-816.

Ryff, C. D., & Migdal, S. (1984). Intimacy and generativity: Self-perceived transitions. *Signs: Journal of Women in Culture and Society.*

Sardello, R. J. (1978). A phenomenological approach to memory. In R. S. Valle & M. King (Eds.), *Existential-phenomenological alternatives for psychology.* New York: Oxford University Press.

Schutz, A. (1967). *The phenomenology of the social world* (G. Walsh & F. Lehnert, Trans.). Chicago: Northwestern University Press.

Spiegelberg, H. (1972). *Phenomenology in psychology and psychiatry: An historical introduction.* Evanston, IL: Northwestern University Press.

Vaillant, G. E. (1977). *Adaptation to life.* Boston: Little, Brown.

Valle, R. S., & King, M. (Eds.). (1978). *Existential-phenomenological alternatives for psychology.* New York: Oxford University Press.

Veroff, J., Douvan, E., & Kulka, R. A. (1981). *The inner American: A self-portrait from 1957 to 1976.* New York: Basic Books.

Wann, T. W. (Ed.). (1964). *Behaviorism and phenomenology: Contrasting bases for modern psychology.* Chicago: University of Chicago Press.

Wrong, D. (1961). The oversocialized conception of man in modern sociology. *American Sociological Review, 26,* 183-193.

Zeren, A. S., & Ryff, C. D. (1984). *Psychological development in men during fatherhood.* Paper presented at the meetings of the Eastern Psychological Association, Baltimore.

3

Socialization in Old Age: A Meadian Perspective

NEENA L. CHAPPELL
HAROLD L. ORBACH

This chapter explores the perspective of George Herbert Mead (1863-1931), highlighting particular concepts of interest to socialization in old age and discussing them in relation to the elderly. Although Mead is assumed to be the forefather of that school of sociological social psychology known as "symbolic interaction" (a term coined by Herbert Blumer, 1937, p. 53; McPhail & Rexcoat, 1979), and it has been symbolic interactionists who have been largely responsible for Mead's recognition in the sociological community (Smith, 1977), it is a Meadian perspective and not a symbolic interactionist perspective that is elaborated here. There are several reasons for this emphasis. There are many differences evident among writers referred to or referring to themselves as symbolic interactionists (Vaughan & Reynolds, 1968), many of which are contradictory to one another. Most important, none of the writers in the school of symbolic interaction provides as detailed and consistent a theory as does Mead.

Most social psychologists claiming allegiance to the writings of Mead have emphasized his role as a social psychologist, focusing on his ideas concerning socialization, self, and social control. The cultural definition and learning of meanings, or, as Farberman (1970) puts it, an understanding of how social factors are intrinsic to mentality while maintaining the selective character of mentality, is recognized as Mead's greatest contribution to the social sciences (Brymer, 1980; Chappell, 1978a, 1978b). Empirical studies, maintaining this emphasis, have tended to concentrate on the specific agents of socialization within society and the roles for which we are socialized. The concomitant

AUTHORS' NOTE: This research was supported in part by a National Health Research Scholar Award (no. 6607-1137-48) to the first author.

neglect of Mead's teaching and writing in education, philosophy, and psychology, especially in comparative and physiological psychology, together with a lack of attention to other aspects of his work, results in a selective and misrepresentative reading of Mead's theoretical contributions.

This selective attention to particular aspects of Meadian theory is perhaps understandable given the time in which he was developing his views. During the first part of this century, sociology was establishing itself as a separate discipline in an academic milieu that traced social experience to elementary human motives referred to variously as "social forces," "interests," and "instincts." This form of explanation began falling into disfavor due to its lack of scientific precision in a time when science was becoming more and more revered. In addition, it was grounded in a particularistic biological determinism that conflicted with basic sociological assumptions about the importance of the social environment for human nature, not to mention the lack of a factual basis supporting the existence and influence of instincts (Hinkle & Hinkle, 1954).

At the same time, within psychology, the functional school pioneered by Dewey, Angell, Mead, and their associates (see Rucker, 1969, chap. 3) was developing a biosocial approach critical of the traditional atomistic approach of associationist and structural psychology. This approach arose out of a sophisticated analysis of the findings of comparative and experimental psychology in the areas of perception, cognition, language, and motivation and a critical application of evolutionary theory in relation to the nature of an organism's environment.

Mead developed his social psychology from the late 1890s on, arguing that the development of the self takes place as an evolutionary process of emergence within social groups through social interaction involving the use of language. He endeavored to show that mind and self as functional processes are social emergents, thereby incorporating the relevance of social groups for individual personality within a framework acceptable to American individualists (Morris, 1934; Reck, 1964).

Our presentation, while not minimizing the importance of Mead's theory of the genesis of the self through human socialization, incorporates in addition a discussion of some of his less well-known ideas that have particular relevance for studying life during old age. Mead himself wrote little specifically about old age, either in his scientific work or in his correspondence (Orbach, 1983). His perspective nevertheless has great relevance for studying socialization through the whole life course.

This chapter begins with a brief presentation of Mead's view of the characteristics of the biological organism at birth and the development of the self in childhood, then proceeds to a discussion of the temporal order and change during adulthood. The prefatory remarks concerning the biological organism at birth and during childhood socialization are relatively well known but are reiterated here, as they are pertinent to understanding a Meadian perspective on socialization in later life.

The main interest of this chapter, however, lies in Mead's ideas concerning later life. Here many insightful and important areas are evident in his writings, but these have received little attention to date, particularly in the area of aging. These include Mead's view of the temporal order and the specious present, which locates our lives in a present that is constantly changing; his views on the problematic situation as that which leads to change in the self; and his views on the uniqueness of each individual. It is argued that these additional ideas can increase our understanding of the human situation. Throughout, examples are designed to highlight the relevance of such an approach for the study of the elderly.

The relevance of a Meadian perspective for research is also discussed throughout. Its use as a conceptual framework guiding the principles of one's research, its use for indicating specific research questions, and its use as a framework within which research data can be interpreted are illustrated. The intent is a greater understanding of a Meadian perspective for studying socialization in old age.

DEVELOPING A SELF

For Mead, although the biological organism as a non-socially organized nature is historically prior to the social process, the social process temporally precedes the individual self and is the context within which the individual self develops and emerges. That is, Mead posits the plasticity of the biological form from birth (1904a, 1907).[1] Although the biological organism is subject to extensive modification through interaction with its environment, it is born with certain basic or "given" characteristics. It possesses biological "stuff," referred to as "impulses" and "primal stuff" in the writings of Mead, which not only exists but seeks expression (1904a, 1907, 1909, 1918, 1929a, 1930). Impulses are the result of biological evolution. Their expression necessarily involves certain social relationships and they become more socially channeled as a consequence of the organization of definite social relationships in the form of "habits" and "institutions."

Mead (1934, p. 337) defines an impulse as "a congenital tendency to react in a specific manner to a certain sort of stimulus, under certain organic conditions." He characterizes this sensitivity to stimuli ("the selective character of attention") as "on its active motor side connot[ing] . . . this relationship of a performed tendency to act to the stimulus which sets the impulse free."[2]

Mead also emphasizes the role of emotion (such as anger, fear, or sympathy), which he claims is a vital part of our experience—the affective as opposed to the "intellectual" or "cognitive" side—that arises out of the inhibition or blocking of our tendencies to act in response to the situations in which our impulses seek expression (1936, p. 375; 1912; 1926).

While there is no systematic treatment of emotion in the work of Mead published to date, his views are consonant with those of Dewey (1894, 1895), which he helped formulate and which are found throughout his works. Essentially, emotion, as the affective side of mind or psychic activity (1903) that arises from the inhibition or blocking of ongoing activity, serves to arouse the organism to solve the problem that is blocking the completion of the ongoing act. It thus serves as a motor basis for the individual's mobilization of resources to solve the problem, because the solution of the problem is what releases the tension created by the emotional state.

Mead, like Dewey, sees specific emotional attitudes as representing biological processes that have emerged and persisted because of their evolutionary survival value. Socialization provides customary and valued forms for the use and control of emotion (habits and manners, for example), but these can break down in extreme situations such as a crowd or mob or other form of collective behavior, when original animal responses take over. The feelings that accompany some forms of emotional excitement and the exhilaration that is felt in certain types of emotional states are treated as essential parts of human life (1934, pp. 216-220). Thus emotion that arises from the release of tension (for example, joy) represents a basis for valuation of successful action and development of interests.

More generally, our own and other people's actions serve as gestures that become symbols that indicate the social meaning and definition of our emotions in relation to given situations (as in joy at success, despair at failure, grief at death, and so on) and come to indicate their content (Mead, 1909, 1910a). We learn the social meaning of emotions in interaction with others, just as other meaning is learned.

Shibutani (1961, pp. 323-366) suggests we respect or despise ourselves in the same manner in which we act toward others when we respect or despise them. Goffman (1955) and Rustin (1971) note that the group socially defines the amount and distribution of emotion that is appropriate in a particular situation. Hochschild (1983) provides an illustration of "emotional" socialization in studying the socialization of airline hostesses, of the emotional side as a vital part of the role and not a separate, dispensable element.

Mead's treatment of the biological and physiologic elements of behavior is always presented in an evolutionary perspective, with particular concern for the plasticity of the human organism to be shaped by the emergent process of "mind" as the outcome of communicative activities originating in the biological organism. He is neither a biological determinist nor a social determinist (Reck, 1964, p. xxxviii; Strauss, 1956, pp. xii-xiii).

From the beginning, then, the biological organism is living in an ongoing social process (Mead, 1909). The basic mechanism that organizes and controls this process is the *gesture*, or the movement of one organism acting as a stimulus calling forth appropriate responses from another organism. The infant initially interacts in a conversation of gestures (natural signs) in which one's movements call out a response in another, that response serves as a stimulus for the first, and so on. Mead (1940b, 1934, pp. 63, 362; 1925, 1929b) refers to the responses that are present in behavior, either in advance of the stimulation of things or already aroused, but not yet fully expressed, as *attitudes*. Attitudes, therefore, are types or aspects of activity and not internal states of readiness for action as many social scientists define them today (Smith, 1977). Attitudes refer to two types of activity for Mead: to the assumed posture of the organism and to the tendency to act in any of a range of ways consistent with that posture. The attitude is the beginning of an act, an encapsulated act, and as gesture comes to represent or mean the act that typically follows.

The term for this *relation* between organism and environment, between stimulus and response, is the "act," and Mead refers to it as the unit of existence. An act is an ongoing event that consists of stimulation and response and the results of the response (Mead, 1938, p. 364; Reck, 1964, p. xix). The responses are meaningful only insofar as they lie inside a conversation of gestures. "Meaning" refers to the later stages of the oncoming act and the objects indicated (Mead, 1910b, 1912, 1922; Morris, 1934, pp. xx-xxi). That is, responses can be meaningful to the observer although not yet to the unsocialized child.

Although these acts are meaningful, the infant is not yet conscious of their meaning, for there is nothing in the mechanism of the act that brings this relation to consciousness (Mead, 1910b). At this point the infant experiences the body, its feelings and sensations, but does not distinguish them from the environment. The significance of this characterization of the biological infant is the fact that the infant is characterized as not yet having a self. For Mead, in this respect (i.e., not yet having self-consciousness), the infant is initially no different from other "lower" animal forms.

It is only with the development of the mind and self that the organism gains human status. The emergence of mind and self takes place within the social process as the outcome of a number of contributing factors. Consciousness of meaning cannot occur unless *images* are formed of responses to gestures. As past experiences accumulate, gestures (both the child's and those of others) become identified with the content of the child's emotions, feelings, and attitudes, and images arise of the response that the gesture of one form will bring out in another (Mead, 1910a). The image, however, cannot be distinguished from the object by its content or function, but only in its appearance in the absence of the object to which it refers. Once images arise, our sensitivity to them serves the same function as does our sensitivity to other perceptual stimulations—namely, that of selecting and building the objects to which we direct our activity (Mead, 1904a, 1903; Meltzer, 1972).

As noted earlier, meaning is not primarily a psychical content and need not be conscious. For Mead, meaning is not conscious until significant symbols evolve. When gestures possess meaning for the child, that is, when the child has a self-consciousness of the meaning of the gesture, the gesture becomes a significant symbol (Mead, 1910b, 1912, 1900). Consciousness of meaning at this stage is the consciousness of one's own attitudes of response as they answer to, control, and interpret the gestures of others (1910a). Crucial for this development are attention and reflexiveness. *Attention* mediates the reference of the act to the self and brings about a conscious organization of the act within the individual as a whole. *Reflexiveness*, the turning back of the experience upon oneself, permits the whole social process to be brought into the experience of the individuals involved in it (1934, pp. 121-122, 134; 1936, pp. 384-385, 1910c).

Consciousness of meaning is the essence of *mind*. "Mind" refers to a process of the importation of the external social processes—the conversation of gestures—into the conduct of the individual so as to meet the problems that arise in ongoing behavior. "The mind is simply the interplay of such gestures in the form of significant symbols" (Mead, 1934, pp. 188-189). When mind arises, the individual becomes self-consciously or reflexively aware of his or her relation to the social process as a whole and to the other individuals participating in it. Through mind, or self-reflexive intelligence, the individual can consciously adjust to that process and modify the resultant of that process in any given social act. In humans, a mediate state or "response of manipulation" brings the ongoing act to a temporary pause prior to completion, out of which control over the act is established. Essential to this mediate state is delayed response, which permits final selection (Mead, 1934, pp. 99-100, 254). It is through thought that the individual interprets experiences (1934, pp. 121-122; 1936, pp. 384-385).

In the development of the child, there are two stages that represent the essential steps in attaining full self-consciousness: play and game. In the play stage, the child "plays at" the role of teacher, mother, pirate, and so on, and thus comes to understand the diverse roles in society. In this stage the child, through the use of language as the mechanism of social conduct, is taking the role of the other by continually arousing in him- or herself the response of others to his or her own acts. Language, in the form of the vocal gesture as stimulus that is common to both the individual and the other(s), becomes the primary system of significant symbols, permitting the child to organize and reorganize his or her own responses and the responses of others to carry on social acts. Through "play"—at first physical and overt and then imaginative and in thought—the child treats the role of the other and his or her own role as "objects" to be manipulated; namely, to be constructed and reconstructed in terms of the constituent units of behaviors. In this way one learns the organization of particular individual behavior, taking one role at a time. At the same time, the process of treating one's own role as an object is the foundation of the ability to be reflexively self-conscious as one takes the attitude of the other toward one's own role. "The self arises in conduct when the individual becomes a social object in experience to himself" (Mead, 1922, p. 160).

In the game stage, the child must assume the various roles of all participants in the game and govern his or her actions accordingly. Here the child must "take" many roles simultaneously. The organized reactions to the child are embedded in the child's own "playing" of different positions, and this organized attitude becomes the "generalized other"; in other words, the crystallization of all the particular attitudes of others into an organized single attitude or standpoint (1934, pp. 90, 158, 364-367; 1925).[3] The complete or full development of the self and self-consciousness appears with this ability to organize all the attitudes—one's own role and the roles of others—toward a social environment from this general standpoint or perspective. The individual now has a generalized or "universal" organization of roles that serves as a standpoint from which any specific act or behavior can be interpreted and understood or constructed and reconstructed in thought. Thought is the "inner" conversation of this generalized other with one's self in the form of specific roles that permit the control of ongoing conduct (Mead, 1922, 1925).

Mead does not speak of roles in the same fashion as many contemporary sociologists. He uses the term primarily in relation to taking the role of the other, which refers to calling forth in oneself the response that the stimulus would call out in others. The term is used interchangeably with "attitude," as in "assuming the attitude of the other" (recall that "attitude" refers to an aspect of activity and not an internal state) and implies the processual fluidity of roles as adaptive responses. This usage refers to a definition of "role" as a constellation of behaviors, actual and potential, related to a position or function (1934, p. 151). Specialized functions lead to different roles, that is, to a different complex of relations. Of particular importance is the fact that "role," for Mead, refers essentially to behavior, not to values or norms. This differs from the predominant usage found in functionalist theories that tend to reify roles as fixed entities (e.g., Riley, Foner, Hess, & Toby, 1969). Rosow defines roles in terms of activities (1976), but also in terms of norms (1974, pp. 38-54). For him, roles incorporate shared expectations about values and behavior (Rosow, 1965; also see George, 1980). For Mead, roles refer to perspectives (see below for an elaboration) and not to values and norms.

It should be noted here that Mead does not consider imitation as an operative process prior to the play and game stages. Rather, imitation becomes possible only after the development of the self as a process of conscious control of behavior. Imitation "becomes comprehensible when there is a consciousness of other selves, and not before" (Mead, 1909; see also 1934, pp. 51ff.). However, others imitate the child's behaviors such that the child makes gestures that bring specific responses from others. Over time, whenever the child makes these gestures in the presence of others, the child receives, to some degree, a consistent set of responses that serve to build the basis for linking these gestures with the imagery of the responses.

THE NATURE OF SELF

The self includes mind, but the two are not synonymous processes. Mind refers to the part of the self that involves self-consciousness. The self includes this reflexive ability to treat oneself as an object and habits (e.g., intonation of voice, accent) that one is not aware of at all. "There are whole bundles of such habits which do not enter into a conscious self" that help make up what is called the "unconscious self"(Mead, 1934, pp. 144, 163). Self-consciousness, the recognition or appearance of the self as an object in consciousness, is the core of the self. This is to be distinguished from the ordinary meaning of consciousness, which is the simple reference to the field of experiences such as those of sight or touch. One can behaviorally respond to the self as an object without a sensuous or physical awareness of this occurrence. Self-consciousness involves our own awareness and response to the same stimuli we use to call forth the responses of others; that is, the awareness of our sharing the attitudes we call out in others (Mead, 1934, p. 163). Only when the individual has developed self-consciousness is one fully human, within a Meadian perspective.

For Mead, the self cannot be located simply as something in the organism. Rather, the term refers to the relation between the organism and its environment. The distinction between the terms "organism" and "environment" is for Mead functional, not metaphysical (1934, pp. 332-333). That is to say, the self is not a substance but a part of a larger social process (1934, p. 178).

This larger, ongoing social process involves two complementary phases or aspects that are paralleled in the structure of the self. The first involves the organization of the relations between the individual and the environment, including other individuals, that is a part of the social acts.

These social relations are represented by the social roles of the individual—the constellation of behaviors engaged in by individuals in the carrying out of the social acts that constitute the ongoing social process. As the individual is socialized into the community, these organized behaviors become a part of the individual's self in the form of what Mead calls the "me" and are its "conventional" phase in the sense that the individual's self incorporates the already-existing attitudes of others as part of one's own self. The "me" thus represents the process of the organization of behavior in the form of group roles, the importation of the social organization of the outer world into the individual by means of which social control is exercised as self-control (Mead, 1934, pp. 90, 163-164, 209; 1925).

The second phase involves the creation of new social relationships through the reconstruction of existing social relations and objects into novel forms of behavior. In an important sense, there is a constant process of creation or construction of new forms of behavior by adaptive responses to previously existing situations. That is, every situation requiring action as it recurs in a new time is potentially one in which previous patterns of response are modified, resulting in the appearance of new social roles and objects or meanings in the environment. The changes occur through the aspect of the self Mead termed the "I," which is the response of the individual to the situation being faced.

Each situation requiring response is a new one in the sense that it occurs in a different time and involves a new organization of behavioral responses. Habit and institutions (the "me") provide continuity and stability of response, but change—either large or small—occurs. The "I" is the source of the new or novel response because as a process it represents the ability of the self in thought to treat itself as an object just as it does other persons and objects, and to consider different, alternative ways of responding to a given situation. It is particularly when traditional ways of responding are unsuccessful in allowing action to proceed that new response *has* to be created (Mead, 1934, pp. 209ff.). It is here that the "I" becomes the source of individual innovation that can transform the larger social process.

THE PRESENT AND THE PASSAGE OF TIME

To understand the self as a process, one must understand Mead's notion of the temporal order. For Mead, the locus of reality is the present. The chief referent of the present is the emergent event, that is, the occurrence of something that is more than the processes that have led up to it and that by its change, continuance, or disappearance adds to later presents a content they would not otherwise have possessed. That is to say, the present includes what is disappearing and what is emerging (Mead, 1934, pp. 197-200; 1932, pp. 23-25, 28-31; Reck, 1964, p. xlvi; Tillman, 1970). Imagery connects the two. The emergent event as present gives us the basic structure of time. We are immediately considering something but we are already going on to something else. We are continually interpreting our present with something that is represented by possible future conduct (Mead, 1932; Reck, 1964, p. xlviii).

The present is the locus of reality throughout life, during old age as well as the middle and younger years. For those who are old, the locus of reality is still their present and its chief referent is the emergent event of the time (preparing a meal, engaging in conversation, reminiscing about past experiences, making cabinets).

A woman now in her early seventies illustrates the meaning and importance of the temporal order, of the present as the locus of reality and its influence on the remembered past. She is and always has been active physically and socially. She spent her earlier years as a wife and mother, believing this was her correct role and trying to fulfill it with pride and zeal. Some time after her husband died, which was well after her children were out of the home, she learned of and became committed to feminism. Her early socialization and early adult years are now remembered as part of a patriarchal enslavement imposed upon her by the structure of our outmoded society. Her past experiences, of course, have not changed. Her interpretation of them has, stemming from her current perspective. Some of the specific events that are remembered have also altered. Furthermore, her perspective and therefore her memory and interpretation of the past are not shared by everyone, least of all her two sons, who disagree vehemently both with the memory of how the events transpired and the interpretation of the events.

In other words, the past that is remembered and reconstructed is done so from the perspective of the present. However, as social scientists, we know little of how our remembered pasts change as we age. Do they change in identifiable ways? Do they vary by gender, by social class, by ethnic group? Although not denying the importance and utility of obtaining reliable and objective historical data, social scientists seldom study the remembered past in terms of what it can tell us about the present situation of the individual. Knowing how the woman referred to above views her past tells us much about her current perspective.

Similarly, the present is responsible for the anticipatory future, recalling that the future exists as alternative possibilities. Depending on the present in which we are living, different possibilities are seen for the future. This too can be illustrated by way of example. A man had a series of minor strokes, heart attacks, and other physical ailments in his late eighties that put him in the hospital almost continuously for just less than two years. During this time, despite his age and various ailments, he never defined himself as having a few years to live or as possibly becoming seriously disabled. He assumed that with the great advances made by medical science, the doctors would be able to cure or mend whatever was wrong with him. He used to write his relatives, with great indignation, that the doctors had the nerve to tell him he was getting old and they could do little for him.

Because of his perspective in the present he anticipated a future in which he would still go to the office every day and continue working very much as before. Much to the amazement of family, friends, and doctors, most of whom were preparing for his retirement, and community organizations that were planning major testimonials to honor him before he died, he not only had no intention of retiring but was quite surprised by the suggestions. In addition, when he returned home from the hospital he refused to stay in bed for several weeks as directed by the medical profession, because in his view he had to ensure the continued use of his "bum leg." He did eventually go back to the office, and it was several years before he "retired." Incidentally, the doctors later said that if he had stayed in bed for as long as they had ordered, he probably would have lost the use of his leg permanently.

Later, when this man was in his nineties, he had both legs amputated and indeed was very ready to die. He was living in a very different perspective, one that was reflected in the future he saw for himself. Having reached the point where he no longer wished to continue living, and having realistically appraised his physical health as leading to death relatively soon, he no longer engaged in acts with long-term consequences. Current affairs, of which he had always been an avid follower, no longer held his interest. He now watched game shows on television, something he had never done. For him, they now held immediate entertainment value with no investment in the future, for which he assumed he would not be around. In other words, as this man's perspective in the present changed, so did the possible courses of action he saw for himself in the future and therefore his actual behavior.

The issue of our limited future once we reach old age was not addressed directly by Mead. How the fact of closeness to death or the concept of finitude affects our perspective is relatively unknown, but of interest for understanding change in the self during old age. As noted elsewhere (Chappell, 1973, 1975), existing research on awareness of death tends to suffer from measurement problems, equating objective measures with the subjective meaning this has for the individual (Gorney, 1968; Chellam, 1964; Falk, 1970; Marshall, 1972). Nevertheless, some research suggests that the respondent's subjective perspective on the future is related systematically to other factors, such as amount of planning, how time is scheduled, and social involvements, but not to amount of time spent thinking about the future or various demographic characteristics (Chappell, 1973, 1975).

The present, then, is not a piece of time cut out anywhere from the temporal dimension of uniformly passing reality. As there is a spatial thickness, so too is there a temporal thickness (sometimes referred to as the "specious present"). We construct our past from the standpoint of the present and as new presents arise we reconstruct different continuities in history. This is not to deny that what is going on would be otherwise if the earlier stages of the occurrence had been of a different character. The temporal order within which things happen and appear conditions what will happen and appear. But the main character of the past is that it connects what is unconnected in the merging of one present into another and provides "elbow room" in our narrow present for coping with the evolving present. That is, we recognize a shape—say a house, a table, a dog—and interpret its meaning based on past experiences. As we extend from the present in memory and history, we similarly extend from the present to the future in anticipation and forecast. The future provides a guide and helps determine our courses of action (Mead, 1938, p. 364; 1932, pp. 23-25, 28-31; 1929c). But the future exists only as alternative possibilities. It is the individual's conceived structure of the immediate present that is responsible for the perceived structure of the remembered past and the anticipatory future.

Of particular relevance here is that the elderly live in the present and remember their past, as do others, from the perspective of their present situations. Their lives continue to be characterized as those of thinking, reflexive individuals as they age. They no more "live in the past" than do others. Even for those who may spend time "reminiscing" (Frenkel-Brunswik, 1968; Erikson, 1968; Butler, 1968), from a Meadian perspective, the life-review is conducted from the perspective of the present, from the individual's current situation (see also Blumer, 1970). The past that is remembered is reconstructed from the perspective of the present, as is the anticipatory future. This process includes not only mind, but the self as well.

Basic to Mead's notion of the temporal order is the idea that change is always taking place. The social process is an evolving process. The self is always "becoming." However slowly, gradually, or subtly, the self is always changing. Within this ongoing process, the novel is always arising (Mead, 1936, pp. 507-509; 1932, p. 90). The basic facts of social life are interaction and the appearance of novelty, emergents from the process.

This understanding of self as a process rather than as a substance is crucial for a correct understanding of Mead and application of his theory to socialization in old age. This must be emphasized because, as

Lindesmith and Strauss (1968, pp. 314-343) point out, the use of the term "self" as a noun seems to imply the existence of a corresponding entity or object. This is as erroneous, however, as it would be to think of "speed" in the same manner. We cannot buy "60 miles per hour" or hold it in our hands. Both terms refer to events and relationships rather than to entities having a definite location in space. It is for this reason that the self has been called a "grammatical illusion." This illusion is reinforced by the fact that the human body can readily be set off as an organic unit, by the continuity of experiences in time, by our identification with a certain act that tends to isolate the self and render it definite, and by our sense of personal autonomy (Mead, 1938, pp. 369-370; Shibutani, 1961, pp. 213-248). However, this sense of being a separate entity, this illusion, is not to be confused with the nature of the self as a process. When Mead refers to the self as an "object" he uses the term to denote a relation that is part of a whole process. The self refers to the objectification of this relation, this process (Mead, 1925; Reck, 1964, pp. l-liii).

An emphasis on the substantive nature of the self is perhaps the most common distortion of Meadian theory. When the substantive aspect is considered its essential and defining character, its processual nature becomes a passive and, in Lichtman's (1970) terms, trivial aspect of life (Glaser & Strauss, 1972). Evidence of this is readily available in many current writings on the self in which it is defined as the totality of a person's self-attributes (such as intelligence and ambition) and/or the roles in which the person participates (such as father or doctor) (Brim, 1966; Sherwood, 1965; Couch, 1966; Kinch, 1968; Stebbins, 1972). Others redefine this aspect of the self as identity, so that, by definition, all other aspects of the self are excluded (Kuhn & McPartland, 1954; Gross & Stone, 1970). In either case, the result becomes a relatively static, socially determined attribute theory of the self as a separate entity. Such views basically select one aspect of the total self and ignore the others (see above).

The fact that change is inherent in the process of living, whether we are particularly aware of it or not, is important to remember in relation to the elderly, whose lives frequently are characterized as standing still. Not only is this characterization false, but it also tends to keep us from recognizing the potential of rich and full lives during old age. It is perhaps better recognized when we compare today to five years ago than today to yesterday. More will be said about this in the following section.

THE SELF IN ADULTHOOD

Mead's account of the development of the self provides a clear conceptual distinction between childhood and adult socialization. During the former, the infant becomes human, develops self-consciousness and, concomitantly, a generalized attitude or standpoint toward others. The rise of mind and self-consciousness can therefore be viewed as the end of childhood socialization and the beginning of adult socialization. The difference between the two is obviously qualitative, as mind and self-consciousness differentiate humans from other animal forms; and quantitative, as the individual now assumes an array of multiple roles and generally, in modern societies, faces a complexly structured environment that requires a large and versatile repertoire of behaviors.

This approach to socialization differs from many other writings in the area. For example, Shibutani (1961, pp. 63-95) describes socialization as the process of learning to participate in social groups and differentiates childhood socialization on the grounds that such learning is more extensive than during adult socialization. Sarbin and Allen (1968) state that "childhood socialization" refers to the acquisition of ascribed roles and "adult socialization" refers to the acquisition of achieved roles. For Mead, of course, the child learns particular roles (both ascribed and achieved) during the play stage even before adapting the viewpoint of the generalized other and the development of a self. There is no reason to assume the child learns only ascribed roles during the play stage. Indeed, Mead's examples of mother, pirate, and teacher clearly include both types.

Even many who agree with Mead's account of childhood socialization as the process of becoming human or of transforming the newly born organism into the basic model of a human being (Wrong, 1970; Cavan, 1970; Rafky, 1973; Berger & Luckmann, 1967, pp. 130-133) depart from him when expounding their views of the nature of adult socialization. For example, Cavan (1970) claims that adult socialization is simply an addition to or an extension of the basic form developed in childhood. Berger and Luckmann (1967, pp. 134-148) say it is less firmly entrenched or is more "artificial" than childhood socialization. Brim (1966) claims that it deals mainly with the acquisition of roles. Others, such as Riley (1976) and Rosow (1976), do not differentiate sharply between childhood and adult socialization, except in terms of transferring between and learning new roles. As noted earlier, these authors define roles primarily in terms of norms and values, rather than activities and relations. It might be noted further, however, that both of these authors, especially the latter, posit change as central.

There are two main reasons Meadian theory opposes the notion of adult socialization as a mere extension of childhood socialization. First, the social process is an evolution, one that becomes a qualitatively different situation when the individual develops a self, but nevertheless continues. The continual emergence of the novel arises through the actions that appear in the social process and necessitates continual reorganization and reconstruction of the self. The individual is always becoming through acts, especially those involving reflexive consciousness that permit identification with the process of development. In other words, one does not perpetuate oneself as is. Furthermore, as the individual adapts to a certain environment, that environment is changed by that action, and a different individual emerges; as one becomes a different individual, the community in which one lives also changes to a greater or lesser degree. The self constantly evolves as part of the ongoing process of interaction among the individual, other persons, and the environment (Mead, 1934, p. 25, 1938, pp. 368-369, 1899a, 1899b, 1903, 1917; Strauss, 1969, p. 25). This is not to say that all changes are sudden, drastic, or even immediately recognized consciously by the individual or by others. Rather, change is part of the individual's day-to-day experience and is often gradual and subtle (Salaman, 1971a; Strauss, 1969, p. 58; Ruitenbeek, 1964, p. 30).

Those maintaining that the self in adulthood is an extension of that formed in childhood may object on the grounds that they do not deny change per se. However, the issue is that they deny qualitative change except on rare occasions or in infrequent cases of resocialization that they distinguish from adult socialization (McHugh, 1970). These authors argue that one's core identity is formed in childhood and changes taking place in adulthood are evidenced in the peripheral or labile identities, or that additional subidentities serve to expand the core identity as the individual enters new roles (Brim, 1966, pp. 14-17; Schein, 1971; Miller, 1963; Ruitenbeek, 1964, p. 10; Sarbin & Allen, 1968).

The reply to the claim that change that takes place in adulthood is not qualitative change is found in Mead's discussion of the self-conscious individual. The person now has use of a mind, reflexive thought, and self-conscious intellect for help in solving problems—abilities not present in childhood. The individual can now use intelligence, sort among various alternatives, reject in favor of those that are in fact carried out or acted upon, and so reconstruct the self and the environment (Mead, 1934, pp. 214ff.). The mediation that occurs in the inhibited act, the process of thinking through the construction of possible futures, provides the basis for the control of the act on the part of the actor. Mead likens this to the adoption of the method of the "working hypothesis" of the experimental scientist, in which provisional futures are continually tested and reformulated.

However, as we noted earlier, Mead's emphasis on the use of rational action, of experiment, does not imply the absence of influence by nonrational, affective, and noncognitive factors, particularly the impulses rooted in the biological organism. The task of intelligence is not to replace the affective and noncognitive dimensions, but rather, through understanding them, to attempt to control them or to use them as part of the process of successful achievement of one's intended goals. This implies intelligent social control of the environment, here including others as a central part of that environment (Mead, 1918; Reck, 1964, p. xxxviii). Humans are active, not passive. The rise of mind engenders an "intellectual competence" to reflect upon and evaluate alternatives (Oestereicher, 1972). The elderly, like other adults, live in a constantly changing world and have the use of mind for choosing among alternatives, subject to the social constraints imposed by the community, which does not recognize or permit such freedom among all theoretically possible alternatives.

It is important to note, in regard to this issue of change and stability in the self, that although change is inherent to Mead's theoretical perspective, he posits the individual's search for continuity. This belief in or search for continuity or consistency extends to the past and to the future. We extend in memory and history and we do so to maintain continuity in the advance toward the goals of our conduct. But we do so in light of the present, in relation to the emergent event in the present situation and as an extension of this present. Furthermore, we find this continuity for every novelty that arises.

A man in his late eighties illustrates this point. He has always been devoted to and very successful at community affairs and business. Although married and the father of four children, he has always seemed to place community organizations and his paid labor ahead of his family. Indeed, when growing up his children had to consult his appointment book for a free evening if they wanted to spend time with their father. It was not unknown for the wait to be as long as three months. As his children grew and had families of their own, he paid two yearly visits to his grandchildren, one in the summertime and one on Christmas Day. In time, this man's perspective changed and he sought more time with his grandchildren, greater communication with his family, and more involvement in primary relationships. As his perspective changed, so too did his interpretation of his past and to some extent of the particular events from his past that he remembered. His stories now contained more people and included not only tasks or activities in which they had been involved, but also relationships between individuals. With his change in perspective came an increased awareness of women as having rightful contributions to make outside of marriage and child-rearing tasks. For the first time, and to the surprise of more than one member of the family, he started telling stories of pioneering women in the history of his family. These pioneering women undertook to initiate and perform tasks that were traditionally male and some of which no one would attempt, not even the men (such as driving one of the first cars up a steep, winding, unpaved, and apparently very hazardous mountain road). These stories were told with great pride and as examples of the "stuff" of which women in this family were made. This man believed and saw a stability and consistency from his past to his present.

As Gerth and Mills (1953, pp. 130-162) note, the influence of childhood experiences may be due to the simple fact that the adult develops temporally after childhood and so has these past experiences upon which to draw. Given that childhood is temporally prior to adulthood, the adult self necessarily develops from that form. Similarly, we project into the future from the present and find continuities there. The future is temporally later than the present and necessarily develops from the present. We are able to make such connections, to maintain a sense of continuity and consistency, through the use of linguistic categories and concepts that unite otherwise diverse things. These categories, with their implied groupings and connections, and even the degree of consistency necessary in the individual's behavior, are socially negotiated, established, maintained, and changed (Lindesmith & Strauss, 1968, pp. 314-343).

Mead's account of social interaction takes account of the large amount of everyday action that is based upon ingrained habit patterns, when mind and thought are not "needed" in the absence of anything that is problematic. Compare the ordinary act of starting an automobile with the same act when the temperature is 30° below zero. One is automatic and "unconscious," the other fraught with concern over the possible response or nonresponse of the automobile. Our habitual interaction with other people is similarly "unthinking" until the routine action is interrupted. These taken-for-granted aspects of the structure of everyday life are based upon both the nonconscious conditioning arising out of our biological and physiological heritage and the successful patterns of past problem solution based on thought and experiment that have now become routine habits: driving an automobile, reading or writing, and so on.

Both the actual continuities that exist and the process of seeking continuities by reconstructing the past and constructing the future are important in Meadian theory. We find such continuities within our constantly changing acts, our environment, and ourselves, but the continuities that we find are themselves constantly being altered by the novelty that emerges in the present. This reconstruction and construction of continuity in the past and in the future, on the basis of their relation to the present, is a determined process in the sense that what has occurred and what is occurring contribute to what will occur; but this should not be misinterpreted as a mechanical or preestablished determinism from the past to the present and the future that permits nothing new or novel to emerge. As Mead (1899a, p. 369) puts it: "It is always the unexpected that happens." The novel does emerge, but the conditions of the emergence are there. The discontinuous is the novel. New forms, qualities, and contexts emerge in the evolutionary process at the physical, biological, and social levels. They are there, but as functions of their contexts, as objectively relative; that is, they are relative to the character of things, and to the sensitivities and capacities of behavior of individual actors and organisms (Mead, 1925, 1929c; Reck, 1964, pp. xlvi, l-lvi).

Emphasizing the influence of the past to the neglect of the effect that the ever-changing presents have on the past and the future can result in what Becker and Strauss (1956) contend is an overemphasis on childhood experiences by Freudians and psychiatrists; and that type of overemphasis leads to a neglect of the dynamics of changes that arise out of the experiences that take place in adulthood and old age.

Wentowski (1981) is one social science researcher who has succeeded in portraying the dynamic ongoing nature of the life of the elderly, however subtle or taken for granted (see also Matthews, 1979; Lopata, 1973, 1979). In her study of social networks among older individuals, with particular focus on reciprocity and coping strategies, she gives examples of the "immediate exchange" and the "deferred exchange" coping strategies.

[Immediate exchange strategy]
Mr. Elder uses the immediate exchange strategy to maintain distance from others and maximize his personal autonomy. He does not own a car and is regularly given rides to local flea markets by Mr. Jones. As

repayment, Mr. Elder calculates a fixed percentage of his daily profits and pays Mr. Jones at the end of each day. He allows no outstanding debts to obligate him to others. Mr. Jones was sick for a while, and I drove Mr. Elder to the flea market a few times. Not as yet understanding the significance of repayments, I refused money for the rides, arguing that I was making the trip anyway. In spite of the fact that he desperately desired the rides, Mr. Elder soon stopped accepting them.

[Deferred exchange strategy]
As a poverty-stricken old person with many health problems, Mrs. Lewis needs much help to live alone. She attempts to obligate a large number of people, each of whom can be called upon for small favors. Her landlady picks her up and takes her grocery shopping each week. After many telephone calls, she can usually locate one of several acquaintances to drive her to cash her SSI cheque and buy food stamps. A partial list of her other helpers would include the doctor at the public health clinic (who visited her home one holiday), the clerks at the discount department store, the man who reads the gas meter, and the women who run the bingo at a nearby nursing home. She always repays these people in some fashion. To those who help her, she gives jars of jelly, left-over portions of desserts, and garden produce (originally given to her). She has only small or token gifts to offer and cannot obligate people to her too heavily. (Wentowski, 1981, p. 607)

These descriptions from field notes serve as excellent examples of ongoing daily activity in the lives of older people that show their lives as dynamic rather than static and inactive. In doing so, they support a Meadian view of old age as dynamic and also illustrate one way this activity can be studied.

ACCOUNTING FOR SITUATIONAL AND TRANSSITUATIONAL BEHAVIOR

Mead's theory of the self accounts for both situational behavior and transsituational behavior. The temporal order and the paramount importance of the specious present require a dynamic conception of the self. The continual emergence of the new, of novelty, and the processual nature of experience necessitate continual reorganization and reconstruction. We are always "becoming" and, through our reflexive consciousness, identify ourselves with the process of development. This is not to say that we are always conscious of our adjustments. Selective attention may be given to different features of the objective field without our pointing them out to ourselves (Mead, 1934, p. 25; 1938, pp.

368-369; 1899b, 1903, 1917). In other words, we do not simply receive impressions and then answer to them. We seek certain stimuli. We act as well as react. We "use" our minds to reconstruct experience and values and consciously direct our conduct. In fact, this process of reconstruction and direction is what is meant by "mind." This process involves the organization of concrete situations into universal categories allowing us to generalize from specific instances to larger acts within which our attention is focused upon the universal relationships in place of the concreteness (Mead, 1934, pp. 215, 388-389; 1938, pp. 372-376; 1930).

Thus actions are not wholly situated in an "objective" or "concrete" present environment. Our individual perspectives are parts of generalized standpoints, common perspectives through which our past comes in to influence our present conduct. However, as previously noted, this is not a fixed determinism, as our present with its vision of the future serves to structure and reconstruct the nature of the past on which we draw. Nevertheless, we carry the influence of our past with us in our individual and common perspectives. We draw on our past through generalization of the identity of responses, through an identification of the new with the old. Given stimuli call out specific responses, and inhibitions are built up through experience so that we avoid selecting those stimuli; consequently those responses tend not to be called out. This influence of the past can be either conscious or nonconscious, that is, habitual.

Mind enables self-conscious selection and purposive conduct. When individuals self-consciously direct attention, that to which we do not direct our attention comes to us in memory images as the familiar and is taken for granted. To the extent that we are living in our well-established habits, we tend not to be conscious of them. The habitual response shows itself in the total response of individuals and not in any isolated memory images. The nonconscious habitual response points to the fact that only a portion of the self is changed at a time, and that it is the part that is relevant to the part of the world that is problematic at the time. The solution to problems is found by considering various alternatives as they present themselves within one's perspective until the best solution is found, or at least one that allows action to proceed (Brymer, 1980). The portion that is unproblematic and unquestioned comes from the past unchanged (Mead, 1934, pp. 114-117, 122-125; 1938, pp. 106-107, 151-153, 548, 607-611; 1907, 1908; Farris & Brymer, 1965). Most of our behavior most of the time is of this character. What once may have been a problematic situation is now an "ingrained" habit.

On the other hand, for an elderly person who has just become widowed, many of the habitual responses are now problematic. Standard ways of thinking and behaving no longer "work," leading to a reorganization of perspective and consequent changes in behavior and thus in the self. Lopata (1973, 1979) has written extensively on the reconstruction of women's lives after widowhood. For many who are active, contributing members of society, retirement marks an event that results in problematic situations. Similarly, selling one's house and moving to an apartment in a new neighborhood will lead to a reorganization of some of the habitual responses that were unproblematic in the past. How much, how frequently, and how noticeably changes are taking place will vary. Graduating from college, moving to a new home, entering into a marriage, having a child, and so on—all are of a similar character with respect to the need to reorganize one's habitual patterns of behavior and one's perspective.

Mead's view of the problematic situation leading to change suggests that one should not expect dramatic changes in the elderly's perspective unless there are such problematic occurrences. Given the tendency toward mandatory retirement and the likelihood of widowhood during this age, however, such known events are likely to point to times of more radical change for the individual. How the individual copes depends on the resulting reconstruction, socially and individually, that takes place and the resources on which the person has to draw (meaning here the multiplicity of perspectives on which the person can draw, and past experiences with similar events or changes in perspectives).

All of the above examples demonstrate change as inherent to Mead's view of the individual and of society. Change, however, can be subtle or it can be dramatic; in the psychologists' terminology it can also be adaptive or disruptive. Gerontological research tends to focus on events that are assumed to result in dramatic change—widowhood, retirement, relocation of residence, and so on—and less on the gradual and oftentimes unnoticeable changes that all of us undergo. What is central to analyzing the actual impact of specific events that result in changed behaviors is the *evaluation* of such change from the point of view of the individual's perspective, not that of the observer. Much gerontological research in the past treated retirement as a disruptive and shattering "crisis" event from an abstract theoretical perspective. Research has shown this to be largely false, yet the bias remains in professional literature (see Friedmann & Orbach, 1974, pp. 626-629).

Regularities in behavior should therefore be evidenced trans-situationally, while recognizing at the same time that each new experience or situation in turn can affect the person's perspective. In other words, behavior is neither totally situationally determined nor totally unaffected by situations (Mead, 1938, pp. 151-153). Rather, perspectives or generalized standpoints are in a continual process of changing, gradually and subtly, into new perspectives.

INDIVIDUALITY AND JOINT ACTION

Mead's discussion of temporality also accounts for the uniqueness of each individual even though the self develops within the same society as others. Each person's perspective is a unique combination of inter-sections in relation to a specific past and future. It reflects a different aspect of the relational pattern of the social process. No one perspective reflects the totality of all relational patterns, but each one represents a different aspect of the whole. The common social origin and constitution of individual selves, then, does not preclude wide individual differences and variations (Mead, 1934, pp. 201-203; Tillman, 1970).

Within this diversity, joint action and cooperation take place because of the capacity of each individual to take on multiple and constantly intersecting views of the group. Insofar as two or more individuals interacting with one another come to share the other's perspective, there is a commonality or basis of identity within which the differences and the different perspectives are irrelevant for the cooperative process in which they are involved. This commonality or identity is referred to as a "universal" that transcends the different perspectives and can become the basis for organizing a common perspective that governs the cooperative activity at hand. As Blumer (1970) notes, it is not the structure of common values and norms that holds society together or controls or regulates activities in an orderly relationship. Rather, society consists of the fitting together of acts to form joint action, and this is dependent on the capacity of the individuals involved through their actions to take the roles of others effectively and to integrate them into a common perspective that is necessary for ongoing cooperative activity (Mead, 1934, pp. 89, 376; 1929a; Reck, 1964, pp. l-lvi; Tillman, 1970). Without this, differences arise between different individuals having different perspectives. Problems arise within our ever-changing experi-ence, causing some disintegration in the organization of the self. In all of these cases the differences or conflicts are settled or terminated by reconstruction. The social situation, the given framework of social relationships, or the self may be reconstructed, and a reconstruction in one of these areas affects the other. The relation between social reconstruction and self reconstruction is reciprocal and internal (Mead, 1934, pp. 307-309; 1913, 1929b).

Some examples are in order. The setting is a seminar in gerontology for first-year medical students. Some videotapes are shown of interviews with elderly individuals living in the community. Discussion ensues. A medical student asks a question about the tendency for the elderly to "wander" in conversation. Asked to explain, he elaborates with an example. Recently he and his wife had their first baby, an exciting event, and one of which he is clearly proud. He telephoned his grandmother, who lives in the country with her husband, has lived there for many years, and whom he sees infrequently. He told her of his joyous news. She apparently congratulated him, but spent more time talking about the fact that they had picked many fresh blueberries and had been enjoying them immensely. She was making blueberry preserves and pies and wanted to know when her grandson would be out for a visit to have some. The student's interpretation of this conversation was that his grandmother's mental health was deteriorating because of her constant "wandering" back to the topic of blueberries.

The student had not entertained the thought that his grandmother was involved mentally in the event of most importance and relevance to her at that time, and that while she offered congratulations on the birth of the new child, that held little consequence for her. Indeed, when it was suggested to the student that he could well have been viewed by her as constantly "wandering" in his attempts to occupy the conversation with the topic of his new child, he was amazed.

Joint activity could have proceeded between the grandson and grandmother, not necessarily if each believed in the value or importance of either children or blueberries, but if one were willing to assume the irrelevancy of differences for the purpose at hand (carrying on a conversational dialogue with each other). If the grandson were willing to discuss the different forms of eating blueberries and looking forward to a visit or if the grandmother were willing to discuss the joys of having children, joint activity could have proceeded. Abstract common values are not necessary. As "abstract," they are of no relevance to the situation at hand. What is relevant is the ability to "situate" given events as concrete exemplifications of universals in a perspective that can be common for the task at hand. It is not the common values as such, but their employment, their application to specific situations that may sometimes make other differences irrelevant and facilitate the creation of a shared perspective for the activity at hand.

The example further illustrates the fact that differences can and do arise normally between individuals. Mead states that the differences or conflicts that arise are settled or terminated through reconstruction of the social situation, the given framework of social relationships, or the self (and change in one results in change in the others). In our example the conflict had not been resolved, and no reconstruction in the self had taken place; rather, the social situation was changed by terminating the conversation. Of course, such reconstructions involve a wide variety of actual social outcomes, from conciliation to battle to the death to isolation, and so on.

One could postulate that it is when a single individual (of interest to us is the elderly individual) is not able to form shared perspective with other persons or with *key* other persons that they become defined as irrational or "senile." For Mead (1934, p. 334), rationality

> implies that the whole group is involved in some organized activity and that in this organized activity the action of one calls for the action of all the others. What we term "reason" arises when one of the organisms takes into its own response that attitude of the other organisms involved. It is possible for the organism so to assume the attitudes of the group that are involved in its own act within this whole co-operative process. When it does so, it is what we term "a rational being."... If the individual can take the attitude of the others and control his action by these attitudes, and control their actions through his own, then we have what we can term "rationality."

That is, "irrationality" refers to a type of conduct between individuals in which each individual involved does not take the attitude of the other or of the group and cannot control his or her action as well as the other's actions by these attitudes. Rationality and irrationality for Mead are not characteristics or personality traits that refer to one person in isolation, but to one person in relation to another, to the interaction between them. Only a rational person can interact in meaningful conduct with others, as one must take the attitude of the other in such a way that those involved understand the meaning of the behavior (Mead, 1934, pp. 7, 44-45, 334-335).

Similarly, Schutz (1971, pp. 23-24) refers to rationality as involving not one person in isolation but one person in relation to the other, and involving communication between them. Chappell (1973, 1978c) applies these concepts to provide an understanding of the meaning and use of "senility."

Perhaps another example will further demonstrate these ideas. As an academic researcher, one converses with one's colleagues in a scientific perspective that assumes a certain amount of specialized knowledge, logic, and argument in the presentation of ideas. It also carries with it specialized jargon, both sociological and gerontological. To decide on the appropriate applicability of research findings concerning the benefits of a particular community program for the elderly, meetings are held with government personnel responsible for the programs, staff operating the programs, and elderly participants in the programs. Common values are not necessary for joint action, that is, meaningful or understandable interchange. Rather, we must adopt a similar perspective that does not necessarily constitute agreement but does constitute a sufficient irrelevancy of differences for meaningful discussion and decision making to proceed.

In sum, Mead not only provides a detailed and comprehensive theory of the self as a social emergent, but does so while providing an understanding of the uniqueness of each individual in joint action and cooperation, of situational behavior and regularities in behavior, and of change and stability in the self. Of particular interest is the relevance of the temporal order and the specious present for the self in later life. There is no doubt that, within a Meadian perspective, change during adulthood is basic and universal. It is inherent in the nature of the social process and, concomitantly, in the self. The specious present as the locus of reality, and as that which determines the choice of pasts on which to draw, supports the view that current adult experiences are more determining of current adult self than childhood or earlier experiences, and that these current experiences in old age for elderly members of society will be most important for their current adult selves and their individual perspectives.

CONCLUSIONS

This chapter has presented a discussion of some of George Herbert Mead's social psychological concepts, attempting to bypass contemporary misinterpretations by returning directly to the works of Mead himself. In doing so, several concepts were elaborated that have particular relevance for studying socialization during old age. This chapter was not intended to present all of Meadian theory, nor all of his concepts that have relevance for this topic. In addition, it was not intended to illustrate in any exhaustive way the types of research questions that can be addressed within such a perspective. Rather, we have attempted to scratch the surface in demonstrating the potential of this particular theory of social psychology for studying old age.

Of primary interest, within a Meadian perspective, is that the maximization of self-development as a process is assumed to be valuable. If we accept the possibility and potentiality for change in older age, a broad research issue is apparent: an analysis of the character of institutions and environments that will help maximize the potentiality for change to become actuality and those that work in the opposite direction. For Mead, the underlying ability of the person, of the self, to make changes is clear. If this idea informed more gerontological research, both the research endeavor itself and the knowledge acquired might be substantially different from a problem-oriented view of the elderly as facing the inevitable process of "disengagement" leading to a uniform pattern of "roleless-roles" while waiting for death. Such research could provide, instead, a framework for studying the lives of the elderly as dynamic and ongoing.

NOTES

1. In all cases, we give the original dates of Mead's own publications. For the posthumous publication of Mead's unpublished writings (1932, 1938) we give the date of publication. These largely can be dated from 1919-1930. For the two volumes based on his lectures (1934, 1936) we give the publication dates, but the reader should note that these are based on courses given in the winter and spring of 1928, respectively.

2. Mead, in many early writings (e.g., 1908), as well as occasionally at later points, also uses the term "instincts." However, even in the early use he tends to view human "instincts" as social in the nature of their expression and as variable in the precise action in which they result, depending on the context of the situation or occasion where a stimulus acts to call them out. Thus he never views them as rigid or fixed, as was the common view of the time. Indeed, in the essay from which the above quotations are taken (written in 1919), Mead says: "They are best termed 'impulses' and not 'instincts' because they are subject to extensive modification in the life-history of the individuals . . . [which] are so much more extensive than those to which the instincts of lower animals are subject that the use of the term 'instinct' in describing the behavior of normal adult human individuals is seriously inexact" (1934, p. 337; see also p. 362).

3. Oestereicher (1972) and Piaget (1943) are examples of two authors who discuss experimental findings supporting the existence and functions of these stages as presented by Mead.

REFERENCES

Becker, H. S., & Strauss, A. L. (1956). Careers, personality and adult socialization. *American Journal of Sociology, 62*, 253-263.
Berger, P. L., & Luckmann, T. (1967). *The social construction of reality*. Garden City, NY: Doubleday.

Blumer, H. (1937). Social psychology. In E. P. Schmidt (Ed.), *Man and society* (pp. 144-198). Englewood Cliffs, NJ: Prentice-Hall.

Blumer, H. (1970). Sociological implications of the thought of George Herbert Mead. In G. P. Stone & H. A. Farberman (Eds.), *Social psychology through symbolic interaction* (pp. 282-293). Toronto: Ginn-Blaisdell.

Brim, O. G. (1966). Socialization through the life cycle. In O. G. Brim & S. Wheeler (Eds.), *Socialization after childhood: Two essays* (pp. 1-49). New York: John Wiley.

Brymer, R. A. (1980). *Mead's sense of problematics and structure.* Presented at the meetings of the Canadian Sociological and Anthropological Association, Montreal, Quebec.

Butler, R. N. (1968). The life review: An interpretation of reminiscence in the aged. In B. Neugarten (Ed.), *Middle-age and aging* (pp. 486-497). Chicago: University of Chicago Press.

Cavan, S. (1970). The etiquette of youth. In G. P. Stone & H. A. Farberman (Eds.), *Social psychology through symbolic interaction* (pp. 554-565). Toronto: Ginn-Blaisdell.

Chappell, N. L. (1973). *Future time perspective among the hospitalized elderly and a phenomenological interpretation of senility.* Unpublished master's thesis, McMaster University, Hamilton, Ontario.

Chappell, N. L. (1975). Awareness of death in the disengagement theory: A conceptualization and an empirical investigation. *Omega, 6,* 325-343.

Chappell, N. L. (1978a). *Work, commitment to work and self-identity among women.* Unpublished doctoral dissertation, McMaster University, Hamilton, Ontario.

Chappell, N. L. (1978b). The social process of learning sex roles: A sociological viewpoint. In H. M. Lips & N. L. Colwill (Eds.), *The psychology of sex differences* (pp. 103-124). Englewood Cliffs, NJ: Prentice-Hall.

Chappell, N. L. (1978c). Senility: Problems in communication. In J. Haas & W. Shaffir (Eds.), *Shaping identity in Canadian society* (pp. 65-86). Englewood Cliffs, NJ: Prentice-Hall.

Chellam, G. (1964). *The disengagement theory: Awareness of death and self-engagement.* Unpublished doctoral dissertation, Western Reserve University.

Couch, C. J. (1966). Self identification and alienation. *Sociological Quarterly, 7,* 255-264.

Dewey, J. (1984, July). The theory of emotion. (I) Emotional attitudes. *Psychological Review,* pp. 400-411.

Dewey, J. (1985, January). The theory of emotion. (II) The significance of emotions. *Psychological Review,* pp. 13-32.

Erikson, E. (1968). Generativity and ego identity. In B. Neugarten (Ed.), *Middle-age and aging.* Chicago: University of Chicago Press.

Falk, J. M. (1970). *The organization of remembered life experience of older people.* Unpublished doctoral dissertation, University of Chicago.

Farberman, H. A. (1970). Mannheim, Cooley, and Mead: Toward a social theory of mentality. *Sociological Quarterly, 2,* 3-13.

Farris, B., & Brymer, R. A. (1965). *Differential socialization of Latin and American youth: An exploratory study of the self concept.* Presented at the meeting of the Texas Academy of Sciences.

Frenkel-Brunswik, E. (1968). Adjustments and re-orientation in the course of the life span. In B. Neugarten (Ed.), *Middle-age and aging* (pp. 77-84). Chicago: University of Chicago Press.

Friedmann, E. A., & Orbach, H. L. (1974). Adjustment to retirement. In S. Arieti et al. (Eds.), *American handbook of psychiatry* (Vol. 1, 2nd ed., pp. 609-645). New York: Basic Books.

George, L. K. (1980). *Role transitions in later life*. Belmont, CA: Brooks/Cole.

Gerth, H., & Mills, C. W. (1953). *Character and social structure*. New York: Harcourt Brace Jovanovich.

Glaser, B. G., & Strauss, A. L. (1972). Awareness contests and social interaction. In J. G. Manis & B. N. Meltzer (Eds.), *Symbolic interaction: A reader in social psychology* (2nd ed., pp. 447-462). Boston: Allyn & Bacon.

Goffman, E. (1955). On face-work: An analysis of ritual elements in social interaction. *Psychiatry, 18*, 213-231.

Gorney, J. (1968). *Experiencing and age: Patterns of reminiscence among the elderly*. Unpublished doctoral dissertation, University of Chicago.

Gross, E., & Stone, G. P. (1970). Embarrassment and the analysis of role requirements. In G. P. Stone & H. A. Farberman (Eds.), *Social psychology through symbolic interaction* (pp. 174-190). Toronto: Ginn-Blaisdell.

Hinkle, R. C., & Hinkle H. J. (1954). *The development of modern sociology*. New York: Random House.

Hochschild, A. R. (1983). *The managed heart: Commercialization of human feeling*. Berkeley: University of California Press.

Kinch, J. W. (1968). A formalized theory of the self-concept. In J. G. Manis & B. N. Meltzer (Eds.), *Symbolic interaction: A reader in social psychology* (pp. 232-241). Boston: Allyn & Bacon.

Kuhn, M. H., & McPartland, T. S. (1954). An empirical investigation of self-attitudes. *American Sociological Review, 19*, 68-76.

Lichtman, R. (1970). Symbolic interactionism and social reality: Some Marxist queries. *Berkeley Journal of Sociology, 15*, 75-94.

Lindesmith, A. R., & Strauss, A. L. (Eds.). (1968). *Social psychology* (3rd ed.). New York: Holt, Rinehart & Winston.

Lopata, H. (1973). *Widowhood in an American city*. Cambridge, MA: Schenkman.

Lopata, H. (1979). *Women as widows: Support systems*. New York: Elsevier.

Marshall, V. W. (1972). *Continued living and dying as problematical aspects of old age*. Unpublished doctoral dissertation, Princeton University.

Matthews, S. H. (1979). *The social world of old women*. Beverly Hills, CA: Sage.

McHugh, P. (1970). A common sense perception of deviance. In H. P. Dreitzel (Ed.), *Recent sociology no. 2* (pp. 151-180). London: Macmillan.

McPhail, C., & Rexcoat, C. (1979). Mead vs. Blumer. *American Sociological Review, 44*, 449-467.

Mead, G. H. (1899a). The working hypothesis in social reform. *American Journal of Sociology, 5*, 367-371.

Mead, G. H. (1899b). Review of LeBon, Psychology of socialism. *American Journal of Sociology, 5*, 404-412.

Mead, G. H. (1900). Suggestions toward a theory of the philosophical disciplines. *Philosophical Review, 9*, 1-17.

Mead, G. H. (1903). The definition of the psychical. *Decennial Publications, University of Chicago, 3*, 77-112.

Mead, G. H. (1904a). Image or sensation. *Journal of Philosophy, 1*, 604-607.

Mead, G. H. (1904b). The relations of psychology and philology. *Psychological Bulletin, 1*, 375-391.

Mead, G. H. (1907). Concerning animal perception. *Psychological Review, 14*, 383-390.

Mead, G. H. (1908). The philosophical basis of ethics. *International Journal of Ethics, 18*, 311-323.

Mead, G. H. (1909). Social psychology as counterpart to physiological psychology. *Psychological Bulletin, 6,* 401-408.

Mead, G. H. (1910a). What social objects must psychology presuppose? *Journal of Philosophy, 7,* 174-180.

Mead, G. H. (1910b). Social consciousness and the consciousness of meaning. *Psychological Bulletin, 7,* 397-405.

Mead, G. H. (1910c). Psychology of social consciousness implied in instruction. *Science, 31,* 688-693.

Mead, G. H. (1912). The mechanism of social consciousness. *Journal of Philosophy, 9,* 401-406.

Mead, G. H. (1913). The social self. *Journal of Philosophy, 10,* 374-380.

Mead, G. H. (1917). Scientific method and individual thinker. In G. H. Mead, *Creative intelligence* (pp. 176-227). New York: Henry Holt.

Mead, G. H. (1918). The psychology of punitive justice. *American Journal of Sociology, 23,* 157-163.

Mead, G. H. (1922). A behavioristic account of the significant symbol. *Journal of Philosophy, 19,* 157-163.

Mead, G. H. (1925). The genesis of the self and social control. *International Journal of Ethics, 35,* 251-277.

Mead, G. H. (1926). The nature of aesthetic experience. *International Journal of Ethics, 36,* 382-392.

Mead, G. H. (1927). The objective reality of perspectives. *Proceedings of the Sixth International Congress of Philosophy,* pp. 75-85.

Mead, G. H. (1929a). National-mindedness and international-mindedness. *International Journal of Ethics, 34,* 385-407.

Mead, G. H. (1929b). A pragmatic theory of truth. In University of California Philosophical Union, *Studies in the nature of truth* (Vol. 11). Berkeley: University of California.

Mead, G. H. (1929c). The nature of the past. In G. H. Mead, *Essays in honor of John Dewey* (pp. 235-242). New York: Henry Holt.

Mead, G. H. (1930). Philanthropy from the point of view of ethics. In E. Faris, F. Laune, & A. J. Todd (Eds.), *Intelligent philanthropy* (pp. 133-148). Chicago: University of Chicago Press.

Mead, G. H. (1932). *The philosophy of the present.* Chicago: Open Court.

Mead, G. H. (1934). *Mind, self and society.* Chicago: University of Chicago Press.

Mead, G. H. (1936). *Movements of thought in the nineteenth century.* Chicago: University of Chicago Press.

Mead, G. H. (1938). *The philosophy of the act.* Chicago: University of Chicago Press.

Meltzer, B. N. (1972). Mead's social psychology. In J. G. Manis & B. N. Meltzer (Eds.), *Symbolic interaction: A reader in social psychology* (2nd ed., pp. 4-23). Boston: Allyn & Bacon.

Miller, D. R. (1963). The study of social relationships: Situations, identity and social interaction. In S. Koch (Ed.), *Psychology: Study of science* (Vol. 5, pp. 639-737). Toronto: McGraw-Hill.

Morris, C. W. (1934). Introduction: George H. Mead as social psychologist and social philosopher. In G. H. Mead, *Mind, self and society* (C. W. Morris, Ed.). Chicago: University of Chicago Press.

Oestereicher, E. (1972). Toward a sociology of cognitive structures. *Social Research, 39,* 134-154.

Orbach, H. L. (1983, June). *George Herbert Mead on aging and old age.* Paper presented at the Centre on Aging, University of Manitoba, Winnipeg.

Piaget, J. (1943). *Main trends in inter-disciplinary research.* New York: Harper & Row.

Rafky, D. M. (1973). Phenomenology and socialization: Some comments on the assumptions underlying socialization theory. In H. P. Dreitzel (Ed.), *Recent sociology no. 5* (pp. 27-43). London: Macmillan.

Reck, A. J. (Ed.). (1964). *George Herbert Mead: Selected writings.* Indianapolis: Bobbs-Merrill.

Riley, M. W. (1976). Age strata in social systems. In R. H. Binstock & E. Shanas (Eds.), *Handbook of aging and the social sciences* (pp. 189-217). New York: Van Nostrand Reinhold.

Riley, M. W., Foner, A., Hess, B., & Toby, M. L. (1969). Socialization for the middle and later years. In D. Goslin (Ed.), *Handbook of socialization theory and research* (pp. 951-982). Chicago: Rand McNally.

Rosow, I. (1965). Forms and functions of adult socialization. *Social Forces, 44,* 35-45.

Rosow, I. (1974). *Socialization to old age.* Los Angeles: University of California Press.

Rosow, I. (1976). Status and role change through the life span. In R. H. Binstock & E. Shanas (Eds.), *Handbook of aging and the social sciences* (pp. 457-482). New York: Van Nostrand Reinhold.

Rucker, D. (1969). *The Chicago pragmatists.* Minneapolis: University of Minnesota Press.

Ruitenbeek, H. M. (1964). *The individual and the crowd: A study of identity in America.* London: New English Library.

Rustin, M. (1971). Structural and unconscious implications of the dyad and triad: An essay in theoretical integration: Durkheim, Simmel, Freud. *Sociological Review, 19,* 179-201.

Salaman, G. (1971). Some sociological determinants of occupational communities. *Sociological Review, 19,* 53-74.

Sarbin, T. R., & Allen, V. L. (1968). Role theory. In G. Lindsey & E. Aronson (Eds.), *The handbook of social psychology* (Vol. 1, pp. 488-568). Reading, MA: Addison-Wesley.

Schein, E. H. (1971). The individual, the organization and the career: A conceptual scheme. *Journal of Applied Behavioral Science, 7,* 401-426.

Schutz, A. (1971). *Collected papers: Vol. I, The problem of social reality* (M. Natanson, Ed.). The Hague: Martinus Nijhoff.

Sherwood, J. J. (1965). Self-identity and referent others. *Sociometry, 28,* 66-81.

Shibutani, T. (1961). *Society and personality: An interactionist approach to social psychology.* Englewood Cliffs, NJ: Prentice-Hall.

Smith, R. L. (1977). *George Herbert Mead: A symbolic interactionist?* Presented at the annual meetings of the American Sociological Association, Chicago.

Stebbins, R. A. (1972). Studying the definition of the situation: Theory and field research strategies. In J. G. Manis & B. N. Meltzer (Eds.), *Symbolic interaction: A reader in social psychology* (2nd ed., pp. 337-356). Boston: Allyn & Bacon.

Strauss, A. L. (Ed.). (1956). *George Herbert Mead on social psychology.* Chicago: University of Chicago Press.

Strauss, A. L. (1969). *Mirrors and masks: The search for identity.* New York: Sociology Press.

Tillman, M. K. (1970). Temporality and role-taking in G. H. Mead. *Social Research, 37,* 533-546.

Vaughan, T. R., & Reynolds, L. T. (1968). The sociology of symbolic interaction. *American Sociologist, 3*, 208-214.

Wentowski, G. J. (1981). Reciprocity and the coping strategies of older people: Cultural dimensions of network building. *Gerontologist, 21*, 600-609.

Wrong, D. H. (1970). The oversocialized conception of man in modern sociology. In G. P. Stone & H. A. Farberman (Eds.), *Social psychology through symbolic interaction* (pp. 29-40). Toronto: Ginn-Blaisdell.

4

Some Contributions of Symbolic Interaction to the Study of Growing Old

DONALD L. SPENCE

This chapter is intended as a theoretical essay on some contributions of symbolic interaction to the creation of a developmental understanding of the problems associated with growing old. By necessity it will be a limited presentation, bringing together ideas only a few of which have been developed specifically in relation to the subject matter of the gerontologist. It will begin with a presentation of some unique characteristics and assumptions of this particular theoretical heritage and will then discuss a series of ideas that, when taken collectively, suggest a developmental model applicable to the study of aging.

This chapter was originally developed as a working document that I use in conjunction with teaching a perspective on adult development and aging grounded in the philosophical tradition of American pragmatism. The opportunity to publish it as a part of a theoretical volume on aging has made me distinctly aware of the intellectual debt that I owe to Anselm Strauss: teacher, colleague, and friend. The origins of this indebtedness are hard to identify, as they began some years before my eight years at the University of California Medical Center in San Francisco. My introduction to social psychology included the reading of Strauss (1956), but as the dominant perspective in sociology during the late 1950s and 1960s was structural functionalism based on philosophical positivism, I spent the years in graduate school suppressing my intellectual inclinations. Even my appointment in psychiatry at UCSF and assignment to the Geriatrics Research Program were a hindrance to the recognition of my commitment to pragmatism. It was the students, shared between human development and the doctoral program in sociology, who triggered this recognition.

The doctoral program was new and working hard to establish its methodological uniqueness. Strauss was serving as chairman and was working to help develop the methodology courses that were based on grounded theory (Glaser & Strauss, 1967). After listening one afternoon to a handful of students complain about their methods course and how they felt that Glaser would be a better teacher than Strauss, as they saw Glaser as more charismatic, I got angry. I told them that they had an opportunity rarely afforded graduate students in any program, and if they failed to take full advantage of this opportunity they did not deserve the Ph.D.

Strauss is both central to the development of symbolic interaction and personally acquainted with the principal scholars of this tradition. The uniqueness of his position made a seminar on symbolic interaction a must for any student of the UCSF sociology program. In short, we arranged an informal evening seminar.

My reward was twofold. I had the opportunity to participate in one of the most intellectually stimulating seminars of my career. It was this seminar that helped me fully recognize my commitment to pragmatism. Second, I was rewarded by the thanks of students who now saw their graduate program with new meaning.

Developmental considerations are central to the interests of symbolic interactionists. Mead and Cooley, however, in their principal writings on the origin of the self, concerned themselves with the early learning of the young, without pursuing the learning of adults in a similar way (see, for example, the extensive review in Chappell & Orbach, this volume). What they had to say is of major importance: "In a sequential fashion, the self develops out of universes of discourse and experience which are routinely confronted by the infant and young child. . . . in each phase, the child is progressively able to differentiate self from other, to view the rules of the game as constructed rather than invariant. . . . as the child moves through the advanced developmental stages, his accommodative and imitative actions give way to reflexive and assimilative conduct. He relinquishes his egocentric views of self, rules, and the world around him. He ceases to think in animistic, artificial, finalistic, and narrow moral terms. In essence, he becomes a reflexive self. . . . This view . . . suggest[s] that a child's reflexive ability varies according to the play-situation (e.g. consecutive vs. singular) and to symbolic abilities" (Denzin, 1972, pp. 293-294).

ADULTHOOD AND DEVELOPMENT

The reflexive behavior of the adult may be more difficult to assess than that of children due to a larger array of choices and to the presence of comparative values, but it is not necessarily different. "[Children] are skilled interactants far beyond what many theories give them credit. Their interactional skills, like those of adults, reflect the situations and objects that they must confront in daily life" (Denzin, 1972, p. 309). The complexity of the dynamics of development in adulthood has deterred most theorists from making more than casual reference to any period past adolescence (e.g., Erikson, 1956).

Several symbolic interactionists have dealt with the concept of identity during adulthood. Stone (1962), for example, focuses on the development of identity in relation to appearance and the self, which clearly has implications for socialization through the life course. Travisano (1970) presents identity development in terms of the difficulties associated with a self-selected identity in conflict with one that is socially ascribed. McCall and Simmons (1966) present us with a systematic account of the way identities grow out of interactions. Most of their examples, however, relate to childhood, and I find their treatment of adult development somewhat structured and without the fullness of complexity or the dynamic properties that the adult life course presents. Without attempting to oversimplify the difficulties of treating the subject matter, Strauss (1969) provides us with a conception of development that allows one to get on with the task. "Development (or the relations between 'permanence and change,' between 'before and after') may be conceptualized as a series of related transformations. Etymologically the term 'transformation' invites us to consider changes in form—changes in being, kind or psychological status" (Strauss, 1969, p. 91).

The definition, like the philosophical tradition from which it emerges, is pragmatic—"a point of view . . . which stresses the crucial role of language for human behavior. It also stresses a kind of openended, partially unpredictable, view of events: interaction is regarded as guided by rules, norms, mandates; but outcomes are assumed to be not always, or entirely, determinable in advance. This indeterminacy need not be a stumbling block to scientific research, but has to be taken into account" (Strauss, 1969, p. 10).

DEVELOPMENTAL FORMS OF BEHAVIOR

It should be noted that the above definition of development challenges any "essential" source of knowledge. Unlike classical empiricism, which insisted that the ultimate source of all knowledge was observation, or rationalism, which insisted that it was in the mind's ability to reason, pragmatism is relativistic. Pragmatism rejects ultimate authority because it sees values and morals as behavior arising through the same interactions of symbols that form and develop any areas of behavior. Mead (1936), in his discussion of how we become selves, suggests a problematic view of society in which individuals take on the roles of others as well as the perspective of their own role to devise collective solutions to generate an evolutionary process toward social development. By attempting to connect the evolutionary process to social organization the "life-process itself is brought to consciousness in the conduct of the individual form, in his so-called self-consciousness" (Strauss, 1956, p. 29). The form is dependent upon the conditions under which the life-process goes on. It is the same process, but it can respond to any number of problems. The recognition of this distinction between process and the form it takes is what gives development its unique and relativistic character.

The central structure that is being transformed through the processes of development is the self, or one's identity. A discussion of the development of the self from a Meadian perspective is included in Chappell and Orbach's contribution to this volume, and would therefore be redundant. A brief look at the work of Becker (1963) on deviance or Goffman (1963) on spoiled identity can, however, highlight the application of symbolic interaction to adult situations. Becker vividly describes the need to learn both a series of behaviors and the language by which to internalize their meaning in the process of becoming a marijuana user or a dance musician. Because these are deviant roles the socialization processes are seen in sharp relief. In Goffman we see how the preconceived notions as represented in the symbols that apply to a stigma, as well as the personal experiences or identity of the stigmatized individual, structure the interactive processes that are the individual's life. Again, because of the nonnormative characteristics of the situation being described, we are made more vividly aware of the processes of self-development.

What must be remembered is that the same processes apply to everyone as his or her identity develops and is transformed through his or her personal history. The socialization process that produces a deviant role is no different from one that transforms us in the sequences of statuses through which we all move. Likewise, every one of us carries a definition of self that predefines the interactive processes as we move through new and familiar interactions. The point is simply that although dramatic and different situations call our attention to process, the nature of that process is essentially the same. John Dewey (1922) put it this way: We are all moving along toward various objectives like an individual walking a path. All of a sudden an obstacle stands in the way. If the objective is important, its importance determined as much by evaluating where we are coming from as well as where we are going, we try to figure a way of getting past the obstacle. To the extent that we are successful (sometimes success means redefining the objective) we have developed or learned an expected response. When the same situation occurs repeatedly, we develop what might be called a "normative" response. More than likely, different types of situations will generate different processes. The normative aspect will be the manner of handling different types of situations. Since norms imply choice, any response that does not involve a conscious choice is, in Dewey's terms, habitual and is not affecting the developmental process. It is like driving a car with a manual clutch—once you have learned how, you do not think about it.

The processes of concern in this chapter are those that effect a transformation in the symbolic meaning of one's identity as it includes age or age-related considerations. The number of such processes, I believe, may be quite substantial. If the few identified here appear useful in our ability to understand or to help people direct age-related changes, then it would appear prudent to develop this approach systematically.

Age as a principal point of consideration will set the limits of this discussion. The focus will be the transformation of identity that results from changes the individual perceives as being age related. The consequences of other social processes may also be developmental to the extent that they involve series of significant transformations, but only insofar as the transformation is perceived as resulting from or involving a new age-related status will it be of concern here. For example, the completion of an advanced degree will more than likely involve a series of transformations of identity that are symbolic of a developmental process. However, whether or not the individual perceives those transformations as involving age-related considerations is dependent on when the individual completes the degree in relation to other courses of development occurring in his or her life—work career, family, and so on.

DEVELOPMENT AS CAREER

The career concept is the principal idea around which the contributions of the various symbolic interactionists have been organized. As a concept it has been useful for understanding certain dynamic aspects of adulthood (Becker & Strauss, 1968), and in this instance is applied to the process of aging. Foote (1956, p. 31) has defined career as "a progression of statuses and functions which unfold in a more or less orderly though not predetermined sequence in the pursuit of values which themselves emerge in the course of experience." The distinction between this definition of aging and the more traditional age grading of the anthropologist is its socially dynamic implications. Although some anthropologists may feel uncomfortable with these implications, they are consistent with the symbolic interactionists' assumption that society and the individual arise simultaneously, that there is no separation, that society is neither more nor less than the individuals of whom it is composed. (For discussion of the implications of this assumption in relation to engagement or disengagement in later life, see Spence, 1975.)

Implicit in the above definition of career are the ideas that form the outline of the theoretical model. First, there is the emergent aspect of the pursuit of values. This implies that the accomplishment of objectives or ends is less important than their pursuit: that it is not the experience of having succeeded or failed that is important for one's psychological well-being, but the sense that one is prevailing, that there is still meaning or purpose to one's existence. Second, there is the dimension of time— "statuses and functions unfold." However, again there is the possibility of active involvement in the establishment of "order" and "sequence." Mead, in *The Philosophy of The Act* (1938), argues that the only reality is what is happening in the present. The past is history interpreted in the pursuit of emergent objectives. Pragmatism focuses on the uses of behavior, including thought, and evaluates behavior in relation to its success. When it is recognized that one may alter the timing of objectives in the pursuit of values then clearly it is possible to "bargain" (Roth, 1963) with oneself in order to maintain the feelings of progress. Bargaining is the third dimension in the model. The fourth dimension involves "statuses and functions." Statuses are units of social structure. Any individual occupies a set of statuses (Merton, 1957) in relation to his or her total contextual situation. Each status in turn involves the individual with others who are also pursuing values over time with their sense of control relative to how well they have been able to bargain with themselves and the significant others of their developing life course.

When we recognize the interdependency of career development within various groups of people, we introduce the possibility of additional processes that result from these interactions. Strauss (1969) identifies several that are quite vivid in their descriptive potential. For example, when we realize that coaching (pp. 109-118) may involve giving up certain aspects of control in some areas of behavior in order to prevail in others, we begin to see the complexity of the model that is being suggested. The pupil, in his or her desire to gain the skills, knowledge, or rewards of a performance currently beyond his or her capabilities, allows the coach to direct the timing of development. Since the steps in this development are blurred to the pupil, he or she cannot progress without expert tutelage. The coach is expected to know when the pupil is ready to advance in the performance process.

Although this chapter is limited to an analysis of the developing individual, one example of how individuals develop interdependently may heighten the insight this perspective can reveal. To prevail in motherhood is ultimately dependent on the behavior of the offspring. The time the offspring's behavior is most critical for the success or failure of the mother is when the mother has the least control over the actions of her child (Spence & Lonner, 1978). The child's career, as he or she reaches independence, is the basis for the mother's sense of her accomplishment as a parent.

Personal, contextual, and sociocultural dimensions are also implicit in the above definition of career. Simply, what this implies is that the researcher should be aware of how the perceptions of the individual with respect to factors of social context and sociohistorical circumstance interact with the age career. Goffman (1952) makes this point in relation to a work career when he suggests that two individuals may have achieved the same objective status over their lifetimes with one perceiving him- or herself a success and the other perceiving him- or herself a failure, the point being that they accomplished these objectives within differentially perceived sociocultural contexts. Lowenthal (1966) made the point twenty years ago in a more dynamic and dramatic sense. She implied that some of the differences in adaptation among her sample of older women, born during the decade of the 1870s, could be explained as a consequence of how they perceived their lives in relation to career expectations that may have been influenced by their social-ization during the feminist movement of the nineteenth century. From an interactionist perspective it is the interpreted past and the projected future present in all situations that make for the dynamic, unpredictable aspect of behavior (see Strauss, 1969, pp. 169-176).

In the sections that follow I will try to flesh out the ideas I have outlined so far. Beginning with the careerlike aspects of development, a section will be presented on the idea of prevailing in life. This will be followed by a section on timing, in which a somewhat unique conception of normative behavior is introduced. Because the perspective is pragmatic, the concept of bargaining is introduced to show how most people are able to manage or control the unexpected as well as the expected events in the developmental course. The three concepts are brought together in a section entitled "The Career Set," in which the multiple career structure of the developmental course is suggested as well as some further implications for career interdependency between significant others.

PREVAILING IN LIFE

The pursuit and accomplishment of a series of expectations mark progress along the life course. Progress, however, is problematic. In a small sample of women, for example, Spence and Lonner (1978) found only 4 out of 27 who felt that the future was unfolding in a truly trouble-free manner. As expectations are thwarted most individuals successfully shift their sights to new targets smoothly and without regret, having reasonable alternatives available. And for most, normal progress through these emergent expectations results in an acceptable and satisfying life. In the above-mentioned sample of women, 18 reported high satisfaction with their present lives, indicating their acceptance of problems as a normal condition of their life courses.

The problematic aspect of prevailing as it relates to one's age can be seen in the lives of men at midlife as they readjust expectations with respect to accomplishments involving their work careers. Chinoy's (1955) portrayal of the inconsistencies between the expectations fostered in "the American dream" and the realities of the work world for most men dramatizes the process of reevaluation necessary for one to feel that one is prevailing. Midlife poses a particularly difficult period for some working-class men who find themselves well beyond their most productive years but somewhat short of being able to retire. Two cases from the Lowenthal (1975) study of transitions make this point quite vividly. Both men had brief periods in their work lives when they had reached positions of some authority in minor companies. At the time of the study, they were both in civil service jobs, doing work that they felt appropriate for the young—namely, dirty, manual work—and looking forward to retirement as a relief but with some apprehension concerning finances. White-collar workers in the same study who perceived themselves several years from retirement but with no likelihood of any further vocational advancement turned their energies to organizing their retirement. Since retirement has become an expected and acceptable age-related status, to be working toward its success can bring rewards as significant as those derived from work.

One of the more dramatic examples of how prevailing in life gets redefined in relation to the realities of any situation can be seen in the behavior of the institutionalized mentally ill. While working to resocialize and relocate long-term institutionalized patients, I saw time and time again individuals brought to a critical point in their resocialization only to revert to the behavior that originally precipitated their institutionalization. I learned from the staff of the institution that this is the way patients exercise control over their situation (for example, see Braginsky, Braginsky, & Ring, 1982, pp. 51-52). Most of these patients had come to see the institution as their home, a place where they were secure. As soon as they figured out that they might have to move, they reverted to a response that produced a known outcome. A locked ward is still a better outcome than having to leave one's home. The project was far more successful with subjects who could think of themselves as patients. Patients, when they get better, are expected to leave the hospital (Siegal & Lasker, 1978).

TIMING

Strauss (1969, p. 43) argues, "It is not change that needs to be explained but its specific directions; and it is not lack of change that needs to be taken for granted, but change itself." Because the processes of change tend to be governed by normative considerations, we are not always aware of the extent to which we participate in shaping our lives and thereby the social order in which we exist. Even to the extent that one accepts another's definition of the situation, it is still an active process in which everyone participates. It is those situations for which there are no norms or in which one exceeds normative expectations where the process is seen in greatest relief. For example, a formal aspect of development appears to involve "timing" (Roth, 1963; Neugarten, Moore, & Lowe, 1965). The timing of one's age career, like the objectives or values that direct its course, is being reconstructed as it develops. Roth's (1963) mostly male tuberculosis patients needed benchmarks to have some feeling that there was progress in the course of their recovery. As they reviewed their progress they would adjust the timing of those benchmarks with respect to the feedback they received from their interactive context. If a patient did not perceive himself progressing as expected, he would reevaluate, telling himself possibly he had been sicker than he presumed. If the individual perceived himself progressing at a greater-than-expected pace, he might attribute this to his general state of health at the time of his hospitalization. What is important from the standpoint of the social scientist is that there were no benchmarks in the recovery from tuberculosis—they had to be constructed by the individual out of his perceptions of his sociohistorical self in the interactive context of the hospital situation.

This immediacy, combined with the emergent properties of developmental behavior, gives a definition to normative behavior that is more flexible than traditional conceptions. There are expectations, but, unlike with structural theories, these expectations are not necessarily shared. There will be a distribution to the timing of events, but there are no necessary mathematical properties to these distributions. Robert Dubin (personal communication, 1960) characterized normative behavior in this tradition as the sewer pipe concept of norms. It is only when a behavior exceeds a boundary that it is problematic, and then only when a stink is made. Since norms are behaviors with their own emergent properties, what produces a stink is changing also.

Timing with respect to aging as one of the more important dimensions in any developing career has been poorly exploited as a research focus. Probably this is because most social scientists feel that to treat time in a developmental sense requires longitudinal data involving sophisticated methodologies (Baltes, 1968; Schaie, 1965). From the standpoint of the interactionist it is the symbolic impingement of the past, as well as the future, on the present that is important. Therefore, when Butler (1963) talks of the "life review" as an adaptive mechanism in relation to the principal late-life transition, the interactionist has anticipated his concept. Rose (1962, pp. 16-17), in a systematic summary of symbolic interaction, called it the "integrated, cumulative, and evaluated character of experience," while Strauss (1969, p. 145) stressed the way in which it gave life "a certain unity and coherence."

There are certain realities to aging that apply to many individuals; for instance, in the United States the social security legislation designates a specific age for eligibility, and companies and unions have fixed-age retirement policies. The point that interests all of us, however, positivist and pragmatist alike, is that no specific age designation has any real generalized meaning (Atchley, 1985, pp. 115-116). What is old for one is not old for another. When one is too old for some things one is not old enough for other things. All this implies is that timing with respect to age interacts with other aspects of life. A 40-year-old football player is old.

A 40-year-old industrialist is young. To be a grandparent at 35 is young. Not to be a grandparent when one's children are 35 is not so young. Knowing this, we still seem hesitant to focus our research on the way subjects perceive certain process characteristics of their existence allowing for the known variability of individual specifics. Aging as a career—timing, in other words—as it has to do with selected other career areas, can be very fruitful in providing insight into transitional dynamics (Spence & Lonner, 1978).

BARGAINING

The temporal dimension of any career provides an area in which bargaining or compromise can take place. In young marrieds, for example, the beginning of family may have to await a certain level of preparation in work or social careers. Throughout life the juggling of our different temporal placements allows us a means of feeling that we are progressing. One may elect to postpone some line of development because another area of consideration is more important at the moment. On the other hand, when a career line is stymied the redirection of energies to other aspects of one's life can give temporary meaning while new life goals and directions are emerging. For example, divorce may be a temporary interlude in the long-term development of one's spousehood career (Spence & Lonner, 1978).

Bargaining over the developmental sequence of any career is not necessarily an intraindividual phenomenon. Returning to young marrieds, we see this exemplified in the bargaining that must occur when there exists between a couple a "differential readiness for parenthood" (Taylor, 1972). In relation to growing older, bargaining can be seen in the resistance or willingness of the aged to relinquish certain behaviors to the young.

The dynamics of intergenerational bargaining can also be seen in the family dynamics surrounding the long-term care of chronically impaired older individuals. Because aging is defined by many in our society as ever-increasing pathology, families feel that to provide any care is tantamount to assuming total responsibility. I believe that this is why the decision to institutionalize, once made, is next to impossible to reverse and why passive euthanasia seems to be growing in acceptance. Given that the condition cannot improve, by definition, and institution-alization itself constitutes a less than acceptable quality of life, why not let an infection or congestive heart failure solve the problem (Miller,

1984)? What such a position fails to recognize is the rehabilitative potential of most older individuals along with the desire to survive that exists in most of us.

THE CAREER SET

The idea of a person occupying a set of careers at any point in the life course adds the fourth and possibly most meaningful dimension to a possible model for the study of adult development. While the consideration of aging as a career points to the interaction of the individual with his or her own past perceptions and future considerations, the idea of the career set places the individual squarely in the middle of an interactive network. The focus is on the individual's perception of this network, however, and more than the objective set of statuses, it includes the attitudes or postures that provide direction for their development. We are still limited by structural considerations, but have chosen to view them dynamically. It is this latter developmental thrust present in the interactionist approach that differentiates the *career set* from Merton's (1957) concept of *status set*. And, as will be shown in a moment, it includes consideration of how an individual perceives the attitude or posture of significant others in relation to their career set development.

As was implied above, one may perceive oneself as aging at different rates in relation to different aspects of the life course. What needs to be done in researching human development in relation to aging is to identify those career areas where the individual perceives age as an important consideration. In most cultures work and family are obvious areas. Culture-specific or even idiosyncratic careers, however, do not make the theoretical considerations relativistic. The theoretical generalizations involve the processes by which identity transformations occur. This is not to imply that one can describe these changes without content, only that this more abstract level of analysis can provide generalization across a wide array of content areas while calling our attention to a kind of detail normally overlooked in most gerontological research.

For example, Rosow (1967) is left to conclude that the best way to explain the differences in age identification between middle-class and working-class members of his study of older persons in Cleveland is to apply different theoretical models. On one hand, the middle-class person's age identification is best explained by a concept of "differential association" with age peers. The working-class individual, on the other hand, identifies with age peers relative to his or her social integration in an age-homogeneous environment.

Implicit in Rosow's analysis is a distinction in the age transformations of the two social classes. The working-class person is seen to have transformed his or her network of social relationships, while the middle-class person has maintained one consistent with an earlier life period. If this were not the case, the integrative differences would be only the integrative modes for the structural differences between the two classes and should not be thought of as relating to aging. Alternatively, it may well be that the middle-class person has transformed his or her age identity by actively avoiding an age-related conception that from his or her perspective is negatively valued. What is important is that the availability of means gives some people alternatives that are unavailable to those who are actually or perceptually constrained.

Family and work careers follow different courses for persons of differing socioeconomic status, with age interacting in ways that provide for major perceptual differences. Take, for example, the intergenerational relationships of men. In the working class, one's productive ability tends to reach its peak earlier than in the middle class. At the time when their own sons are entering the work force, the work careers of working-class men may well be on the decline. Middle-class work careers, on the other hand, peak much closer to retirement, after middle-class workers' sons are well established in their own careers. It has always surprised me that students of social mobility have not examined social classes for the possible perceptual differences in the meaning of work that result from differing career dynamics. Neugarten (1964) has shown that the manner in which one perceives one's work career is related to age and does affect the relationships one has to the succeeding generation.

When men retire they sometimes fail to anticipate how the changes in their career sets will affect the career sets of their spouses. There is the "I married him for life but not for lunch" syndrome that may require what Becker (1968) calls "situational adjustment" or the development of new "interlocking habit systems," placing new unanticipated demands on these couples' relationships (Waller & Hill, 1951). Even more dramatic is the way retirement frees people to make major changes in lifestyle or place of residence. The idea of retiring to the country is quite common. However, in the Lowenthal (1975) study such a move tended to be a man's idea. Women were usually involved in social careers that were unaffected by their husbands' retirement. For a man to pursue a retirement career involving a major relocation may mean that his wife has to give up her social life. If an aspect of his career set is supporting his wife in her activities, then he may well be caught in a double bind. It is not unknown for a couple to relocate when the husband retires, and for the husband to die shortly thereafter, leaving the wife isolated from her past life associations. An understanding of the career set and career set interdependencies could have great utility in retirement planning and in counseling for older adults.

SOME PHILOSOPHICAL COMMENTS

The limitations to this approach are generally tied to one's attitude toward pragmatism. This is particularly true if one equates pragmatism with instrumentalism; that is, the philosophical view that sees theories as nothing more than tools or instruments. When this occurs truth gets equated with usefulness and one must answer the question, Useful for what or whom? Because control of outcomes is generally linked to power, instrumentalism is seen as linked to authoritarian and total-itarian ideas (Popper, 1962, p. 5). It is clear, however, that Mead and Dewey were both liberals. Mead (1936) saw the evolutionary develop-ment of man and society as universal, leading to an increasing openness in society. Dewey (1922) believed also in the rule of law, of equal justice, of fundamental rights, and a free society. His emphasis on education parallels the essential theme of Popper (1950), who argues that only a few have the talent and ability to lead but all (educated) people have the ability to judge the consequences of that leadership (for a fuller discussion, see Mills, 1966, pp. 447-463).

Positivists find the idea of behavior having emergent properties inconsistent with their notions of the reliability and validity of data. This is due to the fact that their focus is on what Simmel (1950, pp. 21-23) would call the content of behavior rather than the form of the relationship, which can be represented by many contents. Glaser (1978) makes a similar distinction between units and processes. It is his contention that the proper subject matter for sociology is the properties of process: "In themselves, the focus on either unit or process sociology is not intrinsically meritorious. The test of their relative worth lies in how well each may contribute to sociology knowledge and the purpose at hand" (p. 109). The circle is complete. The chapter begins and ends with the essential premise of American pragmatism.

A final comment is in order on the predominantly optimistic nature of this presentation. Richard Travisano (personal communication,

1976) has pointed out the particular Western notion of progress implicit in my conception of career. It is my inherent liberalism that makes me believe that things can get better. I realize that many people, if not most, are sufficiently fearful to resist all change. If we believe, however, that change is the given, then anything that will help us understand or influence its direction is of value.

SUMMARY

This chapter has involved a brief exploration into the implications of applying principles of symbolic interaction to the study of the developmental issues of later life. The assumptions of this theoretical tradition are what make this presentation unique. Rather than objectifying the content of behavior, it accepts the subjective, the indeterminate aspects of human existence, focusing on process and changes in identity as one develops. Instead of assuming that goals are external objects pursued by individuals, it assumes that goals are merely an aspect of a person's present state of evaluation. Where one is going loses its importance when compared to the processes of getting there.

Time takes on a new meaning. It is now that is important, but now includes the perceived past and the anticipated future. The structuring of time takes place with its passage. Norms do apply, providing benchmarks for progression or transformation. But benchmarks are constructed. To the extent that this is understood, time becomes a tool rather than a taskmaster.

People can bargain with themselves concerning the importance of where they are going and the schedule of this progress. The greater their awareness of these processes the more likely it is that they can influence their outcome. This perspective recognizes the problematic aspects of human existence, accepting the fact that one may experience the resolution of problems without essentially changing this condition. The implications of these processes become most evident when development is examined from within the perspective of interactive careers.

The career set provides a frame of reference for understanding the development and variability of human pursuits. Where the concepts of role and status have been shown to be inadequate for treating such phenomena as intimacy, intensity, or duration (Turner, 1962), these concepts are central to an understanding of development and to the relationship among the careers composing any career set. This chapter has been an attempt to suggest that the application of these ideas to the study of aging may well lead to the development of new understanding of the problematic aspects of growing old.

REFERENCES

Atchley, R. C. (1985). *Social forces and aging* (4th ed.). Belmont, CA: Wadsworth.

Baltes, P. B. (1968). Longitudinal and cross-sectional sequences in the study of age and generation effects. *Human Development, 11,* 145-171.

Becker, H. S. (1963). *Outsiders: Studies in the sociology of deviance.* New York: Free Press.

Becker, H. S. (1968). Personal change in adult life. In B. Neugarten (Ed.), *Middle age and aging* (pp. 148-156). Chicago: University of Chicago Press.

Becker, H. S., & Strauss, A. L. (1968). Careers personality and adult socialization. In B. Neugarten (Ed.), *Middle age and aging* (pp. 311-320). Chicago: University of Chicago Press.

Braginsky, B. M., Braginsky, D. D., & Ring, K. (1982). *Methods of madness: The mental hospital as a last resort.* Washington, DC: University Press of America.

Butler, R. N. (1963). The life review: An interpretation of reminiscence in the aged. *Psychiatry, 26,* 65-76.

Chinoy, E. (1955). *Automobile worker and the American dream.* Boston: Beacon.

Denzin, N. K. (1972). The genesis of self in early childhood. *Sociological Quarterly, 13,* 291-314.

Dewey, J. (1922). *Human nature and conduct.* New York: Holt, Rinehart & Winston.

Erickson, E. H. (1956). The problem of age identity. *Journal of the American Psychoanalytic Association, 4,* 56-121.

Foote, N. N. (1956). The movement from jobs to careers in American industry. *Transactions of the Third World Congress of Sociology, 2,* 30-40.

Glaser, B. G. (1978). *Theoretical sensitivity.* San Francisco: Sociology Press.

Glaser, B. G., & Strauss, A. L. (1967). *The discovery of grounded theory, strategies for qualitative research.* Chicago: Aldine.

Goffman, E. (1952). On calling the mark out: Some aspects of adaptation to failure. *Psychiatry, 15,* 451-462.

Goffman, E. (1963). *Stigma: Notes on the management of spoiled identity.* Englewood Cliffs, NJ: Prentice-Hall.

Lowenthal, M. F. (1966). Social adjustment in the aged. *Proceedings: 7th international congress of gerontology.* Vienna: International Association of Gerontology.

Lowenthal, M. F., Thurner, M., Chiriboga, C., & Associates (1975). *Four stages of life: A comparative study of women and men facing transitions.* San Francisco: Jossey-Bass.

McCall, G. J., & Simmons, J. L. (1966). *Identities and interactions.* New York: Free Press.

Mead, G. H. (1936). *Movements of thought in the nineteenth century.* Chicago: University of Chicago Press.

Mead, G. H. (1938). *The philosophy of the act.* Chicago: University of Chicago Press.

Merton, R. K. (1957). *Social theory and social structure.* New York: Free Press.

Miller, M. B. (1984). *Long term care paradox: Family survival requires parental death.* Paper presented at the annual meeting of the Gerontological Society of America, San Antonio, TX.

Mills, C. W. (1966). *Sociology and pragmatism.* New York: Oxford University Press.

Donald L. Spence 123

Neugarten, B. (1964). *Personality in middle and later life.* New York: Atherton.

Neugarten, B., Moore, J. W., & Lowe, J. C. (1965). Age norms, age constraints, and adult socialization. *American Journal of Sociology, 70,* 710-717.

Popper, K. R. (1950). *The open society and its enemies.* Princeton, NJ: Princeton University Press.

Popper, K. R. (1962). *Conjectures and refutations.* New York: Basic Books.

Rose, A. (1962). A systematic summary of symbolic interaction theory. In A. Rose (Ed.), *Human behavior and social processes.* Boston: Houghton Mifflin.

Rosow, I. (1967). *Social integration of the aged.* New York: Free Press.

Roth, J. A. (1963). *Timetables.* Indianapolis: Bobbs-Merrill.

Schaie, K. W. (1965). A general model for the study of developmental problems. *Psychological Bulletin, 64,* 92-107.

Seigel, B., & Lasker, J. (1978). Deinstitutionalizing elderly patients: A program of resocialization. *Gerontologist, 18,* 293-300.

Simmel, G. (1950). *The sociology of Georg Simmel* (K. H. Wolff, Ed. and Trans.). New York: Free Press.

Spence, D. L. (1975). The meaning of engagement. *International Journal of Aging and Human Development, 6,* 193-198.

Spence, D. L., & Lonner, T. D. (1978). Career set: A resource through transitions and crises. *International Journal of Aging and Human Development, 9,* 51-65.

Stone, G. P. (1962). Appearance and the self. In A. M. Rose (Ed.), *Human behavior and social processes* (pp. 86-118). Boston: Houghton Mifflin.

Strauss, A. L. (Ed.). (1956). *The social psychology of George Herbert Mead.* Chicago: University of Chicago Press.

Strauss, A. L. (1969). *Mirrors and masks: The search for identity.* San Francisco: Sociology Press.

Taylor, M. C. (1972). *Timing the first child.* Unpublished master's thesis, University of California, San Francisco.

Travisano, R. V. (1970). Alternation and conversion as qualitatively different transformations. In G. P. Stone & H. A. Farberman (Eds.), *Social psychology through symbolic interaction* (pp. 594-606). Waltham, MA: Ginn-Blaisdell.

Turner, R. H. (1962). Role taking: Process versus conformity. In A. M. Rose (Ed.), *Human behavior and social processes* (pp. 20-40). Boston: Houghton Mifflin.

Waller, W., & Hill, R. (1951). *The family: A dynamic interpretation.* New York: Dryden.

5

A Sociological Perspective
on Aging and Dying

VICTOR W. MARSHALL

> We are, from birth on, beings that will die. We are this, of course, in
> different ways. The manner in which we conceive this nature of ours and
> its final effect, and in which we react to this conception, varies greatly. So
> does the way in which this element of our existence is interwoven with its
> other elements. (Georg Simmel, 1908)

In this passage, Simmel sets the stage for a social psychological
approach to understanding the implications of mortality for individuals
and for society. Recognizing the inevitability of death as a fact of life,
Simmel distinguishes between the fact of death and its definition in the
consciousness of individuals; he additionally stresses that the ways in
which people deal with death affect other aspects of social life. In this
chapter an attempt is made to articulate a social psychological
framework along the lines set out by Simmel. I focus on the growing
recognition of mortality that characterizes aging in the contemporary
historical context and on the ways this recognition leads to personal and
interpersonal changes in the lives of the aged. The exercise is grounded,
however, in a concern for the historical and sociodemographic features
that have shaped the present situation.

Death is one of the very few inevitabilities of the human condition.
Nothing is more certain, it is said, than death and taxes. All of us die
eventually and the vast majority of us "face death," in the sense that we
see our family and friends die and we reflect at least occasionally upon
our own mortal state. We are all to some extent conscious of the
"inevitable scarcity" (Moore, 1963) that plagues our existence—our
time will run out.

While cultural recognition of mortality varies dramatically in form
and content (Marshall, 1985), the recognition of mortality is probably a
cultural universal. It is said, for example, that every religion provides an
answer to the question of why humans die.

Some 3000 years ago the ancient people of the Tigris-Euphrates Valley placed their thoughts on the inevitability of death on the tablets of the Epic of Gilgamesh (Heidel, 1963), and at least since then people have been recording their thoughts on mortality and finitude. The Epic of Gilgamesh tells the story of Gilgamesh, who was one-third god and two-thirds man. Being part human, Gilgamesh lamented at the death of his friend, Enkidu. "When I die, shall I not be like unto Enkidu?" he asked. Obsessed with the fear of death, Gilgamesh went through a series of adventures seeking a way to prevent his own death. Enduring the greatest hardships and perils in his ancient quest for a "fountain of youth," he almost succeeded by finding a magical plant. However, a serpent stole the plant and ate it. At last, Gilgamesh realized that he could not transcend his mortality, took consolation in the fact that he had done good and wondrous things in his life, and accepted the inevitability that he, like all of us, would die.

Death has always, then, been something that we human beings have tried to explain and understand, in order that we might come to accept it. The first book of the Old Testament provides an explanation for mortality. Created immortal, the first humans sinned and became condemned to die. Death in the Judeo-Christian tradition thus came, in this interpretation, to be seen as evil but at least understandable, because there was a reason for it. In another cultural tradition with persistent influence to the present time, the Greek Sappho expresses the association between death and evil, writing that death was the greatest evil: "Gods so consider it, else they would die." It is not only the existentialist philosophers who have been concerned with finitude. *Everyman* is concerned with finitude and virtually every thinker in the Western tradition at least has written of it (see Choron, 1963; Toynbee, 1968). The written and orally transmitted myths of diverse religions provide a wide variety of "explanations" for death, as well as recommendations as to how we might face death with greater equanimity (for a historical review in the Western Christian tradition, see Ariès, 1981).

Death is not, however, a problem only for individuals. A major goal of contemporary governments is to ward off death, through public hygiene and health measures, massive medical expenditures, and provisions for national defense. In a world such as ours, survival is frequently problematical at the level not only of the individual but of the society itself. In the terms of the structural functionalist concern for the prerequisites of any society, this means in the most simple terms that no society could survive if all of its members died. This is no trivial concern for small tribal societies numbering perhaps 200 or 300 people in total.

For them, the loss of 10 people through a disaster such as war, famine, or flood seriously jeopardizes their ability to continue to exist. The loss of 10 persons can mean the loss of 10 hunters, 10 warriors, or 10 procreators or childbearers. Robert Blauner (1966) has noted that "in general, the demographic structure of pre-industrial societies results in an exposure to death that appears enormous by the standards of modern western life." Yet in the nuclear age we live with the possibility of complete annihilation not only of societies but of the world population. The meaning of death perhaps assumes a new problematic in such circumstances.

In any society, death removes people from social life and necessitates the institution of mechanisms for recruiting and socializing new members to fill vacancies. It also allows for new individuals to contribute fresh perspectives and thereby contribute to social and cultural change (Mannheim, 1952). Wilbert Moore (1966) has written that men are mortal but societies are, in a sense, immortal and that, in consequence, death poses problems and dilemmas for the organization of societies. At a more everyday level, death disrupts the routine ongoingness of life in society. We have to learn to accept the death of others—including others we love dearly—and keep living ourselves just as we have to learn to accept our own impending deaths and keep on living.

These are then "life and death" issues for both individuals and societies. How can we grasp them? How can we begin to say anything systematic about this pervasive and crucial aspect of our life with others? What has sociology or social psychology to contribute beyond the wisdom of the ages about these matters?

AN INTERPRETIVE PERSPECTIVE ON AGING AND DYING

To begin with, let us distinguish analytically between what people do together and the meanings they share about what they do. This is a distinction between social system (a pattern of action characterizing the behavior of members of a collectivity) and culture (the meanings held in common by members of a collectivity). These definitions are arbitrary and the terms "social system" and "culture" have been defined in many ways, but this distinction is useful (see Inkeles, 1963; Kroeber & Kluckhohn, 1952; Parsons et al., 1961; Spiro, 1961). Culture is retained as a cognitive concept referring to "the framework of beliefs, expressive symbols, and values in terms of which individuals define their world, express their feelings, and make their judgments" (Geertz, 1957, p. 549). Culture thus becomes a resource to be used by people to render their behavior meaningful.

With a number of other scholars whom I shall classify loosely in the "interpretive perspective" (see Chapter 1 of this volume), such as A. Schutz (1967), P. Berger, and G. H. Mead, I would focus on the intentionality of the actor, the active part played by the individual in constructing a sense of the world and his or her life in it. Sense-making activity both relies on and helps to build and sustain culture.

Berger and Luckmann (1967) have emphasized the dialectical relationship between humans as producers of their world and that world as social product. They use the term "externalization" to describe the work of humans, through social interaction, to create and share meaning. Through "objectivation," that humanly produced reality comes to take on a life of its own, "a reality that confronts the individual as an external and coercive fact" (Berger & Luckmann, 1967, p. 58). This is the reification and consequent alienation of which Marx has also written. The third moment in this dialectic between the individual and the social world is "internalization"—the process by which the "objectivated social world is retrojected into consciousness in the course of socialization" (Berger & Luckmann, 1967, p. 61).

The world, not all of our world but a good deal of it and all of our social world, is humanly produced. And our view of that social reality rests on interpretations that are largely shared and thereby social. Our world is in most respects *inter*subjective, even including the fact that our very perception of ourselves is pieced together largely (though not exclusively) from information gathered in social interaction (Breytspraak, 1984, p. 90; Rosenberg, 1981).

The world, intersubjective and socially experienced, is known through typifications or constructs, and the most important vehicle for typifying reality is language itself. As Berger and Luckmann (1967, p. 64) state, "Language provides the fundamental superimposition of logic on the objectivated social world. . . . We can only 'know' reality through the medium of language." Winch (1958, p. 15) puts it thus: "Our idea of what belongs to the realm of reality is given for us in the language that we use. The concepts that we have settle for us the form of the experience we have of the world. . . . The world is for us what is presented through these concepts."

In this "language game" perspective, it follows that, if we know our world through language, then "the most important vehicle of reality-maintenance is conversation" (Berger & Luckmann, 1967, p. 152). The world is not solipsistic. It does not exist simply in the mind of the individual or in the eye of the beholder. It is created through social interaction and its existence transcends those who intersubjectively and interactively sustain it.

A final general theoretical point is that not only do we humans endow our world with meaning, but we have no choice about it. We are not genetically or otherwise preprogrammed to behave in adaptive ways, so we must create the meanings that allow us to make sense of, and to make our way in, the world.

With these preliminaries as a foundation, it is now possible to outline briefly a general thesis concerning the interplay between societal dynamics and individual and interpersonal life as it relates to the fact of death. At a very general level, the outlines of a sociology of aging and dying can be summarized as follows:

(1) For various reasons, death poses "problems" for the survival of any society. The apparent triviality of this assertion is belied by its importance in relatively small societies, by the massive public expenditures in contemporary societies to contain and to ward off death, and by the possibility of nuclear annihilation not only of societies but of the human race.

(2) For various reasons, death poses "problems" for any individual. Death is a universal, it is typically anticipated, and the weight of historical and comparative evidence suggests that people have always and everywhere sought to "explain" it.

(3) People have responded to these social problems (acting, as it were, on behalf of their societies) and to the personal or individual problematics of death and dying by constructing new meanings and new behavior patterns that deal with death and dying. That is, through externalization, they have created both culture and social system patterns (social institutions) that deal with death and dying (see especially Riley, 1983). Religious beliefs about death and the institution of the funeral industry (Pine, 1975) are examples.

(4) These meanings and behavior patterns come to take on a "life of their own," to become traditional or, in sociological parlance, to become "institutionalized." They become "the way it is" through the social process of objectivation.

(5) Objectivated meanings and social institutions then become the context in which individuals must accomplish their own dying. People learn the cultural meanings (internalization) and these meanings, together with such death-relevant social institutions as contemporary medicine and the funeral industry, constrain or place limits on the ways in which individuals can do their own dying.

Each of the above points summarizes a vast topic for analysis. My intention in the following, however, is quite restricted (but see Marshall, 1980). In the section that follows I address the societal problematics of death in something of a comparative context. If nothing else, this will demonstrate through the diversity of meanings and social institutions dealing with death and dying that the subject matter is properly sociological. This discussion will lay the groundwork for an understanding of the situation that older people today experience as they face impending death. In subsequent sections, I will trace out a general theory of aging and dying intended to be generalizable within the so-called modern industrialized world.

THE PROBLEMATICS OF DEATH
IN SOCIETY

Sociologists often speak, very loosely, as if societies had problems. We may be forgiven this sin of reification, perhaps, if it is recognized that we are adopting a type of reification commonly made by members of society. People do speak about their society as if it is more than an abstraction and they do at times work for it. The term "society" refers to membership in a defined collectivity, or group of people who share patterned interaction. Nonpatterned interaction is outside the scope of sociological interest, as is nonsocial interaction (such as, in Weber's example, the accidental collision of two bicyclists who to that point had been unaware of each other; see Weber, 1978, pp. 22-24). Commonsensically, we can think of societies as groups of people, be they tribes or nation-states, who are linked together through direct or mediated interaction.

As noted earlier, if everyone in a society died, the society would not survive and there would be no society left. But this would be true only if everyone died at the same time. Society is in fact very much like the "good ship Lollipop" discussed in undergraduate philosophy courses. Each year Her Majesty's Ship Lollipop puts into dry dock and has one in ten of her planks and beams replaced. Ten years later, is she the same ship? Without venturing into deep philosophical positions, it can be claimed that it is useful to think of her as the same ship. Similarly, it is useful to think of a society as persisting, as having an identity, over time as some of its members are removed by death to be replaced by new members. It is in this sense that Moore (1966) describes societies as, so to speak, immortal despite the mortality of their members.

As events that link humanity with the unknown, both birth and death receive elaborate ritual treatment (De Vries, 1981) and this in turn suggests that both birth and death are highly problematic and call out for meaning. The belief or cultural system of any society provides an answer, or a range of answers, to the meaning of death (although these answers may not be good enough for some people) and, as Riley (1970, p. 31) has said, "in no known society is the individual left to face death completely uninitiated." Peter Berger (1969, p. 51) has argued that "every human society is, in the last resort, men banded together in the face of death." To the degree that this is so, it suggests that death is more than an individual or personal problematic for the person who is to die; it is also problematic at the level of the society.

Malinowski (1948, pp. 52-53) writes:

> A small community bereft of a member, especially if he be important, is severely mutilated. The whole event breaks the normal course of life and shakes the moral foundations of society. . . . Death in a primitive society is. . . . much more than the removal of a member. By setting in motion one part of the deep forces of the instinct of self-preservation, it threatens the very cohesion and solidarity of the group, and upon this depends the organization of the society, its tradition, and finally the whole culture.

We see such disruption in modern societies when heads of state die suddenly while in office. Such deaths are accompanied by large amounts of ritual, both to enable members of society to make sense of the death and to structure the societal reintegration processes.

As noted earlier, if every individual in a society were to die simultaneously, the society would cease to survive. This is not a trivial consideration in many small-scale tribal societies, where famine, flood, pestilence, or war could indeed lead to the annihilation of a society; nor, one might argue, is it a trivial consideration today, when we all live under the threat of nuclear annihilation. Robert Lifton, whose analysis of this phenomenon began with his Pulitzer Prize-winning study of survivors of Hiroshima, *Death in Life* (1967) has said:

> When I say . . . that we are all survivors of Hiroshima, I mean this to be more than a dramatic metaphor. I think we are all involved in struggles to find significance and meaning in a world in which such events can occur. . . . I believe that our best means of reestablishing meaningful boundaries, or at least learning to live with existing ones rendered unclear and uncertain, is to confront those experiences—such as Hiroshima— which have done so much to break those boundaries down. (Lifton, 1967, pp. 16-17)

But in other ways the fact of death calls out for the development of new meanings to deal with it, and of new behavior patterns to contain its impact for the society. The social character of death has changed dramatically, in part because of such efforts, and these changes create new problematics.

Consider, for example, the question of the predictability of death. Today, in the modern industrial societies, we can anticipate that the vast majority of people born will live into the later years. The average age of death is much higher than it was even forty or fifty years ago, and poles apart from, say, the experience of the American colonists (Uhlenberg, 1980). Historian Phillip Greven has analyzed data from colonial Andover, Massachusetts, a healthy community by New England standards of the time, and found that, of 1000 persons born in the last thirty years of the eighteenth century, 132 did not live beyond a year, another 46 died before the age of 10, and 225 in all died before the age of 20. That is to say, over 1 in 5 did not reach the age of 20. Death rates in Boston were, he claims, about double (Greven, 1970, pp. 22, 188-189). With average birthrates on the order of 8 or 9, colonial families could expect that 2 or 3 of their children would die before reaching age 10 (Stannard, 1975, p. 18). In most European countries, life expectancy at birth increased from about 40 years in 1840 to over 50 years by 1900. The infant mortality rate was still over 100 (that is, 100 deaths per 1000 births) in 1900 but is now less than 15, and lower in many areas (see Goldscheider, 1970, p. 110; Marshall, 1980, pp. 12-13). Based on life tables for today, in contrast, a person born has a 96% chance of living to age 25 and even almost a 75% chance of living to age 65. Death is situated in later life in the normal, typical, and predictable case. Statistically, the mean age of death has risen considerably and, in addition, the standard deviation around that mean has shrunk.

If it is necessary to make sense of death, then the nature of what must be made sense of has altered. Not capricious death, but predictable death; not death at an early age, but death as the culmination of life, calls out for meaning. In addition, death now typically comes as the culmination of a protracted period of time when the person can be viewed as "dying." By this, I mean that death follows a period of chronic illness in a much larger proportion of cases than in earlier times. Contrast death in later life from cancer with the swift death of the plagues or, less dramatically, from acute illness in middle life. Pneumonia used to be called "the old man's friend" because it brought a quick and relatively painless death to spare a person from the vicissitudes of old age. But death from pneumonia is today very rare.

The great reduction of death from acute illness is testimony to societal attempts to deal behaviorally with the problematics of death. Massive expenditures for sanitation and preventive health and medical care indicate a societal preoccupation with warding off death. Death is even viewed as "the enemy," and our attack on it is described in terms of "campaigns" or "crusades" to eradicate this enemy.

As a society, we deal with death in bureaucratic ways. The place of death is now typically the hospital, where we make routine of the crisis of death and where, in fact, hospital routines themselves often alter and mold the dynamics of dying (Glaser & Strauss, 1968).

The handling of the dead is similarly turned over to functionaries, who deal with the body but also orchestrate the public ritual for the bereaved, and the funeral industry is a pervasive and massive one. Pine (1975, p. 21) has noted:

> There are approximately 22,000 funeral establishments in the United States and approximately 50,000 people licensed to practice funeral directing. Until the past thirty to fifty years death occurred at home in familiar surroundings in the presence of kin or close friends, and funerals were community events. Times have changed, however. Each year proportionately more people die in institutions instead of their own homes, and almost all of the dead are cared for by funeral directors in funeral homes.

The bureaucratization of death and dying through such institutions as hospital death and the funeral industry has ramifications for other aspects of the society. Robert Blauner was the first sociologist to emphasize this fact. He says:

> This separation of the handling of illness and death from the family minimizes the average person's exposure to death and its disruption of the social process. When the dying are segregated among specialists for whom contact with death has become routine and even somewhat impersonal, neither their presence while alive nor as corpses interferes greatly with the mainstream of life. (Blauner, 1966, p. 379)

Another way to minimize the impact of death and dying on the society, also noted by Blauner, is to reduce the social importance of those who die. Many societies with high infant mortality rates do not grant full human status to infants and have no ritual marking for their deaths. Is there a parallel to the marginalization of older people and their exclusion from full participation in social life? Blauner (1960, p. 383) argues that

> the disengagement of the aged in modern societies enhances the continuing functioning of social institutions and is a corollary of social structure and mortality patterns. Disengagement, the transition period between the end of institutional functioning and death, permits the changeover of personnel in a planned and careful manner, without the inevitably disruptive crises of disorganization and succession that would occur if people worked to the end and died on the job.

At the cultural level, the societal adaptations to death are found in the explanations for death and the conceptions of afterlife that are found in all religions. If we are to understand the contemporary meanings of death in our own society, we must attend to the religious legacy, as this has been modified by the rise of scientism. This legacy can best be described as one of ambivalence (Dumont & Foss, 1972).

At least from the era of the plagues, religion has provided meanings to deal with precipitous and capricious death caused by the Four Horsemen of the Apocalypse (war, famine, strife, pestilence). Death was a sign of God's judgment, the dance of death catching all regardless of rank. Such meanings could find a place in the colonial culture of North America because of the strong religiosity and also because of their appropriateness in accounting for the death of infants, children, and persons still active in the prime of life. Other meanings were also present and more applicable to later-life death: death as reunification with the departed already in heaven, death as relief from earthly suffering or toil, even death as erotic ecstacy. However, the bulk of religious meanings that come down to us today are meanings dealing with the legitimation of death in the young. But, as Talcott Parsons and Victor Lidz (1967, p. 137) have pointed out:

> The problem of the *meaning* of death is coming. . . . to be concentrated about death occurring as the completion of a normal life cycle. . . . This central, irreducible problem is becoming disentangled from the problem of adjusting to deaths that occur earlier in the life cycle, particularly in infancy and early childhood, which was more general in the premodern period.

I would emphasize the newness of this phenomenon. The social location of death has shifted to predictable death in the later years for cohorts born only since the last decade of the previous century. This shift, coupled with the decline of religious belief in many circles, leaves the society without any widely shared set of beliefs about the meaning of death.

The societal response to this, I believe, has become significant in its impact only in the past ten to fifteen years. Lynn Lofland, in her book, *The Craft of Dying* (1978), discusses some of the indications. These include the best-seller status (well over a million paperback copies) of Elisabeth Kübler-Ross's book, *On Death and Dying* (1969), a rapid growth in the number of articles in the nonprofessional literature concerning death and dying, and the growth of university and extension courses in death and dying (Lofland, 1978, pp. 10-11). I would add the rapid spread of the palliative care and hospice movement under the influence of people such as Cecily Saunders, who developed St. Christopher's as a model hospice in England only in the late 1960s. The research in the area of palliative care, which is the attempt to ease suffering and add to the dignity of the dying, exceeds 15,000 articles since 1966 and is expanding exponentially.

In a society such as ours we leave much of the meaning construction (it can perhaps be called the rule making) for anything in the hands of experts, but meaning construction at all levels is active these days. David Gutmann (1977, p. 336) has written:

> Pop psychologists have reduced their production of books on achieving the good orgasm; instead they are now telling us how to compose an aesthetic decomposition—a graceful death. . . . as earnest theology students flock to their bedsides, the dying are treated to the kind of intensive care which, if it does not hasten their demise, may at least make them welcome it.

Lofland (1978, pp. 75-76) calls all this the "happy death movement," a "sprawling, diverse, multi-structured, diffuse assemblage of persons, acting independently and as parts of organizations, engaging in a multiplicity of largely uncoordinated activities and possessing varying degrees of 'consciousness' relative to their participation in a movement." This movement Lofland sees as "promoting a change in American society with regard to its beliefs about death and dying, its emotional responses to death and dying, and its legal and normative practices relative to death and dying" (p. 77). She would include within this movement the intellectual and pop-intellectual writers about better ways of dying such as Kübler-Ross, but also such organizations as the Euthanasia Education Council, the Foundation of Thanatology, the

Forum for Death Education and Counseling, widow-to-widow programs, various similar self-help groups, all the hospice organizations,
the death and dying journals such as *Omega* and *Essence*, and
conferences and workshops on the topic. We seem, in fact, to be
bombarded with verbiage about how people should die properly and the
barriers to the good death. Death, as Lofland (1978, pp. 77-104) points
out, is being recast as a "personal growth experience" (see also Kübler-
Ross's 1974 characterization of death as "the final stage of growth").

This activity is an externalization of meaning construction, in the
sense of Berger and Luckmann's theoretical perspective. It cannot, of
course, be said that this externalization has succeeded in creating a new
social reality of meanings and of patterns of social interaction surrounding death that is as yet widely shared. Rather, there is something
of a social movement and proselytizing flavor to all of this (see Fox,
1981, pp. 49-51). From the point of view of the aging and dying person,
however, the result is a melange of ideas, conflicts over meanings, a
range of behavioral patterns surrounding the process of dying, and the
ritual of bereavement.

From the perspective of the aging and dying individual, orienting to
impending death, then, takes place in a world of meanings and actions
that are ambiguous but, perhaps more important, also ambivalent.
Moreover, the contemporary bureaucratization of death and dying
reduces the opportunity for the aging and dying person to retain
personal control over the last phases of life. Against this context of
ambivalence and loss of control, I want now to consider the process of
aging and dying from the perspective of the individual.

AWARENESS OF FINITUDE

Elisabeth Kübler-Ross (1969) argues that everyone is afraid of
death—she explains this fear through some rather crude psychoanalytic
theories. It makes more theoretical and epistemological sense to view
death itself as a neutral stimulus—something that can be endowed with
meanings of different sorts. Thus, for example, some religious beliefs
have the effect of making death a fearful thing, while others have the
effect of making death something to look forward to (Malinowski, 1948,
p. 50; Radcliffe-Brown, 1965). Any serious look at comparative religions will tell you this.

However, there is another aspect to death that is important to look at,
and I would start my own framework with it: This is what I call

"awareness of finitude," the recognition that one's time on earth is limited and that death is drawing near (Marshall, 1975). Some recent theorists have argued that such a realization comes to all people in the decade between ages 35 and 45, and that the shock of this realization—that my life is now half over, that I now count time in terms of years left to live instead of in years I have already lived—is so pronounced that it initiates a "midlife crisis." This is argued in popular books by Sheehy, (1977), Gould (1978), Levinson (1978), and others.

But this realization does not in fact appear to come in that decade for most people. If it did, and if the midlife crisis theorists were correct, you would expect the evidence to show three things:

(1) a heightened concern for death during that decade of life, as measured on various attitudinal scales
(2) a heightened concern for the self—because the crisis ostensibly stems from the reassessment that one makes of who one is, where one has been, and where one is going
(3) increased pathologies that reflect the negative outcomes of the crises: increased depression, higher suicide rates, greater consumption of psychotropics and antidepressants, greater use of psychiatric services, and so forth

But an examination of the age patterns in these areas shows that in not one of them do you find the pattern you would have if there were in fact a midlife crisis generally experienced by everybody in the society (Marshall, 1980, pp. 107-121). That is, there is not a clustering in that decade of fear of death, or of self-focusing behavior, or of such indicators of "crisis" as alcohol abuse, seeking psychiatric help, prevalance of depression, suicide, and so forth.

So, some people undoubtedly have midlife crises, but most do not. Maybe most of us have lifelong crises, or no crises at all over our lives, but, in any case, few people have a concentration of crisis in that middle decade.

When do people become highly aware of their mortality, then? As John W. Riley (1970) has said, most of us do not really think too much about death except in the case of extreme situations—accidents, disasters, massacres, and the like—and in such circumstances we are likely to see death as something impersonal—as Tolstoy's Ivan Illich acknowledged, he always accepted the validity of the proposition, "All men are mortal"—but he never applied it to himself.

The data are not in fact terribly extensive on this subject, but my best reading of them suggests that recognition of our mortality grows from the middle years and becomes quite strong around the 70s for most people. It grows in relation to deaths of people connected to us, especially our parents (Marshall, 1980, pp. 97-107). Something quite psychologically important happens to people when their first parent dies, and something in addition when the second parent dies. Experiencing these deaths brings people to a fuller sense of their own maturity, and it points to the fundamental truth that people come into the world and pass out of it, that one generation succeeds another (Marshall & Rosenthal, 1982).

There are two other psychological points that I think are also important—although these have not been studied in any depth. I suspect, though, that when a person reaches the age at which one parent died, this is an important life course marker—"I have now lived as long as my father lived"—and that attaining the age by which both parents had died symbolizes, in the typical case, an achievement. The person has now in effect received a just allotment of years. Any additional years of life are, in a sense, a gift, an extra, a plus.

In my own research, with a very small sample, I found that of people who had not yet reached the age at which either parent had died, about two-thirds still gave themselves ten or more years to live (these were older people, average age 80 and minimum age 64). However, of people who had surpassed the age of death of both parents, two-thirds estimated that they had less than five years to live (Marshall, 1975).

This kind of comparison process was a better predictor than was age itself of the length of time people thought remained in their lives, and the relationship was significant when controlling for age. People, then, make mental calculations as to how long they have to live. Pat Keith of the University of Iowa has also studied this phenomenon, and she found, as did I, that not everyone did make such estimates, but those who did, she found, were different from those who did not. They were more likely to see themselves as middle-aged, to have plans for the future, and to have a favorable attitude toward death (Keith, 1982).

Awareness of death, Keith suggests, promotes the organization of time: If you know your time is limited you are more likely to try to put that remaining time to good use. Keith suggests that the fact that those who do give concrete estimates of time remaining also have more favorable attitudes toward death might be accounted for by a refusal to make such estimates in those who are afraid of death.

I have a different explanation. I think that heightened awareness of finitude initiates some social psychological processes of preparation for death that in turn help to reduce anxiety about death and to make people more accepting of it.

LEGITIMATION OF BIOGRAPHY

The first of these social psychological processes, in my scheme of analysis, is what I call "legitimation of biography." The analysis that follows makes use of the following metaphor. When people become highly aware that their time is limited before death, they see themselves in a metaphorical sense as in the last chapters of their autobiography. And they want it to be a story that makes sense. As Kearl (1980, p. 575) states, "Related to the temporal problems of continuity in old age is the problem of biographical culmination. What final biographical chapter or epilogue is one to construct in order to punctuate the meaning of one's life story?"

Erik Erikson (1959) has written about this same process when he talks about the "eighth identity crisis." Identity can be seen as a sense of sameness and continuity of one's selves over time. Identity is an *achievement* that we make, with the help of others. All of us know that we are very different people than we were, say, fifteen or twenty years ago. Yet, paradoxically, we are also the same. Erikson suggests that, late in life, we develop a profound sense of acknowledgment that our lives are basically lived. That is, it is too late to go back and start over again, because death is too near. Therefore, we are left with the possibility of accepting that lived life as meaningful, or of dying with a feeling that life has been meaningless. This recognition, Erikson says, poses the eighth identity crisis—if the person cannot make sense of that past life, he or she will fall into despair; accepting one's own life as having some meaning—even if the life story has not been one of happiness or success—and accepting responsibility for that life as lived leads, alternatively, to the attainment of integrity. And, Erikson says, the person who attains integrity faces death with equanimity.

Robert Butler (1963) has described in some detail a psychological process called the "life review," which people go through to attain integrity. The life review, Butler says, is a naturally occurring, universally experienced process in which the individual who is highly aware of the shortness of remaining life reminisces about his or her past life and tries to make sense of it. The person who is actively reminiscing in the life review process will be focusing on important choice points of the past life that might have been the occasion for a bad choice. In a Kierkegaardian sense, life can be seen as a series of *either/or* choices. Every time we make a choice to go one way rather than another, Kierkegaard says, we accumulate a little bit of *angst* or anxiety: Did I really do the right thing? Should I have married the bum? Was graduate school the right place for me? Why did we not have children? The life review process is one in which the individual surveys the past life and tries to reach a sense of acceptance or rationalization (see Kierkegaard, 1959).

Other theorists in the developmental psychology and social psychology of aging and the disengagement theorists (Neugarten, 1966; Cumming & Henry, 1961) also suggest that sometime after later middle age, people experience a growing sense of "internality" or "interiority" as they try to make sense of their lives as a whole, as they have unfolded over time and as they are drawing now to a close; this process of legitimating one's biography is seen as an adaptation to the profound realization of awareness of finitude.

My own research (Marshall, 1980, chap. 5), and my interpretation of related research, leads to the following conclusions about this process of legitimation of biography:

(1) The process does seem to occur. It is marked by changes in time perspective—a withdrawal of one's orientation to the future and a focusing on the past—and a heightened preoccupation with identity.

(2) The process seems to be at its peak during that period when an individual estimates he or she has between five and ten years left before death. In other words, this is a later-life process and not one of middle age.

(3) The process is initiated by heightened awareness of finitude, it works its way through and, in a sense, it has a conclusion if the person lives long enough. That is, in the normal case, a person will in effect complete the life review and reach a state of integrity. This is measurable. I have found that the person who successfully completes this process is more likely than the person still in it to say that he or she would, if given the chance, like to live life over again, *even if it were to remain the same.* He or she is more likely to say he or she is very happy with life as a whole and less likely to report any continuing disappointments with life as a whole. Finally, completion of the process is marked by a return to a more present- and future-oriented time perspective.

(4) The life review is a social process. Whereas Butler describes the process as psychological and claims that its success depends on individual variables such as ego strength and character, my own research suggests that the process is more sociological. I found that people who said they reminisced and thought about the past a lot privately were not yet through the legitimation process; other people, who reported social reminiscence—that they talked a lot about their own past life with other people—were more likely to demonstrate success in the process. Reconstructing biography is therefore an example of the social construction of reality.

LEGITIMATION OF DEATH

To continue with the metaphor: People who realize they are in the last chapters of their lives not only want their lives to be good stories, they want them to have good endings. This places them in the position of wanting to make sense of death itself, including their own deaths. Most people seem to be successful at doing this. For example, almost no one wants to live to be 100, for reasons such as the following, which were given to me by my respondents:

- I might not be useful then. I might not be able to make other people happy. I don't want to be a burden, I think is what I mean to say.
- So few people who live that long are much comfort to themselves. Very few of them are spry enough to dress themselves, possibly to feed themselves.
- I'd rather be dead than in the infirmary—it would be repulsive—a burden to friends.

In a national survey, John W. Riley, Jr. (1970) asked a sample whether or not they agreed with the statement, "Death always comes too soon." About half of his respondents agreed with that statement. The other half, presumably, thought that death comes either too late or just on time, at least some of the time. In a retirement community, I found few people who agreed with the statement. I also asked, "Under what circumstances does death *not* come too soon?" The reasons given are similar to the reasons people do not want to live to be 100:

- They do not want to be a burden to others.
- They do not want to lose the ability to be active and useful.
- They do not want to remain physically alive while "losing their faculties."
- They do not want to suffer a long siege of illness.

Poet Hans Zinsser (1950) put it very well:

Now is death merciful. He calls me hence
Gently, with friendly soothing of my fears
Of ugly age and feeble impotence
And cruel disintegration of slow years

It is often difficult for young people to believe that the vast majority of older people come to a point where death, and their own dying, makes more sense to them than continuing to live forever. But the data of numerous scholars show that most old people in our society do come to accept their deaths. Arlie Hochschild (1973), in her work, and I in mine (1975), have shown how in congregate residential facilities for the elderly, old people facing impending death as a common problem do in fact develop ways to make sense of death and to both accept the deaths of others with equanimity and anticipate their own the same way. At an interpersonal level, there is some indication that having just one intimate other—such as a spouse—with whom to discuss impending death can increase the likelihood of gaining acceptance of it.

This happens when people try to make sense of the death of other people: "It really was a blessing that Mrs. Jones died," they will say. "She was beginning to lose her faculties." And if this becomes a good reason it is appropriate for Mrs. Jones to die, it becomes a verbal formulation to be applied to oneself for the same purpose. A language game of death legitimation then develops (Wittgenstein, 1953).

This is not to say that old people become suicidal or overly preoccupied with making sense of death. It seems that, just like legitimation of biography, this is a process initiated by heightened awareness of finitude that can, given enough time, reach a sense of completion.

And nothing is more a delight to see than the older person who is ready to die. The acceptance seems to be freeing, a liberation. For if you are ready to die, you become free of the burdens of this world and more able to enjoy those extra days or even years—the gift of life.

AUTHORSHIP

The last part of the metaphor is "authorship"—if people want their lives to be meaningful stories with good endings, they also want to be the authors. This is the taking of responsibility for one's life as a whole, including its ending in death, of which Erikson speaks. In psychological terms, it is "locus of control" (Rotter, 1966). In symbolic interactionist terms in social psychology, it is "status passage control"—having the sense that you are in charge of that life as a whole, as it ends (Marshall, 1980, chap. 7). Hochschild (1973), for example, found that residents of Merril Court, a high-rise occupied by senior citizens, tried to guess how long people had to live as a means of reducing the unpredictability of the timing of death. Other evidence of a desire for control comes from a survey by Kalish and Reynolds (1976), in which almost 80% of respondents said they wanted to be told if they were dying.

Many hospital routines, needless to say, deny to the individual the opportunity to control the very final stages of dying (Glaser & Strauss, 1968; Rosenthal et al., 1980). The ability to plan for the final settling of one's affairs—possible only if a person is in fact told a prognosis that he or she is dying—can enhance personal control. So can freedom from pain. The spread of palliative care programs, which offer open awareness and truth-telling, but also pain relief and social support, may therefore do a great deal to increase the likelihood that an individual will be able to feel "in control" during the final stages.

Commentators on the era of the plagues or "black death" have suggested that the pervasive atmosphere of death at the time contributed to the rise of individualism in the Western tradition. The argument presented here should be seen in the context of individualism as a strong ideological theme in our society. Kearl and Harris, in secondary analyses of national survey data, have in fact shown that an emerging "ideology of death" in the United States has strong associations with individualism on a number of measures. "Authorship" in the metaphor, or internal locus of control, may well correspond to individualism. If so, this sets important cultural limits on the generalizability of the argument being made here. Authorship brings us back to the key aspect of the interpretive theoretical perspective in which this chapter has been grounded, for it speaks to both an intentional originator of social action and a person engaged in meaning construction.

And so we can draw these moments of the social dialectic of aging and dying together. New externalizations seek to change the social patterns and the cultural meanings that provide the context in which the individual must do his or her own dying. The reifications and objectivations of what has been called the "death system" or the "social institution of death and dying" are increasingly challenged. The causes of this continual change in the social organization of death and dying lie partly and importantly in the fact of the changing social character of death and its new location at the end of the life course; but it should be apparent that they lie also in the ever-present and ever-realized quest for meaning that is a species characteristic of the human being.

REFERENCES

Ariès, P. (1981). *The hour of our death.* New York: Knopf.
Berger, P. L. (1969). *The sacred canopy.* Garden City, NY: Doubleday.
Berger, P. L., & Luckmann, T. J. (1967). *The social construction of reality* (2nd ed.). Garden City, NY: Doubleday.

Blauner, R. (1966). Death and social structure. *Psychiatry, 29*, 378-394.

Breytspraak, L. M. (1984). *The development of self in later life.* Boston: Little, Brown.

Butler, R. (1963). The life review: An interpretation of reminiscence in the aged. *Psychiatry: Journal for the Study of Inter-Personal Processes, 26*, 65-76.

Choron, J. (1963). *Death and Western thought.* New York: Collier.

Cumming, E., & Henry, W. (1961). *Growing old: The process of disengagement.* New York: Basic Books.

De Vries, R. G. (1981). Birth and death: Social construction at the poles of existence. *Social Forces, 59*, 1074-1093.

Dumont, R. G., & Foss, D. C. (1972). *The American view of death: Acceptance or denial?* Cambridge, MA: Schenkman.

Erikson, E. (1959). Identity and the life cycle. *Psychological Issues, 1.*

Fox, R. C. (1981). The sting of death in American society. *Social Service Review, 55*(1), 42-59.

Geertz, C. (1957). Ritual and social change: A Javanese example. *American Anthropologist, 59*, 32-54.

Glaser, B. G., & Strauss, A. L. (1968). *Time for dying.* Chicago: Aldine.

Goldscheider, C. (1971). *Population, modernization and social structure.* Boston: Little, Brown.

Gould, R. L. (1978). *Transformations.* New York: Simon & Schuster.

Greven, P., Jr. (1970). *Four generations: Population, land and family in colonial Andover, Massachusetts.* Ithaca, NY: Cornell University Press.

Gutmann, D. (1977). Dying to power: Death and the search for self-esteem. In H. Feifel (ed.), *New meanings of death* (pp. 335-347). New York: McGraw-Hill.

Heidegger, M. (1962). *Being and time* (J. McQuarrie & E. Robinson, Trans.). New York: Harper & Row.

Heidel, A. (Trans.). (1963). *The Gilgamesh epic and Old Testament parallels.* Chicago: University of Chicago Press.

Hochschild, A. R. (1973). *The unexpected community.* Englewood Cliffs, NJ: Prentice-Hall.

Inkeles, A. (1963). Sociology and psychology. In S. Koch (Ed.), *Psychology: A study of a science* (Vol. 6, pp. 317-387). New York: McGraw-Hill.

Kalish, R. A., & Reynolds, D. K. (1976). *Death and ethnicity: A psychocultural study.* Los Angeles: University of Southern California Press.

Kearl, M. (1980). Time, identity, and the spiritual needs of the elderly. *Sociological Analysis, 41*(2), 172-180.

Kearl, M., & Harris, R. (1980-1982). Individualism and the emerging 'modern' ideology of death. *Omega, 12*(3), 269-280.

Keith, P. M. (1982). Perceptions of time remaining and distance from death. *Omega, 12*(4), 307-318.

Kierkegaard, S. (1959). *Either/or* (Vol. 1, D. F. Swenson & L. M. Swenson, Trans.). Garden City, NY: Doubleday. (Original work published 1944)

Kroeber, A. L., & Kluckhohn, C. (1952). *Culture: A critical review of concepts and definitions.* New York: Vintage.

Kübler-Ross, E. (1969). *On death and dying.* New York: Macmillan.

Kübler-Ross, E. (1974). *Death: The final stage of growth.* Englewood Cliffs, NJ: Prentice-Hall.

Levinson, D. J., Darrow, C. M., Klein, E. B., Levinson, M. H., & McKee, B. (1978). *The seasons of a man's life.* New York: Knopf.

Lifton, R. J. (1967). *Death in life: Survivors of Hiroshima.* New York: Random House.
Lofland, L. H. (1978). *The craft of dying: The modern face of death.* Beverly Hills, CA: Sage.
Malinowski, B. (1948). *Magic, science and religion, and other essays.* New York: Free Press.
Mannheim, K. (1952). The problem of generations. In P. Kecskemeti (Ed.), *K. Mannheim, essays on the sociology of knowledge.* London: Routledge & Kegan Paul.
Marshall, V. W. (1975). Age and the awareness of finitude in developmental gerontology. *Omega, 6*(2), 113-129.
Marshall, V. W. (1980). *Last chapters: A sociology of aging and dying.* Monterey, CA: Brooks/Cole.
Marshall, V. W. (1985). Aging and dying in Pacific societies: Implications for theory in social gerontology. In D. Counts & D. Counts (Eds.), *Transformations: Aging and dying in South Pacific societies* (pp. 251-274). Washington: University Press of America.
Marshall, V. W., & Rosenthal, C. J. (1982). Parental death: A life course marker. *Generations, 7,* 30-31, 39.
Moore, W. E. (1963). *Man, time, and society.* New York: John Wiley.
Moore, W. E. (1966). Aging and social system. In J. C. McKinney and F. T. DeVyer (Eds.), *Aging and social policy* (pp. 23-41). New York: Appleton-Century-Crofts.
Neugarten, B. L. (1966). Adult personality: A developmental view. *Human Development, 9,* 61-73.
Parson, T. & Lidz, V. M. (1967). Death in American society. In E. S. Shneidman (Ed.), *Essays in self-destruction* (pp. 133-140). New York: Science House.
Parsons, T., Shils, E., Naegele, K. D. & Pitts, J. R. (Eds.). (1961). *Theories of society* (2 vols.). New York: Free Press.
Pine, V. R. (1975). *Caretaker of the dead: The American funeral director.* New York: Irvington.
Radcliffe-Brown, A. R. (1965). Taboo. In W. A. Lessa & E. Z. Vogt (Eds.), *Reader in comparative religion* (2nd ed., pp. 112-123). New York: Harper and Row. (Original work published 1939).
Riley, J. W., Jr. (1983). Dying and the meanings of death: Sociological inquiries. *Annual Review of Sociology, 9,* 191-216.
Riley, J. W., Jr. (1970). What people think about death. In O. G. Brim, Jr., H. E. Freeman, S. Levine, & N. A. Scotch (Eds.), *The dying patient* (pp. 30-41). New York: Russell Sage.
Rosenberg, (1981). The self-concept: Social product and social force. In M. Rosenberg & R. H. Turner (Eds.), *Social psychology: Sociological perspectives* (pp. 593-624). New York: Basic Books.
Rosenthal, C. J., Marshall, V. W., Macpherson, A. S., & French, S. (1980). *Nurses, patients and families: Care and control in the hospital.* New York: Springer.
Rotter, J. B. (1966). Generalized expectancies for internal versus external control of reinforcement. *Psychological Monographs, 80* (1, Whole No. 109).
Schutz, A. (1967). Common sense and scientific interpretation of human interaction. In M. Natanson (Ed.), *Alfred Schutz: Collected papers* (2nd ed., pp. 7-47). The Hague: Nijhoff. (Original work published 1945)
Sheehy, G. (1977). *Passages: Predictable crises of adult life.* New York: Dutton.
Simmel, G. (1959). The adventure. In K. H. Wolff (Ed.), *Essays on sociology, philosophy and aesthetics* (pp. 243-258). New York: Harper Torchbooks.

Spiro, M. E. (1961). Social systems, personality, and functional analysis. In B. Kaplan (Ed.), *Studying personality cross-culturally* (pp. 93-127). Evanston, IL: Harper & Row.

Stannard, D. E. (1975). Death and the puritan child. In D. E. Stannard (Ed.), *Death in America* (pp. 9-29). Philadelphia: University of Pennsylvania Press.

Toynbee, A. (1968). *Man's concern with death.* New York: McGraw-Hill.

Uhlenberg, P. (1980). Death and the family. *Journal of Family History, 5*(3), 313-320.

Weber, M. (1978). *Economy and society: An outline of interpretive sociology* (G. Roth & C. Wittich, Eds.). Berkeley: University of California Press.

Winch, P. (1958). *The idea of a social science and its relation to philosophy.* London: Routledge & Kegan Paul.

Wittgenstein, L. (1953). *Philosophical investigations* (G. M. Anscombe, Trans.). New York: Macmillan.

Zinsser, H. (1950). Two Sonnets, II. In H. Husted (Ed.), *Love poems of six centuries.* New York: Coward-McCann.

6

The Old Person as Stranger

JAMES J. DOWD

If ever there was a field needing above all else imaginative theory, that field is American social psychology today. (Gerth & Mills, 1953, p. xix)

"Today, everyone born and bred before World War II," Margaret Mead wrote not too long ago (1978), "is an immigrant in time—as his colonizing forebears were in space—struggling to grapple with the unfamiliar conditions of life in a new area. Like all immigrants and pioneers, these immigrants in time are the bearers of older cultures."

This observation, like many of those made by Mead during her lifetime of anthropological research and writing, takes us further along in our attempts to know more of the import of age, time, and generation to human social behavior. At the same time, however, it compels us to question its meaning, to probe its boundaries, and to ascertain the presence of any exceptional or contradictory evidence.

When, for example, did pre-1940 cohorts become immigrants? How is their "older culture" different from the newer cultural practices and beliefs of post-World War II generations? Is it indeed the case that *everyone* among the prewar generations may appropriately be considered an immigrant, the bearer of an older culture? Is there any awareness or appreciation among either pre- or postwar generations of this presumed cultural division of age strata? And, finally, is the cultural estrangement of contemporary age strata historically extraordinary? That is, is it something other than a specific instance of what has been (or what will be) the normal pattern of generational separation? Could it be, perhaps, that World War II constitutes a historically unique occurrence, an anomaly in which the usually slow evolution of cultural change has

AUTHOR'S NOTE: The development of the ideas presented in this chapter has been shaped by discussion with several colleagues, most especially Barry Schwartz and the late Edith Weisskopf-Joelson.

been accelerated and that therefore has become manifest as recognizable age-differentiated patterns of cultural beliefs and idiom?

It is my intent in this chapter to focus on the nature of the cultural separation of generations and, by so doing, to develop more thoroughly our knowledge of intergenerational relationships and age stratification. The differences that separate generations in Europe and America are not solely the lifestyle differences that are associated with biological senescence or the social division of labor. It is by now well understood that age differentiates people in ways that are simultaneously obvious and quite subtle. In addition, however, to the age-related factors that operate as natural mechanisms for selection or allocation in both the public and private spheres of life (such as the age grading of roles and institutions or the reality of biological growth and decline), I wish to argue that there exists a *social psychology* of age relations that has yet to be addressed directly and that in consequence is less than thoroughly understood.

But what does it mean to say that "there exists a social psychology of age relations that has yet to be addressed directly"? Is not the social psychological or individualistic emphasis at present already deeply embedded and widely suffused throughout the field of social gerontology? Apart from its other concerns, gerontology is widely known, is it not, for its preoccupation with the happiness, morale, development, and role synchronization of the aging individual?

While it is certainly true that gerontological studies are characterized by a strong individualistic orientation, it is neither inconsistent nor surprising that it is also a field without the necessary conceptual tools with which to address the social psychological problems inherent in intergenerational social relationships. Social psychology, we all know, has been practiced for at least three-quarters of a century by both psychologists and sociologists. The development of both versions (but particularly the psychological variant) has followed the neopositivistic ideal of the physical sciences by establishing the controlled experiment (or, among sociologists, the probability survey) as the means by which the causal understanding of human behavior may best be developed. The insistence by social psychologists on "correct scientific procedures" (which is to say their insistence on the positivistic agenda of controlled experimentation, operationalization of concepts, statistical analysis, and measured reliability of findings) has had unfortunate consequences for the growth of knowledge and understanding of human social behavior. The emphasis on quantitative measurement has concentrated research attention on those characteristics of the individual that are most readily measured—decisions, verbal assessment of feeling states, mood or opinion, and actual behavior itself. Deemphasized at the same time has been the dialectical reality of an individual who both is affected by and operates on his or her social world, the existence of which may not be verified through direct sensory examination. I refer here to the existence of both structural and cultural forces that impinge upon the individual and yet that resist the operationalized importunities of social psychologists to metamorphose neatly as numerical responses to sets of Likert-type opinion statements. These structural and cultural forces, despite our inability to signify them algebraically, must be addressed if we wish to know the individual.

Before we continue this point, it is necessary that I distinguish between the nature of the critique offered here of both social psychology and individualized "social" gerontology and other more political critiques recently published (compare Wexler, 1983). Whether indeed, as Wexler (1983, p. 15) claims, social psychology attempts "to commoditize and legitimate social ignorance as science" is irrelevant to the arguments developed in this chapter. Whether social psychologists have taken as their "current task" the obfuscation of individuals' understanding of their social worlds is not at issue; the fact, however, that a psychologized understanding of these worlds *is* conveyed tacitly through contemporary social psychological research is at the center of our concerns. The twin dangers of ignoring social class and the social relations of production in our analyses of cognitions, behavior, and social interaction are, on the one hand, to psychologize social and economic relations (to reduce, in the words of Mills [1946, p. 330], class problems to problems "in getting along with each other") and, on the other, to occlude understanding of the relationship between personality and work in contemporary society. Our discipline's research serves to mask, in effect if not in intent, the "causes and even the fact of the flagrant contradictions which characterize personalities within capitalist society" (Sève, 1978, p. 245).

It is also possible to lapse into the opposite error of sociologism, through which individual identity is seen as completely circumscribed by roles, positions, or statuses. The understanding that roles (and role losses or gains) affect the individual's self-conception encourages the reification of the role concept; the resulting hypostatized image of "Homo sociologicus" constitutes part of sociology's share of the obfuscation of the structure-personality relationship.

Agreeing with Lowenthal (1977, p. 117) that the "shortcomings of social and psychological theories in the field of aging reflect a serious deficiency in social psychology itself, namely, lack of systematic conceptualization about the points of articulation between the individual and his society," we would be well advised to consider Adorno's (1967, p. 68) remedial suggestion that we complete social theory by "analytically oriented social psychology." In other words, we must seek our understanding of human actions within the concrete, sociohistorical contexts in which they occur.[1] That such an approach is lacking in social gerontology hardly requires extensive argumentation. Reviews of social psychological theory in the field rarely extend beyond summaries of the oft-tested notion that life satisfaction suffers as a result of role loss (Neugarten, 1977). While preoccupied with morale, social gerontologists ignore the class bases of both aging and age relations. In our search for scientific legitimacy, we participate in our assimilation into what Marcuse has called the "affirmative" culture.

The related focus on *socialization* that has been generated by Riley's general model of age stratification is an important development but one that requires at this point more specific research application. The remainder of the social psychological opus in gerontology (ignoring for the present the considerable literature on life-span human development that, though sharing common roots and concerns with social psychology, has developed a related but different trajectory) includes isolated and noncumulative investigations of subjective traits such as creativity, conformity, religiosity, fear, attitudes toward retirement (among other things), age identity and consciousness, learned helplessness, and locus of control. My criticism of this work is not directed against any particular piece of research or conceptualization; rather, the problem, as Lowenthal (1977) recognized, lies as much with social psychology itself as it does with any application of a social psychological nature within gerontology.

To approach this study of the social psychology of age relations, one first must recognize and then consider the underlying connections among the social psychological phenomena of personality, attitudes, and *Weltanschauung* and the biological and social structural realities that create and sustain them. The German word, *Weltanschauung*, has come into general sociological use through theoretical writings in the sociology of knowledge. Max Scheler, in his 1925 essay "Probleme einer Soziologie des Wissens," described how the views of the individual, which appear to him as "his" views, that is, as natural and unaffected, are actually conditioned by (and therefore relative to) the particular sociohistorical milieu. Scheler described this historically situated perspective as a "relative-natural world view." Although interest in sociology of knowledge issues (like Weltanschauungen) has long characterized the field of political sociology due to Mannheim's influence, American social psychology has only recently focused attention in this area. Berger and Luckmann's (1966) influential work, *The Social Construction of Reality*, has served as one of the principal conduits through which interest in the sociology of knowledge has passed. The possibility of an "unaffected" commitment to an ideological point of view was also suggested by Erikson in his research on psychoanalysis and history (1958). Erikson (1958) considered an ideology to be the *unconscious* tendency (manifest in religious, political, *and* scientific thought) to make facts and ideas mutually amenable, and, by so doing, to "create a world image convincing enough to support the collective and the individual sense of identity" (p. 22). In the present chapter, our understanding of Weltanschauung follows the conventional usage, although to differentiate a "worldview" from the more common "attitude," we append to it the specification of Jung (1948, p. 144) that a Weltanschauung is a consciously formulated attempt on the part of the individual to make clear "why and to what purpose he behaves and lives as he does." An ideology, by contrast, while certainly containing an attitude toward the world, may remain largely hidden from the individual and, as such, would not be identical with the consciously formulated Weltanschauung. The social psychology of age relations becomes then an inquiry into the relationship between personality and social structure.

To illustrate this point, let us consider one aspect of the relationship between generations, one that is continually reinforced both in the research reports of social gerontologists and by our own observations as participants in local provinces of what we know as everyday social life. The aspect I refer to here is the tendency for social interaction to assume different forms depending upon the ages of the particular actors involved. The conversation is different, both in its *structure* (who speaks when and for how long), its *content* (the topics "chosen" to be attended to), and its *style* (ranging from an attitude of familiarity among the actors to one of formality). Social interaction among age unequals resembles, in fact, those situations in which the status characteristics of either sex, class, or race differentiate the participants.

Irrespective of the reasons for such patterning of social interaction (a subject to which I will return later in this chapter), the existence of such patterns has extremely important social psychological effects and implications. We tend to prefer interaction among status equals in that we feel more comfortable in the presence of similar others than we do with dissimilar others. This preference is reproduced in our social institutions that operate in circular fashion to reinforce and legitimate the "preference" by ascribing to it the coercive power of a social norm. The net effect of the institutional reinforcement of individual preference (or, as one may wish to argue in many instances, the net effect of institutional *production* of preference) is a lack of firsthand information concerning those not sharing similar status characteristics. Lacking opportunities for social intercourse, we become more likely to attribute to those of different ages than ourselves stereotypical and usually unflattering characteristics. From the research on prejudice and status generalization, we know, for example, that social interaction, especially the type of interaction in which the situated prestige of the actors is similar, is associated with lower levels of negative attributions of outgroup members.

Archibald (1976) has summarized our knowledge of such interactional patterns with the following three propositions: (1) *the detachment generalization*—"the tendency for persons of different classes, status and powers to avoid each other" (p. 820); (2) *the means-end generalization*—the tendency for status-differentiated social actors to interact "on a narrow, role-specific basis rather than a personal basis" and, by so doing, to *"use* each other" (p. 820); and (3) *the feelings generalization*—"An element of hostility underlies much and perhaps most interaction between 'unequals' and occasionally rebellion occurs" (p. 821). Given such tendencies inherent in unequal social exchange, it is not surprising that *avoidance* becomes a common self-protective strategy. However, since complete avoidance is neither possible nor desired, other mechanisms exist to ensure that the inevitable social encounters among status unequals are at least predictable. Actors involved in such exchange, according to Archibald (1976, p. 822), "try to restrict the . . . cross-position activity to highly circumscribed roles" and also tend to "adhere closely to the prerogatives these roles give to the privileged"

These generalizations are relevant in the present context because equal-status contact among people of different ages who are not related as family members is almost nonexistent. Middle-aged people anticipate deference from the young and usually receive it, as the norm prescribing deference to elders is supported by very salient differences in economic power between the two generations. The accordance of deference to old people by younger age groups, however, is much less certain, as, unlike the previous instance, the normative behavior favoring age and experience lacks consistent and reliable support in the form of economic advantage. *The eventual outcome is a disinclination toward cross-age social interaction.* Such interaction lacks sufficient potential for social rewards to induce the younger person to initiate the exchange. For the old person, the exchange would be too costly, because in mose cases the relationship would be governed by both the rules (the norm of reciprocity, for example) and the grammar of the younger culture (Dowd, 1980). Such interaction requires, in effect, a boundary crossing for the older actor (Anderson & Davis, 1981).

Considered along with the externally imposed factors that encourage age segregation, primary among which are the social constraints that limit the labor market participation of old workers, the greater potential for social profit inherent in same-age social interaction creates a "preference" for the "normal" patterns of age-homogeneous social interaction.

Reluctance to cross age boundaries in the search for satisfying primary relationships has its source, then, in the basic human preference for equal-status interaction *and* in the rational calculation of the lesser profit to be gained in the alternative behavioral option of *unequal* status contact. It seems likely as well, and this is a point of central importance to the current chapter, that such reluctance is rooted also in our irrational fear of those human traits or characteristics that *differentiate* individuals from one another. We have become victims of what Richard Sennett has called an ideal "purified identity." This purification constitutes a refusal to disturb the security of the self by exposing it to contact with the ambiguous "otherness" of different ethnic, age, economic, or cultural groups. The attempt to maintain one's purified identity, an attempt that has come to mark the history of the post-war years, is seen as one of the new possibilities for "self-imposed tyranny" opened up in our modern "communities of affluence" (Sennett, 1970, p. xvi).

Although the focus of Sennett's analysis is the influence of city life on personality, his argument retains considerable vitality in the present discussion of age relations. The generations are indeed separate, and with this separation mutual attributions of strangeness and feelings of social distance have ineluctably followed. Because of their economic marginality and social remoteness, the aged have become strangers to us. Their position as strangers is, however, neither universal nor routine. Rather, it is an unprecedented development, one of the problems "which no society before the twentieth century has had to try to solve" (Gorer, 1966, p. 151). Before leaving this point, it should be emphasized that the present focus on the aged is not meant to suggest that they are the only group to experience loss when the generations separate from one another. When the aged are made marginal to labor markets or to other means of social participation, youth is cut off from firsthand, immediate experience of *tradition*. Societies, as Shils argues so well, are temporally constituted. They exist only through time. As the conduit through which our past is channeled to the present, the aged are of critical importance to society, at least to the one that wishes to remember its past. It is for this reason, then, that "to be cut off from the past of one's society is as disordering to the individual and to the society as being cut off in the present" (Shils, 1981, p. 327). Lacking opportunity for routinized social contact and lacking as well any common basis with which to enrich the contact, the generations in modern capitalism have come to misapprehend the needs and values of one another.

Older generations in the present epoch might thus be considered as immigrants in time and as strangers in their own land. They are strangers not only because, as Mead has told us, the world has changed so significantly it is no longer a world that is recognizable to the aged or one in which they feel "at home." The aged are strangers also because they appear as such to others. The physical features of the older person include stooped posture, wrinkled skin, and a gait that is slow, as well as gray hair and a style of dress that is itself "aged" in appearance. The reduction in physical mobility and agility not only disables old people in social interaction but also has been found to contribute to their social isolation and segregation (Bromley, 1978). Of course, these are the same physical characteristics that have contributed to the exclusion of the aged in *most* known societies. However, the strangeness of the aged in traditional societies is attributed largely to their wizened and "sacred" appearance (and is therefore limited to the physical sphere); under capitalism it transcends the merely physical and enters the ideological realm as well. The aged are "old-fashioned" and cling to antiquated cultural preferences in music, entertainment, and patterns of speech. They participate much less fully in contemporary cultural experience than younger people. They are less knowledgeable about recently arrived cultural heroes, forms of entertainment, and, in many cases, technological innovations that appear first in the workplace. Of course, the longer memories of old people give them valuable access to antecedent political and cultural events; however, such information, although an important and valuable asset, also serves to confirm in the minds of recent generational members the older person's past-situated social identity. The frequently heard (and hardly novel) complaint that old people are prone to disparage the present in favor of the past may be understood as an acceptable means of expressing this perception of the aged as strangers. Or, in the words of the behavioral psychologist, the old person constitutes "a strange sort of stimulus person" (Bromley, 1978, p. 29).

In this brief sketch, I have tried to argue for a fuller understanding of the aged's status as strangers. It would be an error to see this status simply as a purely structural problem (whereby the mandatory retirement policies of the twentieth century have banished them to the social periphery) *or* as a psychological problem (whereby we fear death and therefore attempt to restrict social interaction with those most vulnerable to illness and death). The aged do appear strange to those integrated into the societal mainstream; however, the dominant cultural beliefs and practices that characterize the mainstream are themselves hardly familiar to those who have long since stopped swimming in those fast-moving waters. At the base of the cultural differentiation of the pre- and post-1920 generations of today's world is a difference in ideology.

Participation in a different historical epoch gives birth to an ideological coloring that one may describe as a "generational Weltanschauung." Apart from the physical, social, and psychological differences that separate the generations and that help to sustain the age-stratified access to labor markets, the ideological difference also serves as a boundary that keeps young and old separate.

The set of beliefs and values that distinguish those "born and bred before World War II" from those born later is manifest in the differences in personality and self-presentation that characterize the various generations. These differences are partially captured in Riesman's enduring typology of *traditional-* , *inner-* , and *other*-directed personalities. The modal *Weltanschauung* of those born prior to 1920 compared to that of those born after 1920 is at once more individualistic (rather than narcissistic) and more collectivistic (rather than one-dimensional). That is, one notices more inner-direction among old people (that is not to be confused with eccentricity or with a lessened compulsion to conform) as well as a greater concern for the welfare of social institutions or groups in which one claims membership. The two ideologies differ as well in the credence given to the idea of necessity or "will." In an essay on the subject of will, Trilling (1979, p. 130) underscores the generational factor:

> Those of us who are old enough to have been brought up in the shadow of the nineteenth century can recall how important the will was once thought to be in the conduct of the personal life, how confidently our parents and teachers pointed to the practical as well as the moral advantages of having

a will of developed strength and discipline. Nothing could be more alien to the contemporary style of rearing and teaching the young. In the nineteenth century the will was a central and controlling topic in psychological and ethical theory—as how could it not be, given an economic system in which the unshakeable resolve of the industrial entrepreneur was of the essence.

Ideological differences such as those contained in the perspectives on "willpower" form the core of the analytical social psychology prescribed by Adorno. They are a critical yet ignored aspect of the interrelationship between age cohorts and, consequently, an important aspect of the perception of the old person as a stranger.

For a helpful starting point in this inquiry into generational ideologies, we turn to Mannheim's (1936) argument concerning the sociology of knowledge, in which these questions have been formally, although not substantively, addressed. Thought, according to Mannheim, is a social construct inasmuch as cultural ideas and the means of assimilating these ideas—namely, language—must be *acquired.* Furthermore, although it is true that the cultural content transmitted during socialization tends to reflect the interest of groups in power, it is also true that socialization is never completely successful. The ideologies that support groups in power rarely go unchallenged. Counterideologies, or utopias, inevitably emerge. This is the nature of the relationship between class location and worldview: Ideas follow class boundaries.

From this it can be seen that change in individual perspective is not only possible but highly probable as result of social mobility. And if one considers not individuals but groups such as social classes, the same principle applies: Change in structural location fosters a change in perspective. Consequently, the more stable the structure (and the less mobile the individual's place in the structure), the more stable will be the ideological superstructure. It is for this reason that the collective ideology associated with a particular social class, in the absence of an extraordinary reordering of the class hierarchy (as that that accompanied the events of 1789 in France), changes only slowly, if at all.

The same is not true of the ideological character of generations and age groups. Unlike the class hierarchy, the age structure is continuously replenished and reconstituted as an outcome of the twin processes of cohort flow and human aging. Change occurs simultaneously in the individual as he or she ages and in the society, as the confluence of events, both natural and manmade, pass from the specious present into the commemorated past. The fits and starts of social change, considered jointly with the more predictable pattern of human development and decline, make perspectival differences across generations a matter of certitude. "It has always been true," Trilling (1955, p. 9) has written, "that a chief reason for the alienation of one generation from another lies in their different understanding of what constitutes the past." Mannheim (1936) has argued, and recent research has documented,[2] that because of the recency of their commitment to a particular worldview, younger cohorts tend to be the carriers of new forms of thought. This is the essence of Mannheim's notion of "fresh contact." Change is ongoing because the flow of cohort succession, which introduces into the adult world new recruits who are neither fully informed of nor fully committed to existing institutional requirements, is similarly ongoing. Once formed in the individual, however, Weltanschauung tends to stabilize over the course of life. This is the social psychological basis of the alleged conservatism and inflexibility of old people. Indeed, one may argue that, as economic differentiation is the basis of class conflict, ideological differentiation is the basis of generational conflict. Wilhelm Reich (1942, p. 18) explains this ideological separation in the following passage:

> The basic traits of the character structures corresponding to a definite historical situation are formed in early childhood, and are far more conservative than the forces of technical production. It results from this that, as time goes on, the psychic structures lag behind the rapid changes of the social conditions from which they derived, and later come into conflict with new forms of life.

In other words, both the effects of history and maturation work toward the ideological parting of the generations. Socialization under changed historical conditions tends to produce in later generations a different orientation toward reality than it did with earlier generations. Reinforcing the development of a generationally specific viewpoint is the tendency toward greater commitment to the generational Weltanschauung as individual members move through the life course.

Reich's analysis is supported by Riesman's study of the evolution of character types in the United States.[3] While the inner-directed type of early capitalism preceded the emergence of the twentieth-century other-directed type, such shifts represent only general patterns. Riesman (1950, pp. 31-32) describes his character types as resembling geological or archeological strata, piled "one on top of the other, with outcroppings of submerged types here and there. A cross section of society at any given time reveals the earlier as well as the later character types, the earlier changed through the pressure of being submerged by the later."

I have attempted to provide thus far an outline of the basic elements to a personality and social structure analysis of generational relationships. Following the productive leads of the age stratification theorists, I have noted that the fact of social change requires change in individual perspective because, as Reich (1942, p. 23) has noted, "Every social order produces in the masses of its members that structure which it needs to achieve its many aims." Furthermore, given that social change is reproduced most significantly in the changed consciousness of the young and that ideological thinking or perspective tends to stabilize with entry into the adult world, I have argued that the resulting ideological separation between the generations is a renewable source of intergenerational stress and strain. An important indicator of the generational disjunction is the effect to which aspects of strangeness are attributed to the aged.

At the beginning of this chapter, I distinguished the meaning of generational Weltanschauung from that of ideology, with conscious reflection being the differentiating factor. It becomes necessary at this point to peel away another related concept, that of national or social character. National character, according to Inkeles and Levinson (1969), refers to "the relatively enduring personality characteristics and patterns that are modal among the adult members of the society." Riesman's (1950) study of *social* character differed in that this earlier study was more narrowly focused on aspects of character in "very imprecisely specified parts of the population" rather than with "a more aggregative statement about personality dispositions in a group or nation." Thus, whereas statements about national character are "based mainly on responses cutting across class and ethnic lines to . . . define a commonly held set of dispositions" (Inkeles, 1979, p. 394), those about social character denote a class-related, differentiated set of dispositions. Each view of the concept of character, however, does suggest a set of characteristics, values, or dispositions that is relatively enduring. The American character, for example, continues to reflect the individualism and instrumental attitude toward nature that were critical to our nineteenth-century development as a modern, industrial democracy.

The concept of Weltanschauung, especially when used as we use it (that is, as a generational property), is more fluid than the notion of character in that coexisting generations may hold different worldviews although sharing a common character structure. Given the continual reshaping of societies and their interrelationships as a result of changing historical circumstances, the viewpoint impressed upon a generation as it "comes of age" may quite possibly differ from those of preceding or succeeding generations. At least, this has been the experience of the generations born in the twentieth century.

To complete this exegesis on group consciousness, one may consider the particular viewpoint of the birth cohort, an aggregate more narrowly defined than the generation. Through the technique of cohort analysis, researchers have attempted to uncover significant statistical differences in, for example, the political attitudes or social opinions of different four- or ten-year cohorts. Adjacent cohorts are believed to differ in their levels of political trust presumably due to their different cohort experiences rather than to their different ages (or the accoutrement accompanying age and longevity). Concerning the source of the shared consciousness of cohort members much less is known but this not insignificant problem is hardly noticed among cohort analysts, whose current practice of defining cohorts is typically arbitrary. It is simply assumed, and then argued, that significant "cohort effects" reflect a differing exposure to social, economic, or historical events.

The concept of generational Weltanschauung, in contrast, is not so regularly or so abruptly affected by the events of the day (those tagged by cohort analysts as "period" effects). The differences in the Weltanschauungen of adjacent generations are more subtle, reflecting a gradual evolutionary process rather than an abrupt discontinuity in viewpoint that one may infer is assumed by the cohort analyst. A major shift in economic mode of production, such as the purported arrival of postindustrial society, would likely be reflected in a changing generational viewpoint. Loewenberg's (1983) analysis of the Nazi youth cohort or Wohl's (1979) investigation of the generation of 1914 are good examples of the intended use in this essay of the generational Weltanschauung concept. Newer ideologies do not emerge suddenly as full-blown theoretical systems in dramatic contrast with the Weltanschauungen held by one's parents or children. Differences in meaning are only noticed after many years of gradual accretion of nuanced distinctions, introduced by slowly evolving historical (that is, social and economic) conditions. Cataclysmic disruptions of the social order, such as the French Revolution, should not necessarily be construed as exceptions to the evolutionary rule, as even revolutions as breathtaking and effectual as those occurring in France in 1789 or in Russia in 1917 blossomed only after a long period of subterranean development. So although it may be true that men make their own history, it is important that one remembers Marx's (1977, p. 10) proviso that "they do not make it just as they please; they do not make it under circumstances chosen by themselves, but under circumstances directly encountered, given and transmitted from the past." In his critique of Sennett's (1977) argument concerning the displacement of a public identity by one of narcissism, Abrams (1982, p. 260) notes that, although the change seems undeniable, it nonetheless "has been brought about piecemeal; there are no sudden discontinuities in the face of calamitous events but a prolonged, always exploratory, increasingly affirmed move away from the involvement of individuality in the public domain. As it proceeds the consequences for identity are slowly revealed. At some late point it becomes clear that a new type of individual exists."

In the next several sections, I will discuss the specific structural changes that have taken place in the postwar era, which has produced requirements for a changed character structure or Weltanschauung in its citizenry. Following this, a discussion of the specific generational differences in worldview will be presented.

THE IDEOLOGICAL CONSEQUENCES OF LATE CAPITALISM

The twentieth century has brought to Western societies revolutionary changes in their economic structure and demographic composition. Life as experienced by the citizenry of the modern world has new requirements, pleasures, and problems. The prospect of nuclear war, the increased crime and despotism, the massive size of social institutions that breed a sense of powerlessness, the burgeoning of social welfare programs, and the lessened grip of the ascribed status attributes of race and sex each characterize the present age and contribute, some would argue, to the spirit or morality of our times (e.g., Quinton, 1983). The decisive break from the past generally is agreed to have occurred during the liminal period extending from the end of the Civil War to the 1920s. It was during this period that the conflict between the mercantile classes of the North and the landed aristocracy of the South was settled in favor of the industrial North; the transition from competitive capitalism to its later, oligopolistic form was well under way; the United States fatefully entered as an active participant the military disputes of European nations; Freud uncovered the unconscious; and, most important to some (Johnson, 1983), relativity (as embedded in Einstein's new theory of the universe) was confirmed. The public, however, mistakenly confused relativity with relativism, and, by so doing, "formed a knife, inadvertently wielded by ... [Einstein], to help cut society adrift from its traditional moorings in the faith and morals of Judeo-Christian culture" (Johnson, 1983, p. 5).

Later decades brought their own changes that further contributed to what we now understand as "modernity" or the modern personality. The continued expansion of government services in the twentieth century, especially at the federal level, and the shifting proportion of workers employed in tertiary (or service) industries vis-à-vis the production and manufacturing sectors changed the nature of work and the personality attributes required of workers significantly. To manage the technological requirements and administrative functions of the new bureaucracies, a new class of industrial and academic scientists and planners began to exert a primary influence on the creation of social policy. The growth of this new administrative class accelerated in the post-World War II period. Bell (1973, p. 130) has argued that the great divide between the service and production labor markets began in 1947: "At that time the employment was evenly balanced. From 1947 to 1968 there was a growth of about 60 percent in employment in services, while employment in the goods-producing industries increased less than 10 percent." This shift from business entrepreneur to white-collar employee, along with the decline of the "free farmer," has been described by Mills (1946, p. 437) as the "master occupational change of twentieth-century social structure." This change prompted the Census Bureau in 1950 to introduce the new category of "service workers" as distinguished from unskilled operatives and laborers (Gonos, 1980). The technical and presumably disinterested intelligence of this group has served to sustain its position of influence by providing the necessary "objective" legitimation of social and economic policy decisions. To some observers, however, the intrusion of the ascending class of social engineers into the political institution has had anything but salutary consequences. The potential for more durable family relationships brought by the remarkable decline in human mortality since 1900 has been "negated by rising divorce rates and by deterioration of the parent-child relationship" (Davis, 1979, p. 63). Family breakdown in the past several decades is manifest in the withdrawal of financial support and emotional nurturance from aged family members, and increased rates of both infanticide and child and elder abuse generally. Bronfenbrenner (1974, p. 57) has traced the origins of alienation in the modern world to such family breakdown. To some observers, the dissolution of traditional family forms is the result of the extension of the influence of the ascending class of social engineers into the heretofore private realm of family life. Lasch (1977, p. 18), for example, has argued that "with the rise of the 'helping professions' in the first three decades of the twentieth century, society in the guise of a 'nurturing mother' invaded the family, the stronghold of . . . private rights, and took over many of its functions."[4]

Perhaps most important of all the changes that occurred during the present century has been the demographic revolution within the industrial world. The decline in mortality and fertility rates has created a population age structure in which, by 1980, over 11% were at least 65 years of age. Some demographers believe that the increases in longevity will continue as a function of a developing medical technology that would "alter the genetic constitution of man so as to reduce or banish the aging process" (Davis, 1979, p. 41). Death would come from accidents or violence rather than from chronic disease. The average age of life, predicts Kingsley Davis, "might be 100, or 150."

Considering only the economic and policy developments of the "welfare state" since the 1930s, apart from the attendant rise of the bureaucratic ethos and the new class of social engineers, it is certain that the twentieth century has proved beneficent for old people. Levels of social and financial support for the aged have increased and, with them, the floor marking minimum tolerable limits of human deprivation. The statistics are indeed impressive. From 1960 to 1982, social security (OASDHI) cash benefit payments increased from $10.8 billion (or $727 per person) to $201.2 billion (or $5655 per person). Although part of this increase is due to the inflation of consumer prices, a large part represents real gains by the aged in terms of the emergence of new programs, higher benefits per recipient under existing programs, and increases in the proportion of the older population eligible for existing programs (Clark & Menefee, 1981.) Furthermore, the huge increase in the social security trust funds since 1960 has not only matched but exceeded by a factor of three the expenditures for public assistance programs such as welfare, food stamps, housing subsidies, student aid, and Medicaid (Harrington, 1976).

Developments in the present century have been a mixed blessing, however, for the aged. We are faced with the paradox that a beneficent social policy emerged at the same time that the prestige and respect accorded the aged began to diminish noticeably. Irrespective of the policy attention paid to them, decisive shifts "both in societal definitions of the elderly's status and in the aged's self-image" occurred following the trends toward bureaucratization that characterized the 1890-1920 period in the United States (Achenbaum & Stearns, 1978, p. 310). The ties of commonality and shared sacrifice that bound together the citizens of earlier periods gradually disappeared or became attenuated with the transition of the economy. The corrosion of sacrifice, it is important to note, "did not originate in the deep recesses of the psyche, but in the excesses of that economy. . . . Advanced capitalism requires a programmed hedonism as much as earlier capitalism needed Calvinism and sacrifice" (Jacoby, 1980, p. 64). Willingness of family members to support an aging parent declined as the aged as a group were devalued in recognition of their economic dependency. Beneficent social policy allowed the aged to reproduce their existence; it did not, however, protect them from the devaluation necessitated by their new "leisured" status. No longer "required by capital or the agencies of capital," older workers became superannuated and "dismissed in derogatory terms such as 'obsolescent,' 'unproductive,' and 'inefficient' " (Walker, 1981, p. 88). The aged have become, in effect, both economically and psychologically useless to generations following them. They are tolerated, Sennett (1977, p. 195) has observed, "only so long as they behave submissively."

In response to their devaluation, the aged have come to be considered "problematic." Advocacy for the aged emerged as an occupational specialty in which younger professionals hewed out careers representing the interests of the aged in the various policy arenas. The aged themselves, of course, organized as well and sought to develop their own political influence. It recently has become evident that the aged are *competitors* against other socially peripheral groups for programs and funds. The current political struggles concerning retirement policy and the funding of public pension plans suggest that the issues of age have yet to be completely resolved. The continuing debate over the appropriate levels of societal support of old people indicates that Achenbaum and Stearns (1978, p. 311) were right when they speculated that "a major watershed in the history of old age has unfolded in the past few decades and shall become more manifest." Indeed it seems likely that intergenerational relationships will become increasingly contentious as the economic status of the middle-class members of the younger aged improves with the elimination of mandatory retirement.

The emerging conflict between the generations is based partly in the ideological differences between these groups, which have been socialized in different historical epochs. The term *ideology* is used here in much the same way as Mannheim intended, namely, as a set of ideas that support the structural position of a particular group in opposition to other groups.[5] The groups in question are not economic groups but generational groups; furthermore, the ideology is *consciously* shared by age-group members, although Engels's argument that the impelling motives for ideology remain unknown to the thinker is no doubt correct. Thus, rather than the present witnessing the end of ideology, we have entered a period of heightened generational consciousness, an *age* of ideology. Because of the intercorrelation of age with such important status attributes as income, occupation, gender, and race, there does not exist a single doctrine or issue that defines the generations or marks the temporal boundaries of the contemporary age of ideology. Instead, as Feuer (1975, p. 85) has argued, the age we are in

> abounds in movements, circles, and societies. . . . [It] has its roots in a pervasive generational disaffection. An ideological period therefore overflows with eccentric doctrines and panaceas; youthful sects propagandize their doctrines for the rescue of society through special clothes, foods, personal habits; new faces, new gestures, new speech are advocated. The spirit of rejection of the old diffuses through society.

While Feuer is correct in his observations concerning "pervasive generational disaffection" and "the spirit of rejection of the old," his analysis is incomplete. He recognizes the ideological content in the behavior and attitudes of the young but not those of the old. He implies, in fact, that the aged retain a certain moral superiority vis-à-vis more recent generations even though in terms of social prestige and influence they are certainly inferior. The analysis here differs from that of Feuer on two important points: (1) the aged do have economic and social interests and these interests *are* reflected in historically peculiar Weltanschauungen; and (2) as ideologies reflect social, economic, and historical location, attributions of moral superiority to a particular ideological view reflect personal values rather than a sociological judgment.

In those nonindustrialized societies in which change is slow and consensus on basic values is pervasive, generational Weltanschauungen are less distinct and indeed may not even exist. Because of the homogeneous nature of such systems (their "mechanical" solidarity), the conditions that produce different perceptions of social reality among coexisting generations are not present as they would be in more differentiated societies. Consequently, the elders of *Gemeinschaften* may be successful in socializing the youth of these societies to the traditional value systems that directly benefit the aged. Such values may not be understood by either the young or the old as serving the interests of one group over another. The aged represent the past. Their voice is not simply that of a particular generation but the collective voice of the group's past. Because the aged come from the past yet exist in the present, they carry with them the aura (and derivative influence) of tradition. Shils notes that when the older person legitimates his preference in some matter by saying, "It has always been done that way among us" or "Our forefathers always believed this to be true," the legitimation is explicitly grounded in tradition. Yet there are many other instances in which "they need not offer such legitimation, and the simple fact that they are older than those to whom they proffer the model makes them representative of an ill-defined pastness" (Shils, 1975, p. 189).[6]

The efficacy of tradition as a source of behavioral legitimation has lessened in the twentieth century as technological solutions to everyday problems have proved more reliable. Yet, in the ideological sphere of beliefs, values, and outlook, tradition remains a vigorous source of legitimacy for the aged. The content of the traditional ideology of the aged is, essentially, the idealized images of the American Gemeinschaft: "Keep your promises. Do your job, especially if others depend on it. Look after those whom you are responsible for. Mind your own business, unless asked to help. Don't hurt people unnecessarily. At least listen to those in authority over you. Tell the truth. Above all, think about the consequences of what you do" (Homans, 1982, p. 241). In his essay on traditional values, Shils (1975, p. 197) identified a similar core set of traditional values, including "beliefs in the virtue of authority, of respect for age and the rightful allocation of the highest authority to the aged.... Beliefs in the value of the lineage and the kinship group and in the primacy of obligations set by membership in these groups."

Such beliefs and values are ideological in that the aged, especially the working-class aged, have a particular interest in the maintenance of cross-generational family ties. Such bonds are an important source of aid and nurturance in the daily rounds of everyday life; they are also a valuable source of prestige in the stratification hierarchy of the older person's friendship network. Consequently, the continued viability of norms and values that prescribe selfless caring for an aged parent would tend to benefit old people, even if only to allay fears of institutionalization. For younger generations, however, traditional beliefs, such as the according of deference to the aged, are incompatible with the aged's marginal economic position and the felt need of youth for independence.

In this ideological struggle, the aged must—of necessity—lose. If we view the generations in terms of Shils's distinction between centers and peripheries, peripheral generations (such as the very young, but also the retired old) must be incorporated within the center. Peripheral cultures may resist but they are incapable "under most conditions of modern central government to refuse all permeative influence. The expansion of centers into peripheries results in the modification of the substantive content of traditional beliefs" (Shils, 1975, p. 213). Time is the difference. It is a resource that favors the young and allows them an intangible asset in their exchange relationships with the aged. Consequently, the ideological differences between the generations are rarely accentuated or explicitly stated as such. Such a confrontation would be unnecessarily divisive, given that in the existing ideological war of attrition, the outcome is a *fait accompli*. Recognizing this, the differences in perspective or ideology between generations tend not to be recognized or, if they are, they are regarded with humor, sarcasm, indifference, or silence. On certain occasions, however, generational ideology becomes a salient issue (although even on these occasions, the divisive potential of the ideological difference has been minimal, in part because the actors involved seem to understand that such occasions are indeed exceptions to the routine order of things). Such occasions include elections. During an election, ideologies lurch into public consciousness from their normally tacit state, and skirmishes in the battle between the generations cannot be suppressed. The aged, in Riesman's analysis (1967), feel themselves to be the "displaced persons of contemporary America" who use elections as a form of political resistance. Riesman (1967, pp. 43-44) sees it this way:

> Raised in an era when saving was admired, when Prohibition was preached if not practiced, and when inhibition appeared associated with ascent, the elderly find themselves in a society where the mass media deride such attitudes as old-fashioned and square. . . . The rejected are seldom able to unite on a program vis-à-vis an America that seems to be moving too far and too fast away from them; instead, whether in turning down the fluoridation of water or voting against an issue of school bonds, they express resentment through symbolic gestures of negation.

How did the aged come to feel displaced? And is their commitment to a traditionalist ideology a result of their displaced social status? Although a sense of displacement may be attributable to the specific economic and social developments that began during the critical 1890-1920 period and that continued during the post-World War II period of economic expansion and technological discovery, such obvious economic causes should not blind us to the possible existence of other factors as well. Although norms, beliefs, and ideology do tend to flow from a group's position in the economic structure, the aged's socioeconomic location is relevant but secondary in this regard. One would expect the aged, as a peripheral social aggregate, to hold a nontraditional view of the world. That is, according to Shils's (1975, p. 213) highly regarded analysis, it is the *center*, that is, the rulers, who "are usually more insistent—in their promulgation, recommendation, and exemplification of traditional beliefs—on the observance of traditional norms of the center than are the peripheries, the 'rank and file,' the laity, the working classes, the poor."

The aged contradict these observations, but only if the temporal location of ideological thought is disregarded. Unlike the working class, whose "consciousness" flows from (and is made possible by) their relatively unchanging economic position, the ideological position of the aged must be understood in terms of their earlier location of much closer proximity to the various institutional centers. Their collective movement to the periphery in consequence of their growing old (a generational diaspora) is too recent, and for most too short-lived, to change their traditionalist Weltanschauung significantly.

The movement away from traditional ideology is associated with the end of the nineteenth century and the emergence of modern capitalism in the West. It was during this period of rapid social change that the social and behavioral sciences began to focus on the "abilities" of people to work and produce in the emerging industrial age. This focus required that these abilities be measured in order to be able to gauge the impact of those remedies introduced to render human effort more suitable to the machines people would be attending. Psychologists' fascination with intelligence scores or the interest of personnel managers in industry with time and motion research exemplify the positivistic, enlightened rationalism characteristic of the science of this era. Traditional folk wisdom and other extant elements of the prescientific nineteenth-century culture became suspect for their irrationality. The romantic and traditional ideals of the Gemeinschaft period could not survive the transition to bureaucratic rationality. Television has become "a new folk culture" that confronts and gradually displaces "the wisdom of the old folk culture" (Langman & Kaplan, 1981, p. 107). The "call to heroic virtues," according to Gruman (1978, p. 368) "was supplemented by a vast elaboration of neo-positivistic methods for standardizing human aptitude and traits." As the machine came to embody rationality and efficiency, "individual rationality has developed into efficient compliance" (Marcuse, 1978, p. 144). That is, to get the machine to work, we must follow its instructions. The "mechanics of conformity" spill over from the technological into the social order, rendering irrational any resistance to prevailing modes of thought. The aged were not unaffected by this shifting perception of reality and accompanying efforts to array the population from high to low, good to bad, useful to useless, and so on. What was to come from our need to measure were "such stigmatizing categories as the moron, the 4-F, the odd size and, of course, the 'old fogeys' of sixty-five" (Gruman, 1978, p. 368).[7]

The loss of the intimate connections between the moral and the economic order constitutes, as Habermas has argued, a legitimation crisis. As the nature of the economic substructure changes, its requirements for legitimation in superstructural institutions also must change. In the case under consideration, positivistic science and bureaucratic rationality evolved as elements in the ideological legitimation of oligopolistic capitalism. The traditional legitimacy, "based on a *moral* system of reward rooted in the Protestant sanctification of work" (Bell, 1976, p. 84), persisted, however, in the character and personality of those generations socialized to its virtues. In contrast, the more recent cohorts (that is, those born after 1925) have been raised in a different era, socialized to a different culture, and possess in consequence a different social personality or character. Today's family uses *reason* as a predominant socialization device. This fosters in children "the inculcation of instrumental rationality as a dominating principle" (Langman & Kaplan, 1981, p. 101). Recognizing that socialization produces in the individual a motivational structure "on which the prevailing mode of production is psychologically based" (Dreitzel, 1977, p. 93), the modern family strives to train the child to value self-control over spontaneity and affectivity. The result is a character that is hedonistic, self-conscious, and "modern." It is the personality of the "self-monitor," the manipulative manager of impressions seen in Goffman's dramas of everyday life.[8] It is the personality created, in short, by the culture of narcissism.

The ideological differentiation between older and younger cohorts is made more interesting (that is, more sociologically interesting) by the incongruous fact that it is the older, "descending" generations who espouse an ideology that, when juxtaposed with the technically rational point of view, appears to hold greater relevance for the projected future economic needs of Western societies. The Weltanschauungen of more recent cohorts, in contrast, seem best suited for those societies and historical epochs characterized by economic expansion and surplus. While this is precisely the type of economy that produced the narcissistic self-consciousness of contemporary society, it is not—in the judgments of many contemporary economists—the type of economy one can anticipate for the remainder of this century and the beginning of next. It is for this reason that the theory of alternate generations is applicable in this instance: The old and the young share much in common ideologically that is in joint contradistinction to the views of the middle aged. It is the culture of the middle aged that currently is experiencing self-doubt. The aged, like other strangers, may look upon this culture with a fresh perspective and thus help us to know those aspects of it that may not travel well as we pass into the next century. The continual shortages of energy, "rising unemployment, runaway inflation, and the decline of western colonialism have undermined the economic foundations of hedonistic self-expression" (Lasch, 1979).

The reliance on the technical knowledge of natural scientists spilled over to include the "expertise" of social planners, human relations experts, and, of course, social scientists. The patterned regularities of the physical world were presumed to have their analogues in the social world. And the social engineers, basking in the reflected glory of medical researchers, physicists, and astronomers, were presumed able to generate disinterested, feasible, "objective" solutions to the social problems becoming visible at the time. The wishes of Mannheim and others to the contrary notwithstanding, we know now that the possibility of a class of value-free and free-floating intellectuals is very remote. This is true in both capitalist (Bell, 1973) and socialist societies (Konrád & Szelényi, 1979).

Social engineering (or social pathology, as some know it) grew as an occupational specialty with the growth in the number and size of government agencies in the 1930s.[9] Specialists within this growing group were the intermediating force that translated the cultural requirements of the late capitalistic era (namely, an appetite for new products and the acceptance of alienating work) into the individualistic needs and preferences that formed the modern social character. It was the group of social pathologists, according to Lasch (1977, p. 102), who "played a leading role in undermining Protestant individualism, rural values, and the old-style family." Lasch continues:

> They promoted a "democratic" conception of domestic life, advocated permissive child rearing, defended the rights of women, attacked sexual repression and censorship, and sought to make the members of the family . . . more adept, in short, in the art of interpersonal relations. . . . [This] ideology, rather than harking back to the past, anticipated the needs of a

society based not on hard work but on consumption, the search for
personal fulfillment, and the management of interpersonal relations.
(p. 102)

I do not intend to argue here (and neither does Lasch) that the search
for personal fulfillment (suggested neatly in one or another of the
various forms of the contemporary judgment that one has a *right* to
personal happiness) is the cause of our current social malaise and
cultural crisis. Both the ideological and behavioral aspects of the culture
of narcissism are a *product* of specific historical and economic
developments and not a cause. This can be seen better, perhaps, by
focusing on specific components of the modern ideology. We may
examine, for instance, in the tradition of the sociology of knowledge, the
manner in which intellectual production reflects and legitimates the
existing social and economic order.

An economy based on an endless cycle of growth and destruction
would not only allow but seem to require a nontraditional, individualistic value system. With the passage of time and continued economic
growth, however, the costs of displacing a *social* value system by one
organized around the criterion of personal happiness have been
realized. The outcome of this transition has been alienation, emotional
estrangement, a loss of selfhood, and the diminution of a sense of group
loyalty and collective responsibility.[10] Our crisis in confidence may be
seen in the widespread belief that the self is appropriately understood as
undergoing continual, indeed "endless," development (Lears, 1981,
p. 306). Human development theorists insist, for example, that development continues throughout life as the individual "progresses" through
qualitative stages during which the self is spontaneously reorganized or
transformed (see, for example, Erikson, 1950; Gould, 1978; Levinson,
1978). Adherents to this view, such as Piaget, assume that a general
(universal) theory of cognition is possible. This conception of cognition,
in its disregard of the contention of sociological realism that social
categories affect both the substance and the form of cognition, is
"clearly within the bourgeois, idealist tradition of Immanuel Kant"
(Buck-Morss, 1975, p. 37).

The theory of human development, as part of the intellectual output
of the narcissistic culture of our times, offers an intellectually respectable
legitimation of the present historical moment. With the constant
exception of the work of Klaus Riegel (1973a, 1973b, 1977), one fails to
discern an appreciation of the link between socioeconomic structure and
personality. We read only endless variations on the theme that

individuals have the potential for continual development and, therefore, they have the responsibility as well. The civil amnesia that would result from a society populated by the emancipated individuals whose primary interest is the fulfillment of their own individuality is a *social* problem that is beyond the ken of human development theory.

Underlying the idea of human development are several tacit assumptions concerning human nature and the world in which we live. It presumes, first, that "development" is primarily a function or reflection of individual abilities (an assumption shared by other individualistic theories, like the functionalist theories of stratification and status attainment). Ability to succeed and develop is socially random; in other words, it is undisturbed by the patterning of social institutions along sex, race, or class lines.[11] Second, it assumes that the social world is sufficiently "open" to accommodate individual ability. Therefore, one's placement in an occupational hierarchy, defined by income and control over the labor power of others, is a meaningful indicator of human development. Such assumptions, by identifying occupational success as a reliable measure of adult development (although this blatant materialism would be disavowed by the development theorists themselves), favor the "development" of the appropriate character traits. While capitalism enhances the possibility of self-development through the labor-saving technology it produces, it channels this development along restricted and distorted paths. Those characteristics "that the market can use are rushed (often prematurely) into development and squeezed desperately till there is nothing left; everything else within us, everything nonmarketable, gets draconically repressed, or withers away for lack of use, or never had a chance to come to life at all" (Berman, 1982, p. 96). The theory of personality implicit in the developmental perspective is that self-aggrandizement, profit, personal triumph, and winning constitute the normal and desired course of human activity. Divorce and separation, for example, are considered in the developmental theory of Gould (1978) not as failure but, rather, as "triumphs of love because one partner loves himself enough to risk growth and accept the consequences." Swidler (1980, p. 126) acknowledges that, for Americans, adult commitments are not the fulfillment of the quest for identity but instead represent its defeat.

Finally, the developmental view assumes that the flowering of human abilities and the "growth" of the individual may continue not only into advanced old age but also irrespective of the nature of the social world. Thus the question is never raised concerning how one is to recognize the "developed" social actor should one fall into his or her company.

Although disavowing obviously materialistic criteria, the standard formulation has development tacitly linked with success in human relations if not with success in the economic sphere. We are left with the detritus of a perspective not sufficiently examined. Clearly the developed personalities in the Third Reich would necessitate additional standards for development so as not to confuse them with the upwardly mobile bourgeois technocrats in the service sectors of the postindustrial world. The question not asked is whether human development is even possible in a society that is itself not developed.[12] It appears, at minimum, that democratic political institutions are a prerequisite to human growth on a scale that is sociologically meaningful. This is a firmly established view in the symbolic interactionist tradition of social psychology, clearly present in the writing of John Dewey and others, including many of the writers associated with Frankfurt's Institut für Sozialforschung. Adorno, for example, clearly understood the dangers inherent in psychologized concepts like the "well-integrated" personality. The espousal of an integrated personality is objectionable, he felt, "because it expects the individual to establish an equilibrium between conflicting forces which does not obtain in existing society. . . . His integration would be a false reconciliation with an unreconciled world, and would presumably amount in the last analysis to an 'identification with the aggressor,' a mere character-mark of subordination" (Adorno, 1967-1968). Developmental theory's inattention to this issue helps to illuminate the ideological bias with which it is laden: It constitutes a pseudoscientific rationale for the present preoccupation with the individual needs and feelings of those making their own bourgeois version of the "long march" through the institutions.

THE SOCIAL CHARACTER OF OUR TIMES

The aged are strangers in the modern world primarily because their traditional beliefs are foreign in a world that cultivates "psychologized" personalities and an ideology of bourgeois self-aggrandizement. In this section, I shall review some pertinent work on character and social personality in order to convey an image of the type of character structure that is common in the Western world, especially among those born after 1920.

Characteristics of the modern personality include the following: (1) an intense awareness of and concern with psychological motives and the mental states presumed to cause behavior; (2) a need to disclose information about "true" feelings toward others and the current state of one's own psychological condition (see Sennett, 1977a); (3) a lack of inner-directedness; (4) a lack of spontaneity and a corresponding concern with projecting the appropriate impression or image of the self; and (5) a presumption that what one wants or needs for the continuance of one's own public self is in the public interest. This last characteristic is similar to the infant's learning of language and the corresponding acquisition of social motives that displaces the egocentric world view of the "in-fans" (one without language).

The documentation of the existence of this modern personality began to appear as early as 1947, suggesting that the structural and cultural changes in the immediate postwar period favored (if not actually caused) the modern personality type. Fromm's (1947, p. 67) "marketing personality type," one among several *nonproductive orientations*, emerged as a dominant form "only in the modern era." The marketing orientation describes a personality that is rooted in the *market*, and in the transmogrification of the personality into a commodity under the market system. The experience of oneself as a commodity, which lies at the core of the marketing orientation, is only a short step away from the emergence of social relations that are primarily exchange relations: "The way one experiences others is not different from the way one experiences oneself. Others are experienced as commodities like oneself; they too do not present *themselves* but their salable part. The difference between people is reduced to a merely quantitative difference of being *more or less* successful, attractive, hence valuable" (Fromm, 1947, p. 73).

The result for the individual psyche of the continuous requirement of making the correct impression is a certain amount of nervousness. We cannot rely upon ourselves or any internalized sense of adequacy because what we "produce" in the postwar economy is an image of ourselves as likeable people. Consequently, the standard of success in the evaluation of how well the commodity is packaged lies in the reaction of other people. Self-esteem, Fromm (1947, p. 72) points out, "depends on conditions beyond his control. If he is successful, he is valuable; if he is not, he is worthless . . . with ever-changing conditions, one's self-esteem is bound to be shaky and in constant need of confirmation by others."

Such observations are highly consistent with Riesman's well-known "other-directed" personality type and with the assessments of others as well.[13] Gehlen, for example, noted in the 1950s that "everywhere we observe a need to validate one's worth" (1980, p. 86). Inevitably, those living under such conditions become acutely sensitive to the human relations aspect of success and consequently develop a finely tuned psychological awareness. "If Johnny throws a spit-ball at Mary," Seeley (1967, p. 15) writes, "nothing so ordinary as 'mischief' is afoot. The possibilities have to be (are joyously) entertained that Johnny is 'working off aggression,' compensating for deeply felt 'inferiority,' asserting his 'masculinity' in ways appropriate to his 'developmental stage'" and so on. The later concern with the adult's "mental health" is a predictable corollary of this psychological awareness.

Growth, *development*, and *maturity*—sequentially ordered in a series of stages loosely corresponding to biological age—are terms that have entered the popular consciousness through their diffusion in magazines and other media. Presented as part of a normative schedule aimed at psychological well-being, they have provided an additional motive for anxiety and self-scrutiny. In Lasch's (1979, p. 49) view, the therapeutic ideology of developmental stages has promoted "a view of life as an obstacle course: the aim is simply to get through the course with a minimum of trouble and pain."

Maneuvering through the life course *on time* and in step with one's cohort, if not a little ahead, is greatly aided by the ability to perceive the psychological reactions of other social actors to one's public performance and to control the interaction by a correct anticipation of their reactions. The ability to do just this has been found to be correlated with class background and leadership abilities. The manipulative, highly self-conscious use of such so-called *self-monitoring processes* is justified by the determinedly sophisticated belief that "in the theater of life, appearances and outward images often are more important than reality itself" (Snyder, 1979, p. 86). Failing to appreciate the critical nature of Goffman's seminal work on self-presentation, the self-monitoring theorists propose the management of impressions to be a "basic fact of social life." Laboring in the personality markets of the modern world, in which the self is a commodity to be bought and sold, is taken for granted. Self-aggrandizement, far from being neurotic, is but one of several tactical options open to the guerrilla fighter in the theater of interpersonal relations. The interesting use of language in Snyder's (1979) definitive description of high and low self-monitors deserves careful scrutiny. The prototype of the high self-monitor is one who

> out of a concern for the situational and interpersonal appropriateness of his or her social behavior, is particularly sensitive to the expression of

self-presentation of relevant others in social situations and uses these cues as guidelines for monitoring (that is, regulating and controlling) his or her own verbal and nonverbal self-presentation. (p. 89)

The self-monitor is not, in other words, the ingratiating sycophant who deals with others only insofar as they are useful, only inasmuch as is necessary. Rather this person is "sensitive," a sensitivity born no doubt of a concern for "situational and interpersonal appropriateness." In comparison with the social asset that is the high self-monitor, the low self-monitor is presented as overprincipled to an unseemly degree, too unyielding for his or her own good: "Low-self-monitoring individuals seem to cherish images of themselves as rather principled individuals who wish to live their lives according to the maxim 'believing means doing.' They claim to value congruence between 'who they are' and 'what they do'" (Snyder, 1979, p. 101). Snyder apparently is unwilling to accept the "performance" of the low self-monitors as suggesting inner direction; rather his assumption that self-monitoring is a "basic fact of social life" forces him to characterize the *low* self-monitors as merely *claiming* to be such or *seeming* to act in such a way. From this modernized perspective, there is no possibility of spontaneous behavior or behavior guided by any principle other than self-aggrandizement.

While sharing common ground with the earlier typology of Riesman, the self-monitoring distinction moves us onto new terrain, the contested ground of social psychology in the final quarter of the twentieth century. Riesman was correct in his description of the other-directed personality type as "the typical character of the 'new' middle class" (1950, p. 20), but the narcissistic aspects of this personality were, in the early years after World War II, barely, if at all, visible. Indeed, there is a quality of pathos in Riesman's (1973, p. xxxii) characterization of the other-directed: This is a person who "wants to be loved rather than esteemed; . . . [who] wants not to gull or impress, let alone oppress, others but, in the current phrase, to relate to them."

GENERATIONS AND SOCIAL CHARACTER

In all of the discussion thus far, I have attempted to show how both ideology and social character become changed with the passage of historical events. Often the change is slow, reflecting the insidious evolution of culture as a product of cohort flow. Occasionally, however, the change is paced much faster as the impacts of extraordinary events mark clear differences between age groups resulting from their relative entry into the flow of history. Riesman (1973, p. 169) observed, for example, that the aged in a certain town in Vermont seemed to him heavily inner-directed while the younger generation was "becoming increasingly other-directed."

Whether this generational explanation of the difference in character structure between age groups is accurate, in the sense of illustrating a general pattern of the way in which the flow of cohorts affects the ideational content of culture, cannot be assessed beyond argument at this time. Certainly one may contend that human aging involves a "natural" shift from other- to inner-direction, or from high to low self-monitoring. It is more likely, however, given the irrefutable facts of twentieth-century history, that social character, in its reflection of these facts, would be presented to us in the form of generational differences. Carroll's (1977) assessment of the puritan, paranoid, and remissive social types supports the generational Weltanschauung argument. What Carroll calls "puritan" culture is believed to have attained its maturity in Europe prior to World War I. One of its great achievements, most notably in the United States, was its ability to socialize the young to a "sense of civic duty, of selfless and thoughtful work for the community, or the nation" (Carroll, 1977, p. 31). In contrast, the morality of the remissive type (predominant in the modern industrial world) is sexually hedonistic and hostile to the past. Carroll (1977, p. 50) repeats a theme that is no doubt by now quite familiar: "The industrial state is tooled up to service a culture that operates according to a first principle of rapid change. And remissive man prefers it so: without change in his environment, in his commodities, in his acquaintances, he is quickly bored."

The amoralism of high technology and the self-absorption of those socialized in the postwar epoch make it difficult to understand how a return to the values described here and elsewhere as traditional could be effected. The loathing of old age that is part of our narcissistic culture (Lasch, 1979) perhaps will be tempered as the narcissistic types themselves reach old age. Even this change, however, could only produce a relatively minor personality change in the future aged unless significant change in the culture itself were forthcoming. Given what we know of the direction of social change from Gemeinschaft to Gesellschaft (and not the reverse), future cultural change seems likely to reinforce rather than to redirect this trend.

In the present cultural situation, social attraction and personal social worth are a function of the exchange value of one's personality and individual status characteristics. Even the primary relationships that exist within the family are not immune to the application of the exchange principle. Unless we can commodify a relationship, it is seen to be a threat. The bourgeoisie uses the criterion of economic profit "to prune its own family. . . . All relations are appraised with an eye on the psychic bank account; spending must balance earnings. Consequently the family contracts, eliminating the old and other kin. Requiring more care and attention than they can return, they are herded off to the State agencies and institutions. Psychic bankruptcy is avoided by retrenching, cutting off losing investments: the old, children, the sick, and so on" (Jacoby, 1980, pp. 63-64). In such a culture, old age inspires not love but apprehension (Lasch, 1979). Biological senescence marks both the beginning of the decline toward death and the diminution of social standing. As workers in a capitalist economy, our use value is determined by our exchange value; we are commodities to be sold on the market. Because our success in the personality markets of the present age is a function of our sexual attractiveness, the deterioration of beauty with age undermines the aging person's ability to maintain, if not to increase, his or her value. To compensate for the natural losses in youthful beauty and vitality, the aged may attempt to disguise the physical signs of deterioration. The appearance of age, however, cannot be disguised indefinitely and the fear of growing old is eventually realized. After a lifetime of unconscious internalization of the capitalist ideology of work and value, the aged's idleness renders them superfluous. The result for the narcissist is terror of the aging process. The narcissist's compulsion to be youthful disallows any satisfaction from the thought of growing old. The narcissist understands there to be no wisdom to be gained by aging, only deterioration; he knows that the young will grant him neither deference nor respect, only indifference. And so there is no profit to be gained in the "traditional consolations of old age, the most important of which is the belief that future generations will in some sense carry on his life's work" (Lasch, 1979, p. 210).

The usual strategy for "development" chosen by the middle-aged narcissist is to deny aging as long as possible. Looking young becomes an obsession and making way for new generations becomes unthinkable. The demands of the middle-class "young-old" that they be dissociated in both public perception and public policy from the very old contain an element of narcissism. Hudson (1978) was correct when he noted that the "growing group of economically secure, healthy 'young-old' people will be much more visible to the public at large than will be the smaller group of economically insecure and usually unhealthy 'old-old.'" This is precisely their aim. Through their political influence, the new-old hope to ensure their full participation in societal institutions by elimination of unfavorable restrictions on their participation, such as an arbitrary retirement age. That such an elimination would probably also require a rise in the eligibility age for receipt of social security (and thus would weaken further the socioeconomic status of the working-class members of the young-old) has not deterred the movement against presumably "age-ist" policies such as mandatory retirement.

The intensity of intergenerational conflict varies in direct proportion to the viability of the economy. Beneficent social policies are more likely during periods of increased plenitude and reduced scarcity (Gouldner, 1973). Conversely, the ideological differences between the generations show increase as the economy falters. As the young-old attempt to retain their positions of influence and to delay the ordinary timing of generational succession, the intensity of feeling between the generations will grow more heated. A recent letter to the *New York Times* illustrates this point well. The writer, a young lawyer working as a taxi driver and unable to find employment as an attorney, states he feels "a growing anger and resentment toward anybody 50 years old or older." In his mind, the older generation has had it too good for too long; it is time they stepped aside:

> I am jealous of the 30 years of unlimited prosperity they took for granted.... I'm livid at the virtual unlimited opportunity they enjoyed ... but most of all, I resent the denial of the full use of my talents and the perpetuation of the American dream for a generation that has reaped the benefits for so long! (Olin, 1978).

Such views as expressed in this letter, however misguided, point to the salience of age and generation in the popular view and the inherent relationship between level of economic functioning and the tenor of cross-age social intercourse. During periods of recession and economic decline, the potential for *class* conflict increases considerably. Less appreciated, however, is the greater likelihood for *age* conflict as the recession extends into the occupations dominated by the middle class. Lacking an adequate class explanation for their economic difficulties (it is certainly not the workers from below who constitute the major competition in the tight white-collar, service sector labor market), the "explanation" takes on a generational cast. Out-group hostility against non-age group members is the eventual outcome.

Before leaving the subject of age- versus class-based group conflict, I must not neglect to mention one characteristic feature of age-based social movements that is not shared by class movements. This is the conservatism that so often pervades their ideology. Youth movements, such as the *Jungdeutschlandbund* and the *Wandervogel* of early twentieth-century Germany, are often explicitly antisocialist, while other youth movements, such as the student antiwar movement of the 1960s in America, are conservative in effect. By ignoring the issues of class conflict in industrial society, the student movement was "successful" in diverting public attention from issues of urban decay, poverty, and unemployment toward their predominant concern, namely, the Vietnam war and, more specifically, the military draft. The ease with which college students of the 1960s, like other generations of students before and since, accommodated themselves to the requirements of the workplace points to the undiluted middle-class self-interest that motivates sociopolitical movements based on age. It is in this same context that we should understand old-age movements such as the Gray Panthers. The Gray Panthers have used the strident rhetoric of a 1960s-style "New Left" student movement in order to further the economic interests of the bourgeois aged. Thus far successful in projecting themselves as an admirable, if somewhat naive, group of fighters for economic justice and equality under the law, the Gray Panthers (and other groups in the "aging network" such as AARP/NRTA) are just one among a number of claimant groups (feminists, taxpayers, farmers, new car dealers, consumers, the handicapped, homosexuals, and others) that indirectly compete for a certain share of the national wealth. It is interesting to note that the claims of this politically active segment of the aged population (autonomy, respect, and an end to institutionalized discrimination) are more evocative of the modernist ideological concerns of the post-1920 generations than they are of the "traditional" concerns of the aged themselves. As I have argued elsewhere (Dowd, 1984), the "success" of groups such as the Gray Panthers in their goal of elimination of mandatory retirement and related employment policies such as the social security "retirement test" (a policy, incidentally, supported not only by such advocates as Representative Claude Pepper, but also by the Reagan administration itself), is hardly shared equally by all persons over 65. Indeed, the aging *worker* still hopes for *early* retirement, given the security of an adequate pension. For these workers, the elimination of either the retirement test or mandatory retirement itself is no blessing, especially if the elimination of these policies only presages change in other "protective" legislation such as, for example, the provision of the Social Security Act that allows *early* retirement at age 62 with reduced benefits. *Raising* this age of entitlement to 65 or, worse still, to 68, may secure for the middle-class service worker additional years of high wages, but, for the working-class aged, it may secure instead anxiety and economic destitution.

THE OLD PERSON AS STRANGER

People born and raised prior to World War II are immigrants in time. They appear strange to us, and different. They look different and behave differently. And what is more, they seem to think differently, to believe in different gods and to hold values no longer taken for granted. They are strangers in our midst and we appreciate the boundaries between our lives that keep them as strangers.

To be a stranger, or to be viewed as strange, is not necessarily and never totally a negative experience. Furthermore, the aged have always and everywhere carried with them an aura of strangeness. In certain societies, however, the negative attributions associated with the role of the stranger are less likely to be forthcoming. Gutmann's description of the aged among the Nuniwak Eskimos of the Bering Sea conveys this understanding quite well. The aged represent what Gutmann calls "the internal object," which is some social representation that serves to relate the past to the present. As an internal object, the aged person is regarded apart from his or her immediate physical and social condition. The child, according to Gutmann (1977, p. 315), "does not see in the parent a useless, ugly old person. Rather he still relates to the vigorous, sustaining parent that he once knew, as well as the weak person immediately before him." Gutmann recognizes that the value in this relationship for the old person is to prevent him or her from becoming the *stranger*.

As a bridgehead to society's sacred origins, the aged's strangeness inspires awe, deference, and respect. They are unordinary, special agents who intermediate between this world and other worlds both in the past and in the future; they are "of this world and yet not familiar" (Gutmann, 1980, p. 434). Once their connection to the past is severed, however, the aged stranger arouses not deference but fear and loathing (Gutmann, 1980). In the transition between the traditional and the modern, "the aged have come to be viewed as something new and strange. Instead of symbolizing the reassuringly familiar, they seem threateningly alien" (Gruman, 1978, p. 360). Gutmann (1977, p. 322) considers the narcissistic social character that becomes associated with urban life to be implicated in the aged's changed status:

> The aged are always in danger of becoming the *other*, of being regarded—like strangers everywhere—with a mixture of awe and revulsion. . . . The narcissistic ethos of the city, which asserts that 'nothing strange is human' further crystallizes the tendency to put the aged in this potentially lethal position of the "other."

Gutmann's analysis of the "other" supports the argument that a changed ideology is associated with contemporary perceptions of old people as strange. Character or personality does differentiate generations and is, for this reason, an important variable in the understanding of intergenerational social relationships. We cannot claim full knowledge of the social behavior of the aged until we understand the Weltanschauung they share with other members of their generation. Similarly, we cannot appreciate the origins of age conflict or the etiology of any form of intergenerational exchange without a well-developed analysis of the ideological differences that distinguish the generations and the historical circumstances that gave rise to these ideologies. Such analysis is social psychological in its specific application of the traditional personality and social structure approach to these issues.

I have one final thought on the role of the stranger, especially the aged stranger, in the modern world. It is not new, of course, to argue that one can learn much from old people. Old people claim this continually and, on occasion, their argument is compelling—even to the most insensitive, the most narcissistic among us. Part of the truth of this observation lies quite obviously with the experience and insight that almost invariably accrue with the passage of time in an individual's biography. "Old-timer" is a reference to the aged veteran that connotes this greater understanding quite nicely. Certainly the old-timer *understands* a thing or two better than the rookie, but also he or she has *done* the thing before, and quite probably has done it sufficiently well on sufficiently numerous occasions to be now considered the veteran, the one who has passed an earlier test. The rookie, in contrast, must make up in enthusiasm, strength, or untempered skill what he or she lacks in experience. An appreciation of the different and complementing abilities of the young and the old carries with it the possibility of more humanistic relations between the generations. For, as Simmel (1950, p. 393) notes in his essay on faithfulness, even if "by itself or in response to some external reality, our inner life has made it impossible for us to continue loving, revering, esteeming a person . . . , we can still be grateful to him, since he once gained our gratitude."

There is something else, however, to this bit of folk wisdom that youth can learn from the aged that is much less obvious and therefore less well appreciated. This has to do with the ambivalent status of the old person as stranger. It is precisely because the old person is an immigrant in time, because this person is a stranger to us, that his or her observations may hold much that is of value to us, both individually and collectively. Georg Simmel was the first to recognize this particular potential formally embedded in the role of the stranger. It is because "he is not bound by roots to the particular constituents and partisan dispositions of the group," Simmel (1971, p. 145) reasoned, that "he confronts all of these with a distinctly 'objective' attitude, an attitude that does not signify mere detachment and nonparticipation, but is a distinct structure composed of remoteness and nearness, indifference and involvement."

Part of the stranger's ability to remain disinterested (being indeed unable to do anything but) stems from the stranger's lack of intimate familiarity with the *culture* of the adopted community. Like the student of a foreign language, the stranger is unable to use the cultural pattern "as a natural and trustworthy scheme of orientation" (Schuetz, 1944, p. 504). Like the student who is unable to "think" in the idiom of the new language, the stranger must translate the new culture into the more familiar categories of his or her native culture. This person must question, in effect, all that the native speakers are able to take for granted. Thinking as usual, according to Schuetz, is not a possibility for the strangers.

The aged, like other strangers, become a human variant to the military early-warning system. Because they cannot take any cultural practice or belief for granted, they are able to discern, "frequently with a grievous clear-sightedness, the rising of a crisis which may mean the whole foundation of the 'relatively natural conception of the world,' while all those symptoms pass unnoticed by the members of the in-group, who rely on the continuance of their customary way of life" (Schuetz, 1944, p. 507).

A crisis of this type is currently rising that holds far-reaching implications for the way members of Western industrial societies view themselves. Aspects of this crisis are already apparent, as when psychiatrists note the tremendous increase in narcissistic symptoms among their patients, or when a former president of the United States expresses in a televised speech his concerns about a crisis in confidence raging in the country. The requirements of the new economy for image managers and the reinforcement of the cult of youth and cool beauty in magazines and television have produced a new type of personality or social character. The change, in my view, is neatly summarized in Fromm's distinction between self-love and selfishness. The self-love that characterizes Riesman's inner-directed type is basically a confidence in one's own self-evaluation. It is, in Riesman's (1954) mind, the basis of "true individuality." Selfishness, in contrast, is characteristic of those who, lacking an appreciation or fondness for the self, attempt to gain security in personal conquests, power, or in the esteem of others (Fromm, 1939).

The aged, having been socialized at a different time and to a different set of cultural imperatives, are more frequently able to perceive the change from self-love to selfishness than is the post-1925 generation, for whom self-monitoring and not self-love resonates more strongly. As strangers, the aged, much more than Mannheim's intellectuals, possess the capacity to become "free-floating." Whether the historical moment for realization of this potential has passed awaits future analyses. I suspect that it may have passed, even acknowledging that the aged members of any society may, because of their physical decline and social marginality, be considered remote, different, or like strangers. As strangers, the aged seem to be telling us, as Erikson (1958, p. 22) remarked concerning the youthful Martin Luther, that "in some periods of his history, and in some phases of his life cycle, man needs . . . a new ideological orientation as surely and as sorely as he must have air and food."

NOTES

1. As the reader may have discerned, the "analytically oriented" social psychology proposed by Adorno shares much with social psychology's "third" face, that is, the study of personality and social structure (House, 1977). The argument for an analytical or dialectical social psychology is hardly original, having been made earlier and more thoroughly by other writers, including Max Weber (1949, pp. 88-89). It is important, lest we forget, continually to reassert Gerth and Mills's (1953, p. xiv) judgment that "no matter how we approach the field of social psychology, we cannot escape the idea that all current work that comes to much, fits into one or the other of two basic traditions: *Freud*, on the side of character structure, and *Marx*, including the early Marx of the 1840s, on the side of social structure." In so doing, we cannot help but remember what Archibald (1976) says we must, namely, "that describing characteristics of individuals does not commit one to explaining them psychologically."

2. See, for example, the reports of age-related attitude change by Cutler and Kaufman (1975), Dowd (1979-80), Pederson (1976), and Waite (1978).

3. Social psychological interest in the concept of "character" extends back to the neo-Freudian writers, particularly Erich Fromm (1947, p. 59), who treated character as the "form in which human energy is canalized in the process of assimilation and socialization." The concept received intensive analysis in the work of David Riesman and also in that of C. Wright Mills. In his landmark studies of American character in *The Lonely Crowd* and *Faces in the Crowd* (1952), Riesman helped to establish the sociological counterpart of the culture and personality studies of anthropologists such as Benedict and Mead. His approach considered personality within a particular social-historical structure. For sociologists, character was to be analyzed "by understanding the motivations of men who occupy different positions within various social structures" (Gerth & Mills, 1953, p. xiv).

4. Critics of Lasch's sentimental image of past family forms correctly point out that the traditional patriarchal family was also an authoritarian one. Family authoritarianism was, Jacoby (1980, p. 62) reminds us, "the crucible of fascist and authoritarian character structure. . . . If narcissism is the successor to the authoritarian personality, society has advanced."

5. This usage departs from the definition attributed to Marx and Engels, which restricts ideology to attempts to demonstrate the rationality of the existing distribution of wealth and the social utility of the order in which the wealthy hold positions of power. From this perspective, an ideology is "invariably an apology for institutionalized inequality" (Manning, 1980, p. 3).

6. Mills reports that the Chinese of Mencius's period did not distinguish age in the chronological sense from the pattern of respect and deferent behavior toward those who are old. Consequently, the language does not allow a separation in thought of a person's age and the reverence due because of it (Mills, 1939).

7. Observers such as Herbert Marcuse have argued strongly against the notion that positivistic science is ethically neutral or without a political point of view. Because of the invidious rankings that result from measurement, and because of the source of the *impulse* to measure, Marcuse views *science* as an accomplice in the domination of people. Positivism, because of its delegitimation of traditional values and "its denial of the transcending elements of Reason, forms the academic counterpart of the socially required behavior" (Marcuse, 1964, p. 13). The more conservative analysis of Arnold Gehlen leads nonetheless to the same conclusion. In the shift to industrialization, the dominant source of economic activity shifted from the land (organic) to the machine (inorganic). A decisive fact in this regard, Gehlen (1980, p. 100) believes, is that "one cannot assume an ethical posture toward inorganic nature . . . there are no ethical, but only technical constraints upon the tasks one can set oneself." The most recent discussion of the political bias of technical rationality is given by Urban (1982, p. 23), who sees it as "anything but neutral."

8. Gehlen uses the term "pleonexia" to describe the personality characteristics of the modern character type. As the basic need or requirement of industrial society is consumption, individual attributes such as greed, arrogance, and ambition for power tend to be reinforced. Thus greed or pleonexia should not be considered merely as a failure of *individual* "character" but, rather, as "a most useful term for the social psychological characterization of our age" (Gehlen, 1980, p. 109).

9. The modern evolution of the rule of scientific experts has been scrutinized by Habermas (1965).

10. One senses that our culture has so completely lost the optimism that characterized the pre-1920 generations as to be aptly described as a "survivalist" culture (Lasch, 1984). Similar to the survival strategies adopted by those in adverse circumstances, our approach to daily living is based on a truncation of emotional ties, with the goal of making it through the day. Such techniques of emotional self-management, which may be critical to survival in an emergency, "in more moderate form have come to shape the lives of ordinary people under the ordinary conditions of a bureaucratic society widely perceived as a far-flung system of total control" (Lasch, 1984, p. 39).

11. It has been rightly pointed out in defense of sociology that regardless of "how one-sided sociology, due to its posture within the division of labor of the sciences, may have overemphasized the primacy of society over the individual, still thereby it offers a corrective for the illusion that it is due to his natural disposition, his psychology, and out of himself alone that each single human being has become what he is"(Frankfurt Institute for Social Research, 1972, p. 46).

12. The positivistic concern for establishing lawlike generalizations concerning human behavior has blinded developmental theory to this most important implication of a "personality and social structure" approach to social psychology. It avoids, in other words, dealing with the implication that "the human being is capable of realizing himself as an individual only within a just and humane society" (Frankfurt Institute for Social Research, 1972, p. 46).

13. Mills's portrait of the "competitive personality," though drawn with greater compassion than Fromm's marketeer, is similarly alienated and forced to bargain on a personality market. Such a worker sells not only her time and energy but also herself. The result is self-alienation, because in the personality market, the personality itself, along with advertising, become the "instrument of an alien purpose" (Mills, 1946, p. 440).

REFERENCES

Abrams, P. (1982). *Historical sociology*. Ithaca, NY: Cornell.

Achenbaum, W. A., & Stearns, P. N. (1978). Old age and modernization. *Gerontologist, 18*, 307-312.

Adorno, T. (1967-1968). Sociology and psychology. *New Left Review, 46*, 67-68; *47*, 79-97.

Anderson, B., & Davis, N. J. (1981). Boundary crossing in social networks: A semiotic formulation. In D. Willer & B. Anderson (Eds.), *Networks, exchange, and coercion*. New York: Elsevier.

Archibald, W. P. (1976). Face-to-face: The alienating efforts of class, state, and power divisions. *American Sociological Review, 41*, 819-837.

Bell, D. (1973). *The coming of post-industrial society*. New York: Basic Books.

Bell, D. (1976). *The cultural contradictions of capitalism*. New York: Basic Books.

Berger, P., & Luckmann, T. (1966). *The social construction of reality*. Garden City, NY: Doubleday.

Berman, M. (1982). *All that is solid melts into air*. New York: Simon & Schuster.

Bromley, D. B. (1978). Approaches to the study of personality changes in adult life and old age. In A. D. Isaacs & F. Post (Eds.), *Studies in geriatric psychiatry* (pp. 17-40). Chichester: John Wiley.

Bronfenbrenner, U. (1974). The origins of alienation. *Scientific American, 231*, 53-61.

Buck-Morss, S. (1975). Socio-economic bias in Piaget's theory and its implications for cross-culture studies. *Human Development, 18*, 35-49.

Carroll, J. (1977). *Puritan, paranoid, remissive*. London: Routledge & Kegan Paul.

Clark, R. L., & Menefee, J. A. (1981). Federal expenditures for the elderly: Past and future. *Gerontologist; 21*, 132-137.

Cutler, S., & Kaufman, R. (1975). Cohort changes in political attitudes: Tolerance of ideological nonconformity. *Public Opinion Quarterly, 39*, 69-81.

Davis, K. (1979). The continuing demographic revolution in industrial societies. In S. M. Lipset (Ed.), *The third century: America as a post-industrial society* (pp. 37-64). Stanford, CA: Hoover Institution Press.

Dowd, J. J. (1979-1980). The problems of generations: And generational analysis. *International Journal of Aging and Human Development, 10*, 213-229.

Dowd, J. J. (1980). Exchange rates and old people. *Journal of Gerontology, 35*, 596-602.

Dowd, J. J. (1984). Beneficence and the aged. *Journal of Gerontology, 39*, 102-108.

Dreitzel, H. P. (1977). On the political meaning of culture. In N. Birnbaum (Ed.), *Beyond the crisis* (pp. 81-129). New York: Oxford University Press.

Erikson, E. H. (1950). *Childhood and society*. New York: W. W. Norton.

Erikson, E. H. (1958). *Young man Luther*. New York: W. W. Norton.

Feuer, L. S. (1975). *Ideology and the ideologists*. Oxford: Basil Blackwell.

Frankfurt Institute for Social Research. (1972). *Aspects of sociology* (J. Viertel, Trans.). Boston: Beacon.

Fromm, E. (1939). Selfishness and self-love. *Psychiatry, 2*, 507-523.

Fromm, E. (1947). *Man for himself*. New York: Rinehart.

Gehlen, A. (1980). *Man in the age of technology*. New York: Columbia University Press. (Original work published 1957)

Gerth, H., & Mills, C. W. (1953). *Character and social structure*. New York: Harcourt Brace Jovanovich.

Gonos, G. (1980). The class position of Goffman's sociology: Social origins of an American structuralism. In J. Ditton (Ed.), *The view from Goffman* (pp. 134-169). New York: St. Martin's.

Gorer, G. (1966). *The danger of equality*. New York: Weybright & Tall.

Gould, R. L. (1978). *Transformations: Growth and change in adult life*. New York: Simon & Schuster.

Gouldner, A. W. (1973). The importance of something for nothing. In *For sociology* (pp. 260-299). London: Allen Lane.

Gruman, G. J. (1978). Cultural origins of present-day 'age-ism': The modernization of the life cycle. In S. F. Spicker, K. M. Woodward, & D. D. Van Tassel (Eds.), *Aging and the elderly* (pp. 359-387). Atlantic Highlands, NJ: Humanities Press.

Gutmann, D. (1977). The cross-cultural perspective: Notes toward a comparative psychology of aging. In J. E. Birren & K. W. Schaie (Eds.), *Handbook of the psychology of aging* (pp. 302-326). New York: Van Nostrand Reinhold.

Gutmann, D. (1980). Observation on culture and mental health in later life. In J. E. Birren & R. B. Sloan (Eds.), *Handbook of mental health and aging* (pp. 429-447). Englewood Cliffs, NJ: Prentice-Hall.

Habermas, J. (1965). *Strukturwandel der Oeffentlichkeit: Untersuchungen zu einer Kategorie der burgerlichen Gesellschaft*. Berlin: Luchterland.

Harrington, M. (1976). *The twilight of capitalism*. New York: Touchstone.

Homans, G. C. (1982). Review of Joan Didion's essays. *Theory and Society, 11*, 239-241.

House, J. L. (1977). The three faces of social psychology. *Sociometry, 40*, 161-177.

Hudson, R. B. (1978). Emerging pressures on public policies for the aging. *Society, 15*, 30-33.

Inkeles, A. (1979). Continuity and change in the American national character. In S. M. Lipset (Ed.), *The third century: America as a post-industrial society* (pp. 389-416). Stanford, CA: Hoover Institution Press.

Inkeles, A., & Levinson, D. J. (1969). National character. In G. Lindsey & E. Aronson (Eds.), *Handbook of social psychology* (2nd ed., Vol. 4, pp. 418-506). Reading, MA: Addison-Wesley.

Jacoby, R. (1980). Narcissism and the crisis of capitalism. *Telos, 44*, 58-65.

Johnson, P. (1983). *Modern times: The world from the twenties to the eighties.* New York: Harper & Row.

Jung, C. G. (1928). *Contributions to analytical psychology* (H. G. Baynes & C. F. Baynes, Trans.). London: Routledge & Kegan Paul.

Konrád, G., & Szelényi, I. (1979). *The intellectuals on the road to class power.* Brighton: Harvester.

Langman, L., & Kaplan, L. (1981). Political economy and social character: Terror, desire, and domination. In S. G. McNall & G. N. Howe (Eds.), *Current perspectives in social theory* (Vol. 2, pp. 87-115). Greenwich, CT: JAI.

Lasch, C. (1977). *Haven in a heartless world.* New York: Basic Books.

Lasch, C. (1979). *The culture of narcissism.* New York: W. W. Norton.

Lasch, C. (1984, February 2). The great American variety show. *New York Review of Books*, pp. 36-40.

Lears, T.J.J. (1981). *No place of grace: Antimodernism and the transformation of American culture 1880-1920.* New York: Pantheon.

Levinson, D. J. (1978). *The seasons of a man's life.* New York: Ballantine.

Lowenthal, M. F. (1977). Toward a sociopsychological theory of change in adulthood and old age. In J. Birren & K. W. Schaie (Eds.), *Handbook of the psychology of aging* (pp. 116-127). New York: Van Nostrand Reinhold.

Loewenberg, P. (1983). *Decoding the past: The psychohistorical approach.* New York: Knopf.

Mannheim, K. (1936). *Ideology and utopia: An introduction to the sociology of knowledge.* New York: Harcourt Brace Jovanovich.

Mannheim, K. (1952). The problem of generations. In P. Kecskemeti (Ed.), *Essays on the sociology of knowledge.* London: Routledge & Kegan Paul.

Manning, D. J. (1980). *The form of ideology.* London: George Allen & Unwin.

Marcuse, H. (1964). *One-dimensional man.* Boston: Beacon.

Marcuse, H. (1978). Some social implications of modern technology. In A. Arato & E. Gebhardt (Eds.), *The essential Frankfurt School reader* (pp. 138-162). Oxford: Basil Blackwell.

Marx, K. (1977). *The eighteenth Brumaire of Louis Bonaparte.* Moscow: Progress.

Mead, M. (1978). *Culture and commitment: A study of the generation gap.* New York: Columbia University Press.

Mills, C. W. (1939). Language, logic, and culture. *American Sociological Review, 4*, 670-680.

Mills, C. W. (1946). The competitive personality. *Partisan Review, 13*, 433-441.

Neugarten, B. L. (1977). Personality and aging. In J. Birren & K. W. Schaie (Eds.), *Handbook of the psychology of aging* (pp. 226-249). New York: Van Nostrand Reinhold.

Olin, S. (1978, April 29). Lawyer, 25, wnts Job, Phila.; Drs Clsd. *New York Times.*

Pederson, J. T. (1976). Age and change: The case of California, 1960-1970. *Public Opinion Quarterly, 40,* 153-163.

Quinton, A. (1983). Character and culture. *New Republic, 189,* 26-30.

Reich, W. (1970). *The mass psychology of fascism* (3rd ed.). New York: Farrar, Strauss & Giroux. (Original work published 1933)

Riegel, K. F. (1973a). An epitaph for a paradigm. *Human Development, 16,* 1-7.

Riegel, K. F. (1973b). Dialectical operations: The final period of cognitive development. *Human Development, 16,* 346-370.

Riegel, K. F. (1977). History of psychological gerontology. In J. E. Birren & K. W. Schaie (Eds.), *Handbook of the psychology of aging* (pp. 70-102). New York: Van Nostrand Reinhold.

Riesman, D. (1952). *Faces in the crowd.* New Haven, CT: Yale University Press.

Riesman, D. (1954). The ethics of we happy few. In *Individualism reconsidered* (pp. 39-54). New York: Free Press.

Riesman, D. (1967). Some questions about the study of American character in the twentieth century. *Annals of the American Academy of Political and Social Science, 370,* 36-47.

Riesman, D. (1973). *The lonely crowd: A study of the changing American character.* New Haven, CT: Yale University Press. (Original work published 1950)

Schuetz, A. (1944). The stranger: An essay in social psychology. *American Journal of Sociology, 49,* 499-507.

Seeley, J. R. (1967). *The Americanization of the unconscious.* Philadelphia: J. B. Lippincott.

Sennett, R. (1970). *The uses of disorder.* New York: Knopf.

Sennett, R. (1977a). *The fall of public man.* New York: Random House.

Sennett, R. (1977b). Destructive Gemeinschaft. In N. Birnbaum (Ed.), *Beyond the crisis* (pp. 171-197). New York: Oxford.

Seve, L. (1978). *Man in Marxist theory.* Atlantic Highlands, NJ: Humanities Press.

Shils, E. (1975). *Center and periphery.* Chicago: University of Chicago Press.

Shils, E. (1981). *Tradition.* Chicago: University of Chicago Press.

Simmel, G. (1950). Faithfulness and gratitude. In K. H. Wolff (Ed.), *The sociology of Georg Simmel.* New York: Free Press.

Simmel, G. (1971). The stranger. In D. N. Levine (Ed.), *Georg Simmel: On individuality and social forms* (pp. 143-149). Chicago: University of Chicago Press. (Original work published 1908)

Snyder, M. (1979). Self-monitoring processes. In L. Berkowitz (Ed.), *Advances in experimental social psychology* (Vol. 12, pp. 85-128). New York: Academic Press.

Swidler, A. (1980). Love and adulthood in American culture. In N. J. Smelser & E. H. Erikson (Eds.), *Themes of work and love in adulthood* (pp. 120-147). Cambridge, MA: Harvard University Press.

Trilling, L. (1955). *Freud and the crisis of our culture.* Boston: Beacon.

Trilling, L. (1979). Art, will and necessity. In D. Trilling (Ed.), *The last decade: essays and reviews, 1965-1975* (pp. 129-147). New York: Harcourt Brace Jovanovich.

Urban, M. E. (1982). *The ideology of administration.* Albany: SUNY Press.

Waite, L. J. (1978). Projecting female labor force participation from sex-role attitudes. *Social Science Research, 7,* 299-317.

Walker, A. (1981). Towards a political economy of old age. *Ageing and Society, 1,* 73-94.

Weber, M. (1949). The methodology of the social sciences (E. A. Shils, Trans. and Ed.). New York: Free Press.

Wexler, P. (1983). *Critical social psychology.* Boston: Routledge & Kegan Paul.

Wohl, R. (1979). *The generation of 1914.* Cambridge, MA: Harvard University Press.

7

Social Networks and Social Support: Implications for Later Life

BARRY WELLMAN
ALAN HALL

FROM SUPPORT SYSTEM ANALYSIS TO SOCIAL NETWORK ANALYSIS

The Persistence of Social Support

At one time most commentators feared that large-scale social changes were causing a "loss of community." Although they argued vehemently about the principal cause of this loss—industrialization, urbanization, capitalism, bureaucratization, and technological change have been the principal contenders—they agreed on its consequences: Community ties were becoming few in number, flimsy in structure, and thin in content.

We know now that these fears are not true. Massive empirical evidence has made it clear that networks of "community ties" (i.e., significant interpersonal ties extending beyond the household) continue to flourish and provide supportive resources to almost all members of contemporary societies. Indeed, this finding has become one of the most reliable pieces of knowledge in many areas of sociology, for instance:

- urban studies (Craven & Wellman, 1973; Bell & Newby, 1976; Fischer, 1976, 1982; Warren, 1978; Wellman & Leighton, 1979; Wellman, Carrington, & Hall, in press)

AUTHORS' NOTE: Our thanks to Robert Hiscott and Craig Wilson for their assistance in the research reported here. Research for this chapter has been supported by the Social Sciences and Humanities Research Council of Canada (Strategic Aging Grant and General Research Grant), the National Welfare Grants program of Health and Welfare Canada, the (U.S.) Center for Studies of Metropolitan Problems (NIMH), and the following units of the University of Toronto: the Programme in Gerontology, the Structural Analysis Programme, the Centre for Urban and Community Studies, the Humanities and Social Sciences Research Board, and the Joint Program in Transportation.

- migration studies (Tilly & Brown, 1967; Mayer with Mayer, 1974; Roberts, 1978)
- family studies (Young & Willmott, 1957; Litwak, 1960; Adams, 1968; Firth, Hubert, & Forge, 1969; Gordon, 1978)
- women's studies (Stack, 1974; Tilly & Scott, 1978; Luxton, 1980)
- political sociology (Tilly, 1964, 1978; Oberschall, 1978)
- organizational studies (Thompson, 1967; Benyon, 1973; Aldrich, 1979)

Studies of the community ties of the aged have reflected this broad sociological debate. Until recently, gerontologists feared that the aged's supportive relations with kin and neighbors would wither away as a consequence of a societal "loss of community" (e.g., Parsons, 1949; Burgess, 1960; Nisbet, 1962). These fears were intensified by the more psychologistic argument that role changes—associated with retirement and preparation for death—would cause both the aged and younger members of their communities to "disengage" from many ties (Cumming & Henry, 1961).

Those who made such arguments did so without good data. We know now from many empirical studies that ties with the aged are still abundant and strong, and that such ties are important extrahousehold sources of emotional aid, material assistance, personal services, and help in dealing with bureaucracies (Lemon, Bengtson, & Peterson, 1972; Atchley, 1972; Marshall, 1980). Moreover, historical analysis (e.g., Laslett, 1977) has demonstrated striking similarities of the aged's community ties in preindustrial and contemporary societies. The great transformation in the nature of community and social support appears to have been much overstated by commentators suffused with nostalgia for an idyllic pastoralist past (see White & White, 1962; Marx, 1964; Williams, 1975; Bender, 1979).

The Usefulness of Social Support for Health Care

Social studies of health started by relating the aggregated personal attributes of individuals (e.g., socioeconomic status, gender) to their symptoms and well-being (e.g., Srole et al., 1975). Such studies often sought to explain the observed correlations between personal attributes and health in terms of the various social relationships in which different categories of people were involved.

The next analytic step was to study directly the impact of social relationships on health. Support system research started with the sociological demonstration of the persistence of community ties, and studied how the characteristics of such ties were positively associated with physical and mental health (see the reviews in Mueller, 1980; Gottlieb, 1981; Hammer, 1981; Thoits, 1982). For example, Berkman and Syme (1979, p. 186) found that Alameda County, California, residents "who lacked social and community ties were more likely to die in the follow-up period than those with more extensive contacts." To explain such findings, analysts have suggested four mechanisms by which social support may affect health (adapted from Hammer, 1981; Thoits, 1982):

(1) Support systems may positively promote health-related behavior, such as exercise or the use of medical services. This explanation assumes that community ties are supportive and that health-related activities operate most effectively in a communal milieu.

(2) Support systems serve as a source of support in a crisis, helping to buffer individuals from the harmful effects of stress and strain. This is a reactive rather than a preventive explanation, seeing supportive ties as providing emotional, material, and informational resources that can stop stress and strain turning into distress.

(3) Support systems provide community members with feedback essential to normal behavioral functioning; when this feedback is not forthcoming, behavior is seriously disrupted, and accompanying physiological alterations affect susceptibility to illness. This explanation concentrates on the help-maintaining effects of companionship itself, without necessarily assuming that the community ties provide tangible support.

(4) Such disruptions of support systems as divorce, change of jobs, or long-distance moves may lead to stress. Hence the very abundance of ties may promote well-being. Thus the association of small, sparsely knit support systems with distress may more accurately indicate the impact of such disruptive events rather than the failure of the remaining supportive ties to buffer the stress.

This focus on support systems has had contradictory results. On the one hand, it has been an important analytic step in showing how the nature of community ties can affect health. On the other hand, by oversimplifying the nature of ties and networks, it has weakened and distorted the analysis of social support. Concerned with demonstrating the therapeutic effects of support, researchers have developed refined concepts and measures of acute stress, chronic strain, and consequent physical and mental distress (see Sarason & Sarason, 1985). At the same time, they have left social support itself as much more of an unanalyzed, unidimensional, antecedent "black box."

In order to study the conditions under which individuals do get support, analysts must allow for the possibility that many of their ties are not necessarily supportive. Yet when analysts declare ahead of time that a set of ties constitutes a "support system," they assume in advance precisely that which they should leave open for study:

(a) the assumption that support systems are homogeneous in composition or that variations in their composition are largely irrelevant to the provision of support;
(b) the assumption that all of a person's ties are organized into a single, unitary, densely knit "system";
(c) the assumption that all community ties provide social support; and
(d) the assumption that support itself is a single, broadly based resource.

To state these assumptions—widespread in the social support literature—is to state the analytic problems. We all know from our everyday experience that ties are not always supportive; that support is transmitted in variable, often ambiguous ways; and that people often participate in several social networks in different spheres of their lives. However, the "support system" concept negates this commonsensical knowledge of the complexities of ties and networks by describing a single system composed only of supportive social relationships. Its focus on a simple support/nonsupport dichotomy deemphasizes the multifaceted, often contradictory, nature of community ties. Its assumption that supportive ties form a distinct system analytically isolates such ties from a person's overall network of community ties. Its assumption that all of these supportive ties are connected to one another in one integrated system goes against empirical reality and creates the dubious expectation that unitary systems invariably promote better health. Its assumption that there are no conflicts of interest among "supporters" invokes the dubious and unnecessary premise of a common good.

Our solution has been to use social network analysis, a relatively new research strategy in the social sciences that takes more fully into account the complexities of community ties. A support system *is* a social network: in other words, a set of nodes (persons) connected by a set of ties (relations of emotional support). However, a support system is an analytically constricted social network that only takes into account supportive ties and that assumes that these ties only can form a single, homogeneous, integrated structure.

Our research group is in the midst of a long-term research project to document the variable nature of community ties in Toronto, Canada and to study the changing circumstances under which such ties and networks provide a variety of supportive resources to individuals (see

Figure 7.1). Our project has relevance for the societal care of the aged in a number of ways:

- by delineating the nature of community ties and support, we can better understand the circumstances under which supportive resources come to community members;
- by analyzing the community ties of individuals in different structural positions in society (including different stages of the life course) we can evaluate the extent to which informal support to the aged differs from younger age strata;
- by studying the community ties of individuals *longitudinally* (we have comparable data at two points in time, ten years apart), we can analyze the extent to which potentially stressful changes in the life course (such as life-cycle shifts, job mobility, residential mobility) affect the nature of community ties and the availability of supportive resources during the life-course.

In no way do we presume to boil down this entire research program to a single paper. Indeed, much of this work is still under way. We present here first a brief background description of the nature of social network analysis in an effort to argue its utility for health care research. We then present cross-sectional data from our current East York study on the composition, structure, and content of community ties, in order to show the greater analytic utility of taking the variation of these networks into account when studying informal health care for the aged.

THE NATURE OF SOCIAL NETWORK ANALYSIS

Development

Network as metaphor and concept. Social scientists have used "the social network" as a metaphor throughout this century to connote complex sets of relationships among members of social systems (e.g., Radcliffe-Brown, 1940; Simmel, 1922). Yet it was not until the 1950s that they began to use the term systematically and self-consciously to denote relationships that cut across the bounded groups (e.g., tribes, families) and social categories (e.g., gender, social class) traditionally used by social scientists to organize their data.

These *network analysts* define a social network as a set of *nodes tied* to each other by one or more specific types of strands or relations. While in most health research the nodes are individual persons, they can just as

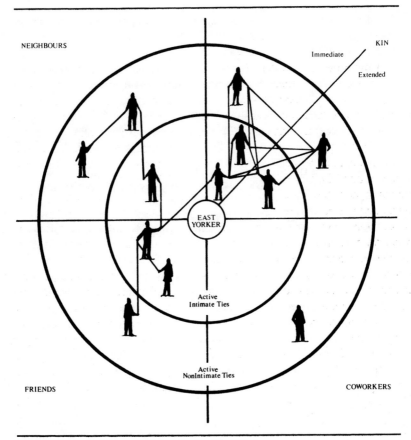

Figure 7.1 Typical Personal Network of an East Yorker

easily be groups, corporations, households, nation-states, or other collectivities. The ties are defined by the flow of resources from one node (or network member) to another. These resources can vary in *quality* (does the tie provide emotional aid or companionship?); in *quantity* (does it provide much emotional aid, frequent companionship?); *multiplexity* (does the tie provide only emotional aid or both emotional aid and companionship?); and *symmetry* (do both parties to a tie exchange roughly equivalent amounts of emotional aid or does the resource tend to go only in one direction?). Thus the criteria for including the nodes and ties that constitute a network are infinitely varied in principle, so researchers must designate the specific relations in which they are interested. For example, to study the influence of social class on the aged's ability to cope with everyday and emergency situations, researchers might want to include measures of role relationships (e.g., kin/friend), structure (e.g., dyadic or structurally embedded tie) and power (e.g., control over which means of day-to-day existence).

Yet many important social relationships cut across such bounded groups and categories. For example, J. A. Barnes (1954) found that he could not describe adequately the social organization of a Norwegian fishing village by using only the traditional categories of class or kin. He needed to examine as well the "network" of concrete ties that cut across class and kinship groups. Not only did the network concept help him describe the village more accurately, it provided a much more powerful way of explaining key social processes (e.g., access to fishing jobs; political activity) than did normative explanations.

Researchers also found the network concept useful in understanding the behavior of Third World migrants from rural villages to big cities and industrial areas. These migrants had left the bounded villages, tribes, and kinship groups that had traditionally provided them with normative guidance. Social scientists and politicians feared that they would wander undirected, isolated, and disorganized in the cities, prone to sink into apathetic despair or seek solace in mindless mobs (e.g., Kornhauser, 1968). Yet researchers soon discovered that not only had these migrants formed strong, supportive ties within their new urban industrial homes, but that they had retained strong ties to their ancestral homelands (e.g., Howard, in press; Mitchell, 1969a; Mayer & Mayer, 1974; Roberts, 1978). Rather than wilting under the impact of urbanization, industrialization, and capitalism, these migrants had constructed complex "social networks" linking city and village, and cutting across tribal, residential, and workplace groups in the cities (see the reviews in Boissevain & Mitchell, 1973; Mitchell, 1969a, 1969b, 1969c; Wolf, 1966).

These studies established the social network concept, developed the practice of studying networks by measuring their structural properties, and produced insightful findings calling attention to the importance of networks in organizing social life. Yet many analysts were cursory in their use of network concepts, content to demonstrate only the importance of networks and to describe the patterns of ties. They often treated ties as residual, forming networks only when they did not fit within bounded groups and categories. Unfortunately, many support system studies refer only to this early work and do not seem aware of more recent network analytic developments (see the review in Hall & Wellman, 1985). Indeed, some only use the term *the social network* to refer to a vaguely defined set of supportive ties (e.g., Beels, 1979; Finlayson, 1976; Henderson, 1977; Silberfeld, 1978).

Network properties as variables. Although the development of the social network concept told social scientists what to look for, it only gave them rudimentary guidance about how to describe social networks and relate their descriptions to other social phenomena. Hence many social scientists have worked since the 1950s to develop sets of variables that would measure network properties. These network analysts have focused on the characteristics of the pattern of ties between actors in a social system rather than on the characteristics of the individual actors themselves. Often using techniques derived from simple graph theory and matrix algebra, they search for regular structures of ties underlying the often incoherent surface appearances of networks and study how these structures constrain network members' behavior (see the reviews in Berkowitz, 1982; Burt, 1980; Rogers & Kincaid, 1981; Wellman, 1983).

In many cases network analysts study *whole networks*: all of the ties linking all of the members of a population. Thus several researchers have analyzed interlocking corporate directorships—who sits on whose boards?—showing that these corporations form densely knit clusters, these clusters are connected in a single overarching corporate elite structure, and that densely knit corporate sectors within this structure have unusually high rates of profit. Other researchers have sought to explain the internal structure of states in terms of transnational links of dependency between states or interest groups, arguing that it has been such asymmetric relations that have caused uneven economic development, and not the internal backwardness of less-developed nations (e.g., Friedmann, in press; Snyder & Kick, 1979).

Whole network analysis permits a simultaneous view of the social system as a whole and of the parts that make up the system. This helps analysts trace lateral and flow of resources and detect structural constraints operating on these flows. Moreover, political economic studies of development have emphasized the ways in which asymmetric ties and hierarchical networks can channel flows of resources to, and constrain the behavior of, individuals and states.

In gerontology, whole network analysis is directly applicable to the study of flows of clients, dollars, and personnel between agencies, as well as to posing broader questions about the political economy of age relations. Moreover, by manipulating matrices representing who is connected with whom, it can discover densely knit clusters of heavily interconnected agencies or find agencies whose similar role relationships show up in a "blockmodel" (White, Boorman, & Breiger, 1976).

Despite their theoretical and technological advantages, whole network studies may not always be feasible. They demand complete lists of all members of a population and all of their ties. Indeed, prior specification of population boundaries often may not be appropriate, as when analysts want to discover the search pathways used by help-seekers (Erickson, 1978; Lee, 1969). Moreover, current techniques for studying whole networks can only comprehend a few types of relations at the same time.

Hence many analysts study *egocentric* or *personal networks*, the composition, structure, and contents of which are defined from the standpoint of (a usually large sample of) focal individuals deemed to stand at the centers of these networks. Thus Elizabeth Bott's (1957) pioneering study related the marital integration of urban English couples to the ways in which they were integrated into kinship networks. She found that those couples who were members of densely knit networks were more likely to act separately from each other (with husband and wife each involved with their respective kin) while those couples who were members of sparsely knit networks were more likely to act jointly and be less involved with kin. (Density is the ratio of the total number of observed ties in a network to the total number of ties possible if all network members are actually linked directly with one another.)

Personal network studies lend themselves readily to large-scale survey research techniques, although investigators often must assume that respondents are accurate reporters of the relevant characteristics of their networks, other network members, and their ties (see Conrath, Higgins, & McClean, 1983). Investigators usually gather information about the networks' composition (e.g., the members' social class or gender), structure (e.g., links between network members), and contents (the resources that flow through these links). Such information provides data not only about dyadic ties (the two-person relationship between a focal individual and a network member treated in isolation) but also about the networks in which these ties are embedded—aggregate information about network composition (e.g., percent kin) and structural information about the arrangement of ties (e.g., clustering).

The personal network approach is especially relevant to gerontological research because it focuses attention on how the properties of networks affect the flow of resources to focal individuals in later life. Thus urban network studies have described the supportive resources available to city dwellers and shown how such ties and networks affect the ways in which these individuals articulate with the resources of larger-scale social systems (e.g., Fischer, 1982; Wellman et al., in press).

Several "search network" studies have shown how network properties affect the ways in which individuals get jobs, social services, and other resources (e.g., Bernard & Killworth, 1978; Granovetter, 1974, 1982; Liu & Duff, 1972).

The Current State of Network Analysis

While many investigators continue to insert network variables as "add-ons" to boost the explained variance of otherwise conventional studies, a number of analysts have been working to interpret all social structures from within a network analytic model. In recent years, the network analytic research traditions have been coalescing into a broadly based approach, comprehensive in its ambitions. Their work has combined the original organizing network concept with a Simmelian (1908) emphasis on the structure of ties affecting behavior, a sociometrically based desire to measure network properties quantitatively (e.g., Burt, 1982), an epidemiological and communications interest in resource diffusion processes (e.g., Rogers & Kincaid, 1981), a contemporary bent for mathematical reasoning (e.g., Fararo, 1981), and a political economic interest in explaining political processes as resulting from the position of interest groups and nation-states in large-scale structures of exchange and dependency (e.g., Tilly, 1978).

Such network analysts no longer look just at friendship and kinship ties but study how relations of power and dependency link together in stratified social systems. They do not restrict their conceptualization of network nodes (or actors) to individual persons; relations between groups, organizations, and clusters of ties (treated as one node) have become an integral part of the model.

The development of this comprehensive network analytic model is influencing the ways in which researchers pose questions, collect information and analyze data. Although the methods these network analysts use are often distinctive, the real difference lies in four fundamental aspects of their analytic approach (for a more extended discussion, see Wellman, 1983).

Relational structures, not aggregated categories. Network analysts organize studies in terms of relations between actors instead of trying to sort actors into categories defined by the inner attributes (or essences) of these actors. This is in contrast to mainstream sociological studies, which have long relied on categorical analyses treating social processes as the sum of individual actors' personal attributes and internalized norms. Such analyses begin with actors as astructural, independent units of analysis, lump them together into social categories (e.g., the elderly, low socioeconomic status) based on similarities in their attributes (e.g., age, education) and norms (e.g., "traditional" values), and then treat the resulting categories as "structural measures." Yet these analyses "have been largely content to aggregate in only two ways: either by positing categorical aggregates (e.g., 'functional subsystems,' 'classes') whose relation to concrete social structure has been tenuous; or by cross-tabulating individuals according to their attributes," for example, what percentage of low-SES aged have traditional values? (White et al., 1976, p. 733).

Such analyses taxonomically group persons with similar attributes and norms into social categories without regard for the structure of relationships among them. They treat inherently structural phenomena such as intergenerational relations and social isolation as personal attributes such as cohort and alienation (see the discussion in Marshall, 1983). This leads analysts to interpret social behavior as the result of individuals' common possession of attributes and norms rather than as a result of their involvement in structured social relationships. Thus analysts can too easily interpret changes in the number and composition of social relations as normative disengagement rather than as post-retirement reductions in the arenas available to recruit and maintain such relationships.

Thus categorical analyses treat each social system member as an astructural, independent unit of analysis. While it is this very assumption of independence which has made standard statistical methods so usable and powerful in the social sciences, the assumption inherently detaches individuals from social structures and forces analysts to treat them as disconnected masses. As such analyses assume random linkages, they cannot take into account the extent to which coordinating ties among category members may be responsible for similar behavior. Aggregating each member's characteristics independently destroys structural infor-mation, just as centrifuging genes destroys structure while providing information about composition. Hence analysts can only measure social structure indirectly by organizing and summarizing numerous individual covariations. They tend to neglect, often unconsciously, social properties that are more than the sum of individual acts. SPSS methods become a worldview.

It has been easier to see what is wrong with categorical modes of analysis than it has been to develop concepts and methods for analyzing social structure directly. Although ethnographic and archival accounts have been important since the early days of network analysis (see the reviews in Barnes, 1972; Mitchell, 1969), most methodological work has been quantitative, using measures derived from simple graph theory and matrix algebra to describe and analyze networks. Some analysts (e.g., Erickson, 1978) have defined populations relationally rather than categorically, tracing chains of network members. Others have manipulated matrices to identify clusters of densely knit ties within networks or used "block-models" to discover members of social systems with similar role relations (White et al., 1976). Some analysts have begun using determinate mathematics (in preference to statistics) to model social structure (e.g., Boorman & White, 1976). Thus most studies of social support and community ties have continued to rely on a few similar measures of tie and network properties, integrating these with traditional statistical databases (Hall & Wellman, 1985).

Structures, not norms. Network analysts interpret behavior in terms of structural constraints on activity instead of assuming that inner forces (internalized norms) impel actors in voluntaristic, sometimes teleological behavior toward a desired goal. They critique as nonstructural those explanations which find sociological regularities when persons in the same social categories (having similar attributes) behave similarly in response to shared norms. While many mainstream sociologists do refer to the structural location of persons to explain their acquisition of norms, these explanations still treat persons as individuals moving compasslike in response to their internalized norms. Such explanations, concerned with aggregated sets of individual motives for action, are ultimately psychological and not sociological, neglecting the ways in which variations in structured access to scarce resources determine opportunities and constraints for behavior. These explanations inherently treat social integration as the normal state, defining the relationship of people to society "in terms of shared consciousness, commitments, normative orientations, values, systems of expectation" (Howard, 1974, p. 5).

In gerontology, "disengagement theory" has been an influential normative explanatory model (e.g., Cumming & Henry, 1961). It assumes that both the aged and other members of their personal networks wind down their ties in response to attitude shifts associated with the aged's retirement, reduced roles, and preparation for death. Yet recent research suggests that normative changes come after shifts in the aged's social relations: movement to a retirement home, loss of job, and illness or death of other network members. Moreover, many aged experience continuity in their relationships; some even obtain more social support (see Hochschild, 1975; Larson, 1978; Lopata, 1978; Maddox, 1970; Marshall, 1980).

Thus network analysts treat norms as effects of structural location, not causes. They study regularities in how people and collectivities behave, rather than regularities in beliefs about how they ought to behave. This leads to the study of how structures of relations of exchange, power, and dependency allocate flows of resources in social systems. It suggests that the study of gerontological care could be aided by analyzing the social distribution of possibilities—the unequal availability of such resources as information, wealth, time, and emotional skills—and the structures through which network members have access to such resources.

Networks, not dyads. Network analyses interpret all two-person (dyadic) relations in the light of the dyadic partners' additional relations with other network members. Many sociological analysts treat dyadic interactions as the basic relational unit of analysis (e.g., Homans, 1961; Berscheid & Walster, 1978). They disregard structural form, making an implicit bet that they can analyze ties adequately in structural isolation without reference to the nature of other ties in the network or how they fit together. For example, some analyses take the number of interpersonal ties, by itself, as an adequate predictor of social support (e.g., Evans & Northwood, 1979). Such studies see support as emerging from multiple duets with separate others.

In contrast, network analysts argue that the pattern of ties in a network affects the flow of resources through specific ties. They point out that investigators cannot discover such emergent structural properties as coalition formation or network density from the study of dyads. Yet the pattern of ties in a network can affect the flow of supportive resources through these ties (Hirsch, 1979). Even ties between aged parents and adult children are affected by the presence or absence of ties to other kin, neighbors, or friends.

Not only does network structure affect dyadic ties, but there are times when the larger network itself is the focus of attention. Each tie gives network members indirect access to all those with whom other dyad members are connected. These compound chains of ties transit and allocate scarce resources, fitting network members into larger social systems.

Networks, not necessarily groups. Network analysts treat social structure as a "network of networks" (Craven & Wellman, 1973) that may or may not be partitioned into discrete groups. They do not assume a priori that tightly bounded groups are the fundamental building blocks of large-scale social systems. Indeed, they caution that a focus on bounded groups produces oversimplified descriptions of complex social structures as organizational trees, when it is the network members' crosscutting memberships in multiple social circles that weave together social systems. They point out that shifts in analysis from small-scale to large-scale systems can be facilitated by considering large-scale systems as "networks of networks" in which clusters of actors in small-scale (interpersonal) systems are treated as single nodes in large-scale (inter-organizational) systems. Such an approach could be used easily to study links among agents, agencies, and clients concerned with care of the aged.

Thus the network model facilitates the study of ties that are not organized into discrete groups while permitting the discovery of those networks that are, in fact, bounded and densely knit enough to be termed "groups." This approach allows analysts to study complex hierarchies of power and not just simple, discrete, social strata (e.g., Breiger, 1979). It has allowed our own research group to discover supportive community ties—often sparsely knit in structure and dispersed in space—when conventional community studies of neighborhoods and kinship groups would have mistakenly suggested a dearth of ties and support (see below; see also Wellman & Leighton, 1979; Wellman et al., in press).

PROCEDURES OF THE EAST YORK STUDY

The East York Context

In the late 1960s, our research group entered directly into the "loss of community" debate. We wondered if English-Canadians continued to maintain communities in a modern metropolis, and if their close community ties were giving them social support to deal with stressful situations (Wellman, 1968; Coates et al., 1970). Rather than studying community, we studied community ties. That is, we did not study a local area comprehensively, but asked a large number of urbanites about their informal relationships with persons outside of their households. This enabled us to find out how both local and more distant ties fit into "personal communities," i.e., networks of community ties providing sociable companionship and supportive resources to participants.

We concentrated on studying the residents of East York, a densely settled, inner residential borough of Metropolitan Toronto (1971 population = 104,785). East York then had a broad housing mix of low-rise and high-rise dwellings. Its population was homogeneously British-Canadian in ethnicity and a mixture of working class and middle class in socioeconomic status. The respondents' relatively homogeneous social backgrounds enabled us to focus on the effects of ties and networks on the provision of support, without having to allow for potentially confounding differences in ethnicity and social class.

Many East Yorkers have seen their borough as a tranquil, integrated community, insulated from the metropolitan hurly-burly. It has had a long tradition of active social service agencies and communal aid. Yet East York has also participated integrally in the postwar transformation of Toronto: it has always been a part of the metropolitan—and North American—economic system; its basic municipal political decisions were taken over in 1954 by a metropolitan government; it has long been integrated into regional transportation and communication systems. Although its British-Canadian residents remain staunchly in their small homes, their children and kin have dispersed throughout North America. Thus the borough and its residents are quite thoroughly knit into larger social structures, despite their insular self-images.

The Original Survey

We based our original study on a two-hour survey of 845 randomly sampled adult East Yorkers. The survey gathered information about each respondent's socially close community ties: their relationship to the respondent, where they lived, how often they were in contact (both in person and by telephone), the strength of their closeness (or intimacy), and whether they helped one another out in everyday or emergency situations.

The survey had a number of strengths: it used a large, well-designed, and well-collected sample; it obtained separate, systematic information about each of the six socially close "intimates"; it did not assume a priori that these intimate community members were kin or neighbors; it enabled some structural analysis by obtaining reports from respondents on the ties between their intimates; it differentiated crudely between everyday and emergency assistance and between the help that respondents and intimates each gave to the other.

The study's basic conceptual strength was that it treated community as a network of ties and not as a local area containing sets of potential relationships. This switch in perspective enabled us to look for community ties that extended well beyond neighborhoods, and it helped dethrone local or group solidarity as the criterion for viable communities. It encouraged us to evaluate different types of ties—kin or friends, strong or weak, local or long distance—in terms of the access they provided to resources. We found that East Yorkers did not count on most of their intimates or neighbors to provide them with assistance in dealing with either everyday or emergency situations, although almost all East Yorkers could count on some intimates and neighbors for help (Wellman, 1979).

In this study, we only crudely differentiated support according to whether it was "Emergency" or "Everyday." Nevertheless, we came up with suggestive evidence as to what causes supportive resources to flow to East Yorkers. To our initial surprise, the availability of social support had little to do with the personal attributes of either the East Yorkers or the members of their networks (Wellman et al., 1973). Rather, it was related to the nature of the ties between East Yorkers and network members, especially the strength of the relationship, the frequency of contact (in person and by telephone), and whether it was a parent/adult child bond (see Figure 7.2). Furthermore, the availability of assistance from intimates in both everyday and emergency situations did not depend on whether they lived in the same neighborhood as the East Yorker, but it did depend on whether they lived somewhere within the greater metropolitan Toronto area.

The New East York Study

Although our original survey had provided some interesting results, we were dissatisfied. Our data were thin. We had asked about only six intimates, and we knew that personal communities were larger and more complex than that. Brief answers to closed-ended survey questions had told us little about the subtleties and details of interactions. For example, we did not know about what kinds of supportive resources network members supplied to one another, or how strong, intimate ties differed from weaker ones (see Granovetter, 1973, 1982).

Hence we designed the new East York study to provide richer, more comprehensive information. Our basic design decision was to reinterview in depth a small subsample of the original East York respondents. This has enabled us to combine more detailed information from the new interviews with more statistically precise information from the original survey. Instead of asking about only six intimates, we asked about all persons with whom the respondents were significantly "in touch." Not only did we obtain information about more ties, we also obtained much more information about each of these ties: how the persons first met, what they do for one another, their present joys and pains, and the

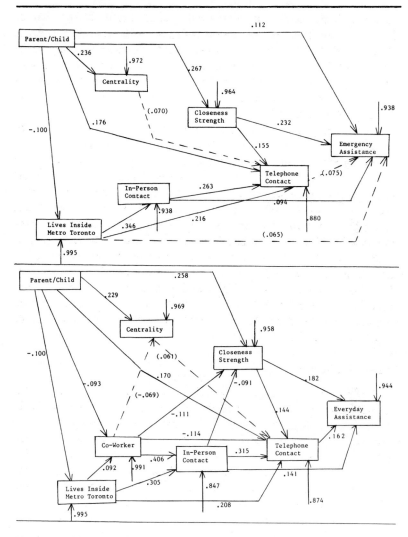

SOURCE: B. Wellman, "The Community Question: The Intimate Networks of East Yorkers," *American Journal of Sociology*, Vol. 84, pp. 1220-1221. © 1979 by The University of Chicago. Reprinted by permission of The University of Chicago Press.

Figure 7.2   Availability of "Social Support" to East Yorkers

specific kinds of help they do and do not give to one another. Moreover, by interviewing the same respondents ten years after the original survey, we now are able to relate longitudinal changes in their personal circumstances to changes in their personal communities.

The tape-recorded interviews usually lasted ten to twelve hours, in four sessions. We used three different methods for recording the information gained. First, we transcribed the interviews completely: Most transcripts are more than 150 pages in length. Second, we constructed qualitative matrices for each personal community. These provide keyword summary information on the composition, structure, and dynamics of each community. Third, we prepared linked computer (SAS) data files for the respondents, their community ties, and the network structures of each personal community.

Our sampling criterion for the interviews was not quite random, as on the one hand we wanted to preserve a longitudinal sample and on the other hand we did not see the point in singlemindedly preserving the ability to generalize to the East York population in 1968. To accommodate one research group member interested in the effects of residential mobility, we randomly selected respondents from among those who had remained in their same East York home, those who had moved elsewhere in East York, those who had moved elsewhere in metropolitan Toronto, and those who had moved farther away. Although slightly more than half of the 33 respondents had moved from East York by the time we interviewed them in 1977-1978, their characteristics are quite typical of East Yorkers and, indeed, of Torontonians in general (see Wellman, 1985b, for details). Almost all still live in or near the metropolitan area, and they retain the moderate-income, predominantly British ethnicity of the 1968 survey sample. The principal changes from the survey sample are that the interview respondents are somewhat more likely to be divorced and to be single parents, and more women have paid employment—all changes consistent with Canadian (and Western industrial) social trends.

While most East Yorkers probably know 1,000-2,000 persons in some way (see the estimates by Boissevain, 1974; Pool & Kochen, 1978), we have not tried to analyze such a comprehensively formidable number. Instead, we have analyzed the 403 active ties with whom the East Yorkers told us they are "in touch." These are the relationships that they actively think about and maintain (although not necessarily with frequent contact). Among these active ties, we have also singled out for special attention the East Yorkers' 164 "intimate" ties: those that they identify as socially close (defined identically to the "intimates" of our 1968 survey).

We analyzed our findings in several complementary ways:

- We aggregate all the 403 active (and 164 intimate) ties of the interviewed East Yorkers. Although this focus on ties does not enable us to study network structure, it does permit us to ask such questions as What proportion of active (or intimate) ties are kin or provide emotional aid?

- We treat the 33 networks of the interviewed East Yorkers as separate units of analysis. This enables us to study the structure of these networks and the ways in which individual networks vary from the overall aggregate (tie-wise) statistics (e.g., what proportions of the networks are predominantly composed of kin or have members who provide major emotional aid?). The networks of the three retired respondents in the interview sample are treated as case studies.

- While these interview data are the principal sources of information in this chapter, we also present data from the more limited set of variables available in the 1968 survey. Our focus here is on the subsample of 67 retired respondents (and their 327 intimate ties) in the survey, but we also provide comparative data on the total survey sample of 845 East Yorkers with their 3930 intimate ties.

In short, when we refer to retired respondents, we are referring to 3 retirees in the 1978 interview sample and/or 67 distinct retirees in 1968 survey.

THE COMPOSITION AND STRUCTURE OF EAST YORKERS' NETWORKS

Composition

Network size and role composition. The great majority of East Yorkers have a sizable number of active ties in their networks. Most have at least eleven such ties; fourteen if ties to married couples (usually interaction occurs as one unit) are counted as two ties (Table 7.1). On the average, four of these active ties are with socially close intimates—enough to fill most dinner tables—and at least three active ties are with persons routinely contacted (in person or by telephone) at least three times per week or more. Moreover, most East Yorkers have at least one socially close intimate tie with whom they are in touch many times per week: a "best friend" or "close sister" who is a reliable source of companionship and aid (see Wellman et al., in press, for more details on many of the findings reported in this section).

Kin play an important but not predominant role in most East Yorkers' lives, constituting 45% of all active ties (Table 7.1). Immediate kin (parents, adult children, siblings) are especially important. Friends are the second most prevalent type of active tie after kin (25%). They are especially apt to be intimates (39% of all intimate ties). Unlike kinship—many of the East Yorkers' kin are tied to them whether they like it or not—friendship is a role that the East Yorkers have more discretion in creating and maintaining. Neighbors, coworkers, and fellow members of formal organizations are active network members in lesser numbers (Table 7.1). In addition, many current friends are former neighbors or coworkers.

Whatever the roles, the East Yorkers' ties are quite long-standing. Their active (and intimate) ties have lasted a median of 19 years, and only one-quarter of their active ties have lasted less than nine years. To be sure, many of these ties are kinship relations into which the two parties were born, but their long duration is an important aspect of these relationships and not an artifact to be explained away. In any event, the median length of active ties with nonkin is a quite durable eight years.

The evidence available for retired East Yorkers shows little psychic disengagement in their lives but some "structural disengagement" (see also Shanas et al., 1968). The role composition of the retired persons in the survey sample is, on the average, quite similar to the overall sample except for the absence of current coworkers (Table 7.1). However, the three retired respondents in the 1978 interview sample (male lab technician, male plumber, female clerk) have fewer neighbors than the other interview respondents (Wellman, 1985b). All three are active, recently retired and happily married. Two have recently moved to winterized rural homes about one hundred miles north of Toronto where they can putter around happily. They are just beginning to develop local ties. The third has remained in Toronto, but spends a good deal of time traveling to visit intimates. Thus it is the sharp discontinuities in their lives—giving up paid labor and moving to a new area— that have significantly affected their networks.[1]

All of the interviewed East Yorkers, including the retirees, have diverse networks containing active ties with persons in at least two roles out of the six analyzed. Indeed the median number of roles present is four; usually Immediate Kin, Extended Kin, Friend, and one of Neighbor, Coworker, or Organizational Contact. Yet this diversity does not necessarily mean that a great variety of network members play a great variety of roles. While intimate ties are mostly with kin and friends, the network members seen several times per week are mostly neighbors and coworkers. In short, most East Yorkers spend much of the week interacting with a few active network members to whom they do not feel very close, and they are in less frequent contact with most of their close intimate ties. Indeed, the most extreme case is the retired clerk, many of whose ties are with kin in West Germany—seen once a year when she makes a Christmas visit, although telephoned more frequently.

TABLE 7.1   Network Size and Role Composition

Dataset	1978 Interviews		1968 Survey	
RESPONDENTS	ALL	ALL	ALL	RETIRED
Type of Tie	Active	Intimate	Intimate	Intimate
Mean number of ties	11	4	5	5
% Immediate kin	22	30	30	30
% Extended kin	23	18	20	20
% Neighbors	18	9	6	10
% Coworkers	7	4	6	0
% Friends	25	39	38	40
% Organizational contact	4	1	_a	_a
Number of networks	33		845	67
Number of ties	403	164	3930	327

a. Not available

These findings suggest that gerontologists may have focused too narrowly on studying supportive ties with kin. Indeed, some such studies have looked only at ties with adult children. Although kin are a natural starting point for analysis—given historic patterns and contemporary norms—studies that look only at kin give up the ability to see how a broad range of network ties may provide access to a variety of supportive resources (see the discussions in Synge & Marshall, 1979; Hagestad, 1981; Johnson & Catalano, 1981; Wood, 1981). Indeed, many East Yorkers have few ties with kin, and many do not contact frequently the kinship ties they do have. And although recent gerontological discussions have raised the question of the "substitution" of nonkin for kin ties, the question has received little empirical attention until now (see the discussions in Atchley, 1972; Dono et al., 1978; Johnson & Catalano, 1981; Marshall, Rosenthal, & Synge, 1983). Moreover, the "substitutability" debate unwarrantedly treats kinship as the normal source of community ties (and social support), rather than asking the more neutral question of the structural conditions under which the aged maintain relationships with different sorts of persons.

Residential dispersion and contact. The largest proportion of active and intimate network members live a short drive or local telephone call away from the East Yorkers, at distances from 1 to 30 miles (Table 7.2). This is true for retirees as well. While one-third of all the East Yorkers' active network members live more than 30 miles away—necessitating a long drive, airplane ride, or long-distance call for contact—less than one-quarter live within a mile's walking distance.

Although most ties of East Yorkers extend outside their neighborhoods, local ties retain real importance. Of the active network members, 17% live on the same block while another 5% live within a mile. Moreover, many coworkers are seen "locally" at work; their effective distance from the East Yorkers is zero. Proximity, in the neighborhood or at work, strongly affects the frequency of both face-to-face and telephone contact, despite the high rate of automobile use, free (i.e., flat monthly rate) telephone calls throughout the metropolitan Toronto area, and low-cost long-distance telephone rates. Thus 41% of those active network members contacted at least 3 times per week live within a mile while another 25% are coworkers (Wellman et al., in press).

Most networks are mixtures of local and distant ties, with even the members of the most local network living a median of 2 miles away. Although some network members tend to cluster together in old hometowns, at workplaces, and in the respondents' former neighborhoods, most members of most networks are dispersed. This locational diversity helps explain why networks tend to interact in small groups rather than as wholes: It is difficult to get them together at the same time, and except for family reunions, there is no English-Canadian tradition of meeting in public or ceremonial spaces.

East Yorkers are in touch with about half of their active network members in an average week, using face-to-face contact somewhat more frequently than telephone contact (Table 7.2). Intimates keep in somewhat more frequent contact and use the telephone more often. This is in part because intimates are less often physically proximate neighbors and coworkers and in part because telephone use is more voluntary than many face-to-face encounters and less dependent on social encounters that others arrange. Rates of face-to-face and telephone contact are positively correlated: As one increases, so does the other. Indeed, the use of one mode of communication often stimulates the other, as when a daughter calls her aged mother to arrange a visit.

Gerontologists have only recently begun to consider how the residential disperson of network members may affect the quality and quantity of sociable contact and interpersonal support (see Longino & Jackson, 1980; Cicirelli, 1981; Marshall et al., 1983). For example, Cantor and McGloin (1977) suggest that long-distance kin are less likely to be in contact with the aged. Such dispersed kin may also be less able to provide physical help, know about local problems, and know about local resources to deal with problems.

Yet research findings suggest that many aged continue to have high rates of interaction. Thus one study has shown that the aged and their

TABLE 7.2   Residential Distance and Frequency of Contact

Dataset	1978 Interviews		1968 Survey	
RESPONDENTS	ALL	ALL	ALL	RETIRED
Type of Tie	Active	Intimate	Intimate	Intimate
% Living ≤ 1 mile	22	18	13[a]	13[a]
% Living > 30 miles	32	32	24[b]	30[b]
% Face-to-face contact				
≥ 1 time per week	35	39	49	53
% Phone contact				
≥ 1 time per week	26	40	53	64
% Overall contact				
≥ 1 time per week	45	58	67	74

a. Percentage living in "same neighborhood."
b. Percentage living "outside metro Toronto."
c. Face-Face + phone contact (interviews); either face-to-face or phone contact > 1 time per week (survey).

adult children often use the telephone for companionship and support (Synge, Rosenthal, & Marshall, 1981), and our survey data show that the aged have higher rates of telephone interaction than other East Yorkers (Table 7.2). Although losses of jobs and homes may disrupt contacts for some aged ("We've moved away and we don't visit so often," says the retired clerk), such structural shocks to the social system may actually facilitate contact. In particular, retired working women, the preeminent community maintainers in most households, may use the reduction of their double work load to intensify ties. In some cases network members may take the opportunity of their freedom from paid labor to move closer together. For example, as a result of the massive retired Jewish migration from northeastern American cities to southeastern Florida, friends and kinfolk probably live closer to one another and have more contact than since childhood.

Structure

Structural embeddedness. Until recently, most studies of social support, nongerontological as well as gerontological, have treated community ties as discrete dyads, using exchange theory as an underlying perspective (see the reviews in Wellman, 1981; Hall & Wellman, 1985; see also Bengtson & Dowd, 1980; Marshall, 1980; Cook, 1982). Often, such analysts have termed the aggregate of these dyadic ties *networks* in a loose, metaphoric way without taking into account the structure of the relationships between network members. Yet the essence of community ties is that they are a structural system; each tie is structurally embedded in a larger social network, and the form of this network can markedly affect the kinds of resources which flow through any specific tie.

The necessity for considering these ties in larger network perspective is shown by our data. For one thing, most networks contain no isolates (persons connected only to the focal East Yorker in the network), and those that do contain isolates almost always have only one or two. In the one measure of structure available in the survey, network density, retired East Yorkers are similar to other respondents (see Table 7.3). Indeed, the median member of the median network is directly linked to 3 other active network members, while in one extreme case, the median member has 10 direct links with others.

Only a minority of active ties are dyadic, existing between the East Yorker and the network member without any mutual reference to third parties (Table 7.3). Indeed, the retired East Yorkers in the interview sample have no dyadic ties: Interactions tend to take place in private homes, with at least one spouse involved. Not only do most ties take mutual links to others into account, most interactions also operate in the actual physical presence of others. For example, 23% of the entire interview sample's active ties usually operate in the presence of one or both spouses, while another 42% usually operate in the presence of other persons with whom the East Yorker and the network member are mutually linked. But ties do not have to operate in the physical presence of others for the interactions between the two parties to be affected significantly by their links to third (and fourth) parties. Thus our coders estimated that 81% of all active ties are "structurally embedded" in this way (Table 7.3). Indeed, the East Yorkers report interacting with fully 46% of their active ties only because they are embedded in such larger social structures as the workplace or kinship group that constrain them to do so (Wellman et al., in press). That most ties are structurally embedded, nearly half involuntary, and a few (4% of all active ties) not even enjoyed clearly calls into question the voluntaristic assumptions by some social psychologists that network members form and maintain ties principally because of "interpersonal attraction" (e.g., Berscheid & Walster, 1978; see also Erickson's, in press, critique).

Clustering. We used the SOCK / COMPLT computer package (Alba, 1973; Alba & Gutmann, 1972) to cluster the active ties of the 33 networks, the first time to our knowledge that this has been done for this large a sample of naturally occurring personal community networks. The typical East Yorker's network contains one large *component* of 8 members, all of whom are directly or indirectly linked to one another (in addition to the direct ties each network member has with the focal East Yorker). These networks also often contain an isolate, dyadic pair or a small, densely knit *cluster* of ties (Table 7.3). The median density of these networks is 0.33; in other words, one-third of all active members are directly linked with one another. Within the largest component, about half of the members are directly linked (median density = 0.56), with a fully linked clique of about 4 persons often being at the core. Yet averages are deceiving: The 33 networks vary from densely knit, cohesive structures to sparsely knit, fragmented structures.

Thus the networks of East Yorkers are more complex structurally than the densely knit solidarities that support system research assumes. Hence, East Yorkers must look for assistance from distinct, often specialized, parts of their networks, and they cannot assume that information about their needs flows easily to all network members. This is as true for the retired members of our sample as it is for the others.

Although making for low communal solidarity, the variety of ties, the multiplicity of parts, and the uneven internal density of their networks provide useful structural bases for dealing with contingencies. While densely knit clusters can provide a basis for cooperative activity, heterogeneous ties organized in the multiple clusters and ties of a network can give East Yorkers indirect access to the connections with others that their network members have. This suggests that such sparsely knit networks may be more than simply a passive rearrangement of interpersonal ties in response to the pressures of large-scale social systems. They may also be active attempts by contemporary individuals to gain access to—and control over—system resources, given differentiated societal divisions of labor.

The implications of such multiple clusters for the aged are profound, if any form of disengagement theory has any validity. If the aged belong to a single unitary network which provides a broad spectrum of support, then disengagement may still leave them with a wide variety of informal assistance. But if the aged belong to multiple clusters, the consequences of disengagement go well beyond cutting down on the number of ties and thinning down the content of those that remain. In the latter case, such cutting and thinning will isolate the aged from some of the diverse social circles to which they had been linked, and hence cut them off from significant sectors of resources. This reduces the flexibility of the aged in obtaining resources for themselves through interpersonal means and makes them more dependent on formal bureaucracies for sustenance.

TABLE 7.3   Network Structure

Dataset	1978 Interviews		1968 Survey	
RESPONDENTS	ALL	ALL	ALL	RETIRED
Type of Tie	Active	Intimate	Intimate	Intimate
% Dyadic ties	36	41	a	a
% Structurally embedded	81	73	a	a
Median network density[b]	33	a	33	31
Median number of clusters	1	1	a	a
Median number of isolates	1	0	a	a

a. Data not available.
b. Percentage actual ties of all possible ties (excluding direct ties with focal East Yorkers).

THE CONTENTS OF EAST YORKERS' TIES

Varieties of Support

When analysts treat all ties as globally supportive or use a simple support/nonsupport dichotomy, they assume that all ties provide a broad range of assistance or that analysts can study all supportive ties in the same ways, regardless of which particular types of resources the ties provide (e.g., Beels, 1979; Finlayson, 1976; Henderson, 1977; Gourash, 1978). These analysts make no distinction between community ties and support ties because they believe that all community ties provide support. Such an approach grows out of the contentions by some social exchange theorists that primary ties are fundamentally based on the dyadic exchange of resources which gratify human needs (e.g., Homans, 1961; Berscheid & Walster, 1978). Yet the use of those contentions by some analysts in developing a global construct of support runs counter to arguments that capitalism, industrialization, and urbanization have forced people to develop specialized relationships with members of their social networks (see the discussions in Wellman, 1981; Hall & Wellman, 1985).

Indeed, although most ties of most interviewed East Yorkers do provide some sort of social support, they report that 7% of their active ties do not provide any of the 15 types of aid or 4 types of companionship we studied (Wellman, 1985a). These nonsupportive ties usually are with persons with whom the East Yorkers interact because they are juxtaposed in the same social contexts (e.g., as coworkers or neighbors) or because they are members of the same social circles (e.g., kinship systems, friendship groups).

Yet documenting that most active ties are supportive does little more than debunk even further the now-discredited tale of contemporary interpersonal isolation and anomie. (It seems as if analysts run the risks of apocalyptic visions, believing that either all or no ties are supportive.) But is "social support" itself a generalized resource ranging over a broad spectrum of assistance or are there important differences in the kinds of supportive resources that specific ties and networks provide? By decomposing support into 15 measures of aid and 4 measures of companionship, we are able to see how broadly diffused each of these types of support are and which types of support tend to occur together in the same ties.

Table 7.4 shows that most networks do provide East Yorkers with several kinds of *companionship* (sociability, discussing things, doing things together), emotional support (minor emotional support, major emotional support, family advice), and *minor services* (in and out of the household). Aid involving major commitments of services is much less common, as are links providing information, dealing with bureaucracies, and helping to find jobs and housing.[2]

Both supply and demand help explain why these types of resources are so abundant in most East Yorkers' networks. Companionship, emotional aid, and minor services are easily supplied and require only small, widely available skills and services. On the one hand, the suppliers of these services do not have to have many material resources at their disposal; on the other hand, most find it easy to be buddies, empathic listeners, and helping hands. Moreover, as these are not zero-sum relationships, supplying these resources does not necessarily cost the giver. Indeed, to give companionship—or even emotional aid and services—may be to gain in companionship as well.

With respect to demand, companionship, emotional support, and helping hands are the resources which most East Yorkers say they want from networks. If they purchased such services, it is not likely that they could get the same combination of frequent, flexible, nuanced, inexpensive services that network members supply. Hence the East Yorkers are more willing to invest in the time and effort necessary to maintain their ties (and their services) than they are to spend the money for equivalent services.

In contrast, East Yorkers often purchase on the open market or seek through bureaucracies the resources that are less abundant in these networks (e.g., large sums of money, major services). Often they do not

TABLE 7.4   Percentage of Active Ties and Networks
Providing Specific Resources to East Yorkers

	Percentage of Ties Sending a Specific Resource			Percentage of Networks in Which East Yorker Receives Resource From	
	to East Yorker Only	to and from East Yorker[a]	from East Yorker Only	at Least a Tie	50% + of Ties
Common resources					
sociability	a	72	a	100	73
doing things together	a	36	a	91	45
discussing things	a	46	a	94	45
minor emotional aid	10	40	7	83	45
family advice	10	29	10	76	28
major emotional aid	10	25	8	69	31
minor services	15	32	7	83	38
minor household aid	12	26	9	90	31
lending household items	7	32	5	83	45
Uncommon resources					
formal group activity	a	18	a	48	6
major household aid	6	9	4	55	3
major services	4	4	3	45	0
small $	8	8	5	62	10
big $ (nonhousing)	2	0.3	4	28	0
housing $	1	0.3	3	28	0
bureaucratic aid	7	6	4	38	3
job opening information	5	1	5	48	0
job contacts	3	1	4	31	0
housing search aid	5	1	3	35	0
Sample size		336 ties		29 networks	

a. "Companionship" variables assumed symmetric, to and from East Yorkers and network members.

even ask network members for these sorts of aid, as they do not consider getting such resources to be part of their relationships. Often network members do not have such specialized resources available in the necessary quantities; for example, time for long-term health care. At times, they want to avoid the increased reciprocal obligations that would come if they called upon network members for such substantial amounts of aid. Nevertheless, these less common forms of support often are important components of those ties that do contain them. Moreover, considered as a property of networks (and not ties), they have been crucial to seeing East Yorkers through major illnesses and emotional breakdowns, and have helped several to get coveted jobs and homes.

Retired East Yorkers participate in exchanges of supportive resources to about the same extent as others. While the survey data show they send emergency aid to fewer intimates (26%) than do other East Yorkers, they receive everyday (21%) and emergency (27%) aid at about the same rate (see also Wellman, 1979; Wellman, 1985b). (Note that the broad survey questions elicited much lower rates of ties sending support than did the more detailed interview questions.) The two retired men in the interview sample, like most other men, give aid principally through the exchange of services (see also Wellman, 1985b). Thus the retired lab technician has helped his closest friend build a garage and has helped his second closest friend put in a new boiler. This is also the way they are getting to know their neighbors. In this way the retired plumber is making friends with the couple next door. He reports: "Debbie is the greatest little borrower you ever saw. She always comes and borrows a shovel or a rake or a hoe or something." (The retired clerk, unlike most other women, seems always to have been quite interpersonally reserved, and does not exchange much emotional aid or services.)

The variety of resources we have observed suggests that "support" must be considered in its variety when planning gerontological care. Ties that provide only emotional support may represent quite different health potentials than those that provide services and material aid (see also the review in Mitchell & Hurley, 1981; Wan, 1982).

Packages of Support

Clustering. We used variable cluster analysis to find out which of the 4 types of companionship and 15 types of aid tend to occur together in the same ties. Variable cluster analysis uses a correlation matrix to divide a set of variables into unidimensional clusters in a way that maximizes the sum of the original variables' variance across clusters, which is explained in turn by the cluster components (see Wellman, 1985a, for more details on our clustering). Unlike a factor analysis search for underlying dimensions, variable cluster analysis is concerned only with producing packages of associated variables. In this case, a 5-cluster solution provides the best balance between increasing explained variance and minimizing single variable clusters. (Attempts to produce more clusters only split single variables out from existing clusters.) These 5 clusters (and their component variables) are as follows (see also Figure 7.3):

- information (job information, job contacts, housing search)
- companionship (sociability, discussing things, doing things together, formal group activities)
- emotional aid (minor emotional aid, family problems advice, major emotional aid, major services)
- services (minor services, lend/give household items, minor household aid, major household aid, organizational aid)
- financial aid (small $, big $, housing $)

The cluster structure shows a distinct hierarchy. Each division stage splits off a single cluster containing three to five specific kinds of support. Although the cluster program is capable of splitting those clusters even further, it never does so here. Rather, at each division stage it splits another specific package of aid from the remaining, more generalized "support" package. The structure and contents of this clustering suggest that the more diffuse kinds of support—information and companionship—often come from different persons than those kinds of support which explicitly supply targeted aid: emotional aid, services, and financial aid. Major services tend to come from the same persons who give emotional aid. Such services are usually given to distressed persons whose families are suffering from acute or chronic illness. The packaging of support in the same ties is clearly substantive: Those who give one sort of emotional aid are apt to give another, and so on. Although this is not surprising, two other likely packaging principles do not seem to operate: There is little tendency for givers of large amounts of one kind of aid to give large amounts of substantively different kinds of aid, and there is little tendency for the common (or uncommon) kinds of resources to be packaged together in the same ties.

Specialization. Because support is separated into many types and packages, it is reasonable to ask about the extent of specialization in these networks. Little specialization (i.e., "broadly based ties"), with the same ties providing many types of resources, would indicate that East Yorkers participate in multipurpose networks providing a broad range of support to members. Extensive specialization would indicate that East Yorkers must move from tie to tie in order to obtain specific kinds of resources. It is the difference between shopping at department stores or boutiques.

Most ties are fairly specialized. Thus the majority of the East Yorkers' active ties provide 4 or fewer of the 19 types of companionship and aid we studied. Indeed, most ties contain 3 or fewer of the 5 broad clusters: typically, Companionship intertwined with some form of Emotional

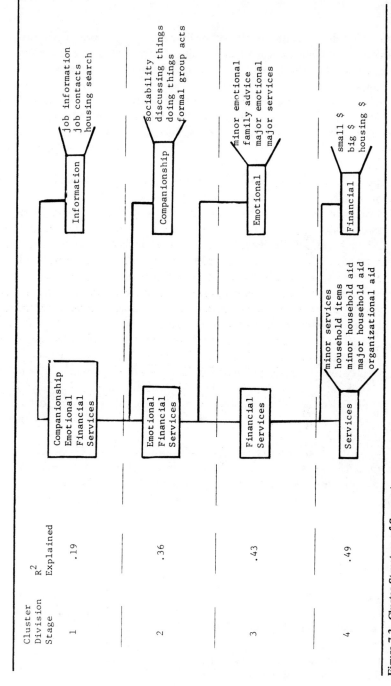

Figure 7.3 Cluster Structure of Support

221

Aid or Services (Wellman, 1985a; Wellman et al., in press). Thus East Yorkers must maintain a diverse portfolio of relationships, maneuvering between several ties in their networks in order to receive different types of support.

Reciprocity. To what extent is the norm of reciprocity (Gouldner, 1960) honored by East Yorkers? That which is given ought to be repaid if only to ensure that more is forthcoming. Such reciprocity might take the form of *specific exchanges*—in which a certain kind and amount of support is repaid precisely; more *generalized reciprocity*—in which support in one area is repaid by support in another (Sahlins, 1965; Cook, 1982); or *network balancing*—in which support given by one network member is balanced by the recipient's support of others (Lévi-Strauss, 1949).

When we asked the East Yorkers about which of the 15 types of support (excluding companionship) they received from each network member, we also asked them about which types of support they themselves had provided to each member. We found many specific exchanges among the more abundant kinds of support: Emotional aid and small services usually flow in both directions (Table 7.5). When almost all East Yorkers, including the aged, give these resources, they usually get them back from the same person, sooner or later. However, the less common forms of support tend to flow in one direction or the other but not in both. Thus persons who have lent mortgage money or have provided long-term or intensive health care rarely get that sort of aid back from the ones they have helped (see Wellman et al., in press, for further details).

In addition to such exchanges, a substantial amount of *generalized reciprocity* exists in the ties. Even if two parties to a tie are not exchanging the same sort of resource with each other, they are sending about the same number of resources to each other. Such reciprocity does not necessarily mean that East Yorkers exchange many, or the same resources with all network members. It does mean, though, that those network members to whom they are sending many resources are quite likely to be sending many back to them, and that those to whom they send few resources are sending few back to them. Moreover, the East Yorkers' networks are even more balanced than their ties are reciprocal. The "Network" correlations in Table 7.5 are almost always higher than the corresponding "Ties" correlations, and usually markedly so. Moreover, the overall support measures are even more highly correlated. Thus the balancing of the networks is much more than the sum of the exchanges and reciprocities between ties.

TABLE 7.5 Correlations Between East Yorkers' Resources Given to and Received from Network Members

| Type of Tie | Active | | Intimates | |
Correlations By	Tie	Network	Tie	Network
Minor emotional aid	.67	.85	.58	.73
Family advice	.58	.79	.56	.76
Major emotional aid	.61	.77	.62	.78
Minor services	.56	.90	.46	.71
Minor household aid	.55	.86	.38	.71
Lending household items	.75	.96	.65	.87
Major household aid	.57	.82	.53	.74
Major services	.48	.89	.43	.87
Small $	.47	.66	.36	.33*
Big $	.07*	−.04*	.10*	−.06*
Housing $	.11	.22*	−.03*	.11*
Bureaucratic aid	.47	.91	.49	.70
Job opening information	.15	.52	.10*	.54
Job contacts	.11	.71	.11*	.63
Housing search aid	.25	.55	.20	.38*
Sample size	337	29	137	29

*Not significant at .05 level.

Three phenomena seem to be associated with network balancing. First, the structural embeddedness of many ties fosters balancing. Thus the networks maintain the individual ties. Second, those who do not receive much support also do not give out much aid. They stand on their own two feet, with their networks balanced at a low level of activity. Third, the East Yorkers who are active senders of support tend to be active receivers as well. Their entire networks are built around sending and receiving resources, over and above exchanges within specific social circles. Indeed, when all network members reciprocate heavily, networks become balanced almost automatically. In short, network members do unto others as they would have their networks do unto them.

Support in a Network-Analytic Perspective

By placing all their emphasis on "support ties," many analysts have conveyed the impression that such ties only play positive roles in health. Yet why are East Yorkers involved with so many significant ties that do not provide much companionship or support? By directing attention toward those ties that are not sources of support, we draw attention to the possibility that a person may maintain relationships for reasons that have little to do with the direct benefits gained from them and yet such ties may play important roles in that person's health. Hence we believe that analysts would profit by developing models of support that mirror the complex and diverse aspects of community ties.

Only recently has the provision of support been treated as a contingency in gerontological research rather than as an a priori assumption (see Cicirelli, 1981; Synge & Marshall, 1979; Tobin & Kulys, 1980). More complex models of community ties are starting to emerge. For example, Bengtson and Dowd (1980) have argued the importance of studying such exchange relationships for the aged, Wentowski (1981) has suggested that kin ties often are based on generalized reciprocity, and Marshall (1980) has argued that intergenerational inheritance is a delayed component of generalized reciprocity. The evidence of specialization in companionship and services in the interactions of the three retired East Yorkers with their network members is suggestive. Quite clearly, the more our measures tease out different aspects of ties— strength, reciprocity, embeddedness, and so on—the more apt we are to develop a fuller understanding of social support and its influence on health.

THE IMPLICATIONS OF
NETWORK STUDIES FOR LATER LIFE

Much research and common sense have now accumulated to show that personal community networks have important, complex implications for the aged. These networks are important for causing stress, preventing stress, preventing stress from turning into distress, providing acute and chronic care, and fostering recovery. They function as complements of formal care systems independently of such systems, and even antagonistically to them, as when prospective clients are steered away from institutions by friends and relatives.

Coming changes in the world system should increase the importance of community ties even more. The demographic aging of the world population will bring greater demands for chronic and acute care while at the same time shrinking the productive base of the population. The consequent fiscal crisis will bring heavy pressures on states for capital and operating funds for formal health care. At the same time requests for such funds must compete with requests for investment in productive industrial and agrarian facilities.

Bolstering informal care through community ties is an attractive option to policymakers, because of the low cost, flexibility, and efficiency of such ties. Most people get a wide variety of help from such ties. In Canada, several government programs work to form and nurture such ties. Meals on Wheels and Home Help enable the aged to contact new friends willing to provide useful services; local information centers bring together mothers who want to give and receive child care in private homes.

Many policymakers have not yet realized that the large-scale societal transformations which make the need for such services so pressing are also transforming the nature of community ties. Policymakers can no longer assume that all ties are broadly supportive, or that all community networks are local and unitary. Hence neighborhood-centered policies will only be of limited value. The trick is to recognize the differentiated nature of networks and supportive resources in contemporary societies and to develop ways of utilizing their more specialized and more flexible divisions of labor. Epidemiological studies of social categories such as gender and occupation will at best give only proxy measures of access to informal health care resources. It makes a lot more sense to study the social networks themselves and the societal factors which differentially allocate access to resources in social systems.

NOTES

1. See Wellman (1985b) for the characteristics of retired East Yorkers' networks compared to the networks of family men principally engaged in paid labor, family women engaged in both paid and domestic labor, family women engaged only in domestic labor, and single men and women.

2. After the 33 interviews were completed, we realized that we needed more systematic information about the varieties of aid that East Yorkers and network members gave to one another. Hence we used a mail questionnaire to ask the respondents systematically about which of 15 types of aid they gave to and received from each network member. (We were able to code the 4 companionship measures from the interviews themselves.) We were able to obtain responses from 29 of the 33 interviewed respondents (reporting about active ties) with this follow-up questionnaire (see Wellman, 1985a; Wellman et al., in press, for details of the questionnaires).

To simplify reporting, we present information only about the aid that active network members send to the East Yorkers. See Wellman et al. (in press) for information about the aid that East Yorkers send to network members and for the aid that intimates send and receive. The data are consistent with those reported here.

We do not have detailed findings on support from the 1968 survey, as we asked simply: "Which of these (intimates) do you rely on for help in everyday matters? Which of these do you rely on for help in an emergency?" The reported help from intimates—22% in everyday matters and 30% in emergencies—is far lower than the percentages obtained through the interviews and mail questionnaire. We suspect that the interviews and questionnaires are much more reliable and valid, given their detailed inquiries into a variety of aid.

REFERENCES

Adams, B. (1968). *Kinship in an urban setting*. Chicago: Markham.

Alba, R. (1973). A graph-theoretic definition of a sociometric clique. *Journal of Mathematical Sociology, 3*, 113-126.

Alba, R., & Gutmann, M. (1972). SOCK: A sociometric analysis system. *Behavorial Science, 17*, 326.

Aldrich, H. (1979). *Organization and environment*. Englewood Cliffs, NJ: Prentice-Hall.

Atchley, R. (1972). *The social forces in later life*. Belmont, CA: Wadsworth.

Barnes, J. A. (1954). Class and committees in a Norwegian island parish. *Human Relations, 7*, 39-58.

Barnes, J. A. (1972). *Social networks*. Reading, MA: Addison-Wesley.

Beels, C. C. (1979). Social networks and schizophrenia. *Psychiatric Quarterly, 51*, 209-215.

Bell, C., & Newby, H. (1976). Community, communion, class and community action. In D. T. Herbert & R. J. Johnson (Eds.), *Social areas in cities II: Spatial perspectives on problems and policies* (pp. 189-207). London: John Wiley.

Bender, T. (1979). *Community and social change in America*. New Brunswick, NJ: Rutgers University Press.

Bengtson, V., & Dowd, J. (1980). Sociological functionalism, exchange theory and life-cycle analysis. *International Journal of Aging and Human Development, 12*(1), 55-73.

Benyon, H. (1973). *Working for Ford*. London: Allan Lane.

Berkman, L., & Syme, S. L. (1979). Social networks, host resistance, and mortality. *American Journal of Epidemiology, 109*, 186-204.

Berkowitz, S. (1982). *An introduction to structural analysis*. Toronto: Butterworths.

Bernard, H. R., & Killworth, P. (1978). A review of the small world literature. *Connections, 2*, 15-24.

Berscheid, E., & Walster, E. (1978). *Interpersonal attraction* (2nd ed.). Reading, MA: Addison-Wesley.

Boissevain, J. (1974). *Friends of friends*. Oxford: Basil Blackwell.

Boissevain, J., & Mitchell, J. C. (Eds.). (1973). *Network analysis*. The Hague: Mouton.

Boorman, S., & White, H. (1976). Social structure from multiple networks II: Role structures. *American Journal of Sociology, 81*, 1384-1446.

Bott, E. (1957). *Family and social network*. London: Tavistock.

Breiger, R. (1979, February). Toward an operational theory of community elite structures. *Quality and Quantity, 13*, 21-57.

Burgess, E. W. (1960). Aging in Western culture. In E. Burgess (Ed.), *Aging in Western societies* (pp. 3-28). Chicago: University of Chicago Press.

Burt, R. (1980). Models of network structure. *Annual Review of Sociology, 6*, 79-141.

Burt, R. (1982). *Toward a structural theory of action*. New York: Academic Press.

Cano, J. E., Falbe, C., Kail, B., Litwak, E., Sherman, R., & Siegal, D. (1978, August). *The structure and function of primary groups in old age*. Paper presented at the annual meeting of the American Sociological Association, San Francisco.

Cantor, M., & McCloin, J. (1977, November). *Friends and neighbors: An overlooked resource in the informal support systems*. Paper presented at the annual meeting of the Gerontological Society of America, San Francisco.

Cicirelli, V. (1981, November). *Adult children's attachment and helping behavior to elderly parents; A path model*. Paper presented at the annual meeting of the

Gerontological Society of America and the Canadian Association of Gerontology, Toronto.

Coates, D. et al. (1970). *Yorklea social environment survey research report*. Toronto: Clarke Institute of Psychiatry, Community Studies Section.

Conrath, D., Higgins, C., & McClean, R. (1983, September). A comparison of the reliability of questionnaire versus diary data. *Social Networks, 5*, 315-322.

Cook, K. (1982). Network structures from an exchange perspective. In P. Marsden & N. Lin (Eds.), *Social structure and network analysis* (pp. 177-200). Beverly Hills, CA: Sage.

Craven, P., & Wellman, B. (1973). The network city. *Sociological Inquiry, 43*, 57-88.

Cumming, E., & Henry, W. (1961). *Growing old: The process of disengagement*. New York: Basic Books.

Dear, M., & Taylor, S. M. (1979). *Community attitude toward neighborhood public facilities: A study of mental health services in metropolitan Toronto* (Research Report). Hamilton, Ontario: McMaster University, Department of Geography.

Erickson, B. (1978). Some problems of inference from chain data. In K. Schuessler (Ed.), *Sociological methodology* (pp. 276-302). San Francisco: Jossey-Bass.

Erickson, B. (in press). The relationship basis of attitudes. In S. D. Berkowitz & B. Wellman (Eds.), *Social structures*. Cambridge: Cambridge University Press.

Evans, R., & Northwood, L. (1979) The utility of natural help relationships. *Social Science and Medicine, 13A*, 789-795.

Fararo, T. (1981). Social activity and social structure: A contribution to the theory of social systems. *Cybernetics and Systems, 12*, 53-81.

Finlayson, A. (1976). Social networks as coping resources. *Social Science and Medicine, 10*, 92-103.

Firth, R., Hubert, J., & Forge, A. (1969). *Families and their relatives*. London: Routledge & Kegan Paul.

Fischer, C. (1976). *The urban experience*. New York: Harcourt Brace Jovanovich.

Fischer, C. (1982). *To dwell among friends*. Chicago: University of Chicago Press.

Friedmann, H. (in press). Form and substance in the analysis of the world economy. In S. D. Berkowitz & B. Wellman (Eds.), *Social structures*. Cambridge: Cambridge University Press.

Gordon, M. (1978). *The American family*. New York: Random House.

Gottlieb, B. (1981). Preventive interventions involving social networks and social support. In B. Gottlieb (Ed.), *Social networks and social support* (pp. 201-232). Beverly Hills, CA: Sage.

Gourash, N. (1978). Help-seeking: A review of the literature. *American Journal of Community Psychology, 6*, 413-423.

Granovetter, M. (1973). The strength of weak ties. *American Journal of Sociology, 78*, 1360-1380.

Granovetter, M. (1974). *Getting a job*. Cambridge, MA: Harvard University Press.

Granovetter, M. (1982). The strength of weak ties: A network theory revisited. In P. Marsden & N. Lin (Eds.), *Social structure and network analysis* (pp. 105-130). Beverly Hills, CA: Sage.

Hagestad, G. (1981). Problems and promises in the social psychology of intergenerational relations. In R. Fogel, E. S. Hatfield, S. Kiesler, & J. March (Eds.), *Stability and change in the family* (pp. 11-46). New York: Academic Press.

Hall, A., & Wellman, B. (1985). Social structure, social networks and social support. In S. Cohen & S. L. Syme (Eds.), *Social support and health* (pp. 23-41). Orlando, FL: Academic Press.

Hammer, M. (1981). *Impact of social networks on health and disease.* Paper presented at the annual meeting of the American Association for the Advancement of Science, Toronto.

Henderson, S. (1977). The social network, support and neurosis. *British Journal of Psychiatry, 131,* 185-191.

Hirsch, B. (1979). Psychological dimensions of social network: A multimethod analysis. *American Journal of Community Psychology, 7,* 263-277.

Hochschild, A. (1975). Disengagement theory: A critique and proposal. *American Sociological Review, 40,* 553-569.

Homans, G. (1961). *Social behavior: Its elementary forms.* New York: Harcourt Brace Jovanovich.

Howard, L. (1974). *Industrialization and community in Chotangapur.* Unpublished doctoral dissertation, Department of Sociology, Harvard University.

Howard, L. (in press). Work and community in industrializing India. In S. D. Berkowitz & B. Wellman (Eds.), *Social structures.* Cambridge: Cambridge University Press.

Johnson, C., & Catalano, D. (1981). Childless elderly and their family supports. *Gerontologist, 21,* 610-617.

Kornhauser, W. (1968). Mass society. *International Encyclopedia of the Social Sciences, 10,* 58-64.

Larson, R. (1978). Thirty years of research of the subjective well-being of older Americans. *Journal of Gerontology, 33,* 109-125.

Laslett, P. (1977). Societal development and aging. In R. Binstock & E. Shanas (Eds.), *Handbook of aging in the social sciences* (pp. 87-116). New York: Van Nostrand Reinhold.

Lee, N. (1969). *The search for an abortionist.* Chicago: University of Chicago Press.

Lemon, B., Bengtson, V., & Peterson, J. (1972). An exploration of the activity theory of aging: Activity types and life satisfaction among in-movers to a retirement community. *Journal of Gerontology, 27,* 511-523.

Lévi-Strauss, C. (1949). *Les Structures Élémentaires de la Parenté.* Paris: Presses Universitaires de France.

Litwak, E. (1960). Geographical mobility and extended family cohesion. *American Sociological Review, 25,* 385-394.

Liu, W., & Duff, R. (1972). The strength in weak ties. *Public Opinion Quarterly, 78,* 361-366.

Lopata, H. (1978). Contributions of extended families to the support systems of metropolitan area widows. *Journal of Marriage and the Family, 40,* 355-364.

Longino, C. F., Jr., & Jackson, D. (1980). Migration and the aged. *Research on Aging, 2,* 205-216.

Luxton, M. (1980). *More than a labour of love.* Toronto: Women's Press.

Maddox, G. (1970). Persistence of life style among the elderly. In E. Palmore (Ed.), *Normal aging: Reports from the Duke Longitudinal Study, 1955-1969* (pp. 329-331). Durham, NC: Duke University Press.

Marshall, V. (1980). State of the art lecture: The sociology of aging. In J. Crawford (Ed.), *Canadian gerontological collection III* (pp. 76-144). Winnipeg: Canadian Association on Gerontology.

Marshall, V. (1983). Generations, age groups and cohorts. *Canadian Journal on Aging, 2*(2), 51-62.

Marshall, V., Rosenthal, C., & Synge, J. (1981). *The family as a health service organization for the elderly*. Paper presented at the annual meeting of the Society for the Study of Social Problems, Toronto.

Marshall, V., Rosenthal, C., & Synge, J. (1983). Concerns about parental health. In E. W. Markson (Ed.), *Older women* (pp. 253-273). Lexington, MA: D. C. Heath.

Marx, L. (1964). *The machine in the garden*. New York: Oxford University Press.

Mayer, P., with Mayer, I. (1974). *Townsmen or tribesmen* (2nd ed.). Capetown: Oxford University Press.

Mitchell, J. C. (1969a). The concept and use of social networks. In J. C. Mitchell (Ed.), *Social networks in urban situations* (pp. 1-50). Manchester: Manchester University Press.

Mitchell, J. C. (1969b). Preface. In J. C. Mitchell (Ed.), *Social networks in urban situations* (pp. v-vi). Manchester: Manchester University Press.

Mitchell, J. C. (Ed.). (1969c). *Social networks in urban situations*. Manchester: Manchester University Press.

Mitchell, R., & Hurley, D., Jr. (1981). Collaboration with natural helping networks: Lessons from studying paraprofessionals. In B. Gottlieb (Ed.), *Social networks and social support* (pp. 277-298). Beverly Hills, CA: Sage.

Mueller, D. (1980). Social networks: A promising direction for research on the relationship of the social environment to psychiatric disorder. *Social Science and Medicine, 14A*, 147-161.

Nisbet, R. (1962). *Community and power*. New York: Oxford University Press.

Oberschall, A. (1978). Theories of social conflict. *Annual Review of Sociology, 4*, 291-315.

Parsons, T. (1949). The social structure of the family. In R. Ashen (Ed.), *The family: Its function and destiny* (pp. 173-201). New York: Harper.

Pool, I., & Kochen, M. (1978). Contacts and influence. *Social Networks, 1*, 5-51.

Radcliffe-Brown, A. R. (1940). On social structure. *Journal of the Royal Anthropological Society of Great Britain and Ireland, 70*, 1-12.

Roberts, B. (1978). *Cities of peasants: The political economy of urbanization in the Third World*. London: Edward Arnold.

Rogers, E., & Kincaid, D. L. (1981). *Communication networks*. New York: Free Press.

Sahlins, M. (1965). On the sociology of primitive exchange. In M. Banton (Ed.), *The relevance of models for social anthropology* (pp. 139-186). London: Tavistock.

Sarason, I., & Sarason, B. (Eds.). (1985). *Social support: Theory, research and applications*. The Hague: Martinus Nijhoff.

Shanas, E. et al. (1968). *Old people in three industrial societies*. London: Routledge & Kegan Paul.

Silberfeld, M. (1978). Psychological symptoms and social supports. *Social Psychiatry, 13*, 11-17.

Simmel, G. (1908). Group expansion and the development of individuality. (R. Albares, Trans.). In D. N. Levine (Ed.), *Georg Simmel on individuality and social forms* (pp. 251-293). Chicago: University of Chicago Press.

Simmel, G. (1922). The web of group-affiliations (R. Bendix, Trans.). In *Conflict and the web of group affiliations* (pp. 125-195). York: Free Press.

Snyder, D., & Kick, E. (1979). Structural position in the world system and economic growth, 1955-1970: A multiple network analysis of transnational interactions. *American Journal of Sociology, 84*, 1096-1126.

Srole, L., Langner, T., Michael, S., Kirkpatrick, P., Opler, M., & Rennie, T. (1975). *Mental health in the metropolis* (Rev. and enlarged ed.). New York: Harper & Row.

Stack, C. (1974). *All our kin*. New York: Harper & Row.

Synge, J., & Marshall, V. (1979). *Generational relations and succession*. Research proposal to the Social Sciences and Humanities Research Council of Canada.

Synge, J., Rosenthal, C., & Marshall, V. (1981). *Phoning and writing as means of keeping in touch in the family of later life*. Paper presented at the annual meeting of the Canadian Association on Gerontology, Toronto.

Thoits, P. (1982). Conceptual, methodological and theoretical problems in studying social support as a buffer against life stress. *Journal of Health and Social Behavior, 23*, 145-159.

Thompson, J. (1967). *Organizations in action*. New York: McGraw-Hill.

Tilly, C. (1964). *The Vendée: A sociological analysis of the counterrevolution of 1793*. Cambridge, MA: Harvard University Press.

Tilly, C. (1978). *From mobilization to revolution*. Reading, MA: Addison-Wesley.

Tilly, C., & Brown, C. H. (1967). On uprooting, kinship, and the auspices of migration. *International Journal of Comparative Sociology, 8*, 139-164.

Tilly, L., & Scott, J. (1978). *Women, work and family*. New York: Holt, Rinehart & Winston.

Tobin, S., & Kulys, R. (1980). The family and services. In C. Eisdorfer (Ed.), *Annual review of gerontology and geriatrics* (Vol. 1, pp. 370-399). New York: Springer.

Wan, T. (1982). *Stressful life events, social-support networks, and gerontological health*. Lexington, MA: D. C. Heath.

Warren, R. (1978). *The community in America* (3rd ed.). Chicago: Rand McNally.

Wellman, B. (1968). Community ties and mental health (working paper). Toronto: Clarke Institute of Psychiatry, Community Studies Section.

Wellman, B. (1979). The community question: The intimate networks of East Yorkers. *American Journal of Sociology, 84*, 1201-1231.

Wellman, B. (1981). Applying network analysis to the study of support. In B. Gottlieb (Ed.), *Social networks and social support* (pp. 171-200). Beverly Hills, CA: Sage.

Wellman, B. (1983). Network analysis: Some basic principles. In R. Collins (Ed.), *Sociological theory 1983* (pp. 155-200). San Francisco: Jossey-Bass.

Wellman, B. (1985a). From social support to social network. In I. Sarason & B. Sarason (Eds.), *Social support: Theory, research, applications* (pp. 205-222). The Hague: Martinus Nijhoff.

Wellman, B. (1985b). Domestic work, paid work and net work. In S. Duck & D. Perlman (Eds.), *Understanding personal relationships: An interdisciplinary approach* (pp. 159-191). London: Sage.

Wellman, B., Carrington, P., & Hall, A. (in press). Networks as personal communities. In S. D. Berkowitz & B. Wellman (Eds.), *Social structures*. Cambridge: Cambridge University Press.

Wellman, B., Craven, P., Whitaker, M., Stevens, H., Shorter, A., DuToit, S., & Bakker, H. (1973). Community ties and support systems. In L. S. Bourne, R. D. MacKinnon, & J. W. Simmons (Eds.), *The form of cities in central Canada* (pp. 152-167). Toronto: University of Toronto Press.

Wellman, B., & Leighton, B. (1979). Networks, neighborhoods and community: Approaches to the study of the community question. *Urban Affairs Quarterly, 15*, 363-390.

Wentowski, G. J. (1981). Reciprocity and the coping strategies of older people: Cultural dimensions of network building. *Gerontologist, 21*, 600-609.

White, H., Boorman, S., & Breiger, R. (1976). Social structure from multiple networks: I. Block models of roles and positions. *American Journal of Sociology, 81*, 730-780.

White, M., & White, L. (1962). *The intellectuals versus the city.* Cambridge, MA: Harvard University Press.

Williams, R. (1975). *The country and the city.* London: Paladin.

Wolf, E. (1966). Kinship, friendship and patron-client relations. In M. Banton (Ed.), *The social anthropology of complex societies* (pp. 1-22). London: Tavistock.

Wolpert, E., & Wolpert, J. (1974). From asylum to ghetto. *Antipode, 6*, 63-76.

Wood, L. (1981). *Loneliness and life satisfaction among the rural elderly.* Paper presented at the annual meeting of the Canadian Association on Gerontology, Toronto.

Young, M., & Willmott, P. (1957). *Family and kinship in East London.* London: Routledge & Kegan Paul.

8

Friendships in Old Age: Biography and Circumstance

SARAH H. MATTHEWS

While analyzing data collected in the early 1970s about the everyday lives of old, widowed mothers, I was struck by the distinction some of them made between old friends and more recently acquired ones. For example, one informant said of her current associates:

> Sunday we played bridge and then went to a coffee shop and had dinner. They're friends, but they're not like the old associates that I had years ago. Now they have their families grown up. Now they have their problems. When my little baby died, I had a friend out and she just jumped right in and did so many things for me. "I'll never forget you for this," I told her, and she said, "Oh, what are friends for." That sort of attitude.... But of all the friends I have now, I don't know of one. . . .

Another informant spoke of her friend of fifty years: "We can trust each other, and that's something. You don't find many people you can trust. I have many acquaintances, but I have very few friends." A third informant explained, "When you're younger you have friends, but as you get older they move away or die or something. . . . And then you make new friends. You have to make new friends, but I don't think there is quite the same feeling as you have with old friends."

These women suggested to me that in order to understand at least some aspects of friendships in old age, it is necessary to know more about individuals' relationships throughout their lives—their "populated biographies"—as well as their interpretations of them. Past friendships affect present friendships of the old with respect to both who their current friends are and the meaning assigned to them. My newly sparked interest in the effects of friendship through the life course on friendship in old age led me to the social science literature to see what others had discovered. I found that there were three characteristics that precluded inclusion of biographical data and interpretations of them. In addition, the meaning assigned to friend relationships simply was left unaddressed.

Following a brief review of the literature to show the areas, hitherto unaddressed in research, into which this chapter attempts to make a small inroad, friendship as a social relationship will be analyzed with an eye toward delineating what is meant by this label. Characteristics unique to friendships in old age will then be discussed in order to describe the circumstances with which the old must deal. Several "styles" of friendship with which social actors come to old age will then be examined. Last, the various ways that biography and circumstance come together in old age will be presented.

Illustrations will be drawn throughout from topical oral biographies collected from 64 old people who participated in a research project in which they related to an interviewer and a tape recorder their life stories, using friendship as a constant referent.[1] Most discussions of data collected using what is termed broadly the "life history method" (Bertaux, 1981) focus on their veracity (Becker, 1970; Job, 1983). The concern is to glean the "truth" by weeding out completely what V. S. Pritchitt (1977, p. 10) attempted to eliminate in his own autobiographical writings:

> My difficulty, looking back after seventy years, was to stop memory sliding into respectable consistency, especially about changes in belief. I mean by that not to pretend that silly beliefs had been smartly dismissed; crises of conscience drag on longer than one likes to admit.

If one is interested in reconstructing the past, accuracy of remembered events is important, but symbolic interactionists and phenomenological sociologists agree that it is not the verifiable events of the past alone that affect an individual's present, but his or her interpretation of them as well (Berger & Luckmann, 1966; Matthews, 1983b; Rosenmayr, 1981). This is not to deny the impact of structure, represented by such things as coming of age during the Great Depression, membership in a large age cohort, or the "untimely" death of a parent, but to emphasize that an individual's assignment of meaning to these events cannot be overlooked in understanding their effects on him or her. For the purpose at hand it is not events or relationships alone that are important, then, but the individual's interpretation of them in old age.

This chapter is suggested in part as an antidote to what is missing, according to Back (1980) and Skolnick (1983, p. 386), in the life-course perspective:

> Much work on the life course is haunted by Wrong's "oversocialized image of man" (1961). The life course is represented as a socially determined trajectory through time, shaped by age norms, economic constraints, institutionalized patterns. The very word "transition" suggests an impersonal, agentless movement. It is true that the life course is socially and biologically conditioned but it is also self-created. People make choices among the options open to them, however limited these may be. Ironically, only the most abstract and mathematical of the social sciences, economics, posits a model of the individual as purposive actor, making life-course decisions on the basis of goals and desires. Economic models, needless to say, have their own limiting assumptions; they do not pretend to reflect the experience of the life course as it is lived by an individual.

By using a qualitative approach to data collection and by focusing on friendship, an area of social life for which transitions are not obviously normative or socially determined, the agency of social actors is not only respected, but emphasized.

FRIENDSHIP IN THE
SOCIAL SCIENCE LITERATURE

Comparisons between present and past relationships have no place in a cross-sectional research design, the one that has been used almost exclusively in studying friendship in general and friendship of the old in particular. Had the three informants cited above been respondents to a structured interview about their current friends, their distinctions would not have been seen as relevant. In a few studies, age groups have been compared in an attempt to uncover variations in number and functions of friends (Candy, 1977; Fischer, 1982; Lowenthal et al., 1975) as well as in composition of social networks (Shulman, 1975) in different stages of the life cycle. However, this modification can only suggest possible changes in individuals' friendships as they age because there is a built-in assumption that explanations for differences are due solely to age or stage in the life course. In addition, individuals' friendships exist through time, often transcending spatial boundaries (see Babchuk &

Bates, 1963), but research questions most often have been formulated in such a way that respondents'friendships are required, in Fischer's (1982) words, to be "active"rather than "latent," availability being the primary concern. Cross-sectional research designs, then, are not only ahistorical, but abiographical as well. One comes away from this literature with the impression that "a friend is a friend is a friend," even though most people would maintain that friendship is one of the most personal relationships in modern societies.

A romp through the research literature on friendship in old age also uncovered another difficulty. Almost all the research is ameliorative in nature, even though claims to the contrary are often made. In Chown's (1981, p. 231) words, "Investigators have been more interested in the social conditions of the elderly than in the investigation of friendship per se." Psychological well-being is used most often as the indicator of social conditions, whether it is conceptualized as morale (Arling, 1976) or mental health (Lowenthal & Haven, 1968; Kahn & Antonucci, 1981). In these studies the effects on psychological well-being of number and availability of friends, and friends' position in the network of social support relative to family, neighbors, and, sometimes, professionals, has been of primary concern. My informants' descriptions of their friends also have no place in this literature.

Implicit in research on the psychological well-being of the old, and the factors that contribute to it, is that the old are more likely than other adult members of society to be "unwell." In the social science literature, as well as in the minds of the general public, in which similarities between old people and children are sometimes drawn, the old often are not conceptualized as social actors, but instead as passive and needy, overwhelmed by the vicissitudes assumed to be inherent in the last stage of life. However, the old persist in being social actors to the ends of their lives, barring dementing illnesses, so that they, like younger social actors, continue to endow their worlds with meaning and have no choice but to do so (Marshall, 1980, p. 5).

To counter the view of the old as passive reactors, Simić and Myerhoff (1978, p. 240) argue that aging should be viewed as a career because it

> constitutes a kind of analogy stressing old age as a period of activity, participation, self-movement, and purposefulness. . . . Stated another way, old age is not necessarily a passive stage, but on the contrary, one evoking dynamic responses to its exigencies.

With respect to friendship, then, an appropriate research question would be: What are the exigencies of this stage of life that evoke response and what are the responses? This research question portrays the old as creative social actors rather than as needy recipients of social support. It does not eliminate psychological well-being as a concern in research, but removes the spotlight from it so that a broader picture of friendships in old age can be discovered.

Research on friendship outside the field of aging is not as likely to focus on psychological well-being, but instead on what psychologists call "attraction" (Huston & Levinger, 1978) and what sociologists describe as "homophily" (Lazarsfeld & Merton, 1954). These abstractions also provide an inappropriate framework for the issues to which my informants had led me. Both are attempts to disprove the old adage, "There's no accounting for tastes," by discovering the attributes of individuals who will "mate" after "meeting" and the conditions under which this will occur (Verbrugge, 1977). This research is concerned with probabilities, with predicting who will be attracted to and/or become attached to whom under what conditions, although sociologists sometimes have begun with established relationships and worked backwards. The thesis that has been supported since Lazarsfeld and Merton's early research report (in which the term *homophily* was coined) is that people who are alike (or perceive that they are alike) and are in situations in which their (apparent) likenesses can become known to one another have a higher probability of becoming friends than those who do not share status attributes or, if they do, have no opportunity to demonstrate this fact to one another. The status attributes that have been demonstrated to be significant include age (Rosow, 1967), gender, social class, race, occupation, and marital status (Blau, 1961; Hochschild, 1978). The condition that promotes "mating" is usually proximity, either residential or occupational, although recent migrants (freshmen in dormitories and first residents of housing developments and apartment complexes) often supply the data and this also may be an important contributing factor.

From the perspective of the individual social actor, however, probabilities are not the major concern. As Bateson (1979, p. 46) has pointed out, "The statement 'The liquid is boiling' is of a different logical type from the statement 'That molecule will be the first to go.'" As far as individuals are concerned, it is not the statement "Birds of a feather flock together" that is important, but the actual "matings" between two (or more) individuals within the homogeneous flock that are of interest.

Probably everyone, at least in modern societies, is familiar with the experience of being in a group of status-homogeneous peers and being unable to find even one other person with whom to form a bond, for however brief a time. It is this experience that prompts agreement with Lord Chesterton's assertion that "there are no words to express the abyss between isolation and having one ally. It may be conceded to the mathematicians that four is twice two. But two is not twice one; two is two thousand times one." After all, it is not simply friendship in general, but friendship with a specific other that is important to the individual.

A summary of what is missing in this literature must state, first, that cross-sectional research ignores time, especially biographical time, as an important dimension of friendships. Second, rather than attempting to discover what friendships are about in old age, most research has assumed that they are primarily important as supports to psychological well-being. Third, categorical explanations of who becomes friends with whom are not appropriate for understanding the specific friendships of individuals, each of whom occupies a unique trajectory of friendships and other social relationships during the course of his or her life.

One problem that is simply ignored in research is that the word *friend* can be and is used in everyday language to describe myriad types of relationships ranging from casual to intense, fleeting to long standing, making the intention of the speaker, whether or not he or she is participating in research, essential for gauging the specific meaning that is to be attached to any reference to a particular relationship. In most cases, social science research has not heeded intention of the speaker, making the nature of the relationships to which respondents refer difficult to know. Most often respondents are asked to identify their closest friends and are then asked questions about each one of them. The criteria employed to decide whom to include are not ascertained. The assumption is that all relationships identified in this way can be treated by the social scientist as essentially the same. Lowenthal and Robinson (1976, p. 439) have concluded that in the research literature "differing concepts of friendship perhaps may account for the inconsistent findings," citing as an example research in which some respondents claimed that their friends included everyone in the community. It is this shortcoming that will be addressed in the following section.

FRIENDSHIP AS A SOCIAL RELATIONSHIP

In everyday language, interpreting the word *friend* is rarely problematic, but for the social scientist doing research on friendships, this is an immediate obstacle. What, exactly, do social actors mean when they describe someone as a friend? To answer this question, I will begin by discussing social relationships very generally, arriving eventually at the particular social relationship of friendship.

Max Weber (1978, p. 26) defines a social relationship as "the behavior of a plurality of actors insofar as, in its meaningful content, the action of each takes account of that of the others and is oriented to these terms." He further specifies that the length of time social actors thus are oriented is not a criterion: "A social relationship can be of a very fleeting character or of varying degrees of permanence" (p. 28). With few exceptions, then, any face-to-face interaction (and some which are not face-to-face) with two (or more) people can be so described.

From the small but influential beginnings with a few primary caretakers, the number of social relationships in which the child participates expands exponentially, with each person's set of social relationships becoming increasingly differentiated from his or her age peers at the same time that it grows in size as he or she moves through the life course. By the time an individual reaches old age in modern societies, the number of people who have qualified as participants with the individual in social relationships is enormous.

Not surprisingly, social actors in all known societies have developed typologies of social relationships so that each need not be treated as unique:

> The reality of everyday life contains typificatory schemes in terms of which others are apprehended and "dealt with" in face-to-face encounters. Thus I apprehend the other as "a man," "a European," "a buyer," "a jovial type," and so on. All these typifications ongoingly affect my interaction with him. (Berger & Luckmann, 1977, pp. 30-31)

In everyday life, then, most of the myriad relationships in which social actors participate are categorized and not by a scheme originated by each individual. Rather, the scheme for the most part predates the individual's arrival and is shared by members of a particular society. Further, some of these typifications are well defined and institutionalized, and others are more open to interpretation. This is one of the characteristics of relationships in which Simmel is interested in his discussion of the dyad.

According to Simmel (1950), as an ideal type, the dyadic relationship is sociologically "trivial." By this he means that it is characterized by "absence of a super-personal unit" (p. 129). Friendship he regards as being very close to the pure form of a dyadic relationship because it is a "relation entirely based on the individualities of its elements" (p. 138). A marital dyad is much more removed from the ideal "because of its traditional forms, its social rules, its real interests. . . . marriage contains many super-individual elements that are independent of the specific character of the personalities involved" (p. 138). In contrast, "triviality" characterizes a dyad that is "inseparable from the immediacy of interaction; for neither of its two elements is it the super-individual unit which elsewhere confronts the individual, while at the same time it makes him participate in it" (p. 126).

Friendships, then, are trivial because they are voluntary and have a content set by their "two elements." Beth Hess (1972, p. 358) echoes Simmel when she writes that one of the reasons that "friendship has often been judged of only minor interest to social scientists" is that it has been seen "as depending more upon idiosyncracies of personality than upon regularities of culture and social structure."

Triviality of friendship dyads also can be equated with the absence for this relationship of some of the elements of "institutionalization," defined by Berger and Luckmann (1966, p. 54) as "reciprocal typifications of habitualized actions by types of actors." They identify a compendium of five interdependent criteria—externality, historicity, legitimation, objectivity, and coerciveness—essential for its existence that can be used to examine a particular pattern of social behavior. By *historicity* they mean that the typification "antedates the individual's birth and is not accessible to biographical recollection" (p. 60). By *externality* they mean that it "exists as a product of human activity" (p. 52). Evidence that historicity and externality are present is found, for example, in Selman's (1980) research on children's definitions of friendship that apparently progress through identifiable stages. That this occurs can be interpreted as meaning that, in a particular society, "children develop until they share the same rules for constructing the world as all other adults" (Kessler & McKenna, 1978, p. 96). Evidence of legitimation, or "ways in which it [friendship] can be explained and justified" (p. 61), is found, for example, in Gold's (1973, p. 47) article in a popular magazine in which he argues that friendship matters because "we long for company unobliged by blood. . . . We choose to have friends because we must; else we'll have no hearts, we'll not feel alive."

With respect to friendship, however, objectivity and coerciveness are absent, or at least not well developed, in most sectors of modern societies:

[Objectivity] means that the institutions . . . are experienced as existing over and beyond the individuals who "happen to" embody them at the moment. In other words, the institutions are now experienced as possessing a reality of their own, a reality that confronts the individual as an external and coercive fact. (Berger & Luckmann, 1966, p. 58)

These are precisely the elements that are missing from the friendship dyad. For example, Allen (1979, p. 4) writes:

The term "friend" is only applied to people who have a personal relationship that is qualitatively of a particular sort. It is the actual relationship itself that is the most important factor in deciding whether someone can or cannot be labeled a friend. . . . Thus, it is a relational label rather than a categorical one.

Friendships, then, unlike kinship relationships, lack definitive criteria that can be used to determine their existence.

In addition, the content of a friendship is set by the two participants, and social pressure to "conform" according to the "rules," or coerciveness, comes only, or at least primarily, from the members of the dyad. Unlike marital dyads, for example, there are no government agencies to enforce the contract signed by the two friends and no grounds for lawsuits for the "injured" friends. Social control is "peculiarly up to each member to accomplish. . . . Because there is only one other member, one cannot 'blow the whistle' on another, calling attention of other members to the offender" (McCall, 1970, p. 27).

Conceptualizing friendship as a social institution, then, is deceptive because to do so makes it appear much more concrete than it is in the world of everyday life. This point is made well by Allan (1979, p. 37) in his treatise on friendship and kinship:

In common usage terms like friend (and mate, pal, chum, etc.) are only vague means of analysis; they serve as resources as well as restraints. People use them as labels and devices for conveying meaning in particular situations, not as rigorous and precise analytical tools.

This lack of a universal definition poses few problems for social actors who are content to rely on context to supply meaning and rarely question whether or not their meanings in fact are shared.

Social scientists, however, have attempted to arrive at clear-cut definitions, in essence, to specify "super-individual elements" or to treat friendship as an institution (Babchuk & Bates, 1963; Kurth, 1970; Lowenthal et al., 1975; Riesman, 1979; Suttles, 1970). As an example,

Brown (1981, p. 25) specifies that friendships are "relationships which are voluntary, mutual, flexible and terminable; relationships that emphasize equality and reciprocity, and require from each partner an affective involvement in the total personality of the other." Probably most people's ideas of friendship contain at least some of these elements, but in everyday life individuals do not run through this list of criteria before deciding whether or not to refer to someone as a friend or whether or not their implicit assumptions about a specific relationship are accurate.

Applying these criteria to a particular relationship may even mean that the person fails to qualify as a friend. For example, one member of a dyad who consciously keeps secrets from the other, in Brown's terms, would not be making available the "total personality," and therefore would not be a friend. An example of such a "betrayal" is cited by Brenton (1974, p. 125):

> A magazine editor told me how upset he was when his closest friend, a man he had gone to high school with, withheld from him the fact that he had cancer "until he was practically on his deathbed. I tried to respect that; I know he was suffering and had his own reasons for not telling me, but—it sounds terrible, I know—I was hurt . . . like he'd let me down."

Had this incident never arisen, however, the friendship would not have been "tested" and the man's assumptions about the friendship not questioned. Further, given that the incident did arise, is this man now an ex-friend? Several informants for the research in which this chapter is grounded had experienced crises in their lives in which friendships had been tested and found wanting. In other cases, however, tested friendships had survived and were found to be even stronger than the individuals had imagined. In still others, relationships that had not been considered friendships prior to a crisis were redefined as friendships because of others' unexpected responses.

The difficulty of dealing with the absence of universally accepted criteria is evident in research on friendship in which Rubin (1981) was not content with her informants' subjective evaluations of relationships, but felt compelled to apply her own. While interviewing a man who claimed to have many close friends, she

> listened with mounting irritation as he told me about his best friend—a man who lives in the east. How often did they see each other? I asked. Well, in fact, they hadn't seen each other since he moved east ten years

ago. Did they talk on the telephone? Not really; maybe a couple of times in the ten years. What makes him a best friend, then? "Trust, that's what it is," he asserted stoutly. "I know I can absolutely trust him." Trust him with what? I asked. "With anything," he replied. "With anything I need. I could land on his doorstep in the cold of winter and the dead of night, and I know he'd be right there." Flippantly, and without really expecting any surprises in the answer, I wisecracked, "And just where is that doorstep on which you'd always be welcome to land?" A moment of silence, and then the answer. "I am not sure. You see, he moved a while back and I don't know exactly where he lives now." "How far back?" "I don't remember exactly—a couple of years maybe." (p. 107)

Lillian Rubin concluded that "the words the informant used to speak about his friendships didn't match his inner reality" (p. 107). To confirm her hypothesis she later called him on the telephone, knowing "that his defenses would not be easily breached so it would be safe to risk a small confrontation" (p. 108). In the course of the conversation, which was intended to gather names of his friends whom she might interview, she suggested to him one reason he might have felt "kind of low" following the initial interview:

"Maybe you didn't feel quite comfortable with everything you told me about your friendships. Maybe they're not as solid as you'd like to think." Silence at the other end of the line for what seemed like a long while, then a sigh, "Maybe you're right." In this instance, I interviewed several of the people this man called intimates in order to check out the stories he told. None of them claimed him among their close circle of friends. (p. 108)

The implication here is that this man has no "real" friends or, at least, not nearly as many as he claims to have. But is Rubin's "truth" better than her informant's? Behind this discussion is the assumption that there is such a thing as friendship with which to compare relationships in order to determine whether or not they qualify. This man's friendships did not meet Rubin's criteria, but he "stoutly" said that they met his. Who is right? The informant or the social scientist who is comparing answers to her own ideal typical definition of friendship?

Lillian Rubin's interviewing of those identified as friends by this informant brings in another criterion, reciprocity, which is included in most definitions of friendship (see Brown, 1981, cited above). In practice, however, few studies actually test this assumption empirically, as is the case with much research in the interactionist perspective (Lofland, 1973). However, what is important here is not reciprocity per se, but *belief* that there is reciprocity, that the other person also regards the informant as a friend. As Weber (1978, p. 27) indicates:

> The subjective meaning need not necessarily be the same for all the parties who are mutually oriented in a given social relationship; there need not in this sense be "reciprocity." "Friendship," . . . on one side, may well be faced with an entirely different attitude on the other. In such cases the parties associate different meanings with their actions, and the social relationship is insofar objectively "asymmetrical" from the points of view of the two parties. It may nevertheless be a case of mutual orientation insofar as, even though partly or wholly erroneously, one party presumes a particular attitude toward him on the part of the other and orients his action to this expectation.

"Reciprocity," like "involvement of the total personality," may be assumed by either member of the friendship dyad until conflicting evidence is presented. Of course, "objective asymmetry" has "consequences for the course of action and the form of the relationship" (p. 27), just as "objective symmetry" does. For friendship dyads, the possibility of "objective asymmetry" is much greater than for dyadic relationships which are institutionalized. That is, it is much less likely for someone to assume "mistakenly" than an individual is her or his spouse than that an individual is his or her friend. Friendship relationships may continue through many years without the subjective assumption of "objective symmetry" being tested.

That institutionalized criteria to determine the existence of friendship are problematic does not justify social scientists' constructing rigid criteria that thereby distort the everyday reality of friendships. Some social scientists have recognized and attempted to leave intact the "triviality" of friendships. For example, Paine (1969, p. 23) writes:

> In as much as friendship is recognized as a social relationship, it is an institution in the limited rather loose sense of bestowal of recognition; and this is commonly the extent of this institutionalization in our culture, where it amounts to a kind of institutionalized non-institution.

Similarly, Suttles (1970), in a paper entitled "Friendship as a Social Institution," includes a definition but describes friendship as an institution that "fills in where the more mechanical and exclusionary institutions fail to define interpersonal affiliations" (p. 96). For him, then, friendship requires the two participants to create their own culture because it is a residual institution or category into which social relationships are placed that have no "super-individual elements" (Simmel, 1950).

Another complicating factor in determining the nature of a relationship that someone describes as a friendship is that social relationships exist through time and therefore are likely to change as the two individuals' lives change. As was suggested above, existing relationships can be redefined as friendships or "recognized" as not being "true" friendships after all. A spouse continues to be a spouse, barring divorce or death, regardless of his or her behavior or the current circumstances of the marriage. It is not so with friendship. As people's lives change, their evaluations of friend relationships are also likely to change. Each of the individuals in the dyad participates in a system of social relationships that affect one another (see Gold, 1973; Lee, 1977). This noninstitutionalized relationship, depending for its existence only on the two members' evaluations of it, may be redefined many times during the course of the two members' lives and even defined out of existence. The present context of each individual's life is, at least for some people, critical to the meaning attached to a particular relationship.

In sum, institutionalized criteria to determine the existence of a friendship are not available, at least not in Western societies (see Reina, 1959, for an example of institutionalized friendships in another culture), so that the existence of one depends on the subjective evaluation of a relationship by at least one of its participants. Therefore, the criteria employed vary from one individual to another and are, at least in part, dependent on the circumstances that are always in process of an individual's life course and on his or her interpretations of them.

OLD AGE AS A
UNIQUE CONTEXT FOR FRIENDSHIP

One of the often lamented consequences of growing old is loss of friends, which is reflected in the declining size of high school and college graduation classes, of bridge clubs and sewing circles, of local chapters of the Veterans of Foreign Wars, and of other groups, like the "Society of the Broken Dish" (Simmel, 1950, p. 125), in which the specific members are not or cannot be replaced. Meeting and talking with those members who have survived may become increasingly difficult due to declining health and decreased mobility. To lose old friends is to lose specific others in whom the old person may have accumulated "investments of the self" (Hess, 1972, p. 300). These are some of the "exigencies," to use Simić and Myerhoff's (1978) term, that must be specified in order to understand friendships in old age. Drawing on analysis of the life stories of the 64 informants, in this section three aspects of friendship unique to old age will be identified and discussed.

Deaths and Disease

The age cohorts to which the old belong are shrinking. This, of course, is the case throughout a cohort's existence, but in modern societies the size of an age cohort drops sharply only when its members reach old age (Marshall, 1980). The future of friendships characterized by "age homophily" becomes increasingly precarious as the members reach their seventh, eighth, and ninth decades. For example, one informant (Margaret Green), after she retired, had spent five summers in Nova Scotia collecting material for a book on folklore. Asked about her friends there, she replied, "I made some good friends, but they are all gone now." Charlotte Dickens explained, "I knew two people when I came into this hotel. Both of them are dead now. That's another thing you run into with us. Our friends are going and we have to get used to the idea and it's not easy." Ethel Thayer lamented, "I had two very nice friends here, but they both died." Avery Clarence, speaking of his college friends, said that

> the friendships were very close. I don't mean with everybody, but certain people who I knew well and our friendships kept up through the years. . . . But most of the class is dead now. There are more widows than there are members of the class.

Anne Livingston described a clique to which she had belonged:

> We had our own little club, just being silly, you know. And we'd meet and use a hammer for a gavel and just act plain crazy. I still remember. And then Elizabeth Morgan died. One morning she died. She was fairly young. It was right on my floor. And we never met after that. We just all felt so sad about that.

Deaths of friends who are also old, then, become a part—though not a welcome part—of the daily lives of the old, at least for those old who have friends.

Another problem confronted by chronologically old friends is that they are likely to experience and to be coping with physical and mental changes (Munnichs, 1964). Granting that stereotypes engendered by the popular press and some social scientists are likely to portray the condition of the aged as considerably more negative than it is in fact, the likelihood of experiencing sensory changes and of having chronic illnesses in old age is very high. Many of these changes limit friends' ability to communicate with one another or to spend time together.

Some of the informants referred to changes in their own physical and/or mental abilities. Charlotte Dickens complained about an effusive woman whom she described as "making passes" at people: "I never liked to be touched. And the more arthritis I get, the less I like to be touched." Referring to a friend with whom her relationship recently had deteriorated, she blamed herself, at least partly: "It's uncomfortable. You can be uncomfortable physically and then to have the mental discomfort right on top of it. . . . I'm not as patient as I used to be because so much of me hurts. And when I hurt I'm likely to get mad."

Anne Livingston was quite ill for the six months preceding the interview, so that when other members of the group of which Elizabeth Morgan had been a member wanted to resume meeting, she did not feel that she could:

> And I think it can't be now because I don't hear. I'm all right when you and I are talking, but if I try to hear anybody's conversation, I just can't enter in. And I can't see very much. And my walking, my balance is affected, and then I get this bad ear. So you can see I have a lot of things against me.

Ethel Thayer had not attended the fiftieth reunion of her college graduation class, which also meant not getting to see her "best friend":

> I just couldn't do it. I can't hobble around campus. I have to walk very slowly. You're always walking, you know, and I can't do it. And I was so fat I didn't want anyone to see me. So I didn't go.

These women, then, spoke of their own physical problems that militated against their continuing to be *actively* involved in or able to form new friendships.

References also were made to changes in friends' behavior or capacities that interfered with maintenance of friendships. Charlotte Dickens spoke of a friend whom she had met each summer for the past decade at a camp that they both attended: "And she won't be going back either. She's younger than I am, but she had a terrific sick spell, awful. She's worse off than I am." About one of her college friends with whom she had maintained a relationship, she said,

I think she has turned out to be a bit forgetful. If I hear from her, it's a Christmas card in March. This is what you are going to run into with us, that we are missing people that we are close to, either because they have fallen apart or dropped dead.

A more recently acquired friend who lives in the same retirement hotel also concerns her:

And this is one of the things about friendship for older people—that our friends start slipping mentally. And we have to get used to it. And part of getting used to it is saying, "Am I getting like that, too?" It's inevitable and uncomfortable. I have a very good friend, a new friend, with whom I eat luncheon and dinner almost everyday. She'll be ninety next month. She's slipping mentally. She scolded the heck out of me after lunch today because she had expected me to eat with her. And I had no idea of eating with her. That is what happens to friendship in this big upper age group.

Physical and mental changes in friends, then, affect the content of relationships. However, the evaluation of the relationship as a friendship may continue. Charlotte Dickens described this woman as "a fascinating study in the mentality of senile disorders":

There is one person that I don't like who bawled her out one day. So I told her, "Let her alone. She's making that up but she doesn't know it. Let her alone. She doesn't know she's lying. Let her have her little story."

It is likely that friends who are old will experience both physical and/or mental changes that interfere with their continued relationships. Anne Livingston described a friend who had recently died: "She had been stone deaf and not seeing anyone much and I haven't been able to get out since I don't drive. And since she's hard of hearing, I couldn't call her up. I had to relay a message and it wasn't very satisfactory." The combination of her friend's deafness and her own lack of transportation made their interaction "unsatisfactory." She continued to think of her as a friend, however: "She's an old friend. Someone I always loved dearly. I think she was a very gracious and lovely woman."

Friendship between two individuals who are both chronologically old, then, is precarious. The continuation of an "active" relationship and the content of the relationship are, to a certain degree, out of the hands of the two individuals who are involved. This removal of responsibility may make continuing to define as friendship a relationship that is no longer satisfactory easier than is the case for young friends.

Extensive Populated Biographies

At any given point in time, individuals possess what Goffman (1963, p. 57) describes as a personal identity, "the unique combination of life history items that come to be attached to the individual." Many, if not all, of these life history items are constructed through participation in social relationships. In Simić and Myerhoff's (1978, p. 231) words, "Aging is the result of an individual's passage through time, through the life cycle, through *a chain of interpersonal exchanges and relationships*" (emphasis added). It is these relationships which constitute the "populated biography" of an individual. Often persons' lives are presented as attributes rather than as relationships with others; for instance, educational status, marital status, employment history. Each of these attributes, however, was acquired through interaction with others, and taken together, they form the "populated biography" of any given person.

The concept of populated biography directs attention to the actual social relationships in which someone participated, rather than to abstract characteristics. For example, Ross (1976, p. 109) points out the importance of social ties from the past when she describes the introduction of newcomers to those already in residence in Les Florelies, the French retirement apartment complex she studied:

> The first day the new arrivals are clearly on display at their separate table. If someone in the community has seen one of them before, on a CNRO-sponsored vacation, or on a job, this is often the moment of recognition. Several new people told me how relieved and excited they were to see a familiar face and to hear someone say "didn't I meet you in the mountains," or "weren't you a mason for Girard and Co.?" New names also begin to circulate as the committee members talk over the morning's experience at their own tables.

> Sometimes a name is recognized when a face has changed or been forgotten. This kind of instant recognition triggers a move, often the next day, to a regular table with other established residents, either the person who knew the newcomer, or someone else chosen by that person.

Clearly, social relationships to which individuals have been party in the past are important in the present context. That someone retired from Girard and Co. may be used by a sociologist to code socioeconomic status, but what is important here is not an abstract job, but that it connected an individual to particular people, some of whom happen to be available in this setting. The title of Ross's book is *Old People, New*

Lives, the implication being that in the move to the retirement complex, the old began their lives anew. By allowing the populated biographies of informants to come into play, it is evident that "new lives" in new settings are related to "old lives" made up of concrete social relationships that the residents bring with them.

The old, relative to others, have longer biographies, more life-history items attached to them (Goffman, 1963). Holding other social variables constant, the old in modern societies probably have participated in more social relationships than younger others. Elapsed time since having met, become friendly, and become friends with someone is also likely to be greater for the old than for the young. Life-long friendships are longer and have weathered more tests successfully. For an 80-year-old, high school friends are people he or she knew initially over 60 years ago. For a 30-year-old or a 50-year-old, the elapsed time is much shorter. All things being equal, then, "more" and "longer" describe the social relationships of the old relative to the young.

Anne Livingston will be used as an illustration of the meaning of populated biographies because of the five distinct periods into which her life can be divided. The first period of her life she discussed was childhood. She had many school friends, but especially one girl with whom she had

> kept in touch for many, many years, until she married a second time. We were very close friends even after we were both married. But circumstances change things. She's moved out to California and has a great deal of money. Her lifestyle is quite different from mine. I hear about her and she about me, but we're not close anymore. I still love her and have many happy memories of our times together.

After she married, she and her husband, a rising young lawyer ten years her senior, lived in the city and moved in a circle that included other lawyers and their wives, most older than she. Several women she had met during this period of her life she still regarded as friends or did until they died: "The Smiths were our closest friends and right straight through until June died about two years ago."

The third period was marked by her move to the suburbs where she reared her four children. She described one friend: "We share lots of happy memories and confidences. I still talk to her. She calls me or I call her, and she came down to visit me last month." Her husband died just as her youngest daughter was launched, forcing a transition in her friendships of which she spoke with regret:

The only thing I thought was kind of too bad when I left there was that I had built up a whole life with everything that you could possibly want. And then after my husband's death, I had to work all day long and I couldn't be chasing back to keep track of my old, original friends. That always pained me, hurt me, but there was nothing for me to do but start fresh. I could see that. They went on. They were busy. They couldn't wait. I couldn't. So we both had to break right off.

Her job, which she was offered by a man with whom she and her husband initially had been friends in the early years of their marriage, brought new friendships, one close one with a fellow employee, Marge, and another with Clare:

When my aunt lived here at this hotel, the last three years of her life she was paralyzed and was in bed and needed round-the-clock nursing. And one of her nurses, the three-to-eleven one, was this Clare. And I used to come right out from my job to see my aunt and have dinner here. I'd have them bring dinner up on a table and the two of us would have dinner together. And we developed a good friendship. Now that was 1957. That's quite a few years. Nearly 25 years. And she has been marvelous to me. I introduced her to Marge and we've had many, many good times together.

The final period of her life was the move to the retirement hotel:

When I came I was a different person. I was so full of pep. I could dance all night. And when I came in, I didn't know anybody. Oh, I knew Mary Allen slightly through Girl Scouts and Evelyn Hooper was an old, old friend. But I just met people all along and I made many friends and had something doing all the time.

This is when she became a member of the club with four other women. By the end of her life, then, she had participated in many of what she considered to be friendships, drawn from five distinct periods of her life.

Anne Livingston had lived in the same city all her life, and had participated in what Moore (1978, p. 26) describes as a "life-term social arena," one in which the personnel remain relatively constant and "the factors that determine entrance to or exit from it are major emotional or physiological life crises." Although her life had sharp transitions and she had acquired friends in each new period, in old age many were still available to her. Some of the relationships that had been dormant were resurrected in old age. The only periods of her life that were not represented well in old age were childhood and early married years, the first because of the demise of a relationship with a woman who had since died, and the second because of the demise of friends. Anne Livingston was somewhat unusual because of the distinct transitions in her life (and because of her personal warmth and optimism), but she illustrates that for some, friendships accumulate through the years so that there are a variety from which to choose in old age depending on the situations of all concerned.

It is possible to move several times and still participate, more or less, in a life-term social arena. Malcolm Avery, for example, even though he had left his hometown, had maintained ties from his early years primarily by attending his college reunions and being an active participant in his alumni group. His earliest friendships had lasted into old age, with few exceptions. Only deaths seemed to rob him of his friends. Others, however, like Ethel Thayer, acquired new friends with each move, leaving behind her old ones so that in old age in a new location she described herself as friendless, unable to acquire friends. In Moore's (1978) terms, Ethel Thayer participated in a "limited-term social arena" because the personnel in each period of her life were temporary.

Relationships do have a way of reappearing throughout individuals' lives. For example, Clarence Avery's best friend from childhood, a wealthy playboy, appeared every three or four years, sometimes more often, to renew their relationship. After middle age, the two men, along with Mrs. Avery and a wife or companion of his friend, often spent vacations together. Although the two men's lifestyles were very different, Mr. Avery's evaluation of his friend and his relationship with him were very positive: "He was a character. . . . We were awfully good friends."

Miss Dickens described being contacted by her first boyfriend:

I hadn't seen him since his family moved to California, but I heard about him from my cousin in my hometown. Whenever she heard about Edward she would tell me because I was devoted to him. It was an adolescent love affair.

[In 1974] Edward decided that he wanted to know if I was still living and he managed to locate me through hometown friends. He sent me an airline ticket. I knew about his wife. I knew he had married dear little sweet Linda who was a baby when I was in high school. I went and had a marvelous week. I didn't know what Linda would think of me. But I reminded her about her nickname of Sweet Linda and we were friends even though she knew that I was Edward's first girlfriend.

In this case, except for a "marvelous week" and an annual Christmas gift, the renewed relationship had little impact on the informant's life.

In another case, the effect of a renewed relationship was much greater. Alex Simak, who had immigrated to the United States in the 1920s, was invited shortly after he retired to attend an international meeting in the late 1960s that was moved at the last minute "to my original homeland. . . . So much to my surprise, I went to Yugoslavia after 40 years and renewed some of my acquaintances there." One of the people he had been able to track down was a woman ("I could almost say a former sweetheart of mine") who had moved to a Northern European country. At the time of the interview he had recently returned from his annual visit with her in Europe. Had he not, "by a quirk," been afforded the opportunity to come in contact with his friend again, he would have had a very different old age.

Moving through a life course means accumulating social relationships, some of which are considered to be friendships. Barring their termination—the abrupt or conscious ending of a relationship, or "breaking up," was very unusual—they continue to be relationships that may be drawn upon again at another time. For some, this was due to fate bringing the two individuals together again, rather than to design. Often, it was a combination of the two. Others, however, actively attempted to maintain relationships, and sought friends with whom they had lost contact. Charlotte Dickens's old boyfriend had no trouble finding her when he wanted. Anne Livingston said of her high school friend, "I hear about her and she does of me," so reestablishing the tie was a possibility until the woman died. Often, only a little initiative is required to track down an old friend.

Related to this is that long-term relationships which are friendships almost may take on a life of their own. "The cumulation over time [of social relationships] may be in the intensifying and strengthening of the relationships in terms of emotional investment, common experience, long-term exchanges" (Moore, 1978, p. 25). Graham Allan (1979, p. 41) writes:

> An assumption entailed in the idea that friendship is voluntary is that it is a relationship based on enjoyment. A friend is someone with whom you enjoy spending time and sharing activities. . . . Conversely, if you do not enjoy interacting with someone they are unlikely to be considered friends.

However, in old age, changes in long-term friendships, and even relatively short-term ones, that may make them less enjoyable and even a burden did not seem to change the designation of them as friendships, as several of the examples cited above indicated. As Naegele (1958, p. 237) points out, "In choosing our friends, we establish ties and connections that are only partly envisaged at the time they are assumed. These, in turn, entrench our friendships and surround them by webs of consequence." Elimination of enjoyment from a relationship may not mark its termination or its redefinition as no longer a friendship.

Charlotte Dickens had two friends in the residential hotel in which she lived whom she had known since the 1930s. One she considered her best friend at the present time, the other a friend who was somewhat troublesome, but a friend nonetheless. She worked with both women at different times during her career:

> So what happens is that each one is a good friend of mine. And one of them can't stand the other and the other one is aware of it and doesn't know what to do about it.... And I don't know quite how to work it out. We used to have a BYO arrangement every Saturday. The other person would serve dips and squeeks. And one time, just before I took sick, Julie was so rude to me that it really stunned me. She's a one-to-one person. If there are three in the group, she eliminates one and addresses herself to the other person. And that's what she had been doing a long time, which made Rachel uncomfortable. But this time Julie was so rude that I wrote her a note saying that I didn't want to have any BYO anymore. She hated that. Oh, she felt terrible. I felt terrible. It was just awful. And it was awful that a third person had been present. Rachel thought it was awful. So.... We're back to normal now, but we've got it worked out that we don't have the BYO anymore. Every Wednesday, buffet luncheon, Julie and I have lunch together. But I still feel that I'm doing her a favor and not myself.

She continues to think of both these women as friends even though her relationship with one of them is not particularly pleasant. In Kurth's (1970, p. 159) words, she has developed "faithfulness," which "serves to maintain the relationship, even if the original reason for forming the relationship no longer remains."

Position in the Age Structure of Society

As people age, an increasing number of those around them are younger than they, while an increasing number of individuals they have known—school teachers, bosses, neighbors from childhood—are dead. In other words, the cohorts that precede a particular age group through time disappear and are replaced by cohorts that follow it through time.

> The social arenas in which people can play out their lives, the circles of persons among whom their views, their actions, their reputations matter, vary very much from one society to another. In no society can the personnel in the social arena be the same throughout life. The fact of death and the succession of generations makes this impossible. (Moore, 1978, p. 25)

The young, then, will have relatively more social relationships—although not necessarily friendships—with persons who are older than they; the old, with persons who are younger than they.

In research focusing on structural explanations or "homophily," similarity in age of the members is found uniformly, making it appear as if the only "changes in personnel" that affect the old are losses. Turning this finding on its head, however, it might be argued that age similarity is thought by many people to be a necessary criterion for a relationship to be described as a friendship:

> Ours is a society in which friends are often presumed in advance to be age-peers. As a consequence, close relationships may exist between age dissimilars, but they may not be labeled friendships, either by the individuals involved or by the researcher. For instance, a close relationship between a younger and an older man may be characterized, not as "he's my friend," but "he's my father figure." (Neugarten & Hagestad, 1976, p. 42)

Social actors, then, may hesitate to describe close, nonkin relationships characterized by age "heterophily" as friendships.

In the course of the discussions of current friendships, as informants attempted to bring in all relationships that were important to them, younger others were often included, sometimes only children who were described as friends to emphasize the quality of relationships, but at other times nonkin relationships with younger people as well. They were generally not the first friendships described, but came into the discussions nevertheless. Margaret Green explained the importance of age in friendships:

> Your period of friendship here [in the retirement hotel] may be fairly short because of your age. But this one person that I'm thinking about is quite a bit younger than I am and the others have been my age or older. So you see that makes a difference in the ending of your friendships, your age contacts.

Anne Livingston did not mention younger friends. All the friends she had acquired were older than she, the same age, or only slightly younger, so that at the age of 82, problems stemming from death and disease described above greatly affected her friendships. Other informants, however, did have what they described as friendships with younger people.

Through a combination of chance and design, some of the informants had friends who were considerably younger than they. Charlotte Dickens described younger friends she had acquired through a college friend who was no longer living:

> I knew her sister very well and I've been friends with her nephew since he was five years old. He's now sixty. He and his wife adopted two children. This is the first year since 1970 that I haven't gone to visit them. I can't do it now. They have a boy and a girl. She asked me to be her pen pal and we are still pen pals. Which means that I was taken on as a substitute aunt. And I was adopted by the two adults, so that's a carried-on-through-the-generations friendship.

She described several other "generations of friendship" and then summarized: "So it keeps on keeping on." By establishing relationships through her initial friends with members of subsequent generations, she continued to have friends even though her friends who supplied the links might have died.

Clarence Avery also had younger friends, men he had taught in law school or other lawyers he had met professionally:

> When I lived in my own home, somebody would drop in [on the way home from work] probably three times a week and we'd have a drink together and then they'd go on home to their wives to dinner. Now I don't have as many, but the one or two that I have have been perfectly marvelous friends. There is one who teaches high school who was one of my students. He claims, and I guess he's right, that he flunked out of law school. But he's bright as the dickens. I think he probably didn't do any work. But he comes in about once a week and we have an awful lot in common because he has a course at the school on the Supreme Court. It isn't a technical course, but he and I both keep up on the decisions. And then he has a gorgeous sense of humor. We always have a lot of fun together.

Mr. Avery referred to these younger men as friends. Others were likely to use, in addition, kinship terms to describe young friends to indicate an age discrepancy. Ties to younger others, then, often existed, but were not described immediately as friendships. These are precisely the kinds of relationships that would be lost in a structured interview about friendships.

These three features unique to friendships in old age are not exhaustive, but ones that suggested themselves in the informants' life stories as important. At the same time, these did not affect the informants uniformly. The next task is to examine the variety of ways in which the informants dealt with friendships in old age.

STYLES OF FRIENDSHIP

The ways in which the context of old age affects the friendships of individual old people varies depending in part on "friendship styles": the expectations about friendships built up through the life course that are brought to old age.[2] Three styles of friendship, and a fourth that is a combination of two, were delineated, each of which will be described in turn. In the following section the way each style is related to biography and circumstances in old age will be addressed.

The Independents

Some of the informants did not identify specific individuals as friends as they related their biographies, even when prompted to do so by the interviewers. Wilbur Evans's comments illustrate this. Referring to his youth, he said,

> Way back when we were children, going to school . . . I made a lot of friends with children, girls and boys. And as long as we were together, we enjoyed ourselves, we went to certain little functions that we had and we were always good friends. I wouldn't say there was any special friend. . . . We just enjoyed what we used to do.

His not having or wanting specific friends he attributes to an incident in late adolescence:

> I love friends. I love people. But I've been stung by friends, and I could never place myself in the position where I'd say, "Well, he or she is a *very* good friend of mine." I won't let myself get hurt anymore. [Can you say something about that?] Well, it happened when I met my wife. The boys that I used to go around with—we used to play ball. And then, suddenly, just like I say, when you fall in love, your life changes. So I didn't have as

much time to give them as I did to give her. I was the catcher on the team, and one day we were supposed to be playing and she was sick, so I didn't go to the ball game. We lost the game. I got blamed for it because I was doing something else. And I couldn't take that. I couldn't do justice to both of them. So I took what I wanted and that's what I went for. After we got married, we spent 55 years together.

About more recent associates he said:

I love'em. I got a lot of friends, too, but I don't say they're friends that I would depend upon. . . . I'm my own man. That's what I want to be. . . . Do I have friends now? I have people that I know.

In this case, the informant's criteria for friendship appear to include absolute commitment and this precluded friendships once he was committed to his wife. There was simply no room for competing relationships. It is interesting to speculate about how different his discussion of childhood friends might have been had he been interviewed at the age of fifteen.

Margaret Green is another case in point. She began the interview by saying:

Let me preface this by saying that I have been thinking a good deal about this since I knew you were going to talk to me about it. And I said, "Well, just how do you make friends?" It seems to me that one way is the neighborhood in which you live. You get acquainted with people. And some of them become your friends and others are just casual acquaintances. And then there is your school. From the time you are a youngster you make contacts there. Again, it's selective. You pick out people who appeal to you because you have something in common besides the fact that you are going to school. And then there is the church, another way in which you make friends, but there again, you are selective. But you form friendships because you are doing things together. And then the other things that occurred to me is the professional connections that you have. And then, of course, that makes me think of friends that I made when I was teaching. And what's become of them? Well, most of them have retired like I have and some of them have moved away. Some of them are gone. And then my last source of new friendships is the people that I have met here [retirement hotel]. And here, you see, circumstances have brought us together, but I'm still selective. I'm not friends with everybody. But I've made some very good friends with people that I never would have had any contact with if I hadn't been part of this group here.

In relating her biography Margaret Green remained true to her initial statement. Through her life she had allowed circumstances to provide her with friends, with only one singled out by name, a current one. In response to my query, "Do you have friends that you went to college with?" she replied,

> No. Not anymore. No, those years are so far behind me. I don't seem to keep close friends. The fact that I only mentioned one person here that I would say is a real friend. . . . But, I'm sort of self-sufficient. I don't seem to need people the way some people do.

About a woman she had lived with for at least a decade when they both worked in the same grade school, she said,

> I guess we separated when I went to the other school to teach because I wanted to be within walking distance of the campus and naturally she wanted to stay where she was. I think that's what caused us to go our different ways.

And of other friends at the grade school, she said,

> When I left, I had to start all over again to get acquainted with people because I didn't see much of those teachers anymore. Some of the depth of your friendship depends on how much you see people and how you are brought together, whether circumstances bring you together or it's altogether a voluntary thing.

These two schools were within three miles of each other. Characteristic of the Independents, then, friendships for Margaret Green apparently were much more circumstantial than personal, and would fall under the heading of "friendly relations" rather than "friendship" (Kurth, 1970) in the minds of many people, including the Discerning and the Acquisitive, described below.

The Discerning

Mary Thompson began the interview by saying, "My two closest friends died quite a long, long time ago."

> I'd say that I formed a very close friendship in high school within a group of girls . . . and there was really close friendship with one of these girls.

She died in her forties and so that ended that. And then another friend was a close friend in college and I married her brother, so that friendship was maintained. Really, it became a family relationship then, too. But she also died about ten years ago.

After we were married, we went to live in New Hampshire and I didn't form any friendships there. Then we moved to Buffalo and I didn't form any friendships there either. And that was sort of hard, not to have any women to talk to. And then eventually we came back to Cleveland and then I did form some new, close friendships here with two women particularly. But I would say that would be about it. We have a lot more casual friends, for instance, that we play bridge with and that sort of thing, but not the type of friends that you are totally unreserved or honest with, that you can let down and say how you really feel about something. I'm pretty on guard most of the time with most people.

Two other nonrelatives were mentioned as friends during the course of the interview. One was a "friend of both my husband and me, a priest who was a really good friend whom we thought of as family." Much to her surprise and disappointment, the friendship, which she assumed to be "symmetric," had ended when the priest was assigned to another parish a relatively short distance away. The other was a college friend who was jealous of her friendship with the woman who was later to become her sister-in-law. The informant felt that she was forced by the woman to choose between the two and that this pressure disqualified her as a "real" friend. Both her husband and one of her daughters were described during the course of the interview as friends, which is in accord with Allan's (1979, p. 41) assertion that when kin are described as friends it is to emphasize the quality of the particular relationship. For this woman, then, there was no question about who her friends were, no gray areas. She speaks of her friends the way one might speak of kin, as if there were institutionalized criteria that could be employed to place individuals in the category. In addition, once she has a friend or two, there is no reason to look for more.

Discerning to Independent

Harry Winter cited three specific individuals whom he considered to be friends. Two were friends from adolescence, one from early adulthood. He described with feeling one of his adolescent friends: "He and I played together. . . . He was, at that time, my very, very best friend." He had stayed in touch with both of these individuals until his early 40s, when both had moved west. Included in the interview somewhat reluctantly was an individual with whom he was still in contact. He and this man had taken classes together in college but he began to think of him, he supposed, as a friend when they both were colleagues in the early years of their professional careers. Among these three, there was a clear ranking, with the "very best friend" from adolescence coming first, the other adolescent friend second, and the colleague a distant third. The first, then, was the standard against which the other two relationships were judged. In describing relationships with others in his life, he explained, "I try to be compassionate. I try to have concern. I try to be just to all the people with whom I am acquainted." With no one else in this man's life had he had a relationship that he would describe as friendship. Even identifying the third person as a friend may have been an artifact of the interview situation. The impression one gets is that when he reached adulthood he had put away childish things, friendships being one of them. During the course of his life, then, he had moved from the Discerning style to the Independent style of friendship.

Acquisitive

The fourth style of friendship includes most of the informants who served as examples in the section of the paper on the unique context of friendships in old age. Malcolm Avery, Anne Livingston, and Charlotte Dickens all continued to acquire relationships that they described as friendships throughout their lives, holding on to old friends and acquiring new ones when their situations changed. Ethel Thayer also continued to acquire friends, although, except for a college friend, no relationship was maintained through the transitions in her life. Lillian Rubin (1981, p. 109) concluded from her experience of interviewing people about their friends that "people will find friendships even where they don't exist." Informants who were Acquisitive led me to conclude that there is no other way to include in conversations those "trivial" social relationships that are subjectively important but for which there is no other label except friend.

FRIENDSHIP STYLES IN OLD AGE: BIOGRAPHY AND CIRCUMSTANCE

Recognition that the old have extensive biographies often clouds the fact that they, like younger social actors, continue to be governed by the "pragmatic motive," that their "attention to this world is primarily determined by what [they are] doing, have done or plan to do in it"

(Berger & Luckmann, 1966, p. 22). Examining friendships by focusing only on biography and ignoring present circumstances with which an old person is faced would therefore give an incomplete picture. With respect to friendship, how do biography and circumstance interact in old age?

Circumstance: The Independents

The Independents are affected primarily by the circumstances that surround them. Because their lives are composed of friendly relations, less personal relationships than those of either the Discerning or the Acquisitive, their participation in social relationships is dependent on the particular "pool" in which they happen to be. Although Margaret Green referred to only one woman she considered a friend in the retirement hotel, she was not isolated:

> I'm involved in a good many activities here. I've always been a people person. I figure when there is something going on at the museum, somebody from here should go on over there. So I call up and make arrangements for transportation and get them over there. We're going to the Shakespeare festival next week.

Later in the interview she said,

> I'm not musical, but I've been going to the symphony with a group of people. I always have somebody that I go with and we have our season tickets. And there's a common interest that brings us together and makes us continue to see each other.

The Independent informant, then, is a friend of "somebody" with whom she shares an interest and, as the above reference to music indicates, she is willing to adopt an interest if necessary.

The more general nature of Margaret Green's biography is important to her current social relationships:

> My people experience is different than that of the women that have had families and family responsibilities, family joys, and family worries. So that is something. I don't have any close friends here that are family people. I think my inclination . . . is to gravitate towards people who have been professional people rather than family people.

Miss Green's populated biography, however, is unrelated to her current friendships. The only problem that might arise for her is living in a place in which there were no people with whom she shared a common interest, but given her willingness to adapt, this seems unlikely.

Biography: The Discerning

The Discerning are least affected by the circumstances of their lives with respect to who their friends are, but the most vulnerable to their friends no longer being available. Loss of these friends will mean that the old person will become friendless, and unlike the Independents for whom lack of friends appears to be no problem, these old people are likely to be very lonely.

Mary Thompson found the period of her life when her two friends were not available to her very painful. The loneliness she felt when she lived in New Hampshire and Buffalo was evident in her voice as she recounted her experiences. Throughout the years, she had relied on her husband as an important source of friendship:

> My husband is the kind of person who is a real friend. I mean, he's the kind of person who loves to talk and he made up for all of that sort of thing [loneliness]. He has sort of, all through the years, been a real friend, very companionable. . . . I think that that's one reason that I haven't really had to seek out friends very much because we're together an awful lot and on a really friendly basis.

At the end of the interview when we were tying up loose ends, she said,

> Wait a minute, I just thought of one other very good friend, my daughter. My daughter moved back to town recently and lives quite close. I really consider that we have a friendship. She's a great person.

She went on to explain that her daughter, who was married and had two children, recently had started graduate school in history. Mrs. Thompson explained that one of the things she had missed in friendships was a friend "whose mind matched mine," someone who was willing to discuss books and ideas that interested her. And now she had her daughter. This informant was relatively young, only 68, but if the rest of her life is continuous with her past, her friendships are very likely to dwindle to the one with her daughter, which will be the only relationship remaining from her biography that she considers a friendship.

Biography and Circumstance: The Acquisitive

For those informants who are Acquisitive, both biography and circumstance contribute to their friendships in old age. They are likely still to have friends from their past, as was evident in the previous descriptions, and to be open to new ones as well. The new friendships arose out of the particular circumstances of this period of their lives. The subset of informants who lived in the same retirement hotel, who shared the same circumstances, will serve as illustrations.

Charlotte Dickens described one of her newer friends:

> One of my best friends in the building is the maid on the sixth floor. We have a gorgeous time together. I know when it is that she can take her rest period and we gossip. And if I get the wrong gossip, she corrects me and if she does, I correct her.

In response to a query about her most recently acquired friend, she said,

> I think it's the person I eat with everyday. You mean a real friend. . . . I know that she fills a need of mine and I know that I fill a need of hers. And we eat luncheon together practically every day and most dinners. And we have fun. She likes *Alice in Wonderland*. She doesn't brag, but she lets you know that she went to boarding school in Switzerland when she was fourteen and was exposed to royalty. Then she forgets she told you that. I think each of us feels a need that the other fills. And it does beautifully for meals. It comes in very handy. "Are you tied up for dinner tonight?" "Well, yes, I'm sorry, I am." Tied up with Ruth. And if we do want to eat with someone else we just tell the other one, "Gee, I'm sorry. I've got to eat with so-and-so tonight." Works out nicely. Now, of course, you run into the age problem. She's almost ninety. How much longer is she going to live?

Providing evidence that "objective symmetry" (Weber, 1978) is not a requisite of friendship, she concluded:

> There are others [recently acquired friends]. Margaret Green I consider a friend, but she's not the most recent. I've been a friend of hers ever since I moved in here.

The circumstances of living in a retirement hotel that includes congregate meals provide the impetus for the initiation and continuation of friendships.

Malcolm Avery responded in a similar way to the circumstances in making his choice of a friend:

> I know who my closest friend is now and that's this Albert Small whom I met here . . . even though I haven't known him nearly as long as some of

the others. I now eat breakfast every day with him. We have become like two brothers. And we now eat dinner together, too, which is great. What I don't particularly want to do is get involved in a series of cocktail parties. I'd rather be with someone that I am very fond of. I've kept out of it and my friend Albert Small has helped me a lot because my natural tendency is to say yes.

These new friendships emerged from the circumstances of the residential setting, which presented these old people with situations that required a particular type of friendship relationship.

Others who were Acquisitive were not as capable of dealing with the setting. They had a passive style of acquiring friends. Ethel Thayer, for example, described herself as the only person in the retirement hotel who had no friends. In going over her life, she identified the various places where she had lived, beginning with her childhood in which she had no friends because, she explained, her family had moved every three years. In college, however, she had acquired several friends ("I generally got along very well with New York and Philadelphia girls"). After that, in almost every place she lived—Boston, Los Angeles, a small town in Indiana, Denver, Knoxville, and a suburb of Cleveland—she felt that she had acquired friends easily and could name one or two individuals in each place whom she had considered close friends, one of whom had even willed a small sum of money to her. She had moved into the retirement hotel in 1975:

And I have made very little progress since then about having friends. At first it surprised me because I'd always had friends. It still surprises me. For instance, if I call up someone and ask them to have dinner with me, they say yes, but they never invite me. No one ever invites me to do anything. To substitute at bridge or to have dinner with them or even lunch with them. If I do anything about it, I'm the one that has to do the inviting. And it seems to me odd. It still does.

Later in her life history she explained:

I was thinking that most of the people who were my friends really sought me out. Bess did. Yes, it seems to me that they were really the initiators. Elizabeth did. And no one here wants to be friends with me. [Have you ever sought out a friendship?] I've always had all the friends I've needed.

Like "the isolates" in Rosow's (1967) research, whose morale was low in age-homogeneous residential settings because they wanted but were unable to make friends, Ethel Thayer found herself lonely, surrounded by likely candidates with whom she would happily have been friends.

An Acquisitive style of friendship is not a guarantee that friendships will be available in old age. Mrs. Thayer had quit writing to her old friends and, therefore, they to her. She described herself as depressed, a term that, as a professional psychologist, she could use legitimately. Although a definitive judgment is impossible with these limited data, one interpretation is that her present circumstances destroyed the significance of her populated biography, leaving her completely bereft in old age.

CONCLUSION

This chapter has addressed old age as a unique context for friendships, populated biographies, and the specific circumstances of particular old people's lives that promote or inhibit friendships. It is intended to contribute in two ways to sociological theorizing in the substantive area of aging and old age. With respect to topic, it is about friendship as a cultural form and about friendship in old age, their biographical origins and their current meanings. More broadly, it is an argument that a better understanding of behavior in old age, regardless of topic, may be attained if the old are conceptualized as social actors who have not simply long biographies, but populated ones, composed of concrete social relationships that they accumulate through the life course and that affect their daily lives in old age. This chapter attempts, then, to follow Back's (1980, p. 2) exhortation that "it is incumbent on all of us to attempt to blend the procedure of the humanist and the social scientist" as, studying the human life course, we search for "systematical regularities in events of unique meaning."

NOTES

1. A total of 64 informants between the ages of 60 and 89 (median age 74) participated in the research. They were recruited in a variety of ways to ensure variation in both biography and social location. Approximately half were men, half women. Although this chapter is based on their life histories, the biographies of nine informants are cited here. Names and personal information have been altered to preserve anonymity. Five of these informants lived in the same retirement hotel and were chosen for this chapter because they share the same circumstances:

- Malcolm Avery, age 86 (b. 1894); widowed, age 82; 2 children; lawyer
- Charlotte Dickens, age 82 (b. 1898); ever single; social worker

- Margaret Green, age 87 (b. 1895); ever single; teacher
- Anne Livingston, age 82 (b. 1898); widowed, age 52; homemaker until her husband's death, social service job thereafter
- Ethel Thayer, age 75 (b. 1905); widowed, age 38; one child; psychologist

The other four informants cited are as follows:

- Wilbur Evans, age 79 (b. 1902); clerk; widowed, age 75; no children; apartment in retirement complex
- Alex Simak, age 86 (b. 1894); widowed, age 72 (?); 2 children; engineer; own home
- Mary Thompson, age 68 (b. 1912); married; 3 children; homemaker and bookkeeper for husband; own home
- Harry Winter, age 75 (b. 1906); married; 2 children; school administrator; apartment

2. In earlier analysis of these data (Matthews, 1983a), definitions of friendship were the focus. Definition of friendship and style of friendship are closely related. Persons whose style of friendship is Discerning are likely to use a "particular person" definition of friendship exclusively; those who are Independent, a "relationship" definition.

REFERENCES

Allan, G. A. (1979). *A sociology of friendship and kinship*. Boston: George Allen & Unwin.

Arling, G. (1976). The elderly widow and her family, neighbors, and friends. *Journal of Marriage and the Family, 38*, 757-768.

Babchuk, N. & Bates, A. P. (1963). The primary relations of middle-class couples: A study in male dominance. *American Sociological Review, 28*, 377-384.

Back, K. (Ed.). (1980). *Life course: Integrative theories and exemplary populations*. Boulder, CO: Westview.

Bateson, G. (1979). *Mind and nature: A necessary unity*. New York: Bantam.

Becker, H. S. (1970). The relevance of life histories. In N. K. Denzin (Ed.), *Sociological methods: A sourcebook* (pp. 419-428). Chicago: Aldine.

Berger, P. L., & Luckmann, T. (1966). *The social construction of reality*. Garden City, NY: Doubleday.

Bertaux, D. (1981). Introduction. In D. Bertaux (Ed.), *Biography and society: The life history approach in social sciences* (pp. 5-15). Beverly Hills, CA: Sage.

Blau, Z. S. (1961). Structural constraints on friendship in old age. *American Sociological Review, 26*, 429-439.

Brenton, M. (1974). *Friendship*. New York: Stein & Day.

Brown, B. B. (1981). A life-span approach to friendship: Age-related dimensions of an ageless relationship. In H. Lopata & D. Maines (Eds.), *Research on the interweave of social roles: vol. 2. Friendship* (pp. 23-50). Greenwich, CT: JAI.

Candy, S.E.G. (1977). *A comparative analysis of friendship functions in six groups of men and women*. Unpublished doctoral dissertation, Department of Psychology, Wayne State University.

Chown, S. M. (1981). Friendship in old age. In S. Duck & R. Gilmour (Eds.), *Personal relationships, 2: Developing personal relationships* (pp. 231-246). New York: Academic Press.

Fischer, C. S. (1982). *To dwell among friends.* Chicago: University of Chicago Press.

Goffman, E. (1963). *Stigma: Notes on the management of spoiled identity.* Englewood Cliffs, NJ: Prentice-Hall.

Gold, H. (1973). Friendship and the lifeboat. *Harper's Magazine, 246,* 44-47.

Hess, B. (1972) Friendship. In M. W. Riley, M. Johnson, & A. Foner (Eds.), *Aging and society: Vol. 3. A sociology of age stratification* (pp. 357-393). New York: Russell Sage Foundation.

Hochschild, A. R. (1978). *The unexpected community.* Berkeley: University of California Press.

Huston, T. L., & Levinger, G. (1978). Interpersonal attraction and relationships. *Annual Review of Psychology, 29,* 115-156.

Job, E. M. (1983). Retrospective life span analysis: A method for studying extreme old age. *Journal of Gerontology, 38*(3), 369-374.

Kahn, R. L., & Antonucci, T. C. (1981). Convoys of social support: A life-course approach. In S. B. Kiesler, J. N. Morgan, & V. K. Oppenheimer (Eds.), *Aging: Social change* (pp. 383-405). New York: Academic Press.

Kessler, S. J., & McKenna, W. (1978) *Gender: An ethnomethodological approach.* New York: John Wiley.

Kurth, S. B. (1970). Friendships and friendly relations. In G. J. McCall (Ed.), *Social relationships* (pp. 136-170). Chicago: Aldine.

Lazarsfeld, P. F., & Merton, R. K. (1954). Friendship as social process: A substantive and methodological analysis. In M. Berger, T. Abel, & C. H. Page (Eds.), *Freedom and control in modern society* (pp. 18-66). New York: Van Nostrand.

Lee, S. (1977). Friendship, feminism, and betrayal. In A. M. Eastman (Ed.), *The Norton reader: An anthology of expository prose* (4th ed., pp. 589-595). New York: W. W. Norton.

Lofland, J. (1973). Interactionist imagery and analytic interruptus. In T. Shibutani (Ed.), *Human nature and collective behavior: Papers in honor of Herbert Blumer* (pp. 35-45). New Brunswick, NJ: Transaction.

Lowenthal, M. F., & Haven, C. (1968). Interaction and adaptations: Intimacy as a critical variable. In B. L. Neugarten (Ed.), *Middle age and aging* (pp. 390-400). Chicago: University of Chicago Press.

Lowenthal, M. F., & Robinson, B. (1976). Social networks and isolation. In R. H. Binstock & E. Shanas (Eds.), *Handbook of aging and the social sciences* (pp. 432-456). New York: Van Nostrand Reinhold.

Lowenthal, M. F., Thurnher, M., Chiriboga, D., & Associates. (1975). *Four stages of life: A comparative study of women and men facing transitions.* San Francisco: Jossey-Bass.

Marshall, V. W. (1980). *Last chapters: A sociology of aging and dying.* Monterey, CA: Brooks/Cole.

Matthews, S. H. (1983a). Definitions of friendships and the consequences in old age. *Aging and Society, 3,* 141-155.

Matthews, S. H. (1983b). Analyzing topical oral biographies of old people: The case of friendship. *Research on Aging, 5,* 569-589.

McCall, G. J. (1970). The social organization of relationships. In G. J. McCall (Ed.), *Social relationships* (pp. 3-34). Chicago: Aldine.

Moore, S. F. (1978). Old age in a life-term social arena: Some Chagga of Kilimanjaro in 1974. In B. G. Myerhoff & A. Simić (Eds.), *Life's career—aging: Cultural variations on growing old* (pp. 23-75). Beverly Hills, CA: Sage.

Munnichs, J.M.A. (1964). Loneliness, isolation, and social relations in old age. *Vita Humana, 7*, 228-238.

Naegele, K. (1958). Friendship and acquaintances: An exploration of social distinction. *Harvard Educational Review, 28*, 232-252.

Neugarten, B. L., & Hagestad, G. O. (1976). Age and the life course. In R. H. Binstock & Shanas (Eds.), *Handbook of aging and the social sciences* (pp. 35-55). New York: Van Nostrand Reinhold.

Paine, R. (1969). In search of friendship: An exploratory analysis in 'middle-class' culture. *Man, 4*, 505-525.

Pritchitt, V. S. (1977). *Autobiography.* London: English Association.

Reina, R. E. (1959). Two patterns of friendship in Guatemala community. *American Anthropologist, 61*, 44-50.

Reisman, J. J. (1979). *Anatomy of friendship.* New York: Irvington.

Rosenmayr, L. (1981). Objective and subjective perspectives of life span research. *Aging and Society, 1*(1), 29-49.

Rosow, I. (1967). *Social integration of the aged.* New York: Free Press.

Ross, J. K. (1977). *Old people, new lives: Community creation in a retirement residence.* Chicago: University of Chicago Press.

Rubin, L. B. (1981). Sociological research: The subjective dimension: The 1980 SSSI distinguished lecture. *Symbolic Interaction, 4*, 97-112.

Selman, R. L. (1981). The child as friendship philosopher. In S. R. Asher & J. M. Gottman (Eds.), *The development of children's friendships* (pp. 242-272). New York: Cambridge University Press.

Shulman, N. (1975). Life-cycle variations in patterns of close relationships. *Journal of Marriage and the Family, 37*, 813-821.

Simić, A. & Myerhoff, B. (1978). Conclusion. In B. Myerhoff & A. Simić (Eds.), *Life's career—aging: Cultural variations on growing old* (pp. 231-246). Beverly Hills, CA: Sage.

Simmel, G. (1950). The isolated individual and the dyad. In K. H. Wolff (Ed.), *The sociology of Georg Simmel* (pp. 118-144). New York: Free Press.

Skolnick, A. (1983). Looking at lives, or "Whose life course is it, anyway?" *Contemporary Sociology, 12*, 386-387.

Suttles, G. D. (1970). Friendship as a social institution. In G. J. McCall (Ed.), *Social relationships* (pp. 95-135). Chicago: Aldine.

Verbrugge, L. M. (1977). The structure of adult friendship choices. *Social Forces, 56*, 576-597.

Weber, M. (1978). *Economy and society: An outline of interpretive sociology* (Vol. 1, G. Roth & C. Wittich, Eds.). Berkeley: University of California Press.

9

The World We Forgot:
A Historical Review of
the Life Course

MARTIN KOHLI

There are several ways of being interested in age and the life course. One is to look at it simply as an additional dimension of variance, to be entered into the larger grid of population breakdowns relevant for the particular questions under study. A second, more direct way consists of focusing on life course processes as a topic in their own right (i.e., on how and why persons move up and change through the life course). As sociologists, we have to go further, however: We have to be interested in the life course as an independent dimension of social structure. What we have before us is not just a temporal variation of other social givens, or a temporal process, but a *social fact* generated by its own system of rules. In this manner, the life course can be conceptualized as a social institution—not in the sense of a social grouping (an aggregate of individuals), but of a pattern of rules ordering a key dimension of life.

What these rules are can best be shown by analyzing how they have changed. As in many other fields—such as the sociology of the family, of the state, or of social movements—the most challenging ideas today come from history: from the large body of sociologically informed historical scholarship that has been accumulating mainly during the past two decades. As in these other fields, a historical analysis can provide better grounding to approaches that have too easily risen to the heights of universal theory, either by universalizing the patterns of the 1950s or by opting for an essentially formal style of theorizing.[1]

There can be no doubt that the process of aging and the limited duration of human life are universal social facts; or rather universal

AUTHOR'S NOTE: This chapter is based on an article in German (Kohli, 1985a). It was completed while the author was a member of the Institute for Advanced Study, Princeton, New Jersey.

problems for which any society has to find a structural solution. But what this solution is and how it articulates with other core structural features of that society cannot be clarified on this level. Neither is there much help to be expected from another formerly popular strategy, namely, the comparison with "primitive" societies as offered by anthropology—not much help, that is, as long as sociologists are not ashamed of throwing together such societies with those of our immediate past under a general label of "traditional."

In this respect, the new historical scholarship imposes on us some healthy restrictions. It reminds us that whatever interesting societies there may be around, we first ought to look at our own case.[2] This is what shall be attempted here. The following considerations will accordingly be limited to the Western modernization process of the last three centuries.[3] To the historian, this is still likely to appear an unmanageably large agenda. As an appeasement, I can only point out that sociology used to be much grander. In addition, there does seem to be some structural unity to the field within these limits, which would warrant treating it as a single case: Among other things, it had a common pattern of household formation rules, the "European marriage pattern" (Hajnal, 1983), and thus a common structure of what was the main unit of both production and reproduction.[4]

A THEORETICAL OUTLINE

The argument set forth here can be summarized in five propositions:

(1) The relevance of the life course as a social institution has greatly increased. There has been a change from a regime in which age was relevant as a categorical status only to a regime in which life-time is one of the core structural features (*temporalization*).

(2) The temporalization of life is largely keyed to chronological age as the basic criterion; this has resulted in a chronologically standardized "normative life course" (*chronologization*).

(3) The chronologization of life is part of the more general process in which the individuals are set free from the bonds of status, locality, and family; becoming, in other words, part of the new social programs that are focused on the individuals as the basic units of social life (*individualization*).

(4) The life course is organized around the *system of labor* that prevails in society. This applies to the shape of the life course—its most obvious temporal ordering today has become the tripartition into periods of preparation, "activity," and retirement—as well as to its organizing principle.

(5) The pattern of rules constituting the life course can be found on two different levels of social reality. One is the movement of individuals through life in terms of *sequences of positions*, or "careers"; the other is their *biographical perspectives and actions*.

The second of these propositions, about chronologization, may be the most obvious and least controversial. That the life course has become more segmented in the transition to the modern regime has been noted by several authors (among them, Winsborough, 1979; Foner, 1982; Hareven, 1982a). It will be useful, however, to distinguish between several levels of this proposition. One is that there is less likeness between the life phases; in other words, they have become more differentiated (as has been asserted by Ariès [1962] in his path-breaking study that started the historiography of childhood). On another level, growing segmentation can mean shorter (and thus more abrupt) individual transitions from one phase to the next. Finally, the transition can become shorter for the population as a whole, which is analogous to saying that it becomes more closely spaced around a common (chrono-logical) standard; it is this process that has received the most attention in the recent studies of the transition to adulthood (see below).

The first and third propositions are more difficult to deal with. Linking the argument to the process of individualization entails a change of perspective from the manner of conceptualizing age that has dominated so far. In the age stratification scheme, focusing on age strata or on the life course are two ways of looking at the same set of phenomena. There is, however, a basic difference between these two foci: Age strata (or age sets) are collective categories with membership rules, while the life course is an individualized life line, being relevant socially in terms of a temporal vector rather than of membership in an aggregate. It is true that the life course rules are partly rules of transition from one position to the next; in other words, of membership change (and that the membership categories have become more clearly separated histori-cally); but above that, they are also rules of organizing these transitions into a comprehensive life process, both in terms of a sequential logic (e.g., of "career," "growth," or "development") and of projects and time perspectives (i.e., anticipation and recollection). In the premodern life course regime, old age may have existed as an age stratum (although with less well-defined boundaries than today), but it did not exist as an expectable stage in the normal life course program. Thus the questions of status and power that have dominated the historiography of old age so far are not the most salient ones when focusing on the life course as the basic unit of social reality and sociological analysis. It might be added that empirically, looking at how people classify themselves, there is not much support for conceptualizing age strata in membership terms, analogous to social class; the relevance of age as a membership category seems to be clearly secondary to that of age, and especially chronological age, as a life course marker.

Another difficulty is posed by the concept of individualization itself. Although it has (again) become popular in sociological discourse, there are as yet no systematic treatments of it on which the argument of the present chapter could be based safely. Although it will not be possible to go into such a systematic discussion, it will be necessary to distinguish between the different levels that the concept addresses, for instance, individuality as a general concept of human agency and accountability versus individuality as personal uniqueness (i.e., referring to interpersonal differentiation), or individualization in terms of labor market status, of resources and lifestyle, or of cultural definition.

The fourth proposition deemphasizes the life domain in which the main body of life-course research has so far had its empirical and theoretical grounding: the family. It is important to give more weight in life-course sociology to work as the key organizing feature of social life. Although the family events have to be considered in constructing a picture of what has changed, and can give rise to striking consequences (see Hagestad, 1984), the focus on work is essential on the level of structural explanation. The impact of work goes far beyond simply assuring material survival; by providing the legitimate basis for the allocation of life chances in a very broad sense, it defines the cultural unity of modern Western society as well as the identity of its members. We may be moving away from it (see below, the section headed "The Present Situation"), but up to now, we are still living in a "work society" (see Matthes, 1983).[5] Historically, of course, the domains of work and family were much less differentiated, so that those emphasizing work and those emphasizing the family branch out from a common reality: the household economy. The emphasis of the present chapter would be shared by those authors who go even farther and assert that structurally, the family was not only organized around but defined by the dynamics of production, so that it makes no sense to distinguish a kinship-based "family" from a production-based "household" (Sieder & Mitterauer, 1983, pp. 337-345).

The fifth proposition calls for simultaneously considering not only two levels of reality but also the two sociological research approaches that have developed in correspondence to them: one, the research on sequences of positions or "life histories" that has grown out of, and can be considered as a generalization of, the models of mobility research and demography (see Featherman, 1981); and the other, research on biographical orientations and action processes—"biographical research" in the more specific sense (see Bertaux & Kohli, 1984). This distinction is close to the more general problem of how to relate social structure and action, or macro- and microsociology. To try to do this is evidently to take on a large project, maybe still the most difficult one in general sociological theory; it will come as no surprise, then, that it cannot be fully accomplished here.[6] As sociologists—even if we are interested in questions of human experience and agency—we are well advised to start with a structural approach, and test how far it takes us (see the section "Toward a Structural Explanation"); it will then become necessary to go into the relation of structure and action in somewhat more detail ("Institutional Program and Subjective Construction").

Constructing such an overall picture of change in the Western modernization process is a task that will require much additional work. The present chapter is intended as a first step. Its point of departure is both under- and overdetermined. On the one hand, there is a lack of research addressing directly the questions posed here. One could expect to find some such research in the new social history of temporal organization and temporal perspectives (see the great panorama by Wendorff, 1980). This, however, turns out be an error; as in the sociology of time more generally, the emphasis in historical analysis has so far been on everyday time (e.g., on the chronologization of everyday time starting in the late medieval period [Le Goff, 1980], or the change of everyday time patterns in the transition to the factory system [Deutschmann, 1983]), while the discussion on changes in the life-time regime has barely got under way.[7] On the other hand, the literature in the various research fields that touch on our topic—from the history of the welfare state to that of autobiography as a literary genre—has grown so enormously that it would be futile to try to summarize it. Even a field like the history of old age, which ten years ago practically did not exist, has grown to the point where it defies easy integration.[8]

Accordingly, there can be no question of giving a complete account of the empirical literature. Instead, I will present some examples of the types of evidence we have, and of the theoretical conclusions that may be drawn from them. I will concentrate on German data and on arguments developed in the German context, but supplement them with American data and arguments, especially where the latter are the only ones available. The procedure followed here implies several theoretical commitments, of which at least three should be briefly mentioned:

(1) I will not go into any regional or social class differentiation of the modernization process, nor go into the problems of temporal sequence (and the patterns of causal sequence that can be derived from them). The latter are critical for some versions of modernization theory; for instance, there is a controversy in the history of old age on whether the status loss of old age preceded or followed industrialization, in other words, whether the cultural or the economic change had precedence (see Achenbaum & Stearns, 1978). For the present argument, this is of no concern; it is limited mainly to a structural before-and-after contrast, assuming a sort of "elective affinity" (Weber) between the different elements of a structure, and leaving open the question of what sets the process in motion and how it proceeds. One thing will be apparent: Most of the population changes in life-course chronology occur rather late, so that at least for them, the temporal and thus the causal sequence is clear. This would suggest that, whatever the prerequisites of industrialization, it is in turn a prerequisite of the new life-course regime becoming a mass phenomenon.

(2) By focusing on structural contrasts, we can avoid another thorny problem, namely, whether the change has been linear or at least continuous. This is essentially the question of the relation of long, middle, and short duration. Much could be said about middle duration, referring to structurally distinct stages of development, such as—in the economic dimension—the stage of protoindustrialization (Kriedte et al., 1977), or—in the demographic dimension—that of the demographic transition (Coale & Watkins, 1985). (An especially challenging thesis now holds that the 1950s were such a distinctive and historically unique phase, demographically [Cherlin, 1980] and even [Lutz, 1984] economically.) And much could be said about short duration—which in sociology is usually conceptualized as "cohort variation." (In fact, my own empirical background would push me in that direction, since Germany has been, among the contemporary Western countries, arguably the one with the highest impact of short-term variation; see Bertaux & Kohli, 1984, p. 221.) But the argument here will be limited to the long run. It is grounded on the assumption that, in spite of all other sources of variation, the transformation from the premodern to the modern form of life and work is still so basic that it makes sense to focus on it.

(3) The procedure of structural contrasting tends to overstate the difference, and this should be kept in mind. Thus speaking of "individualization" does not mean that there was no individuality to start with. Clearly, individuality or personhood in the sense of the basic

competencies required for participation in social interaction is universal. Similarly, "chronologization" does not mean that chronological age had no relevance at all; there are counterexamples (Held, 1985) that would falsify too stark a version of the chronologization thesis but do not cast doubt on its overall validity.

TYPES OF HISTORICAL EVIDENCE

The data presented in this section are examples of the available types of descriptive data on what has changed. What changes are to be taken into account is by no means self-evident; the selection of these examples is intended to show how the changes can be looked at to yield a general pattern.

Duration of Life

Life and death certainly are the basic facts, and so it is appropriate to take them up first. In the dimension of the duration of life (in other words, of age at death), the process of modernization is a transformation from a pattern of relative randomness to a pattern of a predictable life span.

In the premodern demographic regime, the death toll was especially high in the first years, but, for those surviving, death was likely to strike at any time during the possible life course. Now death is concentrated in the upper age brackets. The feature that is decisive for the present argument is not so much the rise of the mean age of death but the drop in variance. One way of looking at it is by way of the cumulative survival curve. For the United States, Fries and Crapo (1980, p. 69) show that between 1840 and 1980 a process of "rectangularization" has occurred. In 1840, there was a high infant mortality, but even after that there was a high death rate remaining fairly constant over most of the adult lifespan. Now the curve is approaching a rectangle. What this shows is that the mean duration of life has risen substantially, while the maximum duration has remained essentially the same. (Fries and Crapo take this as evidence for a biological limit for the human life span.)

For Germany, there is a similar pattern (see Table 9.1). A century ago (at the time of the first nationwide census), one-third of the women lived to age 60, and one-sixteenth to age 80. Today, nine-tenths live to age 60, and still more than half to age 80. Much of this increase is again due to the massive decline of infant and adolescent mortality. But even if we disregard what happens in infancy and adolescence, and take into

TABLE 9.1   Historical Change in Survival Rates for German Women

Age Span	Percentage Surviving Through Specified Age Span	
	1871-1881	*1979-1981*
0-60	36.3	89.6
0-80	6.6	50.1
20-40	82.8	98.5
20-60	52.5	91.2

SOURCE: Statistische Jahrbucher für die Bundesrepublik Deutschland.

account only the adult years—by looking at survival from age 20 to 40 or to 60—the difference between then and now is still dramatic. A century ago, of the women who reached age 20, almost a fifth died before 40 and almost half before 60; today, this is limited to one in 67 and one in 11, respectively. We can say that death has almost disappeared from early and even middle adulthood, and tends to strike in old age only.

Family Cycle

An analogous pattern applies for the events that today comprise what has come to be called the "family cycle": They were less clustered around a specific chronological age. In fact, the concept itself is of questionable value for the premodern family (Mitterauer & Sieder, 1980), because it presupposes a typical sequence of a limited number of distinct configurations of family membership, which occurs only where there is a high standardization of the family events. Instead, the premodern family shows a wide range of kinship and age configurations, and a high amount of short-run fluctuation between them. Similarly, the concepts of "normative life events" (Baltes et al., 1980) in developmental psychology, and of a "normal biography" (Levy, 1977) in life-course sociology are grounded in the present situation; they are not appropriate to the empirical reality of the premodern life-course regime.

In the sociology of the family, it took some time for this to be recognized. Early research on the family cycle tried to trace its historical change by analyzing the change in the mean age at which each event occurred. This led to some interesting results, most notably about the emergence of the "empty nest" as a distinct stage of the modern family cycle—the result of the concentration of births in the early adult years and the increase in life expectancy. However, this type of analysis could

not catch the more basic transformation: the emergence of a standardized general sequence of events.

In the meantime, a growing number of studies have addressed
directly this process of standardization, using several different analytical
strategies (see the overview by Hagestad & Neugarten, 1985; also,
Featherman & Sorenson, 1983). One consists of examining the proportion of people in different types of family event sequences. Thus,
Uhlenberg (1969) has compared the cohorts of women born in
Massachusetts between 1830 and 1920, and found that the proportion of
those in the "normal" life-cycle type (marriage, having children,
surviving to age 55 together with the husband) has increased during this
period from 20.9% to 57.1%. Most of this increase is accounted for by
the decrease in mortality during childhood and adolescence; some of it,
however, is due to the decreasing adult mortality and the increasing
prevalence of marriage. In a later study about the cohorts born from
1890-1931 (Uhlenberg, 1974), the divorce rate is added to the variables
taken into consideration. Although it has increased considerably, there
has still been a strong increase in the proportion of the "normal type."
Thus the historical change up to this point has not resulted in the
dissolution of the family, but rather in the strengthening of the
normative pattern.

Another strategy consists of using some measure of variance of the
age at a transitional event, for instance, the time it takes the two middle
quartiles of a population to go through the transition. It has become
especially popular in studies of the movement from youth to adulthood.
In the first such study, based on census records from Philadelphia,
Modell et al. (1976) found, among other things, that the several
transitions involved (such as ending school, starting the first job, first
marriage) over the last hundred years had moved closer together, so that
the overall transition had become shorter. While this study is limited to
cross-sectional data, others are based on longitudinal or retrospective
data (e.g., Winsborough, 1979; Hogan, 1982). For instance, Winsborough (1979) again shows that, for a nationally representative sample
of men born 1911-1941, the duration of each of the three transitions has
shortened and they also have moved closer together, so that the overall
transition to adulthood (for the middle quartiles) has decreased from 18
to 10 years. In sum, the evidence shows an "increasing segmentalization
of life along the age continuum" (Winsborough, 1979, p. 139). In other
words, there is now more uniformity in the movement along the stages
of life. Having been established by several studies using different
samples and different analytical strategies, this seems to be a rather
robust result.

Another set of family events, referring to intergenerational relations, consists of the death of children and parents (see the studies reported by Hagestad, 1984, pp. 2-4). These events also have become more standardized, and thus more predictable.

To reach farther back in time, we can turn to the data generated by historical demography. Here again, the type of evidence is the same. Imhof (1985) gives a striking example, from one of the Hessian communes that he studies, covering more than two centuries and showing how extensively the age at marriage has become standardized (while the mean has not changed much).

The Constitution of Age Boundaries

The chronologization of the life course has been greatly advanced by the modern age-stratified systems of public rights and duties. Those with the most far-reaching effects are the school system and the old-age pension system; they have created the age boundaries that today constitute the basic tripartition of the life course. Within the boundaries set by the school system, the emergence of age-homogenized classes (see Ariès, 1962) has contributed to further chronological ordering.

In the domain of civil law, it was the Code Napoleon that institutionalized the first comprehensive system of age thresholds (Cain, 1976). In the meantime, we have come to take for granted the age stratification of things like legal responsibility (both in civil and in penal law), right to vote, inheritance, military draft, transportation tickets, and access to public support. Particularly important is the age stratification of the labor market by way of (formal or informal) rules of recruitment, promotion, and protection. These age boundaries have become so elaborate that they require specific studies (see Dohse et al., 1982; Kohli et al., 1983).

The process by which age boundaries have emerged and become generalized is especially clear when focusing on old age (see also Atchley, 1982). It might not be appropriate to speak of the "discovery" of old age, in analogy to what has been claimed for childhood. Age as a cultural category seems to be universal. But as a temporally bounded and structurally distinct phase of life which is part of the "normal" life course, it is quite new. There were some forms of retirement in premodern life, especially the process of turning over the control of the farm to the heir; but they were not clearly tied to chronological age, and their prevalence was quite low. Held (1982), in his careful study of 32 Austrian communities between 1632 and 1909, found that less than 8%

of those aged 51-70 were living as *Altenteiler* (i.e., had turned over their former property). As to the age of those who did retire in this manner, Held reports from a community study that the age at retirement ranged from 37 to 81, and that the "majority" retired between 50 and 65. It should also be noted that retirement had no place in traditional European folk culture; the life-cycle system consisted only of birth-marriage-death, and thus old age was not a distinctive period set off by specific transition rites or other customs (Schenda, 1983, p. 59; see also van Gennep, 1909).

Old age in the modern sense is based on the dominance of salaried labor (see also Myles, 1984, p. 21). The latter was the prerequisite for the processes that culminated in the creation of the public pension schemes. Before their creation, "retirement was completely alien to working class culture" (Stearns, 1977, p. 47). But even after the creation of such pension schemes, retirement proceeded slowly. In the German case—the first of the public systems—it can be shown how it expanded in two dimensions: It covered more and more groups, until it has now become an insurance for the whole population; and a growing proportion of those covered in fact reached the retirement limit; in other words, the point that we now take for granted to be the beginning of old age.

The second dimension is covered by the data on survival (such as those reported above for women). When focusing on men, we find that for 1881-1890 (i.e., immediately prior to the establishment of the old age insurance), 19.7% of German men survived to age 70, which was the pension limit set in 1889; today (1979-1981), 72.2% survive to age 65 (the upper pension limit), and 80.5% to age 60 (the mean factual retirement age being 59). Thus the proportion of those that can possibly benefit from retirement has increased from one-fifth to four-fifths. As to the first dimension, the proportion of those insured has risen from 54% to almost 100% of the economically active population (Mayer & Müller, 1985). An even better indicator of the impact of the pension system is provided by the data on labor market participation, which is a function not only of the proportion covered but also of the level of pensions relative to previous income. Although there are as yet no studies of historical change in the transition to retirement comparable to those of the transition to adulthood, we have at least this simple set of data indicating to what extent there *has* been a transition. As Table 9.2 shows, the decrease in labor force participation of older men in Germany has been dramatic. In the United States, we find a similar evolution: The labor force participation rate of men above age 65 has dropped, in the same period (1890-1980), from 68.3% to 19.1%, with

TABLE 9.2   Historical Change in Labor Force
Participation Rates for German Men

| | Percentage in Labor Force | |
Age	1895	1980
60-70	79.0	25.1
70+	47.4	5.2

SOURCE: Kohli (1985a, p. 10).

most of the decrease occurring after 1930 (Treas, 1981). In other words, the retirement limit set by the public pension scheme has now become the factual limit of labor force participation as well. Only now do we have a structurally distinct phase of life with a relatively uniform beginning and a sizable length for the major part of the population.

Biographical Perspectives

So far, we have been concerned with the external sequencing of life, and have found a straightforward, well-established picture of change. Turning now to biographical perspectives, we face a situation that is more complex. Although there is much work that sheds light on particular aspects of it, there have been as yet no studies integrating these aspects into a coherent whole. To be sure, there is a lot of what could be called "demographic psychology"—arguments of the type, "If the age difference between spouses was so large, this must have meant that marriage had to be based on something other than love," or, "If the duration of life was so unpredictable, this must have meant that there could be no long-range planning." All this may be true, but we certainly would like to see evidence that is more directly to the point.

One aspect of the problem is how age and life course categories are used in everyday social life—in other words, their "social pragmatics" (see Kohli, 1981; Fuchs, 1984). The simplest way to start is with chronological age itself. The emergence of the age-stratified public systems of rights and duties of course presupposes knowing a person's chronological age. Earlier, the need to publicly certify the date of birth arose with the institutionalization of age thresholds in the Code Napoleon (Cain, 1976, p. 351). In modern legal culture, the possibility of referring to age is taken for granted; there are situations, however, in which it is shown to be drastically problematic; in situations of immigration, for example. Thus Israel had to establish legal procedures for formal age determination (Cain, 1976, p. 353), and the administration of age boundaries for immigration into West Germany runs into similar problems. Beyond this level of formal requirements, we would have to study when and how age became an indispensable criterion for assessing oneself and other in everyday life, and thus had to be socially available.[9]

For biographical perspectives proper, some basic features of change are addressed by large-scale studies of mentalities and life forms, such as those by Elias (1969) or Foucault (1977) on the civilizational process, by Weber (1930) on the cultural prerequisites of capitalism, or by Stone (1977) on the history of the family. They differ greatly in the scope of their arguments and in their styles and degrees of documentation, but they show a surprising overall agreement with reference to the emerging concept of the individual. For Elias, the key transformation is from a life form of spontaneity which is bounded by external constraints only (in other words, situationally), to internalized constraint (in other words, self-control). The increasing self-constraint implies a "constraint for long-range perspectives" (1969, 2, p. 336) as the basis for the long-range regulation of behavior. Weber in his ideal-typical characterization of the Protestant ethic emphasizes the same point. He depicts the "medieval Catholic layman" as living ethically "from hand to mouth," in other words, situationally: "His good works did not necessarily form a connected, or at least not a rationalized, system of life, but rather remained a succession of individual acts." In contrast, the God of Calvinism demanded not separate good works but a *system* of being good, in other words, a "consistent method" for the conduct of life as a whole. On the psychological level, the corresponding process is "the destruction of spontaneous, impulsive enjoyment" by systematic self-control (1930, pp. 116-119). Although Weber is interested in the religious roots of this new form of individuality, it has also been studied as a consequence of the changing conditions of work and family life (e.g., Stone, 1977). On the level of social theory, an analogous change is the rationalization of the concept of "passion" into that of "interest" (Hirschmann, 1977).

These considerations are part of the broader topic of the transformation of the person during modernization—that is, part of the general subject matter of historical psychology and historical socialization research. In fact, the changes just mentioned could be reframed in the terms developed to account for social class differences in socialization practices and their outcomes in the 1960s, with "middle-class" practices (orientation to children's motives, to their moral responsibility, and to psychic sanctions such as withdrawal of parental love) contrasted with "lower-class" practices (orientation to children's external behavior, to their compliance with fixed rules, and to physical sanctions). In the historical dimension, the latter could be seen as remnants of a gradually declining tradition, while the former would be the consequence of a style of parent-child relations that has begun earlier in the culturally most advanced strata, and then gradually become more marked and more broadly available. In a detailed analysis projecting these concepts back on the Germany of 1800, Schlumbohm (1981) has shown that the petty bourgeoisie (artisans) socialized their children in a way that produced a traditional collectivity orientation (which corresponded to the primarily collective, noncompetitive type of work in the guild regime), while the upper bourgeoisie were already embarking on practices producing modern individuality.

The importance of long-range thinking and planning in "modern consciousness" has been emphasized by Berger et al. (1973). The life plan—even though typically open-ended and often vague—has become "a primary source of identity" and "a basic organizing principle" for orientation in social reality. Life planning requires a specific mode of temporality: Life is conceived by the individual as a "designed project," in other words, its meanings "derive from future plans rather than from the explication of past events" (1973, pp. 73-75). A related change, in the view of Berger et al., is that the concept of "honor" has become obsolete and has been replaced by the concept of "dignity" (1973, pp. 83-96). Honor links the person to the social aggregate (e.g., family or estate) and thus refers to a membership classification, while dignity refers to claims based on individuality.

Another approach to the changes in the concept of the individual and thus of biographical perspectives is offered by the history of autobiography as a literary genre. In recent years, interest in autobiography and biography has been growing both among the reading public and among historians and literary critics (for the latter, see Müller, 1976; Niggl, 1977). Like most other things, autobiography has a rather complicated evolution, but in the present context one structural change stands out, namely, the change from an "annalistic" conception (Niggl, 1977)—in which life is structured by the sequence of external historical or seasonal events—to a developmental conception, organized around and by the self. In temporal terms, this implies a change from historical, or natural, time as the axis for the life that is being narrated to the time of the individual life course itself. In the first case, the individuals are put into a sequence of events that are connected by a supraindividual logic; in the second case, they constitute a sequential program of their own logic.

This change is parallel to the fundamental change in scientific thinking at the end of the eighteenth century as described by Lepenies (1976). He finds a transition from a spatial or categorical ordering of the objects of science to a temporal ordering; in other words, to a developmental thinking. Thus the process is described not in terms of moving from some form of temporal thinking to another one (e.g., from "cyclical" to "linear"), but more basically, from a static to a "temporalized" conception of reality. For Germany, this coincides with the transformation of autobiographical writing. The first fully developmental text is a heavily autobiographical novel by Karl Philipp Moritz, *Anton Reiser*, which appeared from 1785-1790. It is interesting to note that Moritz was the editor of a yearbook consisting mostly of autobiographical reports, the *Magazin zur Erfahrungsseelenkunde*, which in the historiography of psychology (Reinert, 1979, p. 213) is considered to be the first psychological journal and the beginning of the "formative period" of psychology as a separate discipline. We can take this as an indication that modern psychology and modern autobiography have common roots: the process of individualization, which is also a process of temporalization of life.

A change from a categorical to a temporalized conception of life has also been found by von Kondratowitz (1982) in his study, based on the relevant articles in German encyclopaedias from 1721-1914, of how the stages of life were socially evaluated. These articles draw from a tradition of periodization, the models for which were set in Greek antiquity. This is also true for another well-known genre which may give access to the cultural conception of the life course: the pictorial representation of life stages. It consists of between three and twelve stages and several iconographic types; among them life wheel, life bridge, or (most often) staircase (see Die Lebenstreppe, 1983; Winkler & Cole, 1984). The fact that such depictions in printed form date back to the fifteenth century, and that the basic elements of the iconography were already well in place in the sixteenth and seventeenth centuries, might at first glance seem to contradict the thesis proposed here. As with all cultural genres, however, it would be highly misleading to view this one as a direct mirroring of empirical reality. The stages of life were framed in a system of numbers linking them to the ages of the world, the planets, or the seasons. Accordingly, their iconography was largely allegorical. Also, the early examples linked the life stages to the dance of death, serving as a memento that death could strike at any time, and as a warning against a purely situational life form devoted to worldly pleasures. Thus they did not refer to a conception of a normal life course but on the contrary to the basic insecurity of life. In the following centuries, the theme lost its immediately visible reference to the dance of death; this "secularized" form reached its peak in the nineteenth century, becoming one of the most widespread themes of the new popular imagery, at a time when the individualized life course emerged as the basic code for constructing one's experiences and perspectives.

TOWARD A STRUCTURAL EXPLANATION

Having given a descriptive account of the changes that have occurred, our task now consists of explaining how and why these changes have occurred. The demographic changes would require their own line of explanation; they are not treated here. For the others, there is a wide range of proximate causes, which are the causes that historians usually deal with in retracing the processes of change. The following considerations concentrate on the more distant causes; namely, on a structural argument (which of course has its dangers, and should be complemented and checked by a historical account proper). In other words, the question is not how the institutionalization of the life course has occurred but because of what general structural problems has it become necessary, or more precisely (and less deterministically), for what structural problems is it a solution. We could then go on to ask how solutions have emerged or been found, and how one solution came to be preferred or installed over possible alternatives.[10]

The explanation presented here will focus on the economic sphere, on issues of the social organization of work.[11] The few other authors who have dealt with these questions (Mayer & Müller, 1985; Meyer, 1985) argue that it is the state, especially in the form of the welfare state, that is responsible for the increasing age grading of life. But this seems to beg the question. If the welfare state has produced the modern life course, what has produced the welfare state? Looking for instance at the origin of the German social insurance system (the first of its kind), we will find a complex interplay of political, economic, and cultural interests; there is an extensive body of historical scholarship addressing these issues, and a lively debate as to the relative weight of the various influences (see the excellent concise overview by Ritter, 1983; also Mommsen & Mock, 1982). But surely what is common to all of them is the desire to come to terms with the new forms of organization of work and the problems arising from them. We can tentatively distinguish four structural problems to which the institutionalization of the life course is a solution:

The pressure for rationalization. This is the most obvious dimension when we ask for the structural meaning of chronologization. Chronological age is apparently a very good criterion for the rational organization of public services and transfers. It renders the life course—and by that, the passage of individuals through social systems—orderly and calculable. It is interesting to note, however, that there is an uneasy tension between the formal rationality of such procedures and the substantive rationality that they are supposed to provide. Chronological age is essentially an ascriptive criterion, and thus at odds with the modern emphasis on universalism.[12] These normative implications as well as their empirical relevance have surfaced dramatically in the conflict over mandatory retirement. In a universalistic regime, it is normatively preferable to allocate rights and duties by a criterion based on achievement, such as "functional age." Empirically, on the other hand, the implementation of such a criterion is difficult and may even be self-defeating. Whatever one's normative preferences, it is clear that a replacement of chronological age by "functional age" or "need" as the basis of public policies for older people (see the wide-ranging contributions in Neugarten, 1982) would be very costly in several respects. The prospect of the formal assessment procedures required by the criteria of functional age or need is not likely to generate much enthusiasm beyond the professions of psychology and law; and the replacement of a citizen's right by a means or needs test would be a major setback not only to formal but to substantive rationality as well.

Rationalization means more than that, however.[13] In economic production, it also means that all noneconomic criteria and value orientations are excluded, so that production can be organized exclusively by its own criteria of rationality. With the emergence of an economy differentiated from other spheres of life, noneconomic concerns have been externalized to these other spheres, and economic production thus has reached a higher degree of "thematic purity." This applies not only to the differentiation of life domains (e.g., work/family; public/private) but also to the temporal dimension of life: The preparation for and the consequences of economic activity are externalized to life stages outside the "productive" stage, and are left to be dealt with by appropriately focused institutions.

Finally, rationalization applies to the level of the individual (as discussed more broadly by Kohli, 1981; Meyer, 1985). In the Protestant ethic, life-time is time conferred by God to be put to sensible use. The chronology of the life course is the basic reference line for one's "methodical life-regulation." This by the way required a continuous process of self-examination, which has given rise to accounting procedures such as writing diaries. The Pietist diary can be seen as a key stage in the emergence of the autobiography as a specific literary genre

(Niggl, 1977). In a secularized form, chronological age becomes the criterion for assessing the relation of time passed to time still to go, for drawing the balance of aspirations and achievements, and for planning ahead. Making life decisions based on an instrumentalized calculus of investments and returns (in terms of chronologically measured periods of life) is what the human capital approach assumes to be the normal case; but clearly there are also other forms of orientation (e.g., toward values, or "meanings" of life).

The chronology of the life course is also relevant in our perception of others. As employers, for instance, we want to have a record of the pasts of job applicants not only in terms of achievements but also in order to see whether they have progressed through life in an orderly fashion and complied with the dictates of economic rationality; in other words, whether thay have been consistent members of the moral community of work. Here again, past and future are both relevant; we type others not only on the basis of their past but relate this to the typical future that they can be expected to have.[14]

Social control. This has been an important topic in historical studies of schooling and the social welfare system. In the premodern life form, persons were socialized by being bound to a family and a locality. The transition to the modern regime meant a massive mobilization and pluralization of life, in other words, a process of individualization. As a consequence, social control could not operate any more on the level of stable family and local ties; it had to become more individualized, too. A key part of this new form of social control is the institutionalization of the life course as a sequential program taking a long-range perspective on life. Thus, we could argue that the new life regime is the necessary correlate of individualization. Rules of membership have been replaced by rules of temporal order.

There is some historical evidence for this structural argument in the history of the public social security systems. As is well known, Bismarck repeatedly asserted that nothing would reconcile the workers better with the state, and thus lower the risk of a proletarian revolution, than the perspective of a stable life course with a public guarantee of material security (Ritter, 1983, pp. 28-29, 38). Even before that, the same motif is found in the plans of the bourgeois social reformers, for example, the Centralverein fuer das Wohl der arbeitenden Klassen (Central Association for the Welfare of the Working Classes, founded in 1844). In its project for an old age insurance, developed in 1848(!), the key thought was that the promise of a "modest but secure income during the age of weakness" would turn even the young worker into a "conservative citizen" (Reulecke, 1983, p. 418). Social control is here projected to operate not simply through monetary transfer but through its long-term expectability, in other words, through biographical perspectives.

The German social security system was not simply a continuation of older forms of charity taken over by the new imperial state. While the traditional welfare system (which continued to operate) was means-tested, and deprived its recipients of their public rights, the new system created a "social citizen" with legitimate claims to continuity. The contributions (even those of the health insurance) consisted essentially of wage replacement during the periods of inability to work. By restricting the contributions to those in the (formal) labor force, the system in effect made the worker into a citizen of the new industrial "work society" (and excluded from such citizenship those not continually engaged in salaried work). It is true (Ritter, 1983, p. 65; Myles, 1984, p. 16) that the empirical impact of the old age insurance scheme was at first modest, both in terms of the level of payments and—as noted above—of its effect on labor force participation; but in its basic meaning, it was nevertheless an important step in the institutionalization of the life course.

Succession. Having to replace members as they age or die is a general problem not only on the level of societies, but also on that of organizations of production. In the premodern family-based economic regime, the household had primacy over the individual members. This was especially marked where there were means of production—land, but also positional privileges, such as in the guild regime—to be preserved. For the farmers, life revolved around the property; the persons had little weight by themselves, and were defined essentially by their position in the household (Rosenbaum, 1982). Succession to the head position usually occurred on the basis of the available personnel in the household; family succession and economic succession coincided. In the modern factory, this is not the case. Succession is a process of recruitment from a market of free labor—of workers who are constituted as individuals in their own right. The free external availability of workers creates cohorts with variable spacing and a wealth of different temporal points of reference. In this situation, chronological age is needed for an orderly succession.

That such an order is essential can be shown by newer approaches to the sociology of labor markets (Sorensen, 1983). Internal (within-firm) labor markets are to a large extent "closed" position systems; they are not markets in a true sense. Closed positions become available only when the previous incumbent has left them. The reallocation of the position is therefore not linked to changes in the performance of the incumbent, or to the availability of a better candidate. This mechanism is one of "vacancy competition," very different from the market competition in open position systems. The process of vacancy competition and the ensuing vacancy chains are well known from the academic labor market. In more general terms, they apply to the public sector as a whole;[15] the welfare state has created a large work force that can be conceptualized in terms of internal labor market structures (Rein & Rainwater, 1981; see also Mayer & Muller, 1985). But to a surprising extent, vacancy competition exists in the private economy also, where it operates by formal or informal seniority rules (Dohse et al., 1982; Kohli et al., 1983). For the firms, chronological sequencing is thus not just a marginal concern among others but a constitutive structural dimension of the internal labor market.

Again, there is more historical evidence for the relevance of such considerations in studies of the creation of the old-age insurance schemes, for example, with respect to the interests expressed by the employers and their organizations. A public retirement system allows the firms to get rid of their older workers, and thus to regularize the duration of employment and the flow of cohorts, in a way that is socially legitimate. This becomes especially pertinent when there is a pressure to decrease the size of the work force. The emergence of retirement based on public pensions liberated the firms from paternalistic responsibility for their workers, and thus transformed a human situation into a bureaucratic situation (Graebner, 1980, p. 121; a similar argument is advanced by Haber, 1983). The same can be shown for the contemporary efforts to lower the retirement age (Kohli et al., 1983).

Integration. This problem in this chapter mainly refers to the relation of family and work (see Hareven, 1982b). In a household economy, integration was less a problem. The primacy of the household meant that what counted was its own continuity; it took precedence over the biographical claims of the members. In some cases, pressure could build up, such as when the heir grew older and the father was still not willing to turn control over to him. But there was no need for a general set of temporal criteria for relating separate life domains. Economic and family transitions in the life course were closely intertwined, and resulted directly from the requirements of production and reproduction in the household (e.g., marriage was linked to the availability of a "position"; remarriage was necessary after the death of a spouse). As detailed studies show (Sieder & Mitterauer, 1983), the link between economic position and opportunity or requirement to marry was never complete; but it was sufficiently important to be a matter of legal prescription (which in Germany—with the exception of Bavaria, where it remained effective even longer—was formally revoked only in 1868; see Hubbard, 1983, p. 40).

In the industrial economy, the individual life course becomes the main dimension of regulation. This creates new problems of temporal synchronization. The firms are faced with the task of integrating the individual life-time of their members into their organizational time patterns (see Kohli, 1985b). The individuals are faced with the task of integrating the time dimensions of family and work—a task which poses alternatives with sometimes massive consequences, which may be one of the reasons why this sequence of steps in the work and family careers during the transition to adulthood has become such a popular research topic (see the overview by Hagestad & Neugarten, 1985).

INSTITUTIONAL PROGRAM AND SUBJECTIVE CONSTRUCTION

At this stage of the argument, it is necessary to go back to the starting point, and ask how far a structural approach to the life course can take us; in other words, how far it is sufficient to conceive of the life course as an institutional program, and at what point do we have to take a closer look at what individuals experience and think and do, and by this construct their biographies. As mentioned earlier, this poses the very difficult general problem of how to relate social structure and action, or macro- and microsociology. It will not be addressed here in these general terms, but rather by sketching briefly three models of the relations or tensions between institutional program and subjective construction that lie behind the arguments commonly found in the life course literature.

The first model resolves the tension by focusing exclusively on the institutional programs, and thus implying a picture of actors who by their own interests comply with them (the liberal-utilitarian version), or are subjected to their power (the social control version). The focus is on the opportunity structures or the coercive forces by which the life course is externally shaped; the actors' biographical perspectives are held to be largely irrelevant for the outcome of these processes, and therefore negligible as a topic for investigation (Mayer, 1985). This model is basic to most macrosociological approaches—for example, those that look at career patterns and family cycle in terms of labor and marriage markets;

but it can also be found in some of the interpretive literature, especially in the labeling tradition—for instance, studies of how deviant biographies are produced by the police or other agencies of social control (Cicourel, 1968). It is clear that this model is appropriate for a substantial range of empirical phenomena. Where it is inadequate, however, is in accounting for actors who are motivated by more than simple instrumental rationality, or who resist the pressures to which they are exposed. (Thus, even in situations of overwhelming definitional power, such as mental health institutions, individuals still effectively retain some of their own perspectives; see Riemann, 1984.)

The second model conceives of institutional programming and biographical construction as parallel processes that complement each other. This is essentially the Parsonian (functionalist) view of social reality. Individuality is seen as a necessary component of society. By internalizing the requisite age norms, individuals are socialized to fit into the institutional life course programs and bring them to life. It is indispensable that individuals play their part. There is of course the possibility that they do not—that they deviate. This is considered a failure of socialization, and there have to be sanctions as well as adequate repair mechanisms to deal with these unfortunate cases. Again, this model certainly has its empirical referents; in fact, there are variants of functionalist thinking far beyond Parsonian theory (and far beyond the harmonizing bias of the more vulgar forms of it)—even Marxists sometimes seem to be infused by a belief in the superior logic of the capitalist system to the point where they see everything as falling neatly into its place. But the model reaches its limit in analyzing the conflicts and dynamics of institutionalization itself.

Thus, we need a third model, in which the tension remains alive between the life course as socially ordered reality and biography in terms of individual agency. This requires an approach grounded in a nonnormative action theory, such as that set forth by George Herbert Mead or Alfred Schutz. To them, action is never only the enacting of socially given meanings or the playing of normatively prescribed roles; it is always to some degree a project, designed and emerging into an open future. As to their temporal extension, actions can be ordered hierarchically; everyday actions are part of larger concerns, and ultimately of lifetime idealizations and goals (Schutz & Luckmann, 1973). Thus the biography is the most encompassing time horizon for one's actions, and focusing on biographical perspectives means taking the action approach to its fullest potential.

What has been said so far is seen, in action theory, to be universally valid. However, there is also a level of historical change. Individualization has resulted in openness of action becoming a more central concern. The modern concept of person is that of the full individual, free from the bonds of social programs and able to make his or her own choices. This has been the cultural promise of liberalism and enlightenment. At the beginning of the nineteenth century, German literature had a peculiar genre, the educational novel (Bildungsroman), which dramatized the fight of the developing individual against the social programs into which he (never she) was supposed to grow (Janz, 1980). It is interesting to note that many of these novels stop at the point where the individual has finally achieved a balance, however precarious, between self and world—in a sense, the beginning of mature adult life. Today, a novel could no longer stop at this point. Personal development is projected to continue all through the life course. The key metaphor here is "growth." We want to grow until we fall apart. It is of course tempting to show how highly conventional this desire for growing is (see Bellah et al., 1985), and how well the supplies of the culture industry can take care of it. Thus we can point out that the claim to individual growth is institutionalized in the form of basic cultural codes by which individuals naturally construct their experiences and organize their actions, and in the form of markets for services catering to the resulting needs. But there is a particular historical dynamic: Individuals are provided with legitimate claims to free themselves from the bonds of social programs, and thus to break away from the institutions of the life course (see again the discussion on mandatory retirement). What is institutionalized threatens the institution itself. The consequences of this become apparent when we turn to the present situation.

One qualification is in order: Taking the action approach from the analysis of general life course processes to that of historical changes in the life course regime should not be read as an endorsement of a purely "culturalist" view of such change (just as the structural explanation of the preceding section does not amount to a purely "materialist" view). Claims to individual continuity and development—whatever their cultural genesis—need to be validated by the institutions of the welfare state in order to become socially relevant on a wider scale. We also need to look at whether individuality is curtailed or favored (and even required) in the labor market and workplace. It is critically important whether technological change in the workplace leads to a decrease in skilled work and a growth of highly menial and fractured tasks (as was the conventional wisdom in industrial sociology during the 1960s and 1970s), or whether it leads on the contrary to an increasingly "holistic use" of the worker as a broadly competent subject (as is argued now: Kern & Schumann, 1983; Hirschhorn, 1984). Thus any reasonable approach to the history of the life course has to incorporate material *and* cultural dynamics.

THE PRESENT SITUATION: TOWARD A NEW TRANSFORMATION?

To deal with the present requires one last line of argument. In fact, over the past fifteen years an accumulating number of empirical studies indicate that the process of chronologization has come to a halt or even been reversed.

One domain in which this has become apparent is family behavior (see the interesting discussion by Hagestad, 1985; also Cherlin, 1980; Held, 1985). Since the beginning of the 1970s, several of the processes that resulted in the standardization of the family cycle have stopped or gone into reverse, with most Western countries showing a surprisingly uniform pattern. The age at marriage and at birth of first child has risen; the prevalence of marriage and child rearing has dropped; divorce rates have reached new heights. This means that the process of family formation is lengthened or delayed; that a growing proportion of the younger birth cohorts realize this process in alternative forms, or only partially, or not at all; and thus that there is a growing proportion of household configurations and sequences that depart from the normative pattern that was the point of convergence of historical development until recently.

The second domain is work. We now have lively discussion on models that break up the tripartition of the life course—the "education-work-retirement lockstep," as Best (1980) puts it—and its chronology, by recurrent education, or by various schedules of part-time work and flexible transitions, for example. These models have strong reasons to support them, not only those of individualization (widening the area for personal choices), but also, in the present situation, those of the labor market (distributing the available work among the whole population and on more phases of life instead of concentrating it on a diminishing proportion of full workers with a diminishing proportion of life spent in work). Work time policy along these lines is an important issue today in the interface between the problems of the labor market and those of the welfare state; it is even seen by some authors—especially in the German context—as the only promising way of coping with the structural crisis of the economy (for example, Hinrichs et al., 1984). The work time preferences of the workers tend to go in the same direction. In view of this, it is surprising to note how difficult it is to realize these models. In fact, the most massive change over the last fifteen years has been the decrease in retirement age; and even the provisions for a flexible transition to retirement—which have become an important field of labor negotiations in Germany—overwhelmingly turn out to mean earlier transition (Wolf, 1985). Nevertheless, there is a certain loosening of the chronology of the life course, parallel to the loosening of the boundaries of salaried work or of the formal sector of the economy itself.

Third, formerly strict age norms seem to have become obsolete, for instance, concerning clothing, sexuality, or participation in formal education. We find similar changes in the dimensions of the civilizing process as analyzed by Elias and others—more informality, more freedom of body expression, less control of affect. On the institutional level, there seems to be a general questioning of processes of differentiation and externalization, for instance, in the critique of the professional provision of human services and the call to put them back into the hands of lay people (see the influential books by Ivan Illich), or in the search for "holistic" lifestyles.

It is not clear how far these developments reach; and some of them may have changed again already in the wake of the new conservative mood. This shows how difficult it is to assess whether the changes are but a short-time interruption of the secular trend toward chronologization or whether they represent the beginning of a new structural transformation. Of course it is more interesting to assume the latter, but it is also more risky. We might be induced to some skepticism by the temporal imbalance—three hundred years in one direction, fifteen in the other. Nevertheless, it has become very popular among sociologists to diagnose a structural change, and there is no dearth of general concepts for it, from "late capitalism" or "corporatism" to "post-industrial society" or the simple labels "post-modern" and "post-historic."

Whatever one's sympathy for the rhetoric of crisis and transformation, it seems fair to say that fundamentally our regime is still that of a work society. But let us assume that at least some of the changes do represent a basic turn. This still leaves us with two alternative interpretations. The first would be along the lines of the "end of the individual"—a thesis that has been developed in the tradition of the Frankfurt School. It claims that there has been a transformation from an early capitalist form of socialization by way of individuals with internalized achievement motivation and long-range biographical perspectives to a new form of direct socialization, in which the persons hang by the threads of the centralized media of control (and react instantly). The thesis points to alleged transformations of working conditions that are said to undermine the viability of individualized life planning, and to alleged transformations of socialization conditions that are said to fail to produce the appropriate personality equipment. As evidence for these claims, one can turn to observations on narcissism and value change—topics that have been the object of heated discussions in Germany (see the contributions to Matthes, 1983). On the whole, however, the results of these discussions, as well as the empirical information presented here, seem to contradict the thesis rather than to support it.

It is more plausible, then, to turn to the alternative thesis claiming that we now witness a new thrust of individualization. This again is widely discussed in German sociology at the moment, the notion being that individualization now extends to social groups that have until recently stayed at its margin: women (Beck-Gernsheim, 1983), now breaking away from being a family member only; and blue-collar workers (Beck, 1983), breaking away from class solidarities and lifestyles. More important for the present argument is that—as stated above—individualization in the sense of personal growth now extends over the whole life course. It does not stop any more at the point where we have found our place in life. (Appropriately, socialization research and developmental psychology are not restricted any more to childhood—they now apply to the whole life course.) The evidence for a beginning destandardization of the life course could thus be interpreted not as a reversal of individualization, but on the contrary as a further push, bursting open the chains of chronology. It can be argued that today's individualization process occurs, and can only occur, on the background of a regulated labor market and of functioning public social security systems (Beck, 1983). It is on this background that the modern life course regime has become institutionalized and has led to legitimate individual claims for continuity. The successful institutionalization of the life course is the basis for the present individualizing departure from it.[16]

Here again, however, we should not fall into the trap of a harmonizing functional model. The destandardization of the life course carries with it a high amount of tension and conflict, and is likely to continue doing so for some time. In fact, the difficulty of realizing models that soften the chronology of the life course, especially in the domain of work, is indirect evidence for viewing the present life course regime as one of the core institutions of our type of society.

NOTES

1. A case in point is the "theory of age stratification" (Riley et al., 1972). While this approach has been successful in implementing a comprehensive view of age and the life course as a general feature of social structure, it has not been impressive in analyzing substantive problems of concrete societies. The authors have focused on the formal dynamics of aging and cohort succession, and thus created a framework into which the historical reality and the historical changes of the age organization of societies can only be entered as more or less arbitrary "examples" of the general processes.

2. In fact, this takes us back to the theoretical stance of some of the most enduring "classical" contributions to our discipline. For example, Max Weber started out with careful studies of the development of capitalism in the West, and it was his interest in Western capitalism as a historically unique case that later led him to branch out into the comparative study of the economic ethics of the other world religions.

3. "Modernization" is used here in a very broad sense; as will become clear, it does not imply an endorsement of "modernization theory" in the form of a universal theory of development with a clean hierarchical ordering of stages. The terms "premodern" and "modern" will be used accordingly. Because of the problems of temporal sequence during the industrialization process (see below), they are to be preferred over "preindustrial"/"industrial." It should be noted that "premodern" as used here refers to the epoch that in historical periodization is usually called "early modern." It should also be kept in mind that the terms are constructed as ideal types, in other words, as abstract models that serve to highlight the structural before-after contrast in the manner outlined below.

4. The area in question consists of northwest Europe, including the German-speaking areas and northern France; the rules consist of late marriage, a high proportion of servants, and only one married couple per household (Hajnal, 1983, pp. 66-69). To be sure, there is some disagreement about the unity and geographic extension of the pattern (Laslett, 1983), but this does not affect its general features.

5. It might be objected that the organization of the life course around the system of work applies to women only partially, and more generally, that the argument of the present chapter, by focusing on formal work, is essentially restricted to the male side. My answer would be that it is not so much a male argument as an argument appropriate for a male-dominated and work-dominated society. Women who are not in the labor force have not been constituted socially as full "individuals" but rather as members of a family; this has changed only very recently (Beck-Gernsheim, 1983; see below, last section). Correspondingly, women have developed a moral sense that emphasizes caring for others, while men have constructed a morality that emphasizes individual rights and responsibilities (Gilligan, 1982).

6. For an application in life course research, see Kohli (1985b). It should be noted that looking at sequences of positions is structural only insofar as it goes beyond the descriptive accounting of aggregate movements—conceived as the behavioral result of individual decisions—and tries to identify the features of the system that produce these movements.

(Thus early status attainment research has rightly been criticized as implying an individualistic-reductionist view of social reality, because it did not consider the restraining features of, for instance, labor market structures.) Another difficulty lies in the fact that biographical perspectives can be approached structurally, too, by conceiving of them as the outcome of cultural meaning structures; much of the current sociology of culture focuses more on such basic cultural codes than on how members draw on them to shape their own experiences and actions.

7. Some considerations can be found in the volumes edited by Kohli (1978) and Rosenmayr (1978); more detailed are Hareven (1982a); Mayer & Muller (1985); Meyer (1985); as well as the contributions to Kohli and Meyer (1985).

8. See the review essays by Conrad (1982, 1984).

9. One case in point is the emergence of celebrating one's birthday (see Hopf-Droste, 1979). From measuring a person's progression through life, birthdays now have spread to many more dimensions. An additional example of the relevance of chronology is the modern preoccupation with round numbers in birthdays; we attribute meaning to, say, the fortieth or fiftieth anniversary, even though it is not connected with any status transition outside of the chronology itself.

10. Thus the structural argument tends toward presenting the changes as a necessary outcome of the basic societal dynamics, while the historical narrative reports them as the outcome of the specific circumstances given in the situation, and of the perspectives and strategies of the actors involved. The structural argument stresses the operation of social forces, while the historical narrative stresses the openness of action. For the structural analyst, things are what they need to be, while for the historian, they are one among a number of alternatives—alternatives that would have been possible, but that for a variety of reasons did not materialize. In the present issue, both views—as is the case with structural analysis and action theory more generally—have their points (see Ritter, 1982, p. 10). We can indeed find a substantial amount of variation in institutional arrangements concerning old age among Western nation states; but to the extent that they have converged to share common features (such as generalized retirement based on public pensions), we can see the weight of the basic structural problems common to them.

11. This should not be understood as a purely "materialist" explanation. The "organization of work" consists of a complex pattern of economic and cultural conditions; as stated earlier, the temporal and causal order among them is not a topic here.

12. More precisely, it is ascriptive in the sense that it cannot be influenced by one's own achievements (except insofar as survival is an achievement); it is however different from other typically ascriptive criteria by not being a stable attribute of the person but subject to an ordered sequence of changes.

13. For extensive discussions of rationalization as the key concept in Max Weber's "developmental history" of the West, see the recent works by Schluchter (1981) and Habermas (1984).

14. For a study of how these considerations shape the decisions about the allocation of older workers in industrial firms, see Kohli et al. (1983).

15. Rigidly hierarchized organizations such as armies are particularly good cases of vacancy competition, and members may be quite aware of it (see the nice example reported by Marshall, 1980, p. 40). Keyfitz (1973) has analyzed chances for mobility in peacetime versus wartime armies.

16. Although the new form of the life course in this respect approaches the premodern one again, it has a different structural meaning. However, with the deregulation of the labor market and the cuts in social security, there may also be some reversal to the old

pattern: a non-standardized life course as a result not of individualization but of the need for short-term coping with overriding economic pressures.

REFERENCES

Achenbaum, W. A., & Stearns, P. N. (1978). Old age and modernization. *Gerontologist, 18*, 307-312.

Ariès, P. (1962). *Centuries of childhood*. New York: Knopf. (Original work published 1960)

Atchley, R. C. (1982). Retirement as a social institution. *Annual Review of Sociology, 8*, 263-287.

Baltes, P. B., Reese, H. W., & Lipitt, L. P. (1980). Life-span developmental psychology. *Annual Review of Psychology, 31*, 65-100.

Beck, U. (1983). Jenseits von Stand und Klasse? Soziale Ungleichheiten, gesellschaftliche Individualisierungsprozesse und die Entstehung neuer sozialer Formationen und Identitaten. *Soziale Welt, 2*, 35-74.

Beck-Gernsheim, E. (1983). Vom 'Dasein fur andere' zum Anspruch auf 'ein Stuck eigenes Leben': Individualisierungsprozesse im weiblichen Lebenszusammenhang. *Soziale Welt, 34*, 307-340.

Bellah, R. N., et al. (1985). *Habits of the heart*. Berkeley: University of California Press.

Berger, P. L., Berger, B., & Kellner, H. (1973). *The homeless mind: modernization and consciousness*. New York: Random House.

Bertaux, D., & Kohli, M. (1984). The life story approach: A continental view. *Annual Review of Sociology, 10*, 215-237.

Best, F. (1980). *Flexible life scheduling*. New York: Praeger.

Cain, L. D. Aging and the law. In R. H. Binstock & E. Shanas (Eds.), *Handbook of aging and the social sciences* (pp. 342-368). New York: Van Nostrand Reinhold.

Cherlin, A. (1980). Changing family and household: Contemporary lessons from historical research. *Annual Review of Sociology, 9*, 51-66.

Cicourel, A. V. (1968). *The social organization of juvenile justice*. New York: John Wiley.

Coale, A. J., & Watkins, S. C. (Eds.). *The decline of fertility in Europe*. Princeton: Princeton University Press.

Conrad, C. (1982). Altwerden und Altsein in historischer Perspektive. *Zeitschrift fur Sozialisationsforschung und Erziehungssoziologie, 2*, 73-90.

Conrad, C. (1984). Geschichte des Alterns: Lebensverhaltnisse und sozialpolitische Regulierung. *Zeitschrift fur Sozialisationsforschung und Erziehungssoziologie, 4*, 143-156.

Conrad, C., & von Kondratowitz, H.-J. (Eds.). (1983). *Gerontologie und Sozialgeschichte*. Berlin: Deutsches Zentrum fur Altersfragen.

Deutschmann, C. (1983). Systemzeit und soziale Zeit. *Leviathan, 11*, 494-514.

Die Lebenstreppe: Bilder der menschlichen Lebensalter (Katalog). (1983). Koln: Rheinland-Verlag.

Dohse, K., Jurgens, U., & Russig, H. (1982). *Hire and fire? Senioritatsregelungen in amerikanischen Betrieben*. Frankfurt: Campus.

Elias, N. (1969). *Uber den Prozess der Zivilisation*. Bern: Francke. (Original work published 1939)

Featherman, D. L. (1981). The life span perspective in social science research. In *The five year outlook on science and technology* (Vol. 2, pp. 621-648). Washington, DC: National Science Foundation.

Featherman, D. L., & Sorensen, A. (1983). Societal transformation in Norway and change in the life course transition into adulthood. *Acta Sociologica, 26,* 105-126.

Foner, A. (1982). Perspectives on changing age systems. In M. W. Riley, R. P. Abeles, & M. S. Teitelbaum (Eds.), *Aging from birth to death: Sociotemporal perspectives* (pp. 217-228). Boulder, CO: Westview.

Foucault, M. (1977). *Discipline and punish.* New York: Vintage.

Fries, J. F., & Crapo, L. M. (1980). *Vitality and aging.* San Francisco: Freeman.

Fuchs, W. (1984). *Biographische Forschung.* Opladen: Westdeutscher Verlag.

Gennep, A. van. (1909). *Les Rites de Passage.* Paris: Nourry.

Gilligan, C. (1982). *In a different voice.* Cambridge, MA: Harvard University Press.

Graebner, W. M. (1980). *A history of retirement.* New Haven, CT: Yale University Press.

Haber, C. (1983). *Beyond sixty-five.* Cambridge: Cambridge University Press.

Habermas, J. (1984). *The theory of communicative action* (Vol. 1). Boston: Beacon.

Hagestad, G. O. (1984, November). *Family transitions in adulthood: Some recent changes and their consequences.* Paper presented at the meetings of the Gerontological Society, San Antonio, TX.

Hagestad, G. O. (in press). The aging society as a context for family life. *Daedalus.*

Hagestad, G. O., & Neugarten, B. L. (1985). Age and the life-course. In R. H. Binstock & E. Shanas (Eds.), *Handbook of aging and the social sciences* (2nd ed., pp. 35-61). New York: Van Nostrand Reinhold.

Hajnal, J. (1983). Two kinds of pre-industrial household formation system. In R. Wall, J. Robin, & P. Laslett (Eds.), *Family forms in historic Europe* (pp. 65-104). Cambridge: Cambridge University Press.

Hareven, T. K. (1982). The life-course and aging in historical perspective. In T. K. Hareven & K. J. Adams (Eds.), *Aging and life course transitions: An interdisciplinary perspective* (pp. 1-26). New York: Guilford Press.

Hareven, T. K. (1982b). *Family time and industrial time.* Cambridge: Cambridge University Press.

Held, T. (1982). Rural retirement arrangements in seventeenth to nineteenth-century Austria: A cross-community analysis. *Journal of Family History, 7,* 227-254.

Held, T. (1985). Institutionalization and de-institutionalization of the life-course. In M. Kohli & J. W. Meyer (Eds.), *Social structure and social construction of life stages* [Special Issue]. *Human Development, 18.*

Hinrichs, K., Offe, C., & Wiesenthal, H. (1984, December). *The crisis of the welfare state and alternative modes of work redistribution.* Paper presented to the conference on "The Future of the Welfare State," Maastricht.

Hirschhorn, L. (1984). *Beyond mechanization: Work and technology in a postindustrial age.* Cambridge: MIT Press.

Hirschman, A. O. (1977). *The passions and the interests.* Princeton: Princeton University Press.

Hogan, D. P. (1982). *Transitions and social change: The early lives of American men.* New York: Academic Press.

Hopf-Droste, M.-L. (1979). Der Geburtstag. Ein Beitrag zur Entstehung eines modernen Festes. *Zeitschrift fur Volkskunde, 75,* 229-237.

Hubbard, W. H. (1983). *Familiengeschichte. Materialien zur deutschen Familie seit dem Ende des 18. Jahrhunderts.* Munich: Beck.

Imhof, A. E. (1985). Life-course patterns of women and their husbands, 16th to 20th century. In A. B. Sorensen et al. (Eds.), *Human development and the life course.* Hillsdale, NJ: Erlbaum.

Janz, R.-P. (1980). Bildungsroman. In H. A. Glaser (Ed.), *Deutsch Literatur. Eine Sozialgeschichte, Bd. 5, Zwischen Revolution und Restauration: Klassik, Romantik 1786-1815.* Reinbek: Rowoh t.

Kern, H. & Schumann, M. (1983). Arbeit und Sozialcharakter: Alte und neue Konturen. In J. Matthes (Ed.), *Krise der Arbeitsgesellschaft?* (pp. 353-365). Frankfurt: Campus.

Keyfitz, N. (1973). Individual mobility in a stationary population. *Population Studies, 27,* 335-352.

Kohli, M. (Ed.). (1978). *Soziologie des Lebenslaufs.* Darmstadt: Luchterhand. 1978.

Kohli, M. (1981). Zur Theorie der biographischen Selbst- und Fremdthematisierung. In J. Matthes (Ed.), *Lebenswelt und soziale Probleme* (pp. 505-520). Frankfurt: Campus.

Kohli, M. (1985a). Die Institutionalisierung des Lebenslaufs. *Kolner Zeitschrift fur Soziologie and Sozialpsychologie, 37,* 1-29.

Kohli, M. (1985b). Social organization and subjective construction of the life course. In A. B. Sorensen et al. (Eds.), *Human development and the life course.* Hillsdale, NJ: Erlbaum.

Kohli, M., & Meyer, J. E. (Eds.). (1985). Social structure and social construction of life stages. *Human Development, 18.*

Kohli, M., Rosenow, J., & Wolf, J. (1983). The social construction of aging through work: Economic structure and life-world. *Aging and Society, 3,* 23-42.

Kondratowitz, H. J. von. (1982). Zum historischen Wandel der Altersposition in der deutschen Gesellschaft. *Altwerden in der Bundesrepublik Deutschland* (Bd. 1, pp. 73-201). Berlin: Deutsches Zentrum fur Altersfragen.

Kriedte, P., Medick, H., & Schlumbohm, J. (1977). *Industrialisierung vor der Industrialisierung.* Gottingen: Vanderhoeck und Ruprecht.

Laslett, P. (1983). Family and household as work group and kin group: Areas of traditional Europe compared. In R. Wall, J. Robin, & P. Laslett (Eds.), *Family forms in historic Europe* (pp. 513-563). Cambridge: Cambridge University Press.

LeGoff, J. (1980). Labor time in the 'crisis' of the fourteenth century: From medieval time to modern time. In *Time, work and culture in the middle ages* (pp. 43-52). Chicago: University of Chicago Press. (Original work published 1963)

Lepenies, W. (1976). *Das Ende der Naturgeschichte.* Munich: Hanser.

Levy, R. (1977). *Der Lebenslauf als Statusbiographie.* Stuttgart: Enke.

Lutz, B. (1984). *Der kurze Traum von der immerwahrenden Prosperitat.* Frankfurt: Campus.

Marshall, V. W. (1980). *Last chapters: A sociology of aging and dying.* Monterey: Brooks/Cole.

Matthes, Joachim (Ed.). (1983). *Krise der Arbeitsgesellschaft?* Verhandlungen des 21. Deutschen Soziologentages in Bamberg 1982. Frankfurt: Campus.

Mayer, K. U. (1985). Structural constraints on the life-course. In M. Kohli & J. W. Meyer (Eds.), *Social structure and social construction of life stages. Human Development, 18.*

Mayer, K. U., & Muller, W. (1985). The state and the structure of the life course. In A. B. Sorensen et al. (Eds.), *Human development and the life course.* Hillsdale, NJ: Erlbaum.

Meyer, J. W. (1985). The self and life course: Institutionalization and its effects. In A. B. Sorensen et al. (Eds.), *Human development and the life course*. Hillsdale, NJ: Erlbaum.

Mitterauer, M., & Sieder, R. (1980). *The European family*. Oxford: Blackwell.

Modell, J., Furstenberg, F. F., Jr., & Hershberg, T. (1976). Social change and transitions to adulthood in historical perspective. *Journal of Family History, 1*, 7-32.

Mommsen, W., & Mock, W. (Eds.). (1982). *Emergence of the welfare state in Britain and Germany, 1850-1950*. London: Croom Helm.

Muller, K. D. (1976). *Autobiographie und Roman*. Tubingen: Niemeyer.

Myles, J. (1984). *Old age in the welfare state: The political economy of public pensions*. Boston: Little, Brown and Company.

Neugarten, B. (Ed.). (1982). *Age or need? Public policies for older people*. Beverly Hills: Sage.

Niggl, G. (1977). *Geschichte der deutschen Autobiographie im 18. Jahrhundert*. Stuttgart: Metzler.

Rein, M., & Rainwater, L. (1981). *From welfare state to welfare society: Some unsolved issues in assessments*. Berlin: Wissenschaftszentrum.

Reinert, G. (1979). Prolegomena to a history of life-span developmental psychology. In P. B. Baltes & O. G. Brim, Jr. (Eds.), *Life-span development and behavior* (Vol. 2, pp. 205-254). New York: Academic Press.

Reulecke, J. (1983). Zur Entdeckung des Alters als eines sozialen Problems in der ersten Halfte des 19. Jahrhunderts. In C. Conrad & H.-J. von Kondratowitz (Eds.), *Gerontologie und Sozialgeschichte* (pp. 413-423). Berlin: Deutches Zentrum fur Altersfragen.

Riemann, G. (1984). 'Na wenigstens bereitete sich da wieder etwas in meiner Krankheit vor.' Zum Umgang psychiatrischer Patienten mit ubermac htigen Theorien, die ihr eigenes Selbst betreffen. In M. Kohli & G. Robert (Eds.), *Biographie und soziale Wirklichkeit* (pp. 118-141). Stuttgart: Metzler.

Riley, M. W., Johnson, M., & Foner, A. (1972). *Aging and society, Vol. 3: A sociology of age stratification*. New York: Russell Sage.

Ritter, G. A. (1983). *Sozialversicherung in Deutschland und England*. Munich: Beck.

Rosenbaum, H. (1982). *Formen der Familie: Untersuchungen zum Zusammenhang von Familienverhaltnissen, Sozialstruktur und ozialem Wandel in der deutschen Gesellschaft des 19. Jahrhunderts*. Frankfurt: Suhrkamp.

Rosenmayr, L. (1978). *Die menschlichen Lebensalter: Kontinuitat und Krisen*. Munich: Piper.

Schenda, R. (1983). Bewertungen und Bewaltigungen des Alters aufgrund volkskundlicher Materialien., C. Conrad & H.-J. von Kondratowitz (Eds.), *Gerontologie und Sozialgeschichte* (pp. 59-71). Berlin: Deutsches Zentrum fur Altersfragen.

Schluchter, W. (1981). *The rise of Western rationalism: Max Weber's developmental history*. Berkeley: University of California Press. (Original work published 1979)

Schlumbohm, J. (1981). 'Traditionale' Kollektivitat und 'moderne' Individualitat: einige Fragen und Thesen fur eine historische Sozialisationsforschung. In Rudolf Vierhaus (Ed.), *Burger und Burgerlichkeit im Zeitalter der Aufklarung* (pp. 265-320). Heidelberg: Schneider.

Schutz, A., & Luckmann, T. (1973). *The structures of the life-world*. Evanston, IL: Northwestern University Press.

Sieder, R., & Mitterauer, M. (1983). The reconstruction of the family life course: Theoretical problems and empirical results. In R. Wall, J. Robin, & P. Laslett (Eds.),

Family forms in historic Europe (pp. 309-345). Cambridge: Cambridge University Press.

Sorensen, A. B. (1983). Processes of allocation to open and closed positions in social structure. *Zeitschrift fur Soziologie, 12,* 203-224.

Stearns, P. N. (1977). *Old age in European society.* New York: Holmes & Meier.

Stone, L. (1977). *The family, sex and marriage in England 1500-1800.* London: Weidenfeld and Nicholson.

Treas, J. (1981). *The historical decline in late-life labor force participation in the United States: Policy determinants?* Paper presented to the 12th International Congress of Gerontology, Hamburg.

Uhlenberg, P. (1969). A study of cohort life cycles: Cohorts of native born Massachusetts women, 1830-1920. *Population Studies, 23,* 407-20.

Uhlenberg, P. (1974). Cohort variations in family life cycle. *Journal of Marriage and the Family, 36,* 284-9.

Weber, M. (1930). *The Protestant ethic and the spirit of capitalism.* London: George Allen & Unwin. (Original work published 1920).

Wendorff, R. (1980). *Zeit und Kultur.* Wiesbaden: Westdeutscher Verlag.

Winkler, M., & Cole, T. R. (1984, November). *Aging, death, and the cycle of life: The history of a theme in popular Western art: 1500-1900.* Paper presented at the meetings of the Gerontological Society, San Antonio, TX.

Winsborough, H. H. (1979). Changes in the transition to adulthood. In M. W. Riley (Ed.), *Aging from birth to death: Interdisciplinary perspectives* (pp. 137-52). Boulder, CO: Westview.

Wolf, J. (1985). Flexibler Ubergang in den Ruhestand: Das Beispiel der deutschen Zigarettenindustrie. In M. Dieck (Ed.), *"Freigesetze" Arbeitnehmer im 6. Lebensjahrzent—Eine neue Ruhestandsgeneration?* Berlin: Deutsches Zentrum fur Altersfragen.

10

Comparative Perspectives on the Microsociology of Aging: Methodological Problems and Theoretical Issues

VERN L. BENGTSON

Aristotle suggested that the key to understanding natural phenomena lay in what he called the "method of comparisons": observing and contrasting one group with another, one system with the next. The process of explicit comparison has led to many discoveries, both abstract and practical, in the life sciences. Observing contrasts and similarities between entities/aggregates or classes/phenomena is the cornerstone of most theory building in science. The logic of planned comparisons is so common a part of the scientific method that we frequently take it for granted (see Glaser & Strauss, 1967, p. 21).

In the young but growing field of social gerontology, however, studies involving explicit comparisons among groups are relatively rare. A prominent example is the cross-national comparisons of health status and family life among the aged by Ethel Shanas and her associates (1968). The results suggest some surprising similarities among England, Denmark, and the United States in the frequency of contact between older people and their kin, for example. The replication of the study seven years later in the United States (Shanas, 1979a, 1979b) allows explicit comparison across historical time (but not across these cultures, because funds unfortunately were not available). Contrasts across cultures and over time are the two principal parameters of the comparative research framework in social gerontology.

The Shanas team's work is an exception, however; most contemporary research in gerontology remains noncomparative. Explicit designs for highlighting contrasts between groups are relatively unusual, at least in terms of initial formulation of research questions and in sample definition. Most often, at least in the sociological literature, contrasts are made among individuals and within groups, not across them. In addition, the contrasts often are relegated to statistical controls (such as in multiple regression designs) rather than explicit, theory-based comparison of main effects.

My purposes in this chapter are, first, to present arguments in favor of explicit comparative research design in social gerontology, and, second, to comment on some of the frustrations and difficulties involved in explicitly comparative work. There are considerable advantages to theory development that arise from explicit comparisons among groups, and I will note some surprises that have occurred in examining data within a comparative logic design. Another purpose of this chapter is to indicate some problems that occur in research employing this method, especially in terms of linking the macro to the micro level of analysis. The research projects presented as case studies to illustrate these points are investigations with which I have been personally involved; they are selected for illustration because I know their flaws, as well as their virtues, only too well. Finally, conclusions will be drawn that relate to solving some of the methodological problems noted, and to challenges in linking the micro level to the macro level in social psychological research on aging, reflecting a major theme of this volume.

THEORY AND COMPARATIVE RESEARCH IN AGING

Our goal in employing the scientific method is *theory*. Theory provides an attempt to answer *why*. Good theory consists of logically consistent linkages among constructs, which in turn reflect observable facts (Glaser & Strauss, 1967).

Theories are of extreme importance to any scholarly endeavor. They summarize what is known, predict what will happen, and eventually allow us to manipulate or control desired outcomes (Dubin, 1978). Theory is thus just as important to effective practice and policy in ameliorating social problems as it is to basic research in a field such as gerontology. In a sense, the goals are quite similar, with perhaps more concern for the production of desired outcomes ("amelioration" or "effective policy") in applied gerontology.

Theory building proceeds in four steps that make up what has become known as the scientific method: (a) *observation* of phenomena in the natural world; (b) *classification* of similar events among the welter of phenomena into a much smaller number of constructs or concepts; (c) *prediction* of linkages between constructs that are regular; (d) *control* over naturalistic events by manipulating linkages to achieve desired outcomes. Each of these steps can be pursued most effectively by explicit comparisons among groups.

In the emerging field of social gerontology, the state of theory is primitive. We have a few statements of logically consistent linkages among observable facts that allow us to summarize, predict, and control. We have few universals or lawlike propositions concerning either basic processes or ameliorative intervention.

Scientists and practitioners in social gerontology face pressures to move more quickly than perhaps we should through the steps of theory building in the scientific method. We are called upon to go beyond the initial steps of observation or description and classification to issues of prediction and control. Policymakers and those in the service delivery sector are understandably impatient with the plodding efforts to describe and to classify the bewildering variety of patterns that social aging displays. They want programs—programs that alleviate real needs, that are cost effective, and that have results demonstrable to the voting public.

In the face of such demands for prescriptive statements about aging, our theories, at least today, may constitute something of an embarrassment. What are the mechanisms of socially relevant indicators of age? Which are universal, and which vary from group to group or from individual to individual? Why do some individuals appear to have an easier time adjusting to the social transitions of aging than other individuals? What might be done to help those having difficulty with the adjustment?

The central argument in this chapter is that we should pay more attention to basic logic of explicit comparison—and to the elementary steps of observation and classification—before sweeping onward to the more appealing and satisfying levels of prediction and control. It is useful to be reminded of what the logic of explicit comparative research can offer in the analysis of social aging. It is necessary to acknowledge what the boundaries and limitations of theory building are, and not expect too much before we have an adequate body of empirically based generalizations on which to draw.

I believe that in the course of explicit comparisons between social groups, focusing on the level of observation and classification, we can find elements of linkage among constructs that will lead to theory building and eventually to useful programmatic interventions. We may in fact confirm some universal relationships concerning social aging; or we may find consistent variations across groups that suggest lawlike propositions.

The title of this chapter suggests a focus on *microsociology* within gerontology. By this I mean social-psychological concerns: issues involving the social worlds of individuals that may change with age or with the passage of time. Of course, there is need for macrosocial comparisons—comparing and contrasting broader social aggregates, examining demographic or economic indicators as well as historical contexts as they relate to aging. In sociology, we most often think of comparative research in terms of macrosocial contrasts. In fact the logic of comparative analysis is suited to both the macro- and the microsocial levels of analysis. Many of the problems in undertaking comparative research are the same at both macro and micro levels, as can be seen in other chapters of this volume. But I will limit concerns of this chapter to less frequently considered social-psychological issues, and to case studies in previous published research that focus on individual responses to the changes associated with aging.

OCCUPATIONAL AND CULTURAL DIFFERENCES IN RETIREMENT

The search for "universal" theory that describes processes of aging is one of the more appealing—and perhaps inevitable—quests in gerontology. The first case study illustrating explicit comparative research in the microsociology of aging began with an interest in replicating or disconfirming findings from the disengagement theory of aging suggested by Cumming and Henry (1961).

The disengagement theory suggests that certain processes of aging are universal, inevitable, and developmental. As people grow older, states the first postulate of the theory, there is a mutual withdrawal between the social context and the aging person, seen in decreased interaction or activity outside the primary family group. The individual's withdrawal is accompanied by decreased emotional involvement in the social world; the second major postulate suggests that, in old age, the individual who has disengaged is the person who has high "morale," or psychological well-being.

The data on which disengagement theory was based (prematurely, in the view of other members of the team of investigators involved in the study) involved analyses of role count (the number of active social role relationships), role activity, and "morale" (or well-being) in a sample of 523 middle-aged and elderly persons in Kansas City. The role activity data indeed reflected consistent patterns of low social participation, compared to a presumably high level of activity in middle age. (Unfortunately, because the design was neither longitudinal nor inclusive of younger subjects, no exact cross-age comparisons could be made; the postulate is thus "unfalsifiable" by the data.) Further, with regard to the second major postulate of the theory, the data showed high morale in the presence of low social interaction.

One must applaud the explicit and axiomatic statement that the theory was given by Cumming and Henry. It is a tribute to their insight that two decades later many scholarly analyses in our field routinely refer to disengagement theory as one context within which to view their more focused analysis on social aspects of aging (see, for example, Marshall, 1980; Dowd, 1980; George, 1980). It is one of the few "universal" theories of aging we possess—and therein lies both its attraction and its principal focus of criticism.

However insightful the disengagement theory might have been, however useful a heuristic device it has proven, several important questions remain concerning the validity of the original observations upon which the theory was based. These questions can be addressed only in a comparative research design.

To what extent is the reduction in role activity and involvement during the later phases of life universal? If not universal, the reductions in role activity observed may not be inevitable or developmental, as postulated by the theory. Is the association between low social role involvement and high morale universal, or reflective of this particular sample of Kansas City men and women?

To test the sweeping, if plausible, assertion concerning inevitably decreasing role activity as individuals move into old age, and the correlation between lower activity levels and high life satisfaction, it was necessary to gather data from other social contexts (and incidentally to use more refined concepts and operations in data gathering). In addition, it was necessary to advance a research design that enabled explicit comparison so that the theory could be disproven; as Hochschild (1975) points out, the original theory was "nonfalsifiable" in its test. In contrast to universal processes of disengagement, it may be that patterns of aging vary in direct relation to social setting, reflecting not a universal phenomenon of disengagement, but a systematic variation from one society to the next.

To gather data testing these two assertions, a group of international investigators drawn to the then new International Association of Gerontology set out to design a research program that became known as the Cross-National Study of Retirement and Aging (Havighurst, Neugarten, Munnichs, & Thomae, 1969). The general goals of the study can be summarized as follows:

> There is obvious variability from one aged individual to the next in role activity in retirement. But to what extent are there *group* differences that transcend individual variation—those which stem from differences between occupations and between countries? Does national difference or occupational difference account for the greater proportion of the variance among individuals? (Bengtson, 1969)

The concern, then, was with the extent to which groups from contrasting occupations and contrasting urban societies exhibit different solutions to the problems of aging. If there are universal processes of disengagement, relatively few differences might be expected in patterns of retirement life between a group of retired teachers and a group of retired steelworkers.

A second line of reasoning was that changes in social, psychological, and biological characteristics that accompany aging are of such magnitude as to eliminate, or at least to obscure, previous differences between occupational groups. This might be termed the "age as a leveler" hypothesis (Dowd & Bengtson, 1978): Biosocial processes of aging are so universal as to diminish or eradicate prior socioeconomic distinctions. Similarly, in terms of social or national differences, it is plausible that groups from different nations would experience retirement differently because of contrasts in culture; retirement life patterns would differ accordingly between Poles and Italians, for example. However, it might also be suggested that in technologically advanced, urban social settings, there are greater similarities than differences in adulthood and old age; and that contrasts between groups would reflect universal processes, rather than context-specific ones.

In short, how much of observable social activity in old age reflects universal patterns of disengagement and morale, and how much is specific to occupational style or national culture?

The Cross-National Retirement Study proceeded with two principal expectations or hypotheses in analyzing data (Bengtson, 1969):

(1) Occupational differences—between a sample of retired steelworkers and a sample of retired teachers—will be so pronounced as to overshadow individual differences.

(2) Individual differences will nevertheless be so pronounced as to overshadow differences between countries.

The data compared involved ratings on role activity and life
satisfaction based on open-ended interviews. Thirteen social roles were
defined, and the degree of activity in each of the roles was ascertained in
the semistructured interviews and then rated by at least two judges. On
an 8-point scale (0 = no activity in the role; 8 = frequent and regular
interaction in the role), the role dimensions utilized can be seen in Figure
10.1. Here the two occupational groups sampled from Chicago (N = 25 in
each occupation) are graphed in terms of mean role activity rating
across the thirteen roles. It can be seen that between the two groups there
are considerable differences in the pattern of role activity. The retired
teachers in the Chicago-area sample are highly active in formal and
informal social relations, almost as much as they are in the area of family
roles; the retired steelworkers, however, are much more active in the
family than in the other role areas. It might be inferred that the
structuring of life space following retirement manifests quite different
patterns in the two Chicago groups of retirees.

What then of the comparisons over the twelve groups—six cities
representing national contexts and two occupations? Table 10.1 presents
measures based on total role activity, summing the scores of each individual for each role and taking the mean. The means for each were then
contrasted in a two-way analysis of variance design to determine whether there were significant main effect—national and occupational—differences in total role activity. As can be seen from this summary, there is a
significant difference between the two occupations in mean level of total
role activity. It can be seen that the teachers score higher than the
workers in activity level (4.18 compared to 3.75). This is somewhat
surprising. But even more surprising is the degree of differences that are
significant among the six cross-national urban settings. With the two
occupational groups combined, it appears, for example, that the
Chicago sample (4.42) is substantially higher in mean activity level in
retirement than the Vienna sample (3.30). In addition, there is a
significant interaction effect of city of residence by occupation. The
mean for all the teachers taken together is higher than the mean for all
the steelworkers.

The unexpectedly pronounced contrasts in activity level can be seen
more microscopically when one examines the original grouping of roles
on which the differentiation is based. Table 10.2 presents data on
various clusters of role activity: family role, formal social relations, and
informal social relations. In the family role cluster, the occupational

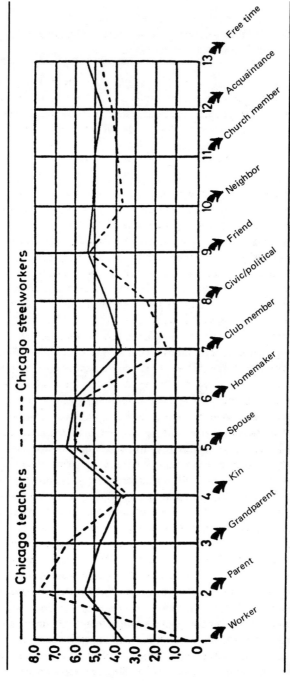

Figure 10.1 Profile of Mean Activity Level Across Roles: Chicago Retired Teachers and Steelworkers

311

TABLE 10.1   Total Role Activity: Means and Analysis
of Variance Summary

	Schoolteachers		Steelworkers		Both Occupations	
	Mean	S.D.	Mean	S.D.	Mean	S.D.
(1) Vienna	3.32	0.75	3.29	0.83	3.30	0.79
(2) Bonn	4.52	0.73	3.83	0.82	4.17	0.76
(3) Nijmegen	4.60	0.70	3.81	0.69	4.20	0.70
(4) Milan	3.47	0.77	3.50	0.71	3.48	0.74
(5) Warsaw	4.29	0.72	4.13	0.94	4.21	0.83
(6) Chicago	4.85	0.72	3.99	0.78	4.42	0.75
Total (N = 300)	4.18	0.73	3.75	0.80	3.97	0.77

Analysis of variance for total role activity level:

	Mean Square	df	P	Intraclass r	
Occupation	12.79	1	.000	.08	.23[a]
Nation	10.30	5	.000	.21	.58[a]
Interaction	2.08	5	.004	.07	.18[a]
Error	0.59	288		.64	

SOURCE: Bengtson (1979, p. 42).
a. This computation considers only the main effects and ignores error variance.

contrasts do not represent a significant difference; steelworkers are not
significantly higher than are the teachers across all the samples. But in
formal social relations as well as in informal social relations there is a
statistically significant difference. On all three parts of the role cluster,
the effect of culture or national difference provides a significant
contrast. There is a wide range of mean activity levels in these twelve
subsamples—the degree of overlap between groups is slight, the degree
of subsample variability is rather large.

This was, of course, a pilot study; the authors repeatedly caution the
reader to view their findings as tentative, in part because the samples
were extremely small and not nationally representative. However, it is
striking how many contrasts were observed in the level of social activity
in various social roles. The findings suggest considerably greater
differences among national groups than had ever been anticipated prior
to this study. Far from there being universal patterns of disengagement
and decline of nonfamily roles in retirement, there appear to be several
patterns of retirement (Table 10.2). These patterns vary not only

TABLE 10.2 Means, Standard Deviations, and Summary
of Analysis of Variance for Role Clusters

	(1) Family Roles Cluster		(2) Formal Social Relations		(3) Informal Social Relations	
	Mean	S.D.	Mean	S.D.	Mean	S.D.
(1) Vienna teachers	4.48	1.02	2.37	1.45	3.92	1.33
Vienna workers	4.90	1.29	2.03	1.43	3.27	1.28
(2) Bonn teachers	5.09	1.12	4.26	0.93	4.48	1.48
Bonn workers	5.45	0.83	2.70	1.10	3.35	1.58
(3) Holland teachers	6.00	0.97	4.67	1.37	3.52	1.17
Holland workers	5.67	1.22	3.28	0.69	2.61	1.35
(4) Milan teachers	5.17	1.27	2.54	1.50	2.85	1.47
Milan workers	4.50	0.92	2.46	1.09	4.03	0.93
(5) Warsaw teachers	5.64	1.45	2.87	1.49	4.20	1.14
Warsaw workers	5.72	1.51	2.29	1.63	4.33	1.29
(6) Chicago teachers	5.01	0.99	4.56	1.37	5.00	1.34
Chicago workers	5.50	1.27	2.96	1.84	3.95	0.97
Total schoolteachers	5.23	1.14	3.55	1.35	4.00	1.32
Total steelworkers	5.29	1.17	2.62	1.30	3.59	1.23

Analysis of variance p of f-value for these role clusters:

Source:	p	p	p
occupation	.679	.000	.011
culture	.000	.000	.000
interaction	.115	.004	.000

SOURCE: Bengtson (1969, p. 44).

between occupations but also between apparently similar urban contexts in Western industrialized societies.

An additional factor of interest concerns the association between role activity and life satisfaction or morale in this study. Across the twelve subgroups, the level of association ($r = .45$) was remarkably similar to that which Cumming and Henry reported in their theory of disengagement—pointing to at least some degree of congruence across social settings in relationship between activity and satisfaction (Bengtson, 1969).

The Cross-National Retirement Study illustrates some of the problems of method encountered in comparative research (Neugarten & Bengtson, 1968). These can be seen in terms of both macro- and micro-level issues. The first and perhaps most obvious challenge involves sampling: selection of respondents or subjects such as to include strictly comparable samples across boundaries of culture and occupation. In the pilot study reported here, it was not possible to obtain a national random sample either in terms of occupation or in terms of the society. The cross-national study by Shanas and associates (1968) was much more successful in obtaining demonstrably representative samples from the three countries under investigation. The danger in irregular sampling across cultures or across occupations—or across any other dimensional sample design—is that the differences observed between groups may be an artifact of sample selection, rather than reflective of substantive contrasts between the two groups.

A second problem in research design involves comparability of data-gathering instruments. Not only is this problematic in terms of linguistic equivalence—the meaning of a question in one language being the same as that in another—but also in terms of interpretation. As Sarah Matthews points out in her chapter in this volume, equivalent meanings can be a significant source of bias in research on aging.

A third and related problem of comparability concerns definitions of the variables themselves. In the study just reported, the role of "friend" initially was seen as quite a different construct by the American investigators, who employed the term quite loosely, as contrasted with the Dutch, for whom the term suggested a lifelong confidant. Similarly, activities that could be termed a "male homemaker role" were considered by the Americans a legitimate social role, with expectations and typical enactments; for some of the more traditional-minded Europeans, however, it had no legitimacy as a role. In the definition of variables, therefore, as well as in the interpretation of the results, it is important in research contrasting cultures to involve members of the groups under study as informants if one is to demonstrate comparability. This can be done by involving investigators from the national groups, cultures, or even occupational backgrounds under investigation; or by using advisory boards; or having graduate students indigenous to the culture involved in the planning, data gathering, and analysis.

Surmounting these three problems of comparability in comparative research requires considerable ingenuity. In this research, however, the results, pointing to the striking variability among ostensibly similar life circumstances in retirement, were highly worthwhile. It does not appear that disengagement is nearly so universal a pattern as the theory Cumming and Henry (1960) originally proposed. The explicit comparative logic, focusing attention on two occupational groups in the context of urban areas in six apparently similar Western nations, resulted in the discovery of markedly different patterns of role activity among retired men. These findings are now well over two decades old; they should be replicated in other social contexts to provide greater certainty of their generalizability. But I, for one, am confident that other studies will replicate the context-specific variability in patterns of aging.

MODERNITY AND PERCEPTIONS OF AGING

One of the oldest studies in the history of social gerontology also involves a search for universals and for general, abstract theory in aging. Four decades ago, Leo Simmons (1945) published his examination of a vast array of ethnographic findings from the nineteenth and early twentieth centuries concerning the status of the aged in preliterate societies. He concluded his investigation with a listing of seven goals or wishes that he suggested older people everywhere and at all times appear to endorse. The most frequently quoted finding of his secondary analysis of ethnographic sources concerns the postulate of a negative association between societal modernity and the prestige or honor afforded the aged.

This "universal" theory that the status of the aged varies inversely with societal modernization has been stated most explicitly by Cowgill and Holmes (1972). As a society moves from a traditional, rural economy to one involving industrialization, and with the increased specialization of knowledge and productivity that characterizes industrialized social systems, the aged in that society possess fewer marketable skills and current information to use as exchange resources in social interaction. Knowledge and control gained by long life are not as important as they once were, and aging loses the value it once had.

The "modernization and aging" theory is intellectually exciting as well as plausible, but it may be questioned on two grounds. First, one might criticize the comparability of the data on which it has been based—single studies, many ethnographic, in which comparisons between "traditional" and "modern" societies are implicit and after the fact. It may be that these studies have not defined "status of the aged" comparably, or have not adequately delimited "modernization" in comparable terms.

The second question has to do with potential confusion in the construct "modernization," reflecting the fact, frequently overlooked, that there are two levels of social context and two levels of analysis involved in the relationship between aging and industrialization. The first is a *macrosocial* perspective, on political-economic development of the nation-state as a whole, indexed by such factors as gross national product, per capita industrial employment, and degree of Westernization—characteristics of a given nation-state that are most appropriately termed *societal modernization*. The other is a *microsocial* perspective: the individual's social experience in terms of his or her exposure to technology, urbanization, and industrial work participation. For this the term *individual modernity* is more appropriate, referring to properties of individuals within societies regardless of the degree of modernization of these societies.

Modern civilization is indeed pluralistic; contemporaneous nations vary in manifestations of modernization, but within each country there are significant differences among individuals in their exposure to modernizing experiences. To gloss over such pluralism is naive. To assert a "universal theory" that with modernization of the national economy the status of the aged declines is an oversimplification, unless data are available to support both macro- and micro-level examination.

Our second case study allows just such bilevel comparison, examining data from the Harvard Project on the Sociocultural Aspects of Development (Bengtson, Dowd, Smith, & Inkeles, 1975; Inkeles, 1983). This study collected interview data from young men in six developing nations varying by degree of societal modernization, with samples defined comparably in each nation to reflect subsamples varying in exposure to modernizing experiences. Thus the countries could be arrayed in terms of gross national product and level of industrialization, from Bangladesh and Nigeria to Argentina and Israel. Within each country samples were defined by occupational groups varying in exposure to industrial, urban culture: rural cultivators, urban nonindustrial workers, and urban factory workers (see Table 10.3).

A total of 5,450 individuals were interviewed for the study, with data collected in 1958-1959 by social scientists indigenous to each country. Respondents were young men between the ages of 18 and 32—the age and sex group thought to be most vulnerable to the direct impact of modernization. (Additional information concerning the sample and data gathering is found in the major reports of this study: Smith & Inkeles, 1966; Inkeles & Smith, 1974; Inkeles, 1983.)

Table 10.3 presents results on one of the variables reflecting perceptions of the aged and aging. The question read, "Some people look forward to old age with pleasure, while others dread or fear the coming of old age. How do you personally feel about the coming of old age?" (Agreement with the former statement indicates a positive attitude toward aging.)

TABLE 10.3   Attitude Toward One's Own Aging:
             Percentage by Occupation and Country Choosing
             "Await or Look Forward to Old Age"

Occupational Group	Bangladesh	India	Nigeria	Chile	Argentina	Israel
Cultivators	32.8	60.5	59.0	16.5	46.9	33.6
Urban nonindustrial workers	37.8	46.1	67.3	24.5	16.4	45.7
Urban factory workers	35.8	44.4	72.2	29.7	29.2	35.4
Totals						
N	334	632	527	242	234	239
%	35.4[a]	49.1	73.3	27.6	28.8	36.5

SOURCE: Bengtson et al. (1975, p. 691).
a. Cell entries can be read as follows: Of the total sample from Bangladesh, 35.4% (334 of 943) respondents chose the "traditional" response; they "look forward to old age."

The first test of the "aging and modernization" hypothesis can be made by looking at between-country score comparisons. Do countries lowest in measures of macrosocial modernization show the greatest proportion of respondents with pro-aging attitudes? In general, the answer is yes. Over twice as many Nigerians (73.3%) as Chileans (27.6%) said they "await or look forward to old age." However, a slightly higher proportion of Israelis (36.5%) than Pakistanis (35.4%) gave the pro-aging response—suggesting less than universal support for the theory.

The second test of the theory involves within-country comparisons among occupational groups, comparing *individual* modernity and attitudes toward aging. The data suggest that rural cultivators—the least modern group—are *not* more likely to give a pro-aging response than are urban factory workers. In fact, in four of the six nations, the cultivators are *least* likely to say they "look forward to old age." Such data do not support the theory of any direct relationship between individual modernity and negative attitudes toward aging.

Taken together with other data (reported in Bengtson et al., 1975), the investigators conclude that the "universal theory that modernization causes a decline in favorable evaluations of aging" is "an unwarranted overgeneralization":

In short, a simple formula suggesting more negative views of the aged with increasing individual modernity is not supported by the evidence. The crucial point . . . is that individual modernity and societal modernization each manifests a different pattern to special aspects of aging. The two hypotheses should be tested separately. (Bengtson et al., 1975, p. 695)

One clear implication of these results is the necessity to differentiate clearly between macro and micro levels of analysis, as is suggested by Quadagno (1980). A second implication is that the linkage between the two levels can be most clearly explicated by theory construction informed by explicitly comparable research designs. This "case study" of the comparative method of research suggests some similar problems in methodology to the cross-national study of retirement. Problems of comparability in sample selection are evident; despite three years of initial fieldwork, working with indigenous social scientists, valid questions may still be raised as to whether the samples of cultivators from India are strictly comparable to samples of cultivators in Argentina, differing only in culture. Problems of comparability in the data-gathering instrument can also be cited, though the fixed-question interview format attempted to assure equivalence of stimuli across language groups.

Perhaps the greatest challenge to future researchers, however, is suggested by the sheer magnitude of this particular study. Spanning six years, involving six developing nations and 5,450 respondents, it is unlikely that this large and exactly comparable sample research design can be replicated in our lifetime. Future researchers can, however, profitably employ smaller, less ambitious, and less costly designs that still involve explicit comparison between comparably defined cultural groups, in testing the plausible and frequently repeated theory that socioeconomic "modernization" invariably erodes the status of the aging.

STRATUM CONTRASTS IN ATTITUDES TOWARD DEATH: SURVEY AND ETHNOGRAPHIC METHODS COMBINED

The third example illustrates a comparative research logic that is much more likely to be replicated in future gerontological research: making explicit contrasts between subsamples that allow exploration of stratification processes within the same large-scale questionnaire survey. Indeed, many survey designs involving implicit contrasts between groups could be modified only slightly in order to allow explicit comparisons similar to those suggested in this example. A third "universal" theory in social gerontology concerns aging and attitudes toward death: Fear of death, and preoccupation with thoughts about death, is postulated to be related directly to age. A plausible proposition (suggested by Jung and others) is that the closer one gets to death, in terms of normal life-span progressions, the more frequent are one's thoughts of dying (Bengtson, Cuellar, & Ragan, 1971).

Two kinds of contrasts are seen in this study. One involves comparison between two modes of data gathering, between results of a questionnaire survey and an ethnographic analysis. The question is whether two quite different modes of data gathering, focusing on the same kinds of respondents and the same dependent variable, afford similar answers to a theoretical issue.

The second contrast is between theoretical constructs, each reflecting different aspects of the key variable in much sociological theory: class or social status. From the founders of modern sociology—Durkheim, Marx, and Weber—down to the present, it has been affirmed and demonstrated that domains of social life appear segmented, layered, or stratified; that access to power, privilege, and prestige is differentially distributed among members of any group, and that the location of individuals in such differential strata or layers predicts their "life chances" and life circumstances (see overview in Bengtson, 1979). From the early statements of social gerontology down to the present, it is suggested that patterns of aging vary according to position in the stratification system (Cain, 1964; Riley, Johnson, & Foner, 1972; Ragan & Wales, 1980; Dowd, 1980). But the problem with an oversimplified statement of class or stratum, like the problem with misrepresented Marxism, is that there are several dimensions of class membership and there are multiple hierarchies of social strata (Bengtson, 1979). Socioeconomic level is an obvious dimension of status, while age, as Riley (1972) points out, is often considered another; ethnicity and gender constitute two other dimensions by which consistent differences in prestige, privilege, or power can be seen in pluralistic societies, with concomitant implications for the structure of individuals' life chances or life experiences.

In any analysis of the effect of aging on behavior, therefore, it is valuable to examine the differentials or similarities that occur in light of socioeconomic contrasts within the highly varied population of the aged. In addition, it is important not to ignore possible gender differences, as the life course of women may be characteristically different from that of men. And, in most pluralistic societies, there are observable contrasts between subcultures defined by ethnicity or language; these too are important variations to examine if one is to construct adequate and generalizable theory.

The focus of the third case study is on a highly personal issue: death. The meaning of death undoubtedly varies from individual to individual, depending on events and situations unique to each person's biography. But attitudes toward death are also the product of collective experience (Marshall, 1975a; 1980; also, see Chapter 5, this volume). To what extent are attitudes toward death predictable from location in the social structure, and to what extent are they individualized, not explainable by such dimensions of collective experience?

In a case study, these propositions about the relationship of death concerns to age were tested on a Southern California sample designed to explore contrasts in orientations between subsamples selected by age, socioeconomic status, and ethnicity (Bengtson, Cuellar, & Ragan, 1977). A fourth dimension, gender, was tested in statistical analysis. Thus four aspects of "multiple hierarchies of status" that may be important in aging could be explored in the survey component of the study.

The findings illustrate the utility of comparative research logic in highlighting differences that may be unexpected in terms of theory. It has been suggested, for example, that fear of death is related to proximity to death—as noted by Marshall (1980) in his review of common suppositions about attitudes toward death and Munnichs in his study exploring "awareness of finitude." Much less, if anything, has been said of socioeconomic or sex differentials in fear of death; but Riley (1968) and Kalish and Reynolds (1976) have presented survey data reporting few contrasts by ethnicity but some differences by level of education.

A multiple-hierarchy stratum analysis of the survey data is presented in Table 10.4. With the sample partitioned to show the four main effect categories, it can be seen that the principal contrast is found in terms of age, but not in the direction predicted. The middle-aged had much higher scores relative to the elderly in the sample. The only other significant main effect found is sex: Females expressed greater fear than did males. Of the interaction effects, only occupational status by sex is significant. These results are better conveyed in Figure 10.2. The results indicate clearly that expressed fear of death tends to *decrease with age*, and is not associated with other factors of stratum location, such as ethnicity.

TABLE 10.4   Perceptions Regarding Fear of Death:
                     Analysis of Variance Summary

Source	df	SS	F
Race (A)	2	0.20	
Age (B)	2	17.73	28.82***
Social status (C)	2	0.04	
Sex (D)	1	1.30	4.22*
A × B	4	1.32	
A × C	4	3.11	2.53*
A × D	2	0.44	
B × C	4	0.85	
B × D	2	0.33	
C × D	2	4.00	6.50***
A × B × C	8	2.97	
A × C × D	4	1.33	
B × C × D	4	0.29	
A × B × C × D	8	2.45	
Error	1,202	0.31	

SOURCE: Bengtson et al. (1977, p. 80).
*p < .05; **p < .01; ***p < .001.

What of the ethnographic findings? Do they support or question the survey results? Ethnographic analysis could not be carried out in all the age-sex-ethnicity groups of the design; but in the Mexican American sample, the fieldwork data support the proposition of an inverse association after middle age between age and fear of death.

For example, the preoccupation with the issue of death in middle age is evidenced in the remarks of a 55-year-old widow whom we will call Mrs. Martinez, who recently moved into an age-segregated housing project:

> Around here I think about death all the time. Two people have died in this building already. And even though they were much older than I am, I can't help but wonder if I'm going to be next. . . . I want to see my grandchildren somewhat grown! I want to enjoy being a grandmother! But if my husband died when he was 59, what can I expect? I *have* to live at least 10 more years, but I'm afraid I won't make it. I don't want to think about dying but what can I do? (Bengtson et al., 1977, p. 251)

Her response typifies the reaction of many middle-aged respondents who have suddenly been faced with the situation of being alone, who sense their personal finitude more pointedly than ever before in their

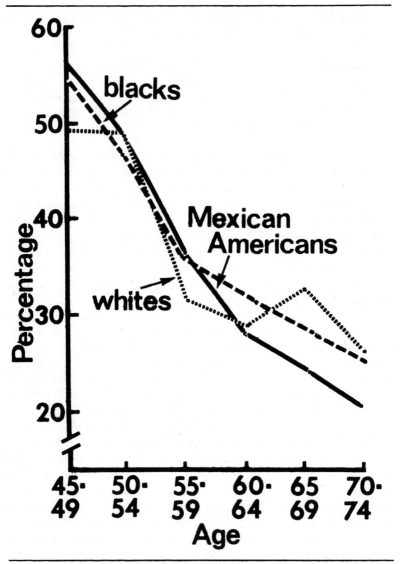

Figure 10.2 Percentage Responding "Very Afraid" or "Somewhat Afraid" of Death,
           by Age and Ethnicity

lives, and who express considerable anxiety about death. As Marshall
(1975b) has pointed out, with middle age occurs a convergence of a
number of "developmental" tasks in connection with awareness of
finitude.

A quite different perspective on mortality is manifested in remarks by a 67-year-old widower whom we will call Mr. Aguilar:

> Although I know I am going to die soon, or rather that I could die at any time, I really try not to think about death. . . . I know I'm going to die, it's something that we all have to go through. When it happens, and there's nothing I can do about it, I'll cross that bridge when I come to it. But for now, I don't think I even want to talk about it.

Some rather unusual problems of method were encountered in this investigation, problems that reflect—perhaps extremely—the centrality of explicit comparison in the research design. The research program was suspended because of protests by members of the groups involved in the study: protests that the research as originally designed was racist and elitist, because it neither explicitly involved members of the ethnic groups under study nor provided for direct benefits to them. But from this confrontation and the subsequent negotiation came an unusual collaborative effort between community and university (Bengtson, Grigsby, Corry, & Hruby, 1977).

For example, the interview schedule was designed over a period of 18 months by the researchers in consultation with the Community Research Planning Committee, composed of representatives from the Los Angeles Black and Chicano communities. This resulted in some critical omissions being rectified before the survey was fielded: One member of the Black caucus pointed out that the researchers had failed to ask questions about children not biologically related whom the respondents may have raised, and who might contribute a potential source of social support in aging. This item was included in the survey, and 51% of the Blacks indicated such a relationship. Moreover, the committee read and gave input to the materials and interpretations published from the project, in order to maximize insight and to minimize possible misrepresentations. Although it has been estimated that one additional year was required to complete the project because of this unique community-university collaboration, there is much evidence that community-academic collaboration can provide unusual insights; its results have been impressive (Bengtson et al., 1977).

COMPARING AGE GROUPS IN VALUE ORIENTATIONS

The fourth case study to be reviewed involves perhaps the most frequent comparison in both macro- and microsocial levels of gerontological research: contrasts between groups defined by age or age-group placement. In this example the social position in terms of social aging is explicit, in terms of generational position within a family; but its boundaries are diverse, in terms of chronological age or birth cohort membership.

The "theory" tested in this example is very informal, and so inexplicit as to be perhaps inappropriate for serious scientific analysis. However, the phenomena involved are both highly topical (as reflected in the mass media) and probably of considerable import to any formal theory concerning the linkage between aging and social change. I am referring to the supposition of a universal, inevitable "generation gap," which involves striking differences between young and older members of a society. This implicit theory was perhaps most formally explicated by Margaret Mead (1970), who suggested that rapid sociotechnological change had, in the 1970s, created a profound chasm between the young and the old in technologically advanced societies.

In 1971, we set out to investigate the nature and extent of age-group contrasts in a variety of behavioral indicators. Data were collected from 2,044 individuals who were members of three-generation families— sampled from among 870,000 subscribers to a prepaid health plan in Southern California (Bengtson, 1975).

One area we investigated involved value orientations. We asked the members of the three family generations to rank, in order of importance to them, 16 items reflecting various goals or orientations. The between-group contrasts are displayed in Figure 10.3. By comparing answers from grandparents, parents, and youth for each item, one sees clear contrasts among generations. The value of "achievement," for example, was ranked highest by the middle-aged parents, significantly lower by young-adult grandchildren, and lower still by the grandparents. "Personal freedom" was ranked very high by youth, but two scale points lower by the grandparents—a pattern seen also in "skill" and "exciting life."

But while value differences between generations are reflected in these data, there are also similarities; and what is most interesting is that many of the differences run counter to usual expectations. The three generations show unexpectedly similar rankings on items such as "respect" and "possessions" as well as "friendship." Also, some contrasts, or lack of differences in the expected directions, are surprising. On the item "a world at peace" we expected the highest ranking to be given by the youngest generation; after all, it was the youth who appeared to be in the forefront of peace demonstrations in the 1960s. But of the three generational groups it was the grandparents who ranked this value

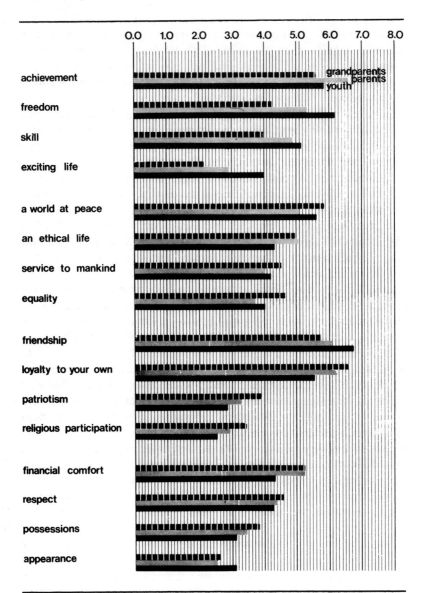

Figure 10.3 Mean of Each Value Ranking, by Generation (N = 1446)

highest. Similar patterns appeared on "service to mankind" and "equality of mankind"—these were valued highest by the grandparents, next by the grandchildren, third by the parents. These scores on humanistic values suggest that some stereotypes about generational differences in orientations are inaccurate. Not only are there similarities in value rankings, but the differences that exist run counter to many expectations.

But contrasts and comparisons between age groups run the risk of methodological difficulties similar to those cited earlier in the examination of contrasts across cultural or ethnic groups. To what extent is there *comparability* in instrumentation, in variable definition, and in interpretation?

In the case of abstract values, there may be a high degree of measurement error caused by lack of *comparability* in meanings of linguistic stimuli. "Freedom" may mean entirely different things to a 70-year-old man and his 17-year-old grandson (Bengtson, 1975). The problem can be solved partially by data-reduction techniques such as factor analysis, which result in an indicator that has higher reliability than the original several scores on individual items.

On these data reflecting values, the factor analysis resulted in two bipolar dimensions: The first reflects the polarity between humanistic and materialistic orientations, and the second encompasses values of individualism versus materialism. Plotting these value scores by generation clearly reveals underlying trends in these data (Figure 10.4). On the first dimension, the major surprise of this analysis can be seen: The young and the old are at similar levels in terms of humanitarianism. The middle-aged, in contrast to either, are far more materialistic. With regard to the second dimension, individualism, there are clearly linear generational contrasts: The oldest generation is more collectivistic; the youngest, more individualistic. These are statistically significant contrasts, with generational contrasts accounting for 21% of the variance on this dimension. Thus the implicit theory, that generational placement is an important predictor of contrast in abstract value orientations, is supported by the observed between-group comparison on one dimension, but not on the other.

Put more colloquially: Yes, there are differences between generations—but not uniformly, across all dimensions of values. In fact on some underlying issues there is much more similarity between the young and the old than one would ever suspect from reading the popular press accounts of the "generation gap." The young and the old may be "generation gap allies" with respect to humanistic values.

But perhaps the most telling message of these data on cross-group comparisons is revealed by portraying these same scores in another fashion (Figure 10.5). Usually we look only at means as characteristic statistics of group distributions. If we examine dispersion, instead of

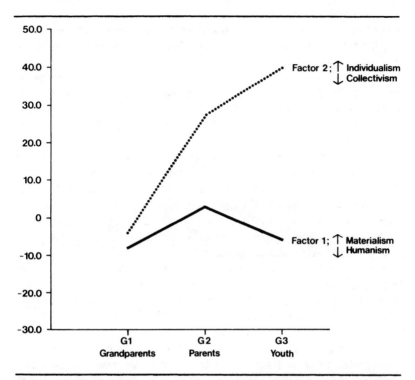

Figure 10.4 Means of Each Factor Score (Representing Two Dimensions of Values),
          by Generation

central tendency, we see a profound degree of overlap among the three
generations in value orientations. Many individuals from each of the
three groups defined by generation are high on values reflecting
humanism; many of each group are high on materialism. There is little in
this graph to support a universal theory of a generation gap in values.

Still another comparative issue that can be addressed in this study is
the question of family lineage (socialization) versus cohort membership
(age) factors in defining value orientations. To what extent are there
patterns of family socialization apparent from the values data—in light
of the generation or age-group contrasts just reviewed?

In an additional analysis of these data (Bengtson, 1975), value
orientations were examined in terms of cohort versus lineage effects. We
found that value similarities could be traced through three generations
of the same family, which suggests lineage continuity in orientations.
However, there was more agreement on values within the grandparent,
parent, and child generations at the aggregate level (which could be

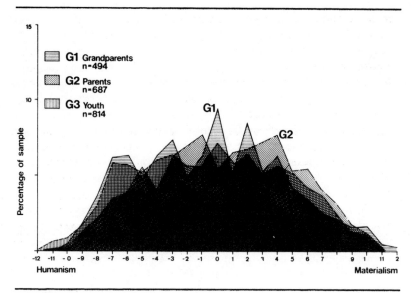

Figure 10.5 Frequency Distribution of Factor Scores, by Generation, on Humanism/
Materialism Value Dimension

interpreted as cohort similarity) than there was among generations within the family. There are two problems of method and interpretation suggested by this example not mentioned in the previous case studies, but germane to each of the four. The first concerns problems of measurement dimensionality: Comparisons of distribution on a particular variable (most often portrayed by means between groups) may mask differences in the underlying dimensions of the variable (Nesselroade, 1970; Nesselroade & Baltes, 1974). In this example, it is possible that the higher mean score on "individualism" for the grandchild sample compared to the grandparents may result from the factor structure on "individualism" being different by the two age groups. This would be a methodological artifact, perhaps related to the fact that the eight individual value variables reflecting "individualism/collectivism" are intercorrelated differentially within the two subsamples. If this were true, the observed differences between the two age groups would reflect not substantive contrasts on similar stimuli, but rather differences between the two on factor structure—an artifact of methodology.

To test the hypothesis that the underlying dimensions of value structure are similar, and that observed differences reflect contrasts in location along a common dimension rather than different underlying dimensions, it is necessary to test "factorial invariance" between the age/generational groups. Any comparative research design contrasting known groups should employ such a test. In this case study, the hypothesis of differences in dimensionality between generations was tested by a simple chi-square procedure examining contrasts in correlations between items constituting the factors (Bengtson, 1975). Given that no significant differences in levels of correlation among the three generations were evident, it was concluded that factorial invariance characterizes these data. Thus one can be confident that the observed between-generation differences do indicate significant contrasts by group in location along a common dimension.

The second problem of method is more difficult to assess empirically. It involves the step of theory building that requires linkages to be expressed that are successful in explanation: to explain "why." These findings suggest an ongoing process of socialization within the family that is bilateral rather than unilateral, in that influence goes both from parent to child and from child to parent, as suggested by Hagestad (1984). The direct parent-child socialization process certainly influences the development of values in the child, but not necessarily those of the parent's original orientation. The difference between parental and child values may derive partly from the social environment, partly from collective relations in peer groups; the similarities come partially from transmission from the older to the younger generation, and partially from the influence of children on their parents (Bengtson & Black, 1973; Hagestad, 1981, 1984).

CONCLUSION

The explicit construction, testing, and refinement of theory is crucial to the development of any scientific field. In the emergence of a new field such as social gerontology, efforts to build cumulative knowledge by directly stating the theory to be tested by empirical data are especially valuable. This chapter has argued that the comparative method, involving explicit tests of propositions that are compared and contrasted using two or more groups, is particularly useful in the development of cumulative theory in the social psychology of aging.

To illustrate this point, this chapter presented four case studies in social gerontology involving the logic of explicit comparisons among groups. Each of the four began with the statement of a "universal" theory reflecting some aspect of aging that served as the impetus for the study, whether or not acknowledged by the authors. Each employed data from comparable groups in order to test whether the law or universal relationship predicted by the theory was reflected in the groups contrasted.

The results of each study indicated the need for important refinements of each theory as had been stated originally. In the Cross-National Study of Retirement, patterns of "disengagement" following withdrawal from primary career involvement were not universal across occupations or cultural groups involved as originally suggested by Cumming and Henry (1961), though the correlation between role activity and life satisfaction averaged across the sixteen groups of men was similar to that in the Kansas City study. In the Harvard study of modernization and modernity, the data from six nations and three occupations within nations partially supported the "aging and modernity" theory suggested by Cowgill and Holmes (1972) in terms of societal levels of modernization, but not at the social psychological level of "individual modernity"—in fact, the cultivators were less likely than the urban factory workers to indicate they "look forward to old age." In the University of Southern California study comparing age cohorts and ethnic groups (as well as contrast by SES and gender) on attitudes toward death and dying, the implicit "universal" theory that preoccupation with themes of dying is directly related to advancing age was not supported; in fact, it was the middle aged, not the elderly, who reported most frequent thoughts about death. (However, this was a cross-sectional survey; longitudinal patterns are more relevant to the theory.) In the USC three-generation study, the theory of substantial generational contrasts among grandparents, parents, and young adults in value orientations was not supported in the explicit comparisons among these age groups on "materialism/humanism," but was evident in "individualism/collectivism" value orientations.

Two general sets of conclusions may be drawn from these case studies in comparative research design, within the context of this volume's discussion of social psychological investigations of aging. The first concerns implications for method in comparative studies undertaken in social gerontology; the second reflects challenges in linking the micro level of social psychology to the macro level of analyzing social structures.

Methodological problems in comparative social psychology. The case studies reviewed have outlined a number of challenges for the investigator courageous enough to employ the comparative method of planned comparisons between groups to test social psychological theories of aging. In general these relate to the methodological problems of obtaining strictly comparable data from groups selected presumably to differ in terms of some independent variable (culture, socioeconomic level within a society, ethnicity within culture, age or generational placement) in order to provide a crucial test of a given theory.

The first and perhaps most obvious challenge involves *sampling:* selection of respondents or subjects so as to include strictly comparable samples across boundaries of culture (or SES levels within culture). The danger of irregular sampling across groups is that differences observed may be an artifact of sampling selection, rather than of substantive contrasts between groups. One solution is to obtain a nationally representative sample from each culture or age group, as was done in the Harvard study of modernity; a second strategy is to focus on groups that appear to have similar locations within and across cultures or nations, utilizing experts indigenous to the culture to select such groups, as was done in the Cross-National Study of Retirement.

A second equally thorny problem involves *equivalence of constructs* in the definition and operationalization of variables. This difficulty can be seen in comparisons across cultures, in which such terms as *family* and *friend* (to say nothing of *social support*) may have quite different meanings from one group to the next. To test theory adequately in a comparative framework requires achieving comparability in constructs and crucial terms, which perhaps can occur only in research design collaboration with experts thoroughly familiar with the cultures or groups involved—even in a pluralistic society such as America or Canada, where the definition of "kin" may vary among ethnic groups. This was done in the Cross-National Study of Retirement, in the Harvard study of modernity, and the USC cross-ethnic study of aging.

Third is the problem of *linguistic equivalence of questions* posed to respondents and of the interpretation of their responses. While this can readily be seen as a problem when more than one language is involved (English and Dutch; *barrio* Spanish and middle-class English), there may be subtle differences among age groups as well in the connotation of questions posed ("freedom"; "an exciting life") that may lead to unintended differences in equivalency between age cohorts. The solution here is extensive pretesting of data-gathering instruments, asking respondents to define in their own terms the crucial questions used, and back-translation of instruments when more than one language is involved. Again, informants representing the groups involved are useful in achieving equivalency.

A fourth problem of between-groups comparability can be solved through the use of appropriate statistical procedures. This is the testing of *uniform dimensionality in the variables selected* for cross-group comparison, seen most readily in factorial equivalence across groups (as was done in the USC examination of generational contrasts in value orientations). If the underlying dimensions of variables are different in the older sample compared to the younger, then any substantive findings concerning differences in levels are akin to the results of comparing apples with oranges.

A fifth problem concerns *levels of analysis.* Comparative research requires the recognition of possible differences in levels of data and interpretation (macrosocial from microsocial). This was illustrated in the Harvard study, in which societal modernization was differentiated from individual social psychological modernity, with quite different results reflecting the two levels of analysis. This same principle applies to much family research in gerontology. Macrosocial considerations reflecting an age cohort's differential placement in historical time must be distinguished analytically from micro-level variables such as generational station within the family (Marshall & Bengtson, 1983; Hagestad, 1981). Both are important in the prediction and understanding of respondents' reactions to questions. However, unless the research design explicitly includes a study component that documents the historical context, it is unlikely that historical time will even be considered in the analysis or that the interindividual behavior at a micro level will be seen as embedded in a macro-social context. The great bulk of survey research in social gerontology can be criticized on these grounds.

A sixth problem involves the *tension between superficiality* (of problems between groups) *and generalizability*, each of which presents problems in interpretation. Multiple methods are particularly useful in comparative research investigations. Qualitative data, collected through ethnographic techniques or open-ended interviews, are helpful in making sense of survey responses (Marshall, 1981). Similarly, surveys— even if utilizing small groups—are helpful in charting the generalizability of findings from intensive ethnographies. The USC study of attitudes toward death illustrates such utility.

Finally, it is particularly necessary, in a developing scientific field such as social gerontology, to avoid premature claims of universality when comparative research is undertaken. As was suggested earlier in this chapter, the search for universals is virtually irresistible in science, as is the tendency toward reduction; but when the claim to universality is made prematurely, as in the case of disengagement theory (and perhaps the modernization theory) and most versions of developmental life-span theory, it can be so seductive as to create overgeneralization. Unfortunately, too few research papers in recent gerontological studies are explicit in stating the logical implications of their findings for lawlike propositions, because they seldom involve explicit comparisons between groups. The comparative research logic is particularly useful in avoiding unwarranted claims to universality.

Challenges in linking the micro level to the macro level. A major theme of this volume is the necessity for social psychological research in aging to be more aware of macrosocial phenomena that shape interactional data. The chapters by Dowd, Wellman and Hall, Ryff, Chappell and Orbach, Matthews, and Marshall give particular illustration to this issue. The case studies cited in this chapter also provide examples of this challenge, whether or not it is adequately addressed by the published results of the research. In any event, explicit comparative designs may be particularly helpful in constructing necessary bridges between the micro and macro levels of analysis in the social psychology of aging.

The first challenge in levels of analysis is in terms of the *ecological fallacy* (Robinson, 1961). This refers to the possibility that observed relationships between two variables may be due to the confounding effect of a third variable related to the ecological placement of the group. The Harvard modernization data's examination of positive or negative attitudes toward old age is a case in point. The variable of exposure to "individual modernizing experiences," such as radio, factory-work organization, and newspapers, was more powerful in explaining attitudes toward aging than was the context of gross national product and indices of social modernization.

A second and related need is to spell out more adequately the *individual-context relationship.* Lawton (1980) has suggested a number of ways in which the individual-environment relationship may be specified in his "environmental press" model of aging. Comparative designs may be particularly helpful in specifying such relationships in terms of developing change in the social world of aging. It should not be assumed that this approach can be taken only with quantitative research. Qualitative studies are equally suited to this task (see Unruh, 1984).

Third, there is greater need for *explicit differentiation within the age categories* frequently employed in gerontological research. Riley (1971) has spoken of "cohort-centric" dangers in interpreting observed differences between groups; others (e.g., Marshall and Dowd, in this volume) have noted the problems attending the failure to examine social class differences among the aged. The case study cited in this chapter involving stratum contrasts in attitudes toward death represents an attempt to recognize four variables of social differentiation that may

predict such attitudes; the Cross-National Study of Retirement examined occupational categories within a retired population in patterns of
"disengagement" from occupational roles. Much more needs to be done
in terms of explicit testing patterns of social differentiation within the
age groups often employed in gerontological research.

A fourth issue might be termed *determinism versus voluntarism* in
examining the individual within comparative contexts. This problem
has been addressed infrequently in gerontological research. However,
most survey research in aging employs an implicitly deterministic
model, leaving less room than desirable for issues such as role making or
the negotiation of relationships. The tensions of social categories are
reflected in several of the case studies presented in this chapter: the
"generation gap" in values, for example, and the "modernization"
approach to attitudes toward aging. The issue is seen in the discussion of
methodological problems (role counts imply a deterministic approach
for Cumming and Henry, 1961, while field data-gathering procedures
imply a more voluntaristic perspective). Certainly qualitative methodologies are more suited to illustrating the negotiation involved in an
aged individual's response to social circumstances and to such personal
realities as impending death.

Finally, there is the question of the *utility in searching for universals.*
Perhaps some of the early preoccupation with universal laws in social
gerontology was due to the influence of related disciplines—biology, for
example—and some would argue that this influence in fact has been
deleterious to good theory building. May it not be more appropriate, at
least for social psychologists, to develop contextual accounts rather
than context-free universal explanations for patterns observed in older
individuals? I would argue that a search for universal principles is an
important characteristic of scientific inquiry and should be more, not
less, explicit in social gerontology; but I would also suggest the
importance of theory that takes into account contextual factors across
groups. This is, it seems to me, the singular advantage of explicit
comparative designs in social gerontology.

The purpose of this chapter has been to argue in favor of explicit
comparative research in social gerontology, as the logic of such designs
has considerable promise in developing and testing cumulative theory.
Many methodological problems are involved in such comparative
designs; the basic issues involve ensuring comparability of methods and
procedures when one group is contrasted with another. Ingenious
solutions and considerable effort are required to ensure comparability
across groups in comparative studies. But the payoff from explicit
comparative logic to cumulative theory building in gerontology appears
impressive.

REFERENCES

Bengtson, V. L. (1969). Cultural and occupational differences in level of present role activity in retirement. In R. J. Havighurst, J.M.A. Munnichs, B. L. Neugarten, & H. Thomae (Eds.), *Adjustment to retirement: A cross-national study* (pp. 35-53). Assen, Netherlands: Van Gorcum.

Bengtson, V. L. (1975). Perceptions of inter-generational solidarity: Attitudes of elderly parents and middle-aged children. In *Proceedings of the 10th International Congress of Gerontology, Vol. I.* (pp. 218-220). Jerusalem, June 22-27.

Bengtson, V. L. (1979). Ethnicity and aging: Problems and issues in current social science inquiry. In D. E. Gelfand & A. J. Kutzik (Eds.), *Ethnicity and aging.* New York: Springer.

Bengtson, V. L., & Black, K. D. (1973). Inter-generational relations and continuities in socialization. In P. Baltes & K. W. Schaie (Eds.), *Life-span developmental psychology: Personality and socialization* (pp. 207-234). New York: Academic Press.

Bengtson, V. L., Cuellar, J., & Ragan, P. K. (1977). Stratum contrasts and similarities in attitudes toward death. *Journal of Gerontology, 32* (1), 76-88.

Bengtson, V. L., Dowd, J. J., Smith, D. H., & Inkeles, A. (1975). Modernization, modernity, and perceptions of aging: A cross-cultural study. *Journal of Gerontology, 30* (6), 688-695.

Bengtson, V. L. Grigsby, E., Corry, E. M., & Hruby, M. (1977). Relating academic research to community concerns: A case study in collaborative effort. *Journal of Social Issues, 33* (4), 75-92.

Cain, L. D., Jr. (1964). Life course and social structure. In R.E.L. Faris (Ed.), *Handbook of modern sociology.* Chicago: Rand McNally.

Cowgill, D., & Holmes, L. (Eds.). (1972). *Aging and modernization.* New York: Appleton-Century-Crofts.

Cumming, E., & Henry, W. E. (1961). *Growing old: The process of disengagement.* New York: Basic Books.

Dowd, J. J. (1980). *Stratification among the aged.* Monterey, CA: Brooks/Cole.

Dowd, J. J., & Bengtson, V. L. (1978). Aging in minority populations: An examination of the double jeopardy hypothesis. *Journal of Gerontology, 33,* 427-436.

Dubin, R. (1978). *Theory-building* (rev. ed.). New York: Free Press.

George, L. K. (1980). *Role transitions in later life.* Belmont, CA: Wadsworth.

Glaser, B., & Strauss, A. (1969). *The discovery of grounded theory.* New York: Aldine.

Hagestad, G. O. (1981). Problems and promises in the social psychology of inter-generational relations. In R. W. Fogel, E. Hatfield, S. B. Kiesler, & E. Shanas (Eds.), *Aging.* New York: Academic Press.

Hagestad, G. O. (1984). The continuous bond: A dynamic multigenerational perspective on parent-child relations between adults. In M. Perlmutter (Ed.), *Minnesota Symposia on Child Psychology* (Vol. 17, pp. 129-158). Hillsdale, NJ: Lawrence Erlbaum.

Havighurst, R. J., Munnichs, J., Neugarten, B., & Thomae, H. (Eds.). (1969). *Adjustment to retirement: A cross national study.* Assen, Netherlands: Van Gorcum.

Hochschild, A. R. (1975). Disengagement theory: A critique and proposal. *American Sociological Review, 40,* 553-569.

Inkeles, A. (1983). *Exploring individual modernity.* New York: Columbia University Press.

Inkeles, A., & Smith, D. H. (1974). *Becoming modern: Individual change in six developing countries.* Cambridge, MA: Harvard University Press.

Kalish, R. A., & Reynolds, D. K. (1976). *Death and ethnicity: A psycho-cultural study.* Los Angeles: Andrus Gerontology Center, University of Southern California.

Lawton, M. P. (1980). *Environment and aging.* Monterey, CA: Brooks/Cole.

Marshall, V. W. (1975a). Socialization for impending death in a retirement village. *American Journal of Sociology, 80,* 1124-1144.

Marshall, V. W. (1975b). Age and awareness of finitude in developmental gerontology. *Omega, 6* (2), 113-129.

Marshall, V. W. (1980). *Last chapters: A sociology of aging and dying.* Monterey, CA: Brooks/Cole.

Marshall, V. W. (1981). Participant observation in a multiple-methods study of a retirement community: A research narrative. *Mid-American Review of Sociology, 6*(2), 29-43.

Marshall, V. W., & Bengtson, V. L. (1983). Generations: Conflict and cooperation. In M. Bergener, U. Lehr, E. Lang, , & R. Schmitz-Scherzer (Eds.), *Gerontology in the eighties: Highlights of the Twelfth International Conference on Gerontology.* New York: Springer.

Mead, M. (1970). *Culture and commitment: A study of the generation gap.* New York: Basic Books.

Nesselroade, J. R. (1970). Application of multivariate strategies to problems of measuring and structuring long-term change. In L. R. Goulet & P. B. Baltes (Eds.), *Life-span developmental psychology: Research and theory.* New York: Academic Press.

Nesselroade, J. R., & Baltes, P. B. (1974). Adolescent personality development and historical change: 1970-72. *Monographs of the Society for Research in Child Development, 39* (1, Whole No. 154).

Neugarten, B. L., & Bengtson, V. L. (1968). Cross-national studies of adulthood and aging. In E. Shanas & J. Madge (Eds.), *Interdisciplinary topics in gerontology: Vol. 2. Methodology problems in cross national studies in aging* (pp. 18-36).

Quadagno, J. (1980). *Aging in early industrial society: Work, family, and social policy in nineteenth-century England.* New York: Academic Press.

Ragan, P. K., & Wales, J. B. (1980). Age stratification and the life course. In J. E. Birren & R. B. Sloane (Eds.), *Handbook of mental health and aging.* Englewood Cliffs, NJ: Prentice-Hall.

Riley, M. W. (1971). Social gerontology and the age stratification of society. *Gerontologist, 11* (1), 79-87.

Riley, M. W. (1976). Aging and social systems. In R. H. Binstock & E. Shanas (Eds.), *Handbook of aging and social sciences.* New York: Van Nostrand Reinhold.

Riley, M. W., Johnson, M., & Foner, A. (1972). *Aging and society: Vol. 1. An inventory of research findings.* New York: Russell Sage.

Robinson, G. O. (1961). The ecological fallacy. *Journal of the American Statistical Association, 43* (2), 241-249.

Shanas, E. (1979a). The family as a social support in old age. *Gerontologist, 19* (2), 169-174.

Shanas, E. (1979b). Social myth as hypothesis: The case of the family relations of old people. *Gerontologist, 19* (1), 3-9.

Shanas, E., Townsend, P., Wedderburn, E., Friss, H., Milhoj, P., & Stehouwer, J. (1968). *Old people in three industrial societies.* New York: Atherton.

Simmons, L. W. (1945). *The role of the aged in primitive society.* New Haven, CT: Yale University Press.

Smith, D. H., & Inkeles, A. (1966). The OM scale: A comparative socio-psychological measure of individual modernity. *Sociometry, 29,* 353-377.

Unruh, D. (1983). *Invisible lives: Social worlds of the aged.* Beverly Hills, CA: Sage.

Name Index

Subject Index

About the Contributors

Vern L. Bengtson is Professor of Sociology and Director of the Gerontology Research Institute of the Andrus Gerontology Center at the University of Southern California. His doctorate was completed at the University of Chicago. He is the past chair of the Behavioral and Social Sciences Division, GSA, and has been elected chair of the Section on Aging, ASA. He was corecipient, in 1984, of the prestigious Reuben Hill Award, given by the National Council of Family Relations for distinguished research in family relations. He has published more than eighty papers and is the author of a text, *The Social Psychology of Aging,* and editor of the Brooks/Cole Series in Social Gerontology. He is coeditor (with Joan F. Robertson) of *Grandparenthood* (Sage, 1985).

Neena L. Chappell is Associate Professor of Sociology and Director of the Centre on Aging, University of Manitoba. She is also a National Health Scholar, with long-standing research interests in aging. Her current research interests are mainly focused on the intersection between informal and formal health care among elderly individuals. A book, *Aging and Health Care: A Social Perspective* (with L. Strain and A. Blandford) has just been published.

James J. Dowd is currently Associate Professor of Sociology at the University of Georgia. With a doctorate from the University of Southern California, he is best known in the sociology of aging for his reformulation and testing of exchange theory in the context of age relations and for his book, *Stratification Among the Aged* (1980). A large number of his publications have appeared in *Human Development, International Journal of Aging and Human Development, Journal of Gerontology,* and other journals. His research interests span the range of methodologies from survey research to participant observation and historical, archival research.

Alan Hall is a doctoral student in sociology at the University of Toronto. He has done considerable work in the area of social support and stress, with a particular emphasis on class issues. At present, he is engaged in dissertation research that attempts to examine the relationships among stress-related disorders, health ideologies, and changes in the social relations of production.

Martin Kohli is a Professor in the Institute for Sociology of the Free University of Berlin. In 1984-1985, while this chapter was being written, he was a Member, Institute for Advanced Study, Princeton. Born in Switzerland, he pursued doctoral studies at the University of Constance. He has published extensively in the sociology of aging, particularly in relation to work and the life course. Among his few publications in English are papers in *Aging and Society* and the *Annual Review of Sociology*, as well as a chapter in the collection edited by Bertaux, *Biography and Society* (1981, Sage).

Victor W. Marshall, Professor of Behavioral Science and of Sociology at the University of Toronto, received his doctorate in sociology from Princeton University. He has been active in developing the sociology of aging in Canada. A founding member of the Canadian Association on Gerontology, he chaired its Research Committee and Social Sciences Division for several years. He is currently Editor of the *Canadian Journal on Aging*. His edited book, *Aging in Canada: Social Perspectives,* will appear in a second edition in 1986. His other publications include *Last Chapters: A Sociology of Aging and Dying* (1980), *Nurses, Patients and Families* (1980), and many articles and chapters. His current research focuses on the family life of older people, aging and long-term care, and work stress in the health professions, especially medicine. He is a National Health Scientist whose work in Canadian gerontology has been honored by his receipt of the Laidlaw Foundation Award in 1984.

Sarah H. Matthews is Associate Professor of Sociology at Case Western Reserve University. She received her doctorate from the University of California, Davis. Her book *The Social World of Older Women* (Sage, 1979) is one of the most popular monographs used in North American social gerontology courses and exemplifies symbolic interactionism and exchange theory as well as an interest in the political economy of aging. She has also published in the sociology of women. Her latest book is

Friendships Through the Life Course: Oral Biographies in Old Age
(Sage, 1986).

Harold L. Orbach is Professor of Sociology at Kansas State University
and one of the senior statesmen in the field of social gerontology, having
contributed to its literature and organizational structure for over two
decades. He was instrumental in the formation of the Aging Section of
the American Sociological Association, has chaired the Research
Committee on Aging of the International Sociological Association, and
has served on the executive board of the Gerontological Society of
America. Generations of doctoral students and postdoctoral fellows
benefited from his guidance through the Midwest Council for Social
Research on Aging. He is currently editing the complete papers and
correspondence of George Herbert Mead.

Carol D. Ryff is Associate Professor of Psychology at the University of
Wisconsin—Madison. Her current research interests include adult
personality development, the impact of critical life events on personality
development, and cultural variations in conceptions of ideal development. Her recent publications include "Personality Development from
the Inside: The Subjective Experience of Change in Adulthood and
Aging," in P. B. Baltes and O. G. Brim, Jr. (Eds.), *Life-Span Development and Behavior* (Vol. 6) and "The Subjective Experience of Life-
Span Transitions," in A. R. Rossi (Ed.), *Gender and the Life Course.*

Donald L. Spence is Professor of Gerontology and Director of the
Gerontology Center of the University of Rhode Island. Following
doctoral studies at the University of Oregon, he was associated for many
years with the "transitions study" at Langley-Porter Neuropsychiatric
Institute and was instrumental in the development of doctoral and
postdoctoral studies at the University of California, San Francisco. His
early work, which is extended in his chapter in this volume, sought to
describe normal processes of aging and human development and
included important papers on the "empty nest." His current interests
focus on social aspects of long-term care. He has been particularly active
in the establishment of the Association for Gerontology in Higher
Education (AGHE) and has held many offices in this organization,
including its presidency.

Barry Wellman has been preoccupied with the nature of social networks
for the past forty years. Now Professor of Sociology at the University of

Toronto, he spends most of his time studying how social networks provide a variety of resources to urbanites. Among his most recent publications are "Domestic Work, Paid Work and Net Work," in S. Duck and D. Perlman (Eds.), *Understanding Personal Relationships, 1*; "Social Networks and Social Support" (also with Alan Hall), in S. Cohen and S. L. Syme (Eds.), *Social Support and Health;* "Network Analysis: Some Basic Principles," in *Sociological Theory* (1983); and "The Community Question," *American Journal of Sociology.*